Modern Studies in Philosophy

MILL

Modern Studies in Philosophy is a series of anthologies presenting contemporary interpretations and evaluations of the works of major philosophers. The editors have selected articles designed to show the systematic structure of the thought of these philosophers, and to reveal the relevance of their views to the problems of current interest. These volumes are intended to be contributions to contemporary debates as well as to the history of philosophy; they not only trace the origins of many problems important to modern philosophy, but also introduce major philosophers as interlocutors in current discussions.

Modern Studies in Philosophy is prepared under the general editorship of Amelie Rorty, Douglass College, Rutgers University.

J. B. Schneewind is a member of the Department of Philosophy at the University of Pittsburgh and the editor of two volumes of Mill's shorter works, *Mill's Essays on Literature and Society,* and *Mill's Ethical Writings.* He previously taught at Princeton University, where he received his Ph.D., and also at the University of Chicago and Yale.

Modern Studies in Philosophy

MILL:
A Collection of Critical Essays

EDITED BY

J. B. Schneewind

Anchor Books
DOUBLEDAY & COMPANY, INC.
GARDEN CITY, NEW YORK

ACKNOWLEDGMENTS

Without the co-operation of the authors and publishers of the works here reprinted the present volume
would not exist: specific acknowledgments are given at
the beginning of each selection, but I wish here to record my general gratitude to all those involved. I am
especially anxious to thank those who have contributed
articles not previously published: Professor Richard B.
Friedman, Professor Maurice Mandelbaum, and Mr.
G. N. A. Vesey. To Mr. Vesey I am also much indebted
for allowing me to see the articles in the "John Stuart
Mill Number" of *Philosophy* (Vol. XLIII, #163, January 1968) prior to publication. Mr. Maurice Cowling
most helpfully chose selections from his book and tied
them together with some additional comments: I am most
grateful to him.

Professor John M. Robson has been very helpful in
bibliographical matters. He sent me the unpublished portions of the comprehensive Mill bibliography on which
he and Professor D. Hascall are working, and the bibliography in the present volume has benefited from it.

Various friends have commented on the different plans
I have had for this book. I thank them all, especially
Professors Richard B. Friedman and George Kateb. It
hardly needs saying that the final selection shows my
personal interests as well as a philosopher's bias. I regret

only that there was not more space: many good things had to be passed by.

My thanks go, finally, to the editor of the series in which this volume appears for her very considerable assistance.

J. B. Schneewind

CONTENTS

INTRODUCTION

John Stuart Mill occupies a unique place in the history of philosophy. He wrote on an extraordinary number of subjects, among them logic, the philosophy of science, ethics, epistemology, metaphysics, economics, psychology, religion, education, literature, history, political theory, social philosophy, and botany. He discussed current affairs and controversial public issues both in his writings and before Parliamentary committees: on problems connected with economics, labor relations, socialism, land tenure, Ireland, and foreign affairs he was considered an expert. It can fairly be said of him that he was not a profoundly original thinker. Yet his views in all these fields were influential, not only among intellectuals and "professional" thinkers but also among plain men, including many in the working class. Mill's popularity cannot be explained—as that of Carlyle and Ruskin can be, in part—by any special charms his writings possess. Mill's style is certainly very serviceable. It is always clear, plain, non-technical, and direct. But it never displays wit, brilliance, or notable concision, and the tepid warmth to which it occasionally rises could hardly be mistaken for passion. The cartoons in *Punch* in 1867 —the year Mill made the first Parliamentary motion to allow women to vote—show him (carrying a book labeled "Logic") as small, pinched, and pedantic. But even if this suggests how the public saw him, it remains true that they read him and allowed their thought to be shaped by him. Mill must be given a high place among the most important influences on the British public mind between 1840 and 1880. No other philosopher, not even Bertrand Russell, has so consistently and strongly appealed to so large and so politically powerful an audience in his own lifetime. And today, nearly a century after his death, Mill's appeal is not yet exhausted. What is at the center of it?

In terms of bulk, Mill probably wrote as much on logic, the philosophy of science, and epistemological and metaphysical problems as he wrote on questions of ethics, society, and politics. For more than half a century after its publication in 1843 the *System of Logic* occupied a pre-eminent position among logic books in English. It was a monumental work of systematization: it brought together the classical main principles, worked out difficulties in them, suggested foundations for them, elaborated details following from them, and applied them to a wide variety of topics. In some areas Mill investigated quite new problems, though even here he was much indebted to other writers. There were very few people in England capable of reviewing the *System of Logic* when it first appeared, and it became, as it deserved to become, the most widely used logic textbook of the century. It has not, however, continued to be a fruitful source of discussion. In deductive logic the book was essentially a culminating, not an innovating, work. It was subjected to severe and sometimes damaging criticism by F. H. Bradley and others,[1] but, more importantly, it began to be outmoded in Mill's own lifetime by

---

[1] F. H. Bradley, *Principles of Logic*, 1883, 2nd ed., London, 1922. Cf. also T. H. Green, *Works*, ed. R. L. Nettleship, Vol. II, London, 1886; G. Frege, *Die Grundlagen der Arithmetik*, Breslau, 1884, translated by J. L. Austin as *The Foundations of Arithmetic*, Oxford, 1950. The best study of Mill's deductive logic is Reginald Jackson's (see Bibliography).

developments of which he took no notice. After 1910, when the first volume of Whitehead and Russell's *Principia Mathematica* appeared, the center of interest in deductive logic lay quite outside the range of Mill's thought. Mill's work in the philosophy of science has had a similar history. Although the treatment of inductive reasoning and experimental methods in the *System of Logic* was in some respects valuable pioneering, it suffered from Mill's lack of any thorough acquaintance with the theories and techniques of the physical sciences. Many generations of students nonetheless accepted Mill's account of the nature and methods of science as authoritative. But with the rise of logical positivism, philosophy came to feel strongly the influence of men who knew more of science than Mill could have had a chance to learn. The work of the logical positivists took the philosophy of science far beyond the point at which Mill left it; and if there is a reaction against their type of view now, it comes from men who are likely to be more sympathetic to Mill's great rival Whewell than to Mill.

Logical positivism again may account for recent neglect of Mill's views in epistemology and metaphysics. In his own times he was the voice of what is now called empiricism. Hume was not read at all, Locke and Berkeley not widely, and Mill's non-skeptical development of Humean principles, suggested in his earlier works and fully presented in his *Examination of the Philosophy of Sir William Hamilton* (1865), had no rivals. The logical positivists, who have represented empiricism most vocally and most clearly in our times, held so many positions similar to Mill's that it seemed quite unnecessary to go back to his work for discussion of important issues; and where they differed (as in Mill's insistence that the problems can only be solved by attention to "ideas" in some psychological sense of the term) Mill seemed to have been simply mistaken, and quite obviously so at that. Hence his work in epistemology, like that in logic and the philosophy of science, has not maintained in contemporary discussion the central and useful place it had in the Victorian period.

With what may be broadly termed Mill's social thought, the situation is quite different. From 1831 on, Mill spoke with a recognizably individual voice on moral, social, and political issues. He held that the fundamental determinant of social change and social stability is men's beliefs. Where a unified body of opinion exists and is widely accepted, there will be a stable society, and where it is lacking, society will be in a process of transition and perhaps of disintegration. He was convinced that none of the doctrines which had been current in his youth, including both Christian belief and orthodox Benthamism, could serve any longer to unify and stabilize society, and therefore he set himself the task of synthesizing a doctrine which could. His goal was not so much originality as comprehensiveness. He believed that on an empiricist and utilitarian basis it would be possible, without being merely eclectic, to bring the different elements of truth grasped by various contending political and social parties into a genuine unity. To work this out in detail was the aim of his more abstract writings. At the same time he dealt with a number of specific issues in terms of his philosophic principles, hoping thereby to demonstrate their applicability and fruitfulness and so to increase their appeal. In the course of doing this Mill was able, as few if any other English writers were, to articulate the views of an important segment of the population, to give them shape and coherence and backing, and to draw out their further implications for practice. It seems clear that his importance in his own times was largely a result of this self-created position as spokesman on social issues—there is reason to believe, for instance, that much of the appeal even of the *System of Logic* was due to recognition of its relevance to practical matters—and in these areas Mill's usefulness as a starting-point for discussion has lasted. If much of his sociological and economic theory is out of date, his general social attitudes are still quite widely held. Hence

examination of his views has a direct bearing on contemporary issues. The relevance of his philosophical positions in ethics and politics has been sustained by the
same similarities between his epistemology and currently
influential positions which have led to the neglect of his
work in the theory of knowledge. He saw problems
where many contemporary philosophers see problems,
and for similar reasons. His social thought—unlike that
of Green or Bradley or Bosanquet—comes to us unen-
cumbered with metaphysical views that are likely to be
rejected with impatience nowadays. He therefore seems
to many to be perhaps the last major English thinker
whose attempt to apply philosophical principles to current issues is still worth examining. Thus in our times as
in his it is Mill's work in ethical, social, and political
philosophy which is central to his significance.

This explanation is borne out by a look at what has
been written about him. The quantity even in the Victorian period was large, and in recent years, after a time
of comparative neglect, it has swollen to gigantic proportions. The bibliography being published in the *Mill
News Letter* (edited by Professor John M. Robson, University of Toronto Press) is enough to depress anyone
who wants a comprehensive idea of what has been or is
being said about Mill. But one feature of this commentary is noticeable throughout the years, though it has
become more marked recently. By far the greater part of
what is written on Mill centers on his social thought
and its foundations. In recent years there have been (to
take one instance) roughly twenty articles and discussions on Mill's alleged proof of the principle of utility.
There have been many more articles than that dealing
with *On Liberty*. But there has been almost nothing
concerning, e.g., his theory of the external world, his
interpretation of the nature of the laws of logic, his understanding of science, or, perhaps surprisingly, his views
on religion. The amount of space given in the present
collection to essays on Mill's moral and social philosophy
is much greater than the space given to articles on his

other views, but even so the proportions here do not accurately represent the proportions in the published literature.

It is quite understandable that comment on Mill's work during his lifetime was almost always animated by some political or sectarian bias. One result of this was that exposition of Mill's views was likely to be—to say the least—not very careful.[2] It may be that this is the price one pays for being a public figure: if so, Mill is still paying it. The caricature of him as a man who abandoned his early philosophic faith because of a nervous breakdown, and who thereafter never ceased to believe he had joined incompatible positions into a harmonious whole when in fact he had really created an enormous muddle, still has wide currency. But it is one of the merits of much recent work on Mill that it refuses to accept this picture without scrutiny. It is increasingly coming to be recognized that one cannot qualify as an expert on Mill by reading *Utilitarianism, On Liberty,* and a chapter or two of the *Logic*. Serious and scholarly attention is now being given to the whole corpus of Mill's writing. Interest in the early essays was stimulated in 1942 by F. A. Hayek's edition of *The Spirit of the Age,* and when the magnificent edition of Mill's works now being published by the University of Toronto Press is completed, students will be able to consult his minor writings more easily than ever before. With broader knowledge, more acute analysis, and more dispassionate scholarship, unsuspected continuities and unexpected depths are already being revealed in Mill's thought. It is of course too soon to predict the results of the revaluation which is beginning. But we can certainly expect

---

[2] There were of course many exceptions. Of the literature of the time, James Martineau's "John Stuart Mill's Philosophy," *National Review,* 1859, reprinted in *Essays, Reviews, and Addresses,* Vol. III, London, 1891, is one of the best general assessments, and John Grote's *Examination of the Utilitarian Philosophy,* Cambridge, 1870, probably the most meticulous philosophical scrutiny.

that critics will now work from full and accurate accounts of Mill's views, instead of from the hasty and partial portrayals which have been all too frequent.

Scholarship is contributing from other sides toward a better understanding and a more informed judgment of Mill. Historians are investigating his influence in politics, literary critics exploring his relation to other Victorian writers.[3] On the philosophic side, something is being done to remedy that "neglect of Victorian philosophy" of which Antony Quinton complained some time ago.[4] At least the most important of the philosophers contemporary with Mill, William Whewell (1794–1866) is being studied. Mill learned much from Whewell's *History of the Inductive Sciences* (1837), and criticized both his *Philosophy of the Inductive Sciences* (1840) and his writings on moral philosophy; but until recently no one bothered to investigate Whewell's side in the disputes. Since 1951 that has begun to change,[5] and now an edition of Whewell's major writings in the history and philosophy of science has been started. There are other philosophical writers who need to be studied more carefully than they have been if we are to obtain a full picture of the influences on and contexts of Mill's views: Bentham, for example (a new edition of his works is in progress), James Mill, a selection of whose economic writings has recently been republished, Sir

---

[3] E.g., Royden Harrison, *Before the Socialists,* London, 1965; John Vincent, *The Formation of the Liberal Party 1857–1868,* London, 1966; and J. Hamburger (see Bibliography). For Mill's position in the positivist movement, see Walter Simon, *European Positivism in the Nineteenth Century,* Ithaca, 1963. For literary critics, cf. F. R. Leavis and E. Alexander (see Bibliography).

[4] *Victorian Studies,* Vol. I, #3, March 1958.

[5] C. J. Ducasse, "William Whewell's Philosophy of Scientific Discovery," *Philosophical Review,* Vol. 60, 1951 (two parts); E. W. Strong (see Bibliography); R. E. Butts, "Necessary Truth in Whewell's Philosophy of Science," *American Philosophical Quarterly,* Vol. II, 1965; J. B. Schneewind, "Whewell's Ethics," *American Philosophical Quarterly Monographs,* #1, 1968.

William Hamilton, and John Austin. It is, moreover, not enough to study the philosophers. Mill did not confine himself to them, and his commentators cannot afford to do so either. A full study of Mill in his times—ambitious task!—will need to draw heavily on the work done by literary and historical investigators of the Victorian period in the last few decades.

There is no lack of passion in recent discussions of Mill, as there was no lack of it in the past. It is to be hoped that the scholarly revaluation of Mill's thought now in process is not a sign that his views are about to lose the life and relevance they have hitherto had.

JOHN STUART MILL

A Chronology

1806 J.S.M. born, May 20, in London.
1807 British slave trade abolished.
      Hegel, *Phänomenologie des Geistes.*
1813 R. Owen, *New View of Human Society.*
1815 Battle of Waterloo, end of Napoleonic Wars.
1809–20 J.S.M. being educated at home by his father.
1817 Coleridge, *Biographia Literaria.*
1819 Byron, *Don Juan.*
      Schopenhauer, *Welt als Wille und Vorstellung.*
1820–21 J.S.M. in France with Sir Samuel Bentham.
1821 Hegel, *Philosophie des Rechts.*
1822 J.S.M. studies law with John Austin and begins
      writing for newspapers.
1823 J.S.M. begins working at India House as clerk.
      Comte's early essays.
1824 J.S.M., article in *Westminster Review,* continuing
      attack begun by his father on the *Edinburgh
      Review.*
      Byron dies in Greece, helping Greek rebels against
      Turkey.

1825   J.S.M. edits Bentham's *Rationale of Judicial Evidence* (5 vols.). J.S.M. helps found London Debating Society.

1826–27   J.S.M.'s "mental crisis."

1828   J.S.M. promoted at India House. He meets F. D. Maurice, John Sterling, and G. d'Eichthal at the Debating Society.

    Repeal of Test and Corporation Acts.

1829   Removal of civil disabilities of Roman Catholics.

    James Mill: *Analysis of the Phenomena of the Human Mind.*

1830   Revolution in France. J.S.M. goes to Paris; begins writing extensively on French affairs. He meets Harriet Taylor.

    Sir John Herschel: *Discourse on the Study of Natural Philosophy.*

    Lyell's *Principles of Geology* (concluded 1832).

    Comte begins publication of the *Cours de Philosophie Positive.*

1831   J.S.M.'s articles on "The Spirit of the Age." He writes but does not publish *Essays on Some Unsettled Questions of Political Economy.*

    Much public excitement about Reform Bill.

    Death of Hegel.

1832   First Reform Bill passes. Deaths of Bentham, Scott, and Goethe.

    Tennyson's *Poems,* reviewed by J.S.M.

    J. Austin, *Province of Jurisprudence Determined.*

1833   Emancipation Act abolishes slavery in British possessions.

    Agitation about reform of Established Church. Start of Oxford Movement.

    Factory Act.

    J.S.M. publishes two essays on poetry.

    Carlyle, *Sartor Resartus.*

1834 New poor law passes.

Deaths of Coleridge, Lamb, and Malthus.

1835 J.S.M. starts and edits *London Review* (continues
     as *London and Westminster Review* until 1840).

J.S.M. reads and reviews de Tocqueville, publishes
article on Sedgwick.

Strauss, *Leben Jesu*.

1836 Deaths of James Mill and William Godwin.

J.S.M. promoted at India House.

Dickens, *Pickwick Papers*.

1837 Accession of Queen Victoria.

J.S.M. reviews Carlyle's *French Revolution*.

Whewell, *History of the Inductive Sciences*.

1838 J.S.M., "Bentham."

Beginning of Chartist movement.

1839 House of Commons refuses to consider Chartist peti-
     tion.

Beginning of Anti-Corn-Law League.

1840 J.S.M., "Coleridge."

Whewell, *Philosophy of the Inductive Sciences*.

1841 Feuerbach, *Das Wesen des Christentums*.

1843 J.S.M., *A System of Logic*.

Joule, "Mechanical Value of Heat."

1844 Factory Act reduces working day.

J.S.M. publishes *Essays on Some Unsettled Questions of Political Economy*, written 1831.

Marx, "Economic-Philosophical Manuscripts" (unpublished).

1845 Potato crop fails in Ireland.

Newman joins Roman Catholic Church, splitting
Oxford Movement.

Whewell, *Elements of Morality including Polity*.

1846 Repeal of corn laws.

1847 Marx and Engels, *Communist Manifesto*.

DeMorgan, *Formal Logic*.

Boole, *Mathematical Analysis of Logic*.

1848   Revolutions in numerous continental countries.

J.S.M., *Principles of Political Economy*.

Thackeray, *Vanity Fair*.

Macaulay, *History of England*.

1850   Spencer, *Social Statics*.

Tennyson, *In Memoriam*.

1851   Opening of Great Exhibition.

J.S.M. marries Harriet Taylor.

Coup d'état of Louis Napoleon.

1852   J.S.M., "Dr. Whewell on Moral Philosophy."

1854   Crimean war begins.

J.S.M. seriously ill, travels extensively in Italy and Greece.

Boole, *Investigation of the Laws of Thought*.

1856   J.S.M. promoted to Chief Examiner of India Correspondence at India House—the position his father had had.

1857   The Mutiny in India. J.S.M. writes defense of East India Company.

1858   Parliament gives administration of India to government. J.S.M. refuses offer of post in government, retires.

Harriet Taylor dies in Avignon. From now on J.S.M. spends about half of each year in Avignon.

Mansel, *Limits of Religious Thought Examined*.

Hamilton, *Lectures on Metaphysics and Logic,* ed. Mansel and Veitch, completed 1860.

Fitzgerald, *Rubaiyat of Omar Khayyam*.

1859   J.S.M., *On Liberty; Dissertations and Discussions,* vols. 1–2; *Thoughts on Parliamentary Reform*.

Darwin, *Origin of Species*.

George Eliot, *Adam Bede*.

Franco-Austrian War.

1860   Lincoln becomes President of U.S.A.

Garibaldi and Cavour struggle to unite Italy.

Tolstoy, *War and Peace*.

1861   Civil War in U.S.A.

J.S.M., *Considerations on Representative Government*; "Utilitarianism" published as magazine articles.

1862   Spencer, *First Principles*.

1863   J.S.M., *Utilitarianism* as book.

Lincoln emancipates slaves in U.S.A.

1865   J.S.M., *Examination of Sir William Hamilton's Philosophy; Auguste Comte and Positivism*.

J.S.M. elected MP for Westminster.

End of Civil War in U.S.A.

J. Grote, *Exploratio Philosophica*, vol. I.

1866   Austro-Prussian War.

J.S.M., article on G. Grote's *Plato*.

1867   Second Reform Bill passes; J.S.M. fails in attempt to amend it to allow women to vote.

J.S.M., *Dissertations and Discussions*, vol. III; publishes also his Rectorial Address to the students of St. Andrews.

Marx, *Das Kapital*, vol. I.

1868   J.S.M. defeated in attempt at re-election.

Browning, *The Ring and the Book*.

1869   J.S.M., *Subjection of Women*; annotated edition of James Mill's *Analysis of the Phenomena of the Human Mind*.

1870   Franco-Prussian War.

Start of Irish Home Rule movement.

J.S.M. publishes writings on Irish land question.

J. Grote, *Examination of the Utilitarian Philosophy*.

1873   J.S.M. dies at Avignon, May 7.

Modern Studies in Philosophy

MILL

JOHN STUART MILL

BY

Bertrand Russell

I

It is not easy to assess the importance of John Stuart Mill in nineteenth-century England. What he achieved depended more upon his moral elevation and his just estimate of the ends of life than upon any purely intellectual merits.

His influence in politics and in forming opinion on moral issues was very great and, to my mind, wholly good. Like other eminent Victorians he combined intellectual distinction with a very admirable character. This intellectual distinction gave weight to his opinions, and was thought at the time to be greater than it appears in retrospect. There are various modern trends which are adverse also to his ethical and moral theories, but in these respects I cannot feel that the world has made any advance since his day.

Reprinted from Bertrand Russell, *Portraits from Memory*, copyright © 1951, 1952, 1953, 1956, by Bertrand Russell. Reprinted by permission of the publishers, Simon & Schuster, Inc. and George Allen and Unwin Ltd.

Intellectually, he was unfortunate in the date of his birth. His predecessors were pioneers in one direction, and his successors in another. The sub-structure of his opinions remained always that which had been laid down for him in youth by the dominating personality of his father, but the theories which he built upon this sub-structure were very largely such as it could not support. Skyscrapers, I am told, cannot be built in London because they need to be founded on rock. Mill's doctrines, like a skyscraper founded on clay, were shaky because the foundations were continually sinking. The new storeys, which he added under the inspiration of Carlyle and Mrs. Taylor, were intellectually insecure. To put the matter in another way: morals and intellect were perpetually at war in his thought, morals being incarnate in Mrs. Taylor and intellect in his father. If the one was too soft, the other was too harsh. The amalgam which resulted was practically beneficent, but theoretically somewhat incoherent.

Mill's first important book was his *Logic*, which no doubt presented itself in his mind as a plea for experimental rather than *a priori* methods, and, as such, was useful though not very original. He could not foresee the immense and surprising development of deductive logic which began with Boole's *Laws of Thought* in 1854, but only proved its importance at a considerably later date. Everything that Mill has to say in his *Logic* about matters other than inductive inference is perfunctory and conventional. He states, for example, that propositions are formed by putting together two names, one of which is the subject and the other the predicate. This, I am sure, appeared to him an innocuous truism; but it had been, in fact, the source of two thousand years of important error. On the subject of names, with which modern logic has been much concerned, what he has to say is totally inadequate, and is, in fact, not so good as what had been said by Duns Scotus and William of Occam. His famous contention that the syllogism in 'Barbara' is a *petitio principii*, and that the argument is really from particulars to particulars, has a measure of truth in certain cases, but cannot be accepted as a general doctrine. He maintains, for example, that the proposition 'all men are mortal' asserts 'the Duke of Wellington is mortal' even if the person making the assertion has never heard of the Duke of Wellington. This is obviously untenable: a person who knows the meaning of the words 'man' and 'mortal' can understand the statement 'all men are mortal' but can make no inference about a man he has never heard of; whereas, if Mill were right about the Duke of Wellington, a man could not understand this statement unless he knew the catalogue of all the men who ever have existed or ever will exist. His doctrine that inference is from particulars to particulars is correct psychology when applied to what I call 'animal induction', but is never correct logic. To infer, from the mortality of men in the past, the mortality of those not yet dead, can only be legitimate if there is a *general* principle of induction. Broadly speaking, no general conclusion can be drawn without a general premiss, and only a general premiss will warrant a general conclusion from an incomplete enumeration of instances. What is more, there are general propositions of which no one can doubt the truth, although not a single instance of them can be given. Take, for example, the following: 'All the whole numbers which no one will have thought of before the year 2000 A.D., are greater than a million.' You cannot attempt to give me an instance without contradicting yourself, and you cannot pretend that all the whole numbers have been thought of by someone. From the time of Locke onwards, British empiricists had had theories of knowledge which were inapplicable to mathematics; while continental philosophers, with the exception of the French *Philosophes*, by an undue emphasis upon mathematics, had produced fantastic metaphysical systems. It was only after Mill's time that the sphere of empiricism was clearly delimited from that of mathematics and logic so that peaceful co-existence became possible. I first read Mill's *Logic* at the age of eighteen, and at that time I had a very strong bias in his favour, but even then I could not believe that our acceptance of the proposition 'two and two are four' was a generalization from experience. I was quite at a loss to say how we arrived at this knowledge, but it *felt* quite different from such a proposition as 'all swans are white', which experience might, and in fact did, confute. It did not seem to me that a fresh instance of two and two being four in any degree strengthened my belief. But it is only the modern development of mathematical logic which has enabled me to justify these early feelings and to fit mathematics and empirical knowledge into a single framework.

Mill, although he knew a certain amount of mathematics, never learnt to think in a mathematical way. His law of causation is not one which is employed in mathematical physics. It is a practical maxim employed by savages and philosophers in the conduct of daily life, but not employed in physics by anyone acquainted with the calculus. The laws of physics never state, as Mill's causal laws do, that A is always followed by B. They assert only that when A is present, there will be certain directions of change; since A also changes, the directions of change are themselves continually changing. The notion that causal laws are of the form 'A causes B' is altogether too atomic, and could never have been entertained by anybody who had imaginatively apprehended the continuity of change.

But let us not be too dogmatic. There are those who say that physical changes are not continuous, but explosive. These people, however, also say that individual events are not subject to any causal regularity, and that the apparent regularities of the world are only due to the law of averages. I do not know whether this doctrine is right or wrong, but in any case it is very different from Mill's.

Mill's law of causation is, in fact, only roughly and approximately true in an every-day and unscientific sense. Nevertheless, he thinks it is proved by an inference which elsewhere he considers very shaky: that of induction by simple enumeration. This process is not only shaky, but can be proved quite definitely to lead to false consequences more often than to true ones. If you find *n* objects all of which possess two properties, *A* and *B*, and you then find another object possessing the property *A*, it can easily be proved that it is unlikely to possess the property *B*. This is concealed from common sense by the fact that our animal propensity towards induction is confined to the sort of cases in which induction is liable to give correct results. Take the following as an example of an induction which no one would make: all the sheep that Kant ever saw were within ten miles of Königsberg, but he felt no inclination to induce that all sheep were within ten miles of Königsberg.

Modern physics does not use induction in the old sense at all. It makes enormous theories without pretending that they are in any exact sense true, and uses them only hypothetically until new facts turn up which require new theories. All that the modern physicist claims for a theory is that it fits the known facts and therefore cannot at present be refuted. The problem of induction in its traditional form has by most theoretical physicists been abandoned as insoluble. I am not by any means persuaded that they are right in this, but I think it is quite definitely demonstrable that the problem is very different from what Mill supposed it to be.

It is rather surprising that Mill was so little influenced by Darwin and the theory of evolution. This is the more curious as he frequently quotes Herbert Spencer. He seems to have accepted the Darwinian theory but without realizing its implications. In the chapter 'on Classification' in his *Logic*, he speaks of 'natural kinds' in an entirely pre-Darwinian fashion, and even suggests that the recognized species of animals and plants are *infimae species* in the Scholastic sense, although Darwin's book on the *Origin of Species* proved this view to be untenable. It was natural that the first edition of his *Logic*, which appeared in 1843, should take no account of the theory of evolution, but it is odd that no modifications were made in later editions. What is perhaps still more surprising is that in his *Three Essays on Religion*, written very late in his life, he does not reject the argument from design based upon the adaptation of plants and animals to their environment, or discuss Darwin's explanation of this adaptation. I do not think that he ever imaginatively conceived of man as one among animals or escaped from the eighteenth-century belief that man is fundamentally rational. I am thinking, now, not of what he would have explicitly professed, but of what he unconsciously supposed whenever he was not on his guard. Most of us go about the world with such subconscious presuppositions which influence our beliefs more than explicit arguments do, and in most of us these presuppositions are fully formed by the time we are twenty-five. In the case of Mill, Mrs. Taylor effected certain changes, but these were not in the purely intellectual realm. In that realm, James continued to reign supreme over his son's subconscious.

II

The *Principles of Political Economy* was Mill's second major work. The first edition appeared in 1848, but it was followed by a substantially modified edition in the next year. Mr. Packe, in his admirable biography, has said most of what needs to be said about the difference between these two editions. The difference was mainly concerned with the question of socialism. In the first edition, socialism was criticized from the point of view of the orthodox tradition. But this shocked Mrs. Taylor, and she induced Mill to make very considerable modifications when a new edition was called for. One of the most valuable things in Mr. Packe's book is that he has at last enabled us to see Mrs. Taylor in an impartial light, and to understand the sources of her influence on Mill. But I think perhaps Mr. Packe is a little too severe in criticizing Mill for his change as regards socialism. I cannot but think that what Mrs. Taylor did for him in this respect was to enable him to think what his own nature led him to think, as opposed to what he had been taught. His attitude to socialism, as it appears in the later editions of the book, is by no means uncritical. He still feels that there are difficulties which socialists do not adequately face. He says, for example, 'It is the common error of socialists to overlook the natural indolence of mankind'; and on this ground he fears that a socialist community might stagnate. He lived in a happier age than ours: we should feel a joyful ecstasy if we could hope for anything as comfortable as stagnation.

In his chapter 'on the Probable Futurity of the Labouring Classes' he develops an Utopia to which he looks forward. He hopes to see production in the hands of voluntary societies of workers. Production is not to be in the hands of the State, as Marxian socialists have maintained that it should be. The socialism to which Mill looks forward is that of St. Simon and Fourier. (Robert Owen, to my mind, is not sufficiently emphasized.) Pre-Marxian socialism, which is that of which Mill writes, did not aim at increasing the power of the State. Mill argues emphatically that even under socialism there will still have to be competition, though the competition will be between rival societies of workers, not between rival capitalists. He is inclined to admit that in such a socialist system as he advocates the total production of goods might be less than under capitalism, but he contends that this would be no great evil provided everybody could be kept in reasonable comfort.

For readers of our time, who take it as part of the meaning of socialism that private capitalists should be replaced by the State, it is difficult to avoid misunderstanding in reading Mill. Mill preserved all the distrust of the State which the Manchester School had developed in fighting the feudal aristocracy; and the distrust which he derived from this source was strengthened by his passionate belief in liberty. The power of governments, he says, is always dangerous. He is confident that this power will diminish. Future ages, he maintains, will be unable to credit the amount of government interference which has hitherto existed. It is painful to read a statement of this sort, since it makes one realize the impossibility of foreseeing, even in its most general outlines, the course of future development. The only nineteenth-century writer who foresaw the future with any approach to accuracy was Nietzsche, and he foresaw it, not because he was wiser than other men, but because all the hateful things that have been happening were such as he wished to see. It is only in our disillusioned age that prophets like Orwell have begun to foretell what they feared rather than what they hoped.

Mill, both in his prophecies and in his hopes, was misled by not foreseeing the increasing power of great organizations. This applies not only in economics, but also in other spheres. He maintained, for example, that the State ought to insist upon universal education, but ought not to do the educating itself. He never realized that, so far as elementary education is concerned, the only important alternative to the State is the Church, which he would hardly have preferred.

Mill distinguishes between communism and socialism. He prefers the latter, while not wholly condemning the former. The distinction in his day was not so sharp as it has since become. Broadly speaking, as he explains it, the distinction is that communists object to *all* private property while socialists contend only that 'land and the instruments of production should be the property, not of individuals, but of communities or associations, or of the Government'. There is a famous passage in which he expresses his opinion on communism:

> If, therefore, the choice were to be made between Communism with all its chances, and the present state of society with all its sufferings and injustices; if the institution of private property necessarily carried with it as a consequence, that the produce of labour should be apportioned as we now see it, almost in an inverse ratio to the labour—the largest portions to those who have never

worked at all, the next largest to those whose work is almost nominal, and so in a descending scale, the remuneration dwindling as the work grows harder and more disagreeable, until the most fatiguing and exhausting bodily labour cannot count with certainty on being able to earn even the necessaries of life; if this or Communism were the alternative, all the difficulties, great or small, of Communism would be but as dust in the balance. But to make the comparison applicable, we must compare Communism at its best, with the régime of individual property, not as it is, but as it might be made. The principle of private property has never yet had a fair trial in any country; and less so, perhaps, in this country than in some others.

The history of words is curious. Nobody in Mill's time, with the possible exception of Marx, could have guessed that the word 'communism' would come to denote the military, administrative, and judicial tyranny of an oligarchy, permitting to the workers only so much of the produce of their labour as might be necessary to keep them from violent revolt. Marx, whom we can now see to have been the most influential of Mill's contemporaries, is, so far as I have been able to discover, not mentioned in any of Mill's writings, and it is quite probable that Mill never heard of him. The *Communist Manifesto* was published in the same year as Mill's *Political Economy*, but the men who represented culture did not know of it. I wonder what unknown person in the present day will prove, a hundred years hence, to have been the dominant figure of our time.

Apart from the pronouncements on socialism and communism, Mill's *Political Economy* is not important. Its main principles are derived from his orthodox predecessors with only minor modifications. Ricardo's theory of value, with which on the whole he is in agreement, was superseded by Jevons's introduction of the concept of marginal utility, which represented an important theoretical improvement. As in his *Logic*, Mill is too ready to acquiesce in a traditional doctrine provided he is not aware of any practical evil resulting from it.

III

Much more important than Mill's longer treatises were his two short books *On the Subjection of Women* and *On Liberty*. In regard to the first of these, the world has gone completely as he would have wished. In regard to the second, there has been an exactly opposite movement.

It is a disgrace to both men and women that the world should have had to wait so long for champions of women's equality. Until the French Revolution nobody except Plato ever thought of claiming equality for women, but when the subject came to be raised, incredibly ridiculous arguments were invented in support of the *status quo*. It was not only men who argued that women should have no part in politics. The arguments were equally convincing to women, and especially to political women such as Queen Victoria and Mrs. Sidney Webb. Very few seemed capable of realizing that the supremacy of man was based solely upon a supremacy of muscle. The claim for women's equality was regarded as a subject of ridicule, and remained so until three years before it achieved success. I spoke in favour of votes for women before the First World War and in favour of pacifism during it. The opposition which I encountered in the first of these causes was more virulent and more widespread than that which I encountered in the second. Few things in history are more surprising than the sudden concession of political rights to women in all civilized countries except Switzerland. This is, I think, part of a general change from a biological to a mechanistic outlook. Machinery diminishes the importance of muscle. Industry is less concerned with the seasons than agriculture. Democracy has destroyed dynasties and lessened the feeling of family continuity. Napoleon wanted his son to succeed him. Lenin, Stalin, and Hitler had no such desire. I think the concession of equality to women has been rendered possible by the fact that they are no longer regarded primarily in a biological light. Mill remarks that the only women in England who are not slaves and drudges are those who are operatives in factories. Unaccountably, he forgot Queen Victoria. But there is a measure of truth in what he says, for the work of women in factories, unlike child-bearing, is such as men are capable of doing. It seems that, however admirable the emancipation of women may be in itself, it is part of a vast sociological change emphasizing industry at the expense of agriculture, the factory at the expense of the nursery, and power at the expense of subsistence. I think the world has swung too far in this direction and will not return to sanity until the biological aspects of human life are again remembered. But I see no reason why, if this occurs, it should involve a revival of the subjection of women.

Mill's book *On Liberty* is more important to us in the present day than his book on the *Subjection of Women*. It is more important because the cause which it advocates has been less successful. There is, on the whole, much less liberty in the world now than there was a hundred years ago; and there is no reason to suppose that restrictions on liberty are likely to grow less in any foreseeable future. Mill points to Russia as a country so dominated by bureaucracy that no one, not even the individual bureaucrat, has any personal liberty. But the Russia of his day, after the emancipation of the serfs, had a thousand times more freedom than the Russia of our day. The Russia of his day produced great writers who opposed the autocracy, courageous revolutionaries who were able to carry on their propaganda in spite of prison and exile, even liberals among those in power, as the abolition of serfdom proved. There was every reason to hope that Russia would in time develop into a constitutional monarchy, marching by stages towards the degree of political freedom that existed in England. The growth of liberty was also apparent in other countries. In the United

States slavery was abolished a few years after the publication of Mill's book. In France the monarchy of Napoleon III, which Mill passionately hated, came to an end eleven years after his book was published; and at the same time manhood suffrage was introduced in Germany. On such grounds I do not think that Mr. Packe is right in saying that the general movement of the time was against liberty, and I do not think that Mill's optimism was irrational.

With Mill's values, I for my part find myself in complete agreement. I think he is entirely right in emphasizing the importance of the individual in so far as values are concerned. I think, moreover, that it is even more desirable in our day than it was in his to uphold the kind of outlook for which he stands. But those who care for liberty in our day have to fight different battles from those of the nineteenth century, and have to devise new expedients if liberty is not to perish. From the seventeenth century to the end of the nineteenth, 'Liberty' was the watchword of the radicals and revolutionaries; but in our day the word has been usurped by reactionaries, and those who think themselves most progressive are inclined to despise it. It is labelled as part of 'rotten bourgeois idealism' and is regarded as a middle-class fad, important only to those who already enjoy the elegant leisure of the well-to-do. So far as any one person is responsible for this change, the blame must fall on Marx, who substituted Prussian discipline for freedom as both the means and the end of revolutionary action. But Marx would not have had the success which he has had if there had not been large changes in social organization and in technique which furthered his ideals as opposed to those of earlier reformers.

What has changed the situation since Mill's day is, as I remarked before, the great increase of organization. Every organization is a combination of individuals for a purpose; and, if this purpose is to be achieved, it requires a certain subordination of the individuals to the whole. If the purpose is one in which all the individuals feel a keen interest, and if the executive of the organization commands confidence, the sacrifice of liberty may be very small. But if the purpose for which the organization exists inspires only its executive, to which the other members submit for extraneous reasons, the loss of liberty involved may grow until it becomes almost total. The larger the organization, the greater becomes the gap in power between those at the top and those at the bottom, and the more likelihood there is of oppression. The modern world, for technical reasons, is very much more organized than the world of a hundred years ago: there are very much fewer acts which a man does simply from his own impulse, and very many more which he is compelled or induced to perform by some authority. The advantages that spring from organization are so great and so obvious that it would be absurd to wish to return to an earlier condition, but those who are conscious only of the advantages are apt to overlook the dangers, which are very real and very menacing.

As a first example, let us take agriculture. In the years immediately succeeding the publication of Mill's *Liberty*, there was an immense development of pioneering in the Middle West of the United States. The pioneers prided themselves upon their 'rugged individualism'. They settled in regions which were well wooded, well watered, and of great natural fertility. Without excessive labour, they felled the trees, thereby securing log cabins and fuel, and when the soil was cleared, they procured a rich harvest of grain. There was, however, a Serpent in this individualist paradise: the Serpent was the railroad, without which the grain could not be got to market. The railroad represented a vast accumulation of capital, an enormous expenditure of labour, and a combination of very many persons, hardly any of them agriculturists. The pioneers were indignant at their loss of independence, and their indignation gave rise to the Populist movement, which, in spite of much heat, never achieved any success. In this case, however, there was only one enemy of personal independence. I was struck by the difference when I came in contact with pioneers in Australia. The conquering of new land for agriculture in Australia depends upon enormously expensive schemes of irrigation, too vast for the separate States and only practicable by the Federal Government. Even then, when a man has acquired a tract of land, it contains no timber, and all his building materials and his fuel have to be brought from a distance. Medical attention for himself and his family is only rendered possible by an elaborate organization of aeroplanes and wireless. His livelihood depends upon the export trade, which prospers or suffers according to the vagaries of distant Governments. His mentality, his tastes, and his feelings, are still those of the rugged individualist pioneer of a hundred years ago, but his circumstances are totally different. However he may wish to rebel, he is tightly controlled by forces that are entirely external to himself. Intellectual liberty he may still have; but economic liberty has become a dream.

But the life of the Australian pioneer is one of heavenly bliss when compared with that of the peasant in communist countries, who has become more completely a serf than he was in the worst days of the Czardom. He owns no land, he has no right to the produce of his own labour, the authorities permit him only a bare subsistence, and any complaint may land him in a forced-labour camp. The totalitarian State is the last term of organization, the goal towards which, if we are not careful, we shall find all developed countries tending. Socialists have thought that the power hitherto vested in capitalists would become beneficent if vested in the State. To some degree this is true, so long as the State is democratic. Communists, unfortunately, forgot this proviso. By transferring economic power to an oligarchic State, they produced an engine of tyranny more dreadful, more vast, and at the same time more minute than any that had existed in previous history. I do not think this was the intention of those who made the Russian Revolution, but it was the effect of their actions. Their actions had this effect because they failed to realize the need of liberty and the inevitable evils of despotic power.

But the evils of which the extreme form is seen in communist countries exists in a lesser degree, and may easily increase, in many countries belonging to what is somewhat humorously called the 'Free World'. Vavilov, the most distinguished geneticist that Russia has produced in recent times, was sent to perish miserably in the Arctic because he would not subscribe to Stalin's ignorant belief in the inheritance of acquired characters. Oppenheimer is disgraced and prevented from pursuing his work largely because he doubted the practicability of the hydrogen bomb at a time when this doubt was entirely rational. The F.B.I., which has only the level of education to be expected among policemen, considers itself competent to withhold visas from the most learned men in Europe on grounds which every person capable of understanding the matters at issue knows to be absurd. This evil has reached such a point that international conferences of learned men in the United States have become impossible. It is curious that Mill makes very little mention of the police as a danger to liberty. In our day, they are its worst enemy in most civilized countries.

IV

It is an interesting speculation, and perhaps not a wholly idle one, to consider how Mill would have written his book if he had been writing now. I think that everything he says on the *value* of liberty could stand unchanged. So long as human life persists, liberty will be essential to many of the greatest goods that our terrestrial existence has to offer. It has its profound source in one of our most elementary instincts: new-born infants fall into a rage if their limbs are constricted. The kinds of freedom that are desired change with growth in years and knowledge, but it remains an essential source of simple happiness. But it is not only happiness that is lost when liberty is needlessly impaired. It is also all the more important and difficult kinds of usefulness. Almost every great service that individuals have ever done to mankind has exposed them to violent hostility extending often to martyrdom. All this is said by Mill so well that it would require no alteration except the supplying of more recent instances.

Mill would, I think, go on to say that unwarrantable interferences with liberty are mostly derived from one or other of two sources: the first of these is a tyrannical moral code which demands of others conformity with rules of behaviour which they do not accept; the other, which is the more important, is unjust power.

Of the first of these, the tyranny of moral codes, Mill gives various examples. He has an eloquent and powerful passage on the persecution of the Mormons, which is all the better for his purposes because no one could suspect him of thinking well of polygamy. Another of his examples of undue interference with liberty in the supposed interests of a moral code is the observance of the Sabbath, which has lost most of its importance since his day. My father, who was a disciple of Mill, spent his brief Parliamentary career in a vain endeavour to persuade the House of Commons that T. H. Huxley's lectures were not entertaining, for, if they could be considered as entertainment, they were illegal on Sundays.

I think if Mill were writing now he would choose in further illustration two matters which the police have recently brought to the fore. The first of these is 'obscene' literature. The law on this subject is exceedingly vague; indeed, if there is to be any law about it, it cannot well help being vague. In practice, anything is obscene which happens to shock a magistrate; and even things which do not shock a magistrate may become the subject of prosecution if they happen to shock some ignorant policeman, as happened recently in the case of the *Decameron*. One of the evils of any law of this sort is that it prevents the diffusion of useful knowledge if such knowledge was not thought useful when the magistrate in question was a boy. Most of us had thought that matters were improving in this respect, but recent experience has made us doubtful. I cannot think that the feeling of shock which an elderly man experiences on being brought in contact with something to which he is not accustomed is a sufficient basis for an accusation of crime.

The second matter in which Mill's principles condemn existing legislation is homosexuality. If two adults voluntarily enter into such a relation, this is a matter which concerns them only, and in which, therefore, the community ought not to intervene. If it were still believed, as it once was, that the toleration of such behaviour would expose the community to the fate of Sodom and Gomorrah, the community would have every right to intervene. But it does not acquire a right to intervene merely on the ground that such conduct is thought wicked. The criminal law may rightly be invoked to prevent violence or fraud inflicted upon unwilling victims, but it ought not to be invoked when whatever damage there may be is suffered only by the agents—always assuming that the agents are adults.

Of much greater importance than these remnants of medievalism in our legislation, is the question of unjust power. It was this question which gave rise to the liberalism of the eighteenth and nineteenth centuries. They protested against the power of monarchs, and against the power of the Church in countries where there was religious persecution. They protested also against alien domination wherever there was a strong national sentiment running counter to it. On the whole, these aims were successfully achieved. Monarchs were replaced by Presidents, religious persecution almost disappeared, and the Treaty of Versailles did what it could to realize the liberal principle of nationality. In spite of all this, the world did not become a paradise. Lovers of liberty found that there was less of it than there had been, not more. But the slogans and strategies which had brought victory in the past to the liberal cause were not applicable to the new situation, and the liberals found themselves deserted by the supposedly progressive advocates of new forms of tyranny. Kings and priests and capitalists are, on the whole, outmoded bogies. It is officials who represent the modern danger. Against the power of officials, single individuals can do little; only organizations can combat organizations. I think we shall have to revive Montesquieu's doctrine of the division of powers, but in new forms. Consider, for example, the conflict of labour and capital which dominated the minds of socialists. Socialists imagined that the evils they were combating would cease if the power of capital was put into the hands of the State. This was done in Russia with the approval of organized labour. As soon as it had been done the trade unions were deprived of independent power, and labour found itself more completely enslaved than ever before. There is no monolithic solution of this problem that will leave any loophole for liberty. The only possible solution that a lover of liberty can support must be one in which there are rival powers, neither of them absolute, and each compelled in a crisis to pay some attention to public opinion. This means, in practice, that trade unions must preserve their independence of the executive. Undoubtedly the liberty enjoyed by a man who must belong to his union if he is to obtain employment is an inadequate and imperfect liberty; but it seems to be the best that modern industries can permit.

There is one sphere in which the advocate of liberty is confronted with peculiar difficulties: I mean the sphere of education. It has never been thought that children should be free to choose whether they will be educated or not, and it is not now held that parents ought to have this freedom of choice. Mill thought that the State should insist that children should be educated, but should not itself do the educating. He had, however, not very much to say about how the educating should be done. I will try to consider what he would say on this subject if he were writing now.

Let us begin by asking the question of principle, namely, what should a lover of liberty wish to see done in the schools? I think the ideal but somewhat Utopian answer, would be that the pupils should be qualified as far as possible to form a reasonable judgement on controversial questions in regard to which they are likely to have to act. This would require, on the one hand, a training in judicial habits of thought; and, on the other hand, access to impartial supplies of knowledge. In this way, the pupil would be prepared for a genuine freedom of choice on becoming adult. We cannot give freedom to the child, but we can give him a preparation for freedom; and this is what education ought to do.

This, however, is not the theory of education which has prevailed in most parts of the world. The theory of education which has prevailed most widely was invented by the Jesuits and perfected by Fichte. Fichte states that the object of education should be to destroy freedom of the will, for why, he asks, should we wish a freedom to choose what is wrong rather than what is right? Fichte knows what is right, and desires a school system such that, when the children grow up, they will be under an inner compulsion to choose what Fichte considers right in preference to what he considers wrong. This theory is adopted in its entirety by communists and Catholics, and, up to a point, by the State schools of many countries. Its purpose is to produce mental slaves, who have heard only one side on all the burning questions of the day and have been inspired with feelings of horror towards the other side. There is just one slight divergence from what Fichte wanted: although his method of education is approved, the dogmas inculcated differ from country to country and from creed to creed. What Fichte chiefly wished taught was the superiority of the German nation to all others; but on this one small point most of his disciples disagreed with him. The consequence is that State education, in the countries which adopt his principles, produces, in so far as it is successful, a herd of ignorant fanatics, ready at

the word of command to engage in war or persecution as
may be required of them. So great is this evil that the
world would be a better place (at any rate, in my opinion) if State education had never been inaugurated.

There is a broad principle which helps in deciding
many questions as to the proper sphere of liberty. The
things that make for individual well-being are, broadly
speaking, of two sorts: namely, those in which private
possession is possible and those in which it is not. The
food that one man eats cannot be also eaten by another;
but if a man enjoys a poem, he does not thereby place
any obstacle in the way of another man's enjoyment of
it. Roughly speaking, the goods of which private possession is possible are material, whereas the other sort of
goods are mental. Material goods, if the supply is not
unlimited, should be distributed on principles of justice:
no one should have too much if, in consequence, someone else has too little. This principle of distribution will
not result from unrestricted liberty, which would lead to
Hobbes's war of all against all and end in the victory
of the stronger. But mental goods—such as knowledge,
enjoyment of beauty, friendship and love—are not taken
away from other people by those whose lives are en-
riched by them. There is not, therefore, any *prima facie*
case for restrictions of liberty in this sphere. Those who
forbid certain kinds of knowledge, or, like Plato and
Stalin, certain kinds of music and poetry, are allowing
Government to intervene in regions where it has no
locus standi. I do not wish to over-emphasize the importance of this principle, for there are many cases in
which the distinction between material and mental goods
cannot be sharply drawn. One of the most obvious of
these is the printing of books. A book is as material as a
plum pudding, but the good that we expect to derive from
it is mental. It is not easy to devise any sound principle
upon which even the wisest authority could decide what
books deserve to be printed. I do not think that any improvement is possible upon the present diversity of publishers. Wherever there is an authority, whether secular

or ecclesiastical, whose permission is required before a book can be printed, the results are disastrous. The same thing applies to the arts: no one, not even a communist, will now contend that Russian music was improved by Stalin's intervention.

Mill deserved the eminence which he enjoyed in his own day, not by his intellect but by his intellectual virtues. He was not a great philosopher, like Descartes or Hume. In the realm of philosophy, he derived his ideas from Hume and Bentham and his father. But he blended the harshness of the Philosophical Radicals with something of the Romantic Movement, derived first from Coleridge and Carlyle and then from his wife. What he took over, he made rational in assimilating it. The follies and violences of some Romantics made no impression upon him. His intellectual integrity was impeccable. When he engaged in controversy, he did so with the most minutely scrupulous fairness. The people against whom his controversies were directed deserved almost always the urbanely worded strictures which he passed upon them.

In spite of his purely intellectual deficiencies, his influence was very great and very beneficent. He made rationalism and socialism respectable, though his socialism was of the pre-Marxist sort which did not involve an increase in the powers of the State. His advocacy of equality for women in the end won almost worldwide acceptance. His book *On Liberty* remains a classic: although it is easy to point out theoretical defects, its value increases as the world travels further and further from its teaching. The present world would both astonish and horrify him; but it would be better than it is, if his ethical principles were more respected.

JOHN STUART MILL

BY

Noel Annan

Why should those who love and study English literature read Mill? It is not quite enough to say that everyone who is moved by Victorian poetry and novels and who tries to criticize them should enlarge his understanding of the age by becoming acquainted with its philosophers. It is not even enough to point out that literature is concerned among other things with morality and society, and that Mill (1806–1873) wrote about both. But what did he write that compels a critic or a student to study him? Since the war four Cambridge critics have answered this question, and perhaps it is of interest in passing to note that their answers were given in response to the challenge that teaching literature makes. In literary studies—unlike the natural sciences—the best research often springs from the delight and the despair of teaching.

From *The English Mind*, edited by Hugh Sykes Davies and George Watson, Cambridge University Press, 1964. Reprinted by permission of the Cambridge University Press.

Basil Willey's memorable essay on Mill[1] sprang from the lectures that he gave for the paper on the English Moralists in the English Tripos. In it he painted the picture of a man continually forced to repudiate the principles on which he founded his philosophy of life. We must, he said, admire the honesty of the utilitarian rationalist who had seen the errors of his creed; but is it not all the more pathetic that Mill was unable to cut himself adrift from it? To attempt to inject feeling into the adamantine doctrines of Bentham was praiseworthy; but what did the attempt amount to? Mill in the *System of Logic* (1843) set down the rules for establishing a science of society, but then had to admit that his elaborate structure neglected all that is most valuable and strange and curious in man. Mill was a perfectionist, yet the *Political Economy* (1848) led inescapably to a scene where the mass of men were forced to live on the brink of starvation. His lofty injunctions to them to reform and improve society were a mockery when improvement was limited by the operation of the iron law of wages. How odd that Mill, the evangelist of progress, was so terrified by the rise in population that he argued in favour of arresting the growth in productivity and of settling for a static State! He praised liberty, he asserted that the individual must not be engulfed by the tide of vulgar prejudices and deplorable social conventions; yet what hope was there of preserving individuality when in the same breath he declared that all the tendencies of the times ran against it, and when his own better judgement made him move slowly towards socialism? It was all very well to pronounce that the gross utilitarian morality of self-interest was inadequate and could not be reconciled with the principle of promoting the greatest happiness of the greatest number, but in performing his dissection of utilitarian ethics he so mangled the carcass that he left a shambles. Finally, when we turn to ob-

---

[1] Basil Willey, *Nineteenth Century Studies* (London, 1949), pp. 141–86.

serve what Mill made of religion, the maze of contradiction that meets our eyes reveals why all along the line
he failed. His religion is devoid of what matters most in
religion. It is devoid of love.

> All through his life, like some ungifted Moses, he had
> tried to strike water out of dry rocks—altruism out of self-
> love, liberty out of bondage—and now here, in culminating
> frustration, he tries to draw faith out of reason. The rod
> taps and taps; the rock yields no drop; while—hidden from
> his short-sighted eyes—the spring bubbles up close at his
> back. If any proof were needed of St Paul's proposition
> that by wisdom (reasoning) no man finds God, here is an
> admirable one.

It is sad yet fitting that one so grave, so grey, so like a
power-loom, with lack-lustre eye, so full of joyless knowledge, 'his earnest, exemplary face turned persistently
in the wrong direction', should display an incomprehen-
sion in discovering Christianity that becomes almost
sublime in its perversity.

That was in 1949. A year later F. R. Leavis published
his introduction to Mill's essays on Bentham and Coleridge.[2] It was born out of his exasperation with the
syllabus of the English Tripos and the lack of discipline
that enfeebled background studies to literature. The
reconciliation that Mill made between what he called
'the two great seminal minds of the age' was magnificent.
The mind that saw both these doctrines as necessary and
complementary was—unlike Coleridge's—a disciplined
mind. It was the mind of a man of integrity whose
'intellectual distinction is at the same time a distinction
of character'. Mill, moreover, was a great representative
figure of the Victorian age, and Leavis proceeded to trace
an educational trail that would lead the student from
Mill to George Eliot, who shared Mill's belief in the

---

[2] F. R. Leavis, *Mill on Bentham and Coleridge* (London, 1950),
pp. 1–38.

Religion of Humanity. The trail led past the far less important Carlyle and Sterling, moved in sight of F. D. Maurice, the Broad Church movement and early socialism, to link Mill's own leanings to socialism with a social scientist of the next generation—Beatrice Webb. *My Apprenticeship* was the corollary to the *Autobiography* (1873). Having made this connexion, the student would recall that Mill and Beatrice Webb both rejected materialism and believed that men and women should dedicate their lives to service and high seriousness: in a sense, Beatrice Webb's life was the child of Mill's denunciation of the subjection of women. Yet he would also note the strength of the hold that Benthamism exercised over Mill. For though it is true that Benthamism inspired the movement for reform, it was also inextricably entangled with Adam Smith's economics. The student therefore must hold in his mind not only the image of Mill, the dedicated modifier of utilitarianism. He must also retain the judgement that Dickens passed on 'enlightened' utilitarianism through the character of Gradgrind in *Hard Times*.

Eight years passed. Then, in exploring how the notion of culture had arisen in England and how writers related it to society, Raymond Williams returned to Mill.[3] In his view Mill had recognized well enough what Coleridge was doing. He understood that the social philosophy which ran in rivulets through the morass of Coleridge's writing fed a theory of culture. In this theory culture did not mean the acquisition of a cultivated mind: it was not an eighteenth-century aristocratic virtue, a facet of the personality that enabled a man to move at ease in polite society. Coleridge thought of culture as a vision of life or a moral habit. But Mill, though he was to develop Coleridge's idea of the clerisy or intellectual élite, made nothing of Coleridge's notion of culture. He remained intellectualist in manner and in method. If in

---

[3] Raymond Williams, *Culture and Society 1780–1950* (London, 1958), pp. 49–70.

his youth he appreciated that Bentham and Coleridge
should be reconciled, as he grew older he moved further
from reconciling them. The notion of culture entails fus-
ing entities. Mill did not fuse anything, he opposed sets
of abstract principles one against the other, never realizing that doctrines become alive only through what they
are attached to and through what they pronounce to
be valuable, never realizing that values are 'different
orders of expression which arise from different ways of
life'. It was characteristic of Mill—and of the English—
to think of political activity as a pendulum that swings
between two extremes. This mechanical metaphor reveals their misunderstanding of life because it shows how
they thought of life as a series of disjointed parts and
not as a whole. And this same disjunction appears in
Mill's view of art. His *Autobiography* indeed described
his realization in youth that to work for social reform
was by itself an inadequate ideal: man needed poetry as
a source of inward joy and a perennial source of happiness to sustain him when the treacheries of politics be-
trayed him. But, Williams objects, this was to make
poetry a substitute for feeling. Once again Mill was
operating by posing antitheses: feeling versus mind; subjective, intuitive apprehensions versus logical, mechanical reasoning. He never learnt from Coleridge that what
men needed was not merely to enlarge the mind by
recognizing differences. They needed to change their
mode of thought by reasoning, not from abstracted experience cast into principles but from their own living,
hard, personal experience. It was this that should mould
their attitude to social institutions. What, after all, was
Mill but a more humane utilitarian with all the desperate
inadequacies of that creed?

The disastrous inadequacy of utilitarian ethics was
again one of the themes of Dorothea Krook's book,
which appeared in 1959. She discerned three main traditions in moral thought, of which the basest was the
worldly utilitarian ethic of Aristotle, Hobbes or Hume,
which substituted self-sufficiency, or fear, or sympathy

for love as the central moral concept.[4] Yet she singled
Mill out not as the exemplar of utilitarian morality but
as a humanist who made perfectly legitimate criticisms
of the Christianity of his day. She set out to rescue him on
this score from Basil Willey's strictures. It was true that
Mill was too much the social scientist and too little the
humanist to be flexible or imaginative enough. But, at
any rate, he did not fall into the complacent morality of
the club-man that made Hume's morality so despicable.
He might criticize Christianity in a wooden way, but if
he had got hold of the wrong end of the stick he was
surely holding it by the same end as the Victorian Christian apologists. It was they who repeated the two-
centuries-old arguments for the existence of God from a
First Cause or from Design or from Consciousness or
from the General Consent of Mankind. It was they who
entangled themselves in moral dilemmas by declaring
God omnipotent and then maintaining that his mercy
must be limited to the Elect. If Mill was disabled from
understanding the innermost meaning of Christianity,
he at least did a good job of demolition in pulverizing
these arguments. But he went further. He asked questions which must be asked by those who are serious. He
asked what fundamental needs of the human spirit were
supplied by Christianity and how far it redeemed men's
corrupt consciousness. When, for instance, he considered
the claim for immortality, his scrupulous honesty admitted that there was nothing in human knowledge or
experience to disprove it—and that therefore it might be
true. He also admitted that the terror of death was a
reality and that the only possible way of diminishing it
was to improve society so that more human beings could
lead happy lives. 'They who have had their happiness
can bear to part with existence; but it is hard to die without having lived.' Dorothea Krook did not deny Mill's
limitations. His scientific habit of mind—a habit which

---

[4] Dorothea Krook, *Three Traditions of Moral Thought* (Cambridge, 1959), pp. 181–201.

imposes disastrous restrictions when the mind is working
on moral problems—impeded the spiritual resources that
undoubtedly lay within him and produced a thin gruel
of humanism that was infinitely less impressive than that
of Arnold; but he had grace within him.

Now, different as these four accounts of Mill are, they
have certain things in common. All praise Mill's conversion to Coleridge, Wordsworth and the life of the spirit:
all welcome his recognition that happiness cannot be
attained by making it the direct end: all deplore the
backsliding towards utilitarianism and laissez-faire. To
Basil Willey the spectacle is pathetic, to Leavis it is an
example of distinction in moral bearing, for Williams
and Dorothea Krook it demands both sympathy and
regret that a man who understood so many of the limitations of the creed that he inherited could not break
through it to perceive the moral profundities that it concealed. All of them see in Mill an illustration of what
social philosophers might be if only they would expose
themselves to the full experience of literature and life
that criticism analyses. They judge Mill by his criticism
of his age—what he thought were its vices, what virtues
he particularly prized and what he conceived to be the
purpose of life: they judge him by his answers.

But is it really apposite to judge Mill solely in terms of
culture? He worked in a philosophical tradition that is
not susceptible to judgements of this kind. Very severe
criticism can be made of him as a philosopher; but although he may not sound as impressive as the sages who
prophesied over the bones of Victorian culture, he contributed certain notions which are as important as any
of theirs. Mill adorns a famous tradition of thought and
he cannot be seen in perspective until we stop regarding
him as the man who tried and failed to spiritualize utilitarianism. He was not merely the heir to Bentham. He
stood at a turning-point in the history of ideas when
the social sciences were beginning to detach themselves
from philosophy. He stood at the end of a tradition of

thought which was established by Hobbes and Locke, and he looked far more to the past than forward to the future. What had begun as an exploration in the mid-seventeenth century of the political conditions that would enable a minority to be free developed into a systematic analysis of society and of human behaviour. In this newly constructed model of the world, the older hier-archical society of feudal obligation and custom and Christian duty disappeared and was replaced by a bustling collection of individuals, each free to own and to accumulate an unlimited amount of property and wealth, each free to pursue his own goals, none owing duties to another apart from those imposed by law, none de-flecting himself from the pursuit of his own goals in order to conform to the purposes of others. Each man was responsible for his actions and chose the means to achieve his ends, but each chose different ends because he had been given freedom of conscience. Why then was there not chaos? The famous answer given by Locke was that there existed in Nature a law of the natural identity of interests, whereby men did not consciously co-operate or pursue a common end but where the efforts of each striving on his own behalf were reconciled with the efforts of everyone else. What clinched this argu-ment was the work of the classical economists. For the first time one aspect of human behaviour was analysed as a system of interrelated variables that embodied all sorts of factors such as tariffs, price-levels or the division of labour, and it appeared to be established that men, by pursuing their own self-interested diverse ends, could in fact achieve a common end, i.e. the highest level of wealth possible. It was, as a theory, immensely satisfying, because it explained social behaviour in terms of indi-vidual psychology and hence in terms of personal be-haviour; it was coherent, in that literature, philosophy and scientific inquiry seemed for a time all to be moving in harmony; and it was heartening, in that it suggested that, as education spread and men grew wiser, they would choose their goals and the means to achieve them

in a rational and scientific manner. Above all, it settled
what to the pioneers of the model in the seventeenth century seemed all-important, namely the problem why order and not chaos in society would ensue if men were
free to choose their own goals at random—for instance
to dissent in religion.

Theories, however water-tight and convincing, generate their own doubts, and the positivist theory of social
behaviour was no exception. If Hartley provided it
with a more rigorous conception of psychology, Hume
almost destroyed it by his separation of fact and value.
Godwin carried it to the brink of absurdity by arguing
that, if men's interests were really identical, then unnatural institutions such as Church and State could be
abolished, since education would provide men with all
the knowledge that they needed to understand the situation in which they lived. Meanwhile Malthus and
Ricardo began to paint a gloomier picture of the economics of competition, and doubted whether competition
alone was sufficient to stabilize social relations: perhaps, after all, everything could not be explained in terms
of rational self-interest, perhaps social institutions such
as marriage, property and custom were also required to
explain why men behaved as they did. Against these
doubts could be set Bentham's brilliant, clear and simple
explanation of the principles that governed institutions
and their reform—principles which were sustained by
an analysis of human behaviour. Until Mill's time every
theoretical weakness that was exposed seemed to find its
counter in some new exposition of part of the theory.
What finally put the theory into a hopeless state of confusion were social events which it could not explain
satisfactorily in its own terms. These events were the
population explosion and the effects of the industrial
revolution on the lives of human beings. Now it was no
longer self-evident that order could be maintained by
putting political power into the hands of a small number
of property-owners. Now men could no longer believe
that whatever economic inequalities were produced by

the operations of the market were more than outweighed by the political equality that the freedoms won in the seventeenth century guaranteed. Society was being transformed by industrialism and it was inevitable that the way it worked and the behaviour of the human beings in it would also be transformed.

This revolution in thought is, of course, associated first and foremost with the name of Marx. It was Marx who denied that social phenomena could be reduced to laws about human nature. Mill, standing at the end of the positivist explanation of social behaviour, was still arguing that since men make their own environment and traditions, their institutions and customs must be explicable in terms of the mind and of human nature. For how else had they arisen other than through men's will? Every institution had a motive behind it, everything was purposeful or it could not have been instituted by man. Even though the purpose that lay behind a custom or tradition or institution had long been forgotten or had been perverted, one had only to discover the original motive in order to provide an explanation. This was the theory that Marx destroyed. 'It is not the consciousness of man that determines his existence—rather it is his social existence that determines his consciousness.' Man was the product of society and a slave to the impersonal laws of history that governed society.

What then did Mill contribute to this remarkable tradition of thought which had shown such coherence and vitality? His writings, in particular *The System of Logic* during the fifties and sixties, captured the minds of a strong minority among the young men of those decades, and when he died one of them canonized him as the 'saint of rationalism'. But does the saint still work miracles? His treatise on logic, the great counterblast against Whewell's intuitionism, was less revolutionary than it seemed at first sight, technically only slightly more interesting than was Whateley's work and slightly less interesting than those of De Morgan, Venn or Boole. His inquiry into the methods of the natural sciences was

certainly more original once he had set aside his argument about causation and had seen that tests, prediction
and probability theory were the important concepts in
the logic of the natural sciences. But the greater part of
his work was connected with the social sciences, and
here he added little. His *Political Economy* ran into
many editions, but it made no contribution of importance to any part of economics. He did not appreciate
the part that mathematics or statistics were to play in
economics or in social inquiry. In common with most
contemporary social philosophers, including Marx, he
thought his task to be the discovery of the laws that governed human behaviour and the progress of society. He
admitted that, in order to be significant, *a priori* deductions from abstract principles must be checked against
empirical data obtained by observing history. But he realized neither how detailed and statistical such observations had to be if they related to the present, nor how
boldly and powerfully they had to be analysed if they
were extracted from the past. His *a priori* studies derived, as we have seen, from the positivist theory that all
social events are ultimately the product of human motives, and the analysis that he made of history was feeble
in comparison with that of Marx, Hegel or even the
utopian socialists or Comte.

There is indeed a feebleness and timidity in Mill. He
has not the same courage as his predecessors in the positivist tradition. He has not their assurance that even
when they were criticizing the tradition in which they
worked they were enhancing it. Nor has he their political confidence that reforms which were to give reality to
popular rights, such as the right to vote, would not destroy order and prosperity. To some critics these limitations seem to be virtues. Gertrude Himmelfarb, for
instance, argues that there are two Mills: the blinkered
radical under the spell of Harriet Taylor, who repudiated
his youthful criticisms of utilitarianism and wrote the
dogmatic essays on Liberty and the Utility of Religion;
and the mature man who returned to the spirit of the

essays on Bentham and Coleridge and wrote the works on Representative Government and Theism.[5] Yet if we set Mill's anxieties about the effect of democracy against those of Tocqueville, or his analysis of government and finance against Bagehot's *English Constitution* and *Lombard Street*, we must admit that he is neither as profound as the first nor as independent as the second. Mill works away plugging holes, reorganizing his defences, admitting defects, modifying virtues, patching and darning. It is not in this way that advances in philosophy or the social sciences are made. Nor do these modifications and criticisms of radicalism impress. Many of them, such as plural voting, were the sort of safeguards that were put forward by the Whigs and Liberal-conservatives whom he despised. Others, such as proportional representation, produced in practice the very opposite of what Mill desired. Although Mill was often trying to see through the formulae of radicalism to discover what would make government not more democratic but better, and although he deplored individuals pursuing their own personal or class interests, he never understood the play of social forces. If his essays had been really searching criticisms of the styles of life in his times, surely one of them would have been concerned with urbanization and industrialization and their appalling problems? He applied Tocqueville's analysis of democracy in America to England, oblivious for the instant of the immense strength of aristocratic and upper-middle-class power. He could not imagine that for the next hundred years the intellectual minority, which he was so concerned to protect, was in danger not of being stifled by the masses but of being gelded by the upper classes.

Imagination! *That* has never been the quality that comes first to mind when one reads the rationalist philosophers. There is no need to tell again the failings of the middle-class liberal thinkers. They did not under-

[5] *Essays on Politics and Culture by J. S. Mill*, ed. Gertrude Himmelfarb (New York, 1962).

stand that their political reforms would in practice have
the effect of transferring power from an aristocracy to a
plutocracy. They ignored the destruction by the cash
nexus of whatever gains had been made by political action in achieving equality. Their non-historical and de-
humanized creed could not take account of the new
historiography of dynamic history and daemonic man.
Their reform programme of mechanized devices and governmental adjustments was inadequate to meet the new
formulations of power politics and revolution. Finally, in
psychology they neglected the startling notion of the
Unconscious whether it operated in individuals or in the
mass. Beside the German Idealists or the utopian socialists, or the Marxists or the historians, Mill seems de-
plorably unoriginal and uninventive, staid and sedate.
He seems to be fiddling with small methodological points
or constitutional and financial reforms.

And yet, however much at first sight the Cambridge critics' assessment of Mill seems to be substantiated, a
shadow falls across it. Is empirical philosophy or social
science susceptible to their cultural criteria? Is Mill primarily intending to advocate a style of life? It is true that
a philosopher's style—the way he constructs his system,
the way he moves from premises to conclusions, perhaps
the metaphors he uses—can be as personal a statement
of reality as a poem. Plato, St Augustine, Hobbes and
Hegel composed unforgettable dramas concerning the
nature and purpose of life. But not all philosophy is
concerned with penetrating reality. Indeed most philosophers start their inquiries not in order to answer the
riddle of the universe but because they are puzzled by
specific logical or epistemological problems, such as induction or meaning; and some such as Mill, who concern themselves with ethics or social theory, indignantly
deny that they are ontologists or metaphysicians. Those
who study literature should admit that many philosophers
do not believe that anything profitable can be said about
the whole of life. Critics have a predisposition to prefer

metaphysicians because, like poets, they appear to speak to our present condition. Empirical philosophers and social scientists, on the other hand, come to transitory conclusions that are superseded the day after tomorrow. They are the victims of time; but that does not mean that they can be shrugged off—they have made too many damaging criticisms of metaphysics.

There is indeed an innate antagonism between the cultural mode of thought that critics employ and the operations of empirical philosophy and social science. The artist, the metaphysician and the critic who judges them, are all trying to obtain a single vision of life, the empiricist to place life under a prism so that he can study its component parts. The Cambridge critics suggest that if Mill had only broken with utilitarianism he would have been less the slave of abstraction, more able to fuse the insights of Bentham and Coleridge instead of laying them side by side. But this is not so. In Victorian times it became no longer possible for a rationalist philosopher to fuse the various recognized ways of analysing what human beings do. Gradually new academic disciplines were hardening and becoming autonomous and could no longer be subsumed under a super-theory of knowledge. All they could do was occasionally to lighten one another's darkness. The Victorian intelligentsia were puzzled and distressed that this appeared to be so, and they were all too apt to applaud efforts to re-establish the unity of knowledge. Mill made such efforts, but in retrospect it is as just to criticize as to praise him for making them. For in attempting to reconcile Coleridge with Bentham, or good with democratic government, or agnosticism with theism, Mill so far from becoming a better became a worse social scientist.

Social scientists can work only within the concepts and techniques of their own discipline. Alfred Marshall introduced into his *Principles of Economics* many high-sounding passages about thrift and self-reliance and poverty; and these admirable sentiments may have inspired him to tackle the problem of the redistribution of

wealth. But they did not affect the logic of his economic
theory; the passages could be removed and the theory
would be unaffected. Keynes believed that capitalism was
grossly inefficient and unemployment a blot upon civilization, but it took long years of controversy and experiment to hammer out the *General Theory*, which did not
rely as a theory on moral considerations. As a contribution to social science, Mill's revision of utilitarian ethics
—except in so far as it produced confusion—is irrelevant.
His successors were far more to the point. They recognized utilitarian ethics for what it was: either it was a
matter of technical philosophy to be treated with great
rigour as Sidgwick and Moore treated it; or it was a
shorthand common-sense guide to political and social reform, not purporting to cover the whole of moral activity
and capable of being set to work, as it was at the end of
the century, with economic theories opposed to laissez-
faire justifying programmes of State interference.

Mill, then, was a social philosopher—which is something more and something less than a critic of culture.
His flat undistinguished tone of voice was quite distinct
from the peculiar powers of persuasion that the Victorian
sages exercised. Arnold quite rightly claimed for the
critic an autonomous mode of discourse. He was for ever
wringing his hands at his own lack of erudition, his deplorable incompetence in abstract argument, his inability
to be precise or to be a good party man or to grasp the
principles of science or theology; and we know, of course,
as his good humour bubbles over, that he is delighted
to have imposed upon his readers a style of thinking
that does not rely for its power on erudition, scientific
principle, precision or orthodoxy. So much so that when
F. H. Bradley used the techniques of philosophy to dis-
sect Arnold's concepts, we feel that, despite his shrewd
blows, he was not moving on the same plane and the
brilliant exhibition leaves Arnold untouched. Just so with
Mill. The philosopher and political reformer does not
have to be a critic of culture. On that score he is im-
measurably inferior to Arnold and even to Carlyle. But,
in representing the strain of rationalism, he made several

notable contributions to the culture of his own times that still echo in ours.

Mill's social theory is simple. There is one end in life to which all others are ultimately subordinate, the progress of society—that is to say, the discovery of the laws by which men can realize their better selves. We cannot progress unless we find truth, and we shall not find truth unless we realize that it is clothed in new ideas. It is with these new ideas that men shape history and tame the ethnological and economic forces that in the past have been beyond their control. In modern society truth is discovered by the intellectual élite; they do not govern, they point the way. The force most likely to hamper the élite in their search is society itself—the stupidity, vested interests, shibboleths and bigotry of various classes and groups. That is why intellectual and political liberty are paramount: a free élite is free to disturb the rest of society with its new truths. These truths, if acted upon, will in fact conflict with the selfish private interests of some individuals. Sometimes we must not force individuals to conform to these truths but allow them to continue to act selfishly and foolishly, because it is so important to preserve freedom of conscience and action. At other times the State will be justified in interfering so that society as a whole may benefit. Such interference can be justified on the grounds that no individual shall be allowed palpably to harm others. In other cases individuals will have to be persuaded by education and argument to change their ways. Is there any argument which can persuade a man that this is better than that, or that will disprove Bentham's assertion: 'Quantity of pleasure being equal, push-pin is as good as poetry'? Only the reason that 'it is better to be Socrates dissatisfied than a fool satisfied', and that if the fool is of a different opinion it is because he has experienced only the pleasure of push-pin, whereas Socrates has experienced the pleasure of both push-pin and poetry and knows that the latter is a higher and better form of pleasure.

Out of this theory three notions ought to live for the

critic and student of literature: Mill's call to truth, his
passion for intellectual freedom and his belief in the
clerisy.

Truth for Mill was almost a tangible entity. You feel
that for him it was composed of hard, gritty particles
which needed to be poured into a centrifuge in order to
be redistributed correctly. Truth in its primitive state
was not necessarily exact. 'Mankind', he said, 'have many
ideas, and few words. Two consequences follow from
it; one, that a certain laxity in the use of language must
be borne with, if a writer makes himself understood; the
other that, to understand a writer who uses the same
words as a vehicle for different ideas, requires a vigorous
effort of co-operation on the part of the reader.'[6] At one
time he thought that Truth was sown and germinated in
the mind and was not to be 'struck out like fire from a
flint' by the collision of opinions. Later he came to believe the reverse, and held that Truth did not always
emerge in the right shape—it had to be hammered until
it rang true, it could 'establish itself only by means of
conflict.' Truth mounted at compound interest. 'The
progress of opinions is like the advance of a person climb-
ing a hill by a spiral path which winds round it, and by
which he is as often on the wrong side of the hill as on
the right side, but still is always getting higher up.'[7] That
was why militant discussion was valuable: that was why
Mill argued that a government that suppressed discussion unjustifiably assumed itself to be infallible; and
that was why he often returned to the deadening effect
that custom, convention, taboos and social disapproval
can have on intellectual life.

Mill's insistence on the sacredness of truth had the
force of a religious commandment; and it had an immense influence not only upon his rationalist followers

---

[6] 'Review of Use and Abuse of Political Terms', *Tait's Edinburgh Magazine*, I, (1832), p. 299.

[7] *Letters of Mill*, ed. H. Elliott, vol. II (London, 1910), Appendix A.

but throughout the Victorian clerisy. It forced people to consider the grounds for their beliefs, it compelled them to give reasons for these beliefs where formerly they had not needed to do so, it put a premium upon intellectual honesty and scrupulousness. A literary critic may object that Mill's criteria for establishing truth are excessively scientific; and his criteria, no less than those of Arnold, have of course dated. So, perhaps, has Mill's hunger for truth. There are in every academic discipline or activity in life today innumerable accommodations that enable men to treat other qualities such as goodness or scepticism as more important. But during the nineteenth century the notion that truth was tangible and in some degree, however small, attainable was an element in culture. There are novels which owe a direct debt to Mill—Mrs Humphry Ward's *Robert Elsmere* (1888) is certainly a document, and Olive Schreiner's *The Story of a South African Farm* (1883), which is almost a Millite tract, at one point presents Mill's conception of the search for truth in the form of an allegory. But to search for far-fetched examples of Mill's influence is unprofitable. It is much more important for the student of literature to see how the theme of truthfulness—not in regard to abstract beliefs but in personal relations—is handled by novelists such as Jane Austen, Constant, George Eliot, Forster or the great Tolstoy. The theme of untruthfulness and self-deception in the relationship between one person and another is endemic in nineteenth-century literature, with Emma or Adolphe, between Lydgate and Rosamund Vincy, or Dorothea and Casaubon, in the Schlegel family or with poor Ricky, above all between Anna and Vronsky. 'To tell the truth', wrote Tolstoy, 'is a very difficult thing; and young people are rarely capable of it.'

The essay *On Liberty* (1859) is often referred to as a classic defence of individual freedom, yet very few of its arguments stand up to criticism. Only one of them is utilitarian, the others are assertions that a man must always be responsible to himself for his actions—which is a religious notion. Time and again we can think of instances which contradict Mill's reasons—for instance, those who care most deeply about the truth are often those most ardent in suppressing it, because they mistakenly believe that they, and they alone, have attained it. Time and again, to justify freedom today, we would use arguments that Mill would have disliked, such as the argument that good ends conflict, or that diversity of opinions and of moral standards are good in themselves. Time and again we have seen political situations arise that justify the suppression of certain freedoms that Mill thought should never be suppressed. Mill did not appreciate how greatly social factors determined freedom: how freedom in Britain, for instance, rested on the supremacy of the mid-Victorian Royal Navy, and the absence of any internal subversive movement willing to aid an external enemy.

And yet Mill's essay continues to exist as a monument to belief in intellectual liberty. It is a solemn reminder how important it is to keep alive the idea of *negative* liberty, that is to say the right to allow people to go their own way even if it is to hell. For although Mill thought that it was of importance not only what men do but what manner of men they are that do it, he also thought that individual spontaneity had a value in itself and he was not prepared to coerce men to realize their better selves. The Essay burnt itself into the consciousness of each succeeding generation of liberals: whatever else they discarded from mid-Victorian radicalism, they retained the Essay—it troubled the conscience of converted Marxists and mellowed the convictions of British socialists. Its spirit was one of the challenges to the prudery and podsnappery that Thackeray complained hamstrung the novel in England. It still provides some of the standard arguments against censorship and the burning of books, because it insists that the onus of proving that a book or some poisonous opinions will cause irreparable social harm must fall on the prosecution. The prosecutions which were uppermost in Mill's mind were those for blasphemy made in defence of religion; he did not live long enough to see the most notorious ones made against birth-control, a cause which he fearlessly advocated. But the piece of cultural history that is already being forgotten was the series of prosecutions or refusals between 1880 and 1930 to publish poetry and novels on grounds of obscenity that was part of the savage outburst of philistinism and hatred of artists that met the great revolution in the arts. How far it has been forgotten was well shown by the debate that followed the prosecution in 1960 of the publishers of *Lady Chatterley's Lover*. The book there on trial was as much the essay *On Liberty* as Lawrence's novel: and what was interesting was that those who criticized the witnesses for the defence forgot that Mill cared less whether a book was good or bad literature than that its suppression meant suppressing truth—the truth that the conflict of opinion about the merit or worthlessness of the book would throw on sexual love and its portrayal in a novel, and upon Lawrence's status as a novelist. How far Mill's principle of freedom affects the writing of good literature is still almost wholly obscure. We know that much of the greatest art—certainly nineteenth-century Russian literature, which was the greatest of all national literatures in Mill's lifetime—has been produced under severe censorship. All we know is that artists hate censorship.

Mill's third contribution to culture was his notion of an intellectual élite, which he developed from Coleridge's woolly concept of a national clerisy. It is understandable that he should have created this class in his own image, picturing it as centred educationally on University College London and the dissenting academies rather than on Oxford and Cambridge and the Clarendon schools, and on the high-minded liberal families of the provincial cities such as the Rathbones of Liverpool or the Frys of Bristol. He saw it manning the civil service which, as government became more complex, the aristocracy were unable any longer to treat as a field of patronage, being forced to employ middle-class men of ability such as himself. In the last years of his life he could see representatives of this class gathering to deliver the unsparing anticlerical attack of the seventies. It was natural enough for him to envisage the intelligentsia as a class that would keep their distance from the rulers of the country whom they would chide and guide as occasion saw fit, if only for the fact that as a class it is always separated from the main body of society. Intellectuals create society's art, they make its past explicit, they interpret its religion and morality and customs, they provide it with new political constitutions. It is they who protest in times of revolution or deep political dissatisfaction that the rulers have no legitimate authority to act as they are doing. Society and its rulers are often enraged by them, and their taste conflicts with intellectual expressions in art, religion and politics. The things that intellectuals ask people to believe, respect and enjoy lie outside people's experience, and therefore they will reject these things in times of stress and blame the intellectuals for forcing them to accept them. Similarly, while it is to the advantage of rulers to get the intellectuals on their side, particularly since many of the intelligentsia are bureaucrats or scientists or journalists or manipulators of the mass media that influence public opinion, the rulers' interests will always diverge from those of the intelligentsia. Intellectuals purport to regard their work as concerned with sacred subjects such as truth and goodness; and some even do so regard it. This alienates them from rulers and businessmen, who are interested primarily in whether things will work and who are obliged to compromise and make innumerable political adjustments that seem to the intellectual corrupt and cowardly. This conflict between ideal solutions and practical politics in turn sets up a conflict within the intelligentsia itself—between administrators and those who are divorced from making or executing policy, between churchmen and theologians, labour politicians and socialists, the organizers of science and research scientists, publishers and authors, editors and journalists, or corporations and technologists.

At the same time, although intellectuals are always to some extent opposed to the various forms of social and political authority, it is an error to imagine that they are permanently in revolt. Some of them advise the rulers and their bureaucracy; others, as we have seen, are part of the machine of government; a few may even be politicians, as Mill was in one Parliament. Some kinds of politics, e.g. liberal and constitutional or socialist politics, are the creation of intellectuals, who are therefore deeply implicated in them and have an interest in making them work. Intellectuals never completely reject the central value system of their country. The Marxist conclusion that intellectuals must feel alienated in a bourgeois society is untrue: intellectuals can feel much at home even when sensing the tension between themselves and those who are the guardians of the central institutional system. What is impossible to achieve is a situation (which figures often in intellectuals' dreams) in which the intelligentsia stands quite aside from the vulgar activities of rulers, middle-men and the populace who, however, prove to be docilely willing to accept their prognostications and dictates, to do their best to put them into practice, and meekly to accept criticism of their efforts.

Mill was under no such illusion, but even so he overestimated the independence of the British intelligentsia and underestimated their desire to assimilate and use the reformed ancient institutions of the Establishment, such as Oxford and Cambridge and the public schools. Many of his intellectual élite were only too anxious to ally themselves to the ruling class. There were always sources of radicalism and discontent—collectivist liberalism, anticlericism, Fabianism, syndicalism, anti-industrialism—but the sources were always drying up and changing, especially in the area in which Mill expected them to gush: the provinces. The intelligentsia as a whole became most disaffected in the period between the two wars, when the revolution in the creative arts went hand in hand with

bitter attacks on imperialism and public schools, capitalism and advertising, popular entertainment and subur-
banism—indeed on the whole of English society. But
this was an interlude, and in the post-war years the intelligentsia has been tamed and has fragmented.

Nevertheless Mill's spirit is still at work among them.
There have always been many ready to analyse and reform social evils: if they do not share Mill's faith in the
perfectibility of man in its pristine form, they act as if it
might be true. Indeed a double portion of his spirit falls
on a few, they inherit Mill's moral temperament and, in
a new form, his religion of humanity. As Leavis correctly
points out, it descended on Beatrice Webb. But the student of literature, as he reflects on the writers of importance during the past hundred years, will come to a
melancholy conclusion. They have loathed and rejected
Mill's vision of life. Whether it is Tolstoy or Dostoievsky,
Flaubert or Proust, Yeats or Joyce, Nietzsche or Rilke,
Henry James, Lawrence or T. S. Eliot, none has any
love for this abstract description of human behaviour and
prediction of moral and material improvement. The only
novel of any merit I know which realizes in fictive form
some of Mill's emotion is Gorki's *A Confession*: the only
outstanding figure whose criticism of progressive humani-
tarianism shows how much of it an artist in the liberal
tradition has to reject is Forster. Nor has the gospel of
progress gripped any writer of importance today.

There are many reasons, some of them highly complex,
why this should be so. Perhaps something not entirely
pleasant, which artists are quick to sense, emanates from
high-minded and dedicated human beings such as Mill
and Beatrice Webb. There is a censorious, waspish tone
of voice, a lack of sympathy and humour, a contempt for
living foolish human beings (as distinct from humanity),
an inability to see people except as material to be
moulded and exploited, a mind which, if at first open to
arguments and facts, closes like a rat-trap once it has
digested them—a temperament which in fact is at variance with their creed. One remembers Mill's venomous

reference to 'that creature Dickens' who had dared to satirize blue-stockings in *Bleak House*. Creative writers, moreover, may also recognize in the social scientists' description of human behaviour something that is a genuine challenge to their art. In Mill's time the method was still crude, but with the revolution in sociology at the beginning of this century their description of human behaviour is more penetrating. As sociologists no longer tried to discover grandiloquent social laws in the style of Mill or Marx, and as they explored how family, class, age-group, occupation and a maze of other social institutions conditioned human behaviour and moulded the morality of society, so a new and no less inimical way of depersonalizing life and discarding the living individual in favour of the group acquired prestige. Yet although sociology abstracts and categorizes life, it also sometimes brings to life the way in which living people describe their style of life and the institutions through which they live. So much so that Lionel Trilling noted that no American novel of recent years had given the sense of actuality that David Riesman's essays were able to convey.[8] Whereas once artists were confident that their vision of life was a whole vision which did not have to break up life into a spectrum as the social scientist did, now their vision is partly focussed by the findings of the social scientists: the Coleridge of today is panting after Bentham. One thing only is certain. We know little about the relation of art to society and practically nothing about the reasons why it flourishes or declines. Dogmatic assertions about the superiority of 'organic' communities are as fanciful as the sketches that Mill's contemporaries made of the Middle Ages. If we see in Mill the ominous portent of a method of looking at society which at the moment coincides with a decline in the arts, we must admit that this method seems the most likely to explain why this decline has occurred.

---

[8] Lionel Trilling, *A Gathering of Fugitives* (London, 1957), p. 92.

THE LOGIC OF J. S. MILL

BY

R. P. Anschutz

I

Mill distinguishes three periods in his life. The first was devoted to education and youthful Benthamite propagandism and ends with his breakdown of 1826-27. In the second the influences of "the reaction of the nineteenth century against the eighteenth" streamed in upon him from France and from Germany, from Coleridge and from Carlyle. They did not on the whole, he thought, induce him to ignore "that half of the truth which the eighteenth century saw". The fight between the eighteenth and the nineteenth centuries reminded him rather of the battle about the shield, one side of which was white and the other black. And Goethe's device, "Many-sidedness", was one which he would most willingly have taken for his own at this period. Nevertheless he gradually became aware that the impetus with which he had detached himself "from whatever was untenable in the doctrines of Bentham and of the eight-

From *Mind*, 58, 19 July 1949. Reprinted by permission of the author and the Editor of *Mind*.

eenth century" had perhaps carried him too far in the opposite direction. And in the third period he determined to remedy this tendency.[1]

He dates the beginning of this period from his *Political Economy* which was published in 1848, five years after the *Logic*. But these periods shade into each other. And the *Logic*, unlike the *Political Economy*, was a book which took many years to write. Some parts of it were drafted before Mill had really felt the new influences of the nineteenth century. Others were written after he had begun to repudiate them. Furthermore, it is noticeable and this is perhaps the most important point about it, that Mill's development, unlike that of most other men, did not carry with it the obliteration of old landmarks. Whichever course he was pursuing, the two schools of thought which he associated with the eighteenth and the nineteenth centuries were the fixed poles of his intellectual world. And these schools were regarded as including all possible differences of opinion, not only on the obviously controversial subjects of politics and ethics but also on those, like logic and theory of knowledge, which one might be tempted to regard as neutral. It was indeed a leading tenet in the doctrine of the two schools that in philosophy there are no neutral subjects; that all other differences of opinion are, if not reducible, at any rate related to, political differences. And it is significant that Mill's most explicit account of the two schools is to be found in his twin essays on Bentham and Coleridge whose main work lies on the fringes of philosophy as it is generally understood.[2]

For Mill, however, they were the most significant figures of the preceding generation. To Bentham it was given to discern the truths with which existing doctrines

---

[1] *Autobiography* (World's Classics), pp. 136 ff., 194 f., 198 ff.

[2] The quotations in the next few paragraphs are all taken from the essays, *Bentham* (1838) and *Coleridge* (1840). They are reprinted in *Dissertations and Discussions*, Vol. I, and the main references are pp. 397, 331, 394, 396, 403 ff.

and institutions were at variance; to Coleridge, the neglected truths which lay *in* them. And Mill considered
that "whoever could master the premises and combine
the methods of both would possess the entire English
philosophy of their age". Moreover with all their differences, they were in complete agreement about one thing.
Both made it their occupation "to recall opinions to first
principles", taking no proposition for granted without
examining its grounds and ascertaining that it possessed
"the kind and degree of evidence suitable to its nature".
Hence they both agreed in perceiving that the groundwork of all other philosophy must be laid in "a theory
respecting the sources of human knowledge and the objects which the human faculties are capable of taking
cognizance of".

Now the prevailing theory of the eighteenth century
was that proclaimed by Locke, "that all knowledge consists of generalisations from experience"; or what in the
opinion both of Locke and of Mill comes to the same
thing, that "sensations and the mind's consciousness of
its own acts, are not only the exclusive sources but the
sole material of our knowledge". And according to this
theory there is no knowledge *a priori*—"no truths", as
Mill puts it, "cognizable by the mind's inward light and
grounded on intuitive evidence". Coleridge, however,
along with the German philosophers since Reid, takes
the opposite view. He admits that no knowledge is possible without experience but he holds that in some cases
the visible appearances of nature excite in us by an inherent law ideas of the invisible things on which they
depend. And thus he believes that it is possible by direct
intuition to perceive things and recognise truths not cognizable by our senses.

Among the truths which are thus known *a priori* according to Coleridge are "the fundamental doctrines of
religion and morals, the principles of mathematics and
the ultimate laws even of physical nature". And it was
indeed precisely because it promised to save these things

from the destructive analysis of Locke and his followers that Coleridge valued the intuitionist theory of knowledge. The intuitionists believe with Hume that it is impossible to prove the existence of God from experience. But they do not therefore conclude that we know nothing of God. They prefer to conclude that some of our knowledge is not derived from experience. The derivation of all knowledge from experience, they hold again, can only end in the denial of morality. It will then, they argue, be reduced either to the blind impulses of animal sensibility or to a mere calculation of prudential consequences. And either reduction results in the annihilation of moral obligation. Finally, they hold that even science, on the theory of Locke, loses its character and becomes empiricism, for a fact is only scientifically accounted for, according to them, "when we are made to see in it the manifestation of laws which as soon as they are perceived at all are perceived to be necessary".

On the other hand the followers of Locke retort that the intuitionists "lay down principles under which a man may enthrone his wildest dreams in the chair of philosophy". And even if with gross inconsistency the private revelations of a Boehme or a Swedenborg are disavowed (or in other words outvoted) this is still only substituting as the test of truth the dreams of the majority for the dreams of each individual. Indeed it is the peculiar danger of intuitionism that it provides a ready means by which whoever is on the stronger side may dogmatise at his ease and instead of proving his propositions may rail at all who deny them as bereft of "the vision and the faculty divine" or blinded to its plainest revelations by a corrupt heart. Thus in the battle of the two schools neither side is sparing in its imputation of horrid consequences to the creed of its antagonists. "The one doctrine is accused of making men beasts, the other lunatics." And although at this period of his life Mill deprecated such imputations, it was not long before he was again indulging in them.

II

Mill declares, however, that his *Logic*, which is by far the most important of his philosophical books, is neutral in regard to the two schools. "Logic", he says, "is common ground on which the partisans of Hartley and of Reid, of Locke and of Kant may meet and join hands. . . . And I can conscientiously affirm that no proposition in this work has been adopted for the sake of establishing, or with any reference to its fitness for being employed in establishing, preconceived opinions in any department of knowledge or of inquiry on which the speculative world is still undecided". Hence he refuses to define logic as "the science of the operations of the understanding in the pursuit of *truth*", because that would imply that it is concerned with "the original data or ultimate premises of our knowledge". And he chooses instead to define it as "the science of the operations of the understanding which are subservient to the estimation of *evidence*", because this restricts it to the consideration of "that portion of our knowledge which consists of inferences from truths previously known".[3]

In the *Examination of Hamilton*, however, Mill takes a very different line. Logic, he now says, is concerned with valid thinking and as the end of thinking is truth, he argues that we can never satisfy ourselves that the end has been attained "by looking merely at the relation of one part of the train of thought to another". He concedes indeed that we may sometimes discover that an inference is *invalid* without ascending to the original sources of our knowledge. A concept or judgment, for example, may involve a contradiction or a syllogism may have travelled from premises to conclusion through an ambiguous term. And he is quite prepared to segregate from the remainder of the theory of the investigation of truth "as much of it as does not require any reference

---

[3] *Logic*, Introduction, Sections 7, 3, 4.

to the original sufficiency of the groundwork of facts or the correctness of their interpretation". But he emphatically denies that this portion of logic is the whole of it. There are, he holds, in fact, two logics—the Logic of Consistency and the Logic of Truth, which includes the Logic of Consistency. (His followers sometimes speak of them as Formal or Conceptualist Logic and Material Logic respectively.) And the province of the Logic of Truth is not confined to the truths which are known through the medium of other truths but includes also the consideration of the processes by which first truths are obtained.[4]

Although this revised account of logic was not published until twenty years after the publication of the *System of Logic*, it is assumed throughout that work. In the Sixth Edition Mill actually adds a footnote directing readers to the discussion in the *Examination of Hamilton* and he never respected the distinction between logic and metaphysics which he originally laid down. There is indeed scarcely a proposition in the *Logic* which has *not* been laid down for the sake of establishing a preconceived opinion in some department of knowledge on which the speculative world was still undecided. And Mill himself was well aware of this. "You have very rightly judged", he writes to his German translator, "that to give the cultivators of physical science the theory of their own operations was but a small part of the object of the book; and that any success in that attempt was chiefly valued by me as a necessary means towards placing metaphysical and moral science on a basis of analysed experience in opposition to the theory of innate principles so unfortunately patronised by the philosophers of your country". And in the *Autobiography* he is equally explicit. "The German or *a priori* view of human knowledge", he says, "is likely for some time longer to predominate. But the *System of Logic* supplies what was

---

[4] *Examination of Hamilton*, pp. 470 ff.

much wanted, a textbook of the opposite school—
that which derived all knowledge from experience."[5]

III

The idea of the two schools of thought was not peculiar to Mill or to the Utilitarians. It was widely held in
the early nineteenth century that a belief in progress
naturally went with the inductive philosophy of Bacon
or the new way of ideas of Locke; a belief in order with
the intuitive philosophy of Descartes or Kant. The germ
of the idea was found in the two political parties which
had crystallised out of the troubles of the seventeenth
century—the Tories being regarded as the conservative
party, the Whigs as the progressive. Thence it was gen-
eralised into a division between conservatives and progressives in general—"not only", as Macaulay puts it, "in
politics but in literature, in art, in science, in surgery
and mechanics, in navigation and agriculture, nay even
in mathematics". A systematic age next considered how
conservatives and progressives have generally endeavoured to recommend themselves to the public. And it was
thought that the progressives have encouraged people
to weigh the secular advantages of the reforms they
advocated, while the conservatives have appealed to their
feelings, and particularly to their religious and moral
feelings. Thus the conservatives were regarded as the
party of religion, the progressives as the party of irreli-
gion. And this provided an easy bridge to a distinction in
terms of the arts; the conservatives were the romantics,
the progressives the classicists.

This was how the distinction appealed to Mr. Crotchet in Peacock's *Crotchet Castle*. "The sentimental
against the rational, the intuitive against the inductive,
the ornamental against the useful, the intense against
the tranquil, the romantic against the classical; these",

---

[5] Mill to Gomperz (19/8/1854) quoted "New Letters of J. S.
Mill", *Times*, 29/12/1938; *Autobiography*, p. 190.

says Mr. Crotchet, "are great and interesting questions which I should like before I die to see satisfactorily settled." And this, more or less, was how the situation still appeared to Mill a few years later. "The Germano-Coleridgian doctrine", he says, "expresses a revolt against the eighteenth century. It is ontological because that was experimental; conservative because that was innovative; religious because so much of that was infidel; concrete and historical because that was abstract and metaphysical; poetical because that was matter-of-fact and prosaic."[6]

Nevertheless Mill does seem to be introducing a new note into the distinction. The conservative school, we have all along been assured, is intuitive or *a priori*; the progressive is inductive or experimental. But the conservative school we are now told is "concrete and historical", while the progressive is "abstract and metaphysical". Thus the progressive school is inductive and at the same time abstract and metaphysical, the conservative is *a priori* and at the same time concrete and historical. And if this seems hard to understand, it becomes no easier when Mill goes on to say that members of the Coleridge school were "the first who inquired with any comprehensiveness or depth into the inductive laws of the existence and growth of human society"—"the first who pursued in the spirit of Baconian investigation a philosophy of society in the only form in which it is yet possible, that of a philosophy of history".[7]

IV

There are several senses in which the school of Bentham may be described as "abstract and metaphysical"; several corresponding senses in which the school of Coleridge may be described as "concrete and historical".

---

[6] Peacock, *Crotchet Castle* (1831); Mill, *Dissertations*, Vol. I, p. 403.

[7] Mill, *ibid.*, p. 425 condensed.

(i) One of the standing marks of a conservative theory of morals is the tendency to connect a person's duties with his station in society. Burke, for example, assumes that God having "disposed us and marshalled us, by a divine tactick, not according to our will but according to his, he has in and by that disposition virtually subjected us to act the part which belongs to the place assigned us". Progressive moralists, on the other hand, make a point of ignoring station when defining duty. And no one has ever gone further in this direction than Bentham. According to him "the standard of right and wrong by which alone the propriety of human conduct can be tried" is "the greatest happiness of all those whose interest is in question". And among those, he includes the lower animals on the same terms as men, since they also can suffer.[8]

(ii) It is one thing to say that in a matter of duty we should pay no attention to a person's station in society; quite another to say that in point of fact the whole idea of station is unreal because society consists simply of the multitude of persons who compose it. Nevertheless people are prone to connect their ideas of what is and what ought to be. And Bentham's abstract theory of morals is accompanied by an equally abstract theory of society. "The community", he says, "is a fictitious body composed of the individuals who are considered as constituting as it were its members. The interest of the community then is, what?—the sum of the interests of the several members who compose it."[9]

(iii) As the utilitarian ethics is based on the single principle that men and other animals are susceptible of happiness, so the utilitarian theory of government is based on the principle that men pursue their own interests and the utilitarian economics on the principle that they

---

[8] Burke, *Appeal from the New to the Old Whigs* (1791), p. 121; Bentham, *Principles of Morals and Legislation* (Oxford), pp. 1 footnote, 310 f. footnote.

[9] Bentham, *ibid.*, p. 3.

prefer a greater gain to a smaller. And its procedure in these studies defines a third sense in which Bentham's school may be described as "abstract" and the most intelligible sense in which it may also be described as "metaphysical". As a follower of Locke and Berkeley, Mill regularly uses the term 'metaphysical' as a synonym for 'psychological'. And the method pursued by the Utilitarians is, then, abstract and metaphysical so far as it attempts to explain and evaluate "social phenomena" on the basis of a few leading principles of human nature.

Now one of the characteristic features of Mill's middle period, when he aimed at many-sidedness, was the series of essays[10] in which he recommended the work of some of the men who were then, in the golden age of history, revolutionising its study. Mill had originally learned something of what history might be from Carlyle. But he soon came to consider that the sort of history Carlyle wrote—"the essence of innumerable biographies"—was by no means the highest sort. At a further stage, he considered, history might come to be regarded as "a progressive chain of causes and effects", or rather as "a gradually unfolding web". And although nobody had yet succeeded in constructing "a science of history" along these lines, he thought that some progress towards it had already been made.

It was on the basis of his discovery of history that Mill characterised the philosophy of Bentham as abstract and metaphysical. "Bentham's idea of the world", he wrote, "was that of a collection of persons pursuing each his separate interest and pleasure." And it was precisely because the *philosophes* of the eighteenth century had the same idea that they failed in their attempt to new-model

---

[10] De Tocqueville on Democracy in America (1840); Michelet's History of France (1844); Guizot's Essays and Lectures on History (1845). These are all reprinted in *Dissertations*, Vol. II, and Mill's best statement about the stages of historical study is in *Michelet*, pp. 124-130.

society. Ignoring the host of civilising and restraining influences by means of which society is sustained, they
did not recognise in many of the institutions which they
assailed "necessary conditions of civilised society though
in a form and vesture no longer suited to the age".
Hence they involved many great truths in a common
discredit with the errors which had grown up around
them. And among these neglected truths Mill thought it
particularly necessary to emphasise the fact that in any
permanent political society there must always be a general feeling that there is "in the constitution of the state
something which is settled, something permanent and
not to be called in question whatever else might change".[11]

It was at this stage of Mill's development that the
orthodox Utilitarians began to be seriously alarmed about
him. Grote regarded this last remark as nothing but "an
expression of the standing intolerance of society towards
unpopular opinions". And his admiration for Mill was
always subsequently to be "tinged with fear", because
he never knew what unexpected turn Mill might take.
Mrs. Grote acquired the habit of referring to Mill now
as "the Lama", now as "that wayward intellectual deity".
And Francis Place was writing, with all the unction of
a man beyond the reach of temptation, "I think John
Mill has made great progress in becoming a German
metaphysician. Eccentricity and obscurity must necessarily be the result."[12] If, however, Grote and his
friends had looked a little closer, they might have found
grounds for comfort. Mill does indeed repudiate Bentham's doctrine that a community is a fictitious entity
reducible to the individuals who compose it. But he
continues to accept both the ethics and the method of
the Utilitarians. Thus of the three senses in which Bentham's philosophy may be described as abstract and metaphysical, Mill accepted the criticism of the Coleridge

---

11 *Dissertations*, Vol. I, pp. 362, 424, 461 ff.

12 Graham Wallas, *Francis Place*, p. 91 and footnote; Bain,
J. S. Mill, pp. 57, 83.

school only in regard to one. And even on this point he soon saw reasons for modifying his attitude.

V

The trouble with historians, from the reformer's point of view, is that they find it difficult to believe that social arrangements can be different from what they actually are. Few of them indeed go to the lengths of Carlyle and assert that whatever is, is right. In order to arrive at that conclusion a man needs also to have a very lively sense of the presence of God in the things of this world. But even a historian with as purely secular an outlook as Macaulay is apt to be impatient with the discussion of rights which are unaccompanied by mights. And it is not difficult to understand why this should be so. The first principle of the historian must be that nothing happens accidentally and so he will regard forms of government as a sort of "organic growth" or "spontaneous product" of any given state of society. Hence he will tend to conclude that in the main we must take governments as we find them. Whatever is the strongest power in any society, he will argue, will obtain the governing authority; and a change in the political constitution cannot be durable unless it is preceded or accompanied by an altered distribution of power. Therefore, apart from details, political organisation or re-organisation is not susceptible to the direction of philosophical reformers. According to Macaulay, for instance, "Constitutions are in politics what paper money is in commerce. They afford great facilities and convenience. But we must not attribute to them that value which really belongs to what they represent. They are not power, but symbols of power, and will in an emergency prove altogether useless unless the power for which they stand be forthcoming."[13]

---

[13] Macaulay, *Utilitarian Theory of Government* (1829), reprinted *Miscellaneous Writings* (1860), Vol. I, p. 375.

Now this "organic" or "naturalistic" view of government, as Mill calls it, is plainly not one to which he could subscribe. He might refuse to go the whole way with Bentham and his father who looked upon a "constitution in the same light as a steam plough or a threshing machine". But he could not but believe that within certain limits "institutions and forms of government are a matter of choice" and that therefore "to inquire into the best form of government is not a chimerical but a highly practical employment of scientific intellect". He admitted indeed that political machinery has to be worked by men and even ordinary men; and that it would be a great mistake, accordingly, for any legislator not to take advantage of existing habits and feelings. Nevertheless he held that people can acquire new habits and feelings, particularly when they are incited thereto by enlightened leaders. And it is this consideration which provides him with the basis of his reply to Macaulay. "It is what men think," he says, "that determines how they act and though the persuasions and convictions of average men are in a much greater degree determined by their personal position than by reason, no little power is exercised over them by the persuasions and convictions of those whose personal position is different and by the united authority of the instructed. When therefore the instructed in general can be brought to recognise one social arrangement as good and another as bad, very much has been done towards giving to the one or withholding from the other that preponderance of social force which enables it to subsist."[14]

A radical reformer, that is to say, may find it useful to point to the accidental genesis in interest and experience of the opinions of the "average men" who are his opponents or potential converts. But he must believe that he himself, as one of "the instructed" whose convictions are founded upon "reason", has gone to the root of the

[14] *Considerations on Representative Government* (1861), pp. 15 f.

matter. Otherwise he will be unable to sustain the fervour or exercise the authority required of him. And this consideration suggests that in regard to political theory the position at the beginning of the nineteenth century was rather more complex than Mill usually allowed for. To begin with there was a certain incoherence in both the schools he describes. The radical school held that all knowledge is derived from experience and yet based its political theory on statements regarding human nature which it regarded as having a validity far beyond that which attaches to the empirical generalisations of the conservatives. The Tory school of Coleridge and Carlyle, for all its *a priori* theory of knowledge relied largely on observation of the actual behaviour of man for its formulation of those statements regarding the course of history which formed the immediate basis of its political programme. Moreover there was a third school of Whigs of a sufficiently conservative turn of mind to be consistently opposed to radicalism, who yet managed to dispense largely or altogether with the *a priori*. They included such men as Burke, Mackintosh and Macaulay, who although seldom mentioned by name in Mill's writing, occupied a large place in his thoughts. One of them, Macaulay, was the author (in Mill's words) of "the bitterest and ablest attack" ever publicly made on his father. Another, Mackintosh, was the recipient of an equally whole-hearted attack by his father. And the standing charge levelled by the Utilitarians against these men was precisely the same as the charge levelled by the intuitionists against them—that namely of empiricism.[15]

VI

It has been so much the fashion to talk of "the empiricism of Mill"—Höffding even speaks of his "absolute

[15] *Autobiography*, pp. 133 f. See also Mill's Preface to his father's *Analysis of the Phenomena of the Human Mind* (1869), p. xvii.

empiricism"—that some surprise may be occasioned by the statement that empiricism was not only a charge levelled against Mill but also one that he levelled against other people. And yet his own usage on the point is completely consistent. He always proclaimed himself an adherent of the School of Experience as against the School of Intuition. Nevertheless he always used the term "empiricism" to denote a theory which he did not hold but which Macaulay, for instance, did. Thus he speaks of "empiricism and unscientific surmise"; of "bad generalization or empiricism properly so-called"; of "knowledge both scientific and empirical"; of "direct induction usually no better than empiricism"; of "the empirical method of treating political phenomena which would have recognised Kepler but would have excluded Newton and Laplace". And had he foreseen the way in which his own name would be linked with empiricism, he would doubtless have said of himself what he said of Bacon—"The philosopher who laboured to construct a canon of scientific induction, by which the observations of mankind, instead of remaining empirical, might be so combined as to be made the foundation of safe general theories, little expected that his name would become the stock authority for disclaiming generalization and enthroning empiricism, under the name of experience, as the only solid foundation of practice."[16]

In Mill's opinion, then, his position is "experiential" but not "empirical". And this seems to mean that while he holds that experience provides all the material of knowledge, he also holds that there are various ways of dealing with this material, some of which lead to bad and unscientific, others to safe and scientific generalisations. He suggests further that it is unscientific and unsafe to deal with the observations of experience directly and piecemeal; scientific and safe to deal with them more

---

16 *Logic*, VI. 10, 8, V. 5, 3; *Political Economy*, V. 7, 2; *Comte and Positivism*, p. 121; *Autobiography*, p. 157; *Examination of Hamilton*, p. 627 footnote.

indirectly and in combination with one another. And, finally, he regards as an empiricist a man who, failing or refusing to recognise any distinction between scientific and unscientific ways of treating experience, inevitably treats it in the unscientific way.

Now Mill's use of the terms 'empirical' and 'empiricist' is, I take it, comformable to common usage.[17] If, moreover, an appeal is made to precedent it is plain that a man need not be, or at least need not *choose* to be, an empiricist even although he is an experientialist. Locke's is an obvious case in point. Nobody has ever insisted more strenuously than he that all our ideas are derived from experience. Nobody has ever at the same time drawn the line more sharply between certain knowledge and probable opinion. Bacon's is an even more interesting case. For one thing his general position is extremely close to Mill's. Both begin by recognising a single alternative to the method of experience; but in both cases this divides into two as soon as the method of experience is elaborated; and the result is that the one and only true method of experience finds itself with an enemy on the left as well as an enemy on the right. Bacon writes, for example, "Those who have practiced the sciences have been either empiricists or dogmatists. The empiricists, like the ants, merely collect and use: the rationalists, like spiders, spin webs out of themselves. But the way of the bee lies in between: she gathers materials from the flowers of the garden and the field and then by her own powers transforms and digests them. And the real work of philosophy is similar."[18]

The other interesting point about Bacon is that, unlike Mill, he distinguishes a legitimate and an illegitimate

---

[17] Thus Venn in the Preface to his *Empirical Logic* says, "By the introduction of the term Empirical into the title, I wish to emphasise my belief that no ultimate objective certainty, such as Mill for instance seemed to attribute to the results of Induction is attainable by any exercise of the human reason."

[18] Bacon, *Novum Organum*, Lib. I, Aph. 95, 64.

method of experience without having had much opportunity of seeing what they would produce in practice, and indeed without fully availing himself of the limited opportunity he had. It was in fact by the sort of anticipation of nature that he most deprecated that Bacon arrived at the conclusion that the empirical kind of philosophy would produce "even more deformed and monstrous theories than the rationalist kind". All the later philosophers of experience had Newton's *Principia* before them as a norm of science and scientific method. It was on this model accordingly that they attempted to create the new science of political economy. And their appreciation of Newton's work was heightened by the fact that some of their most eminent and successful opponents attacked them not in the name of intuition at all but rather in the name of experience. Hence it became necessary for the Utilitarians to argue that the principles taught by these men were not derived from experience in the correct way. And as they, however mistakenly, made much of Bacon, the Utilitarians tended to shelter under the rival authority of Newton.

VII

The general position, then, is that Mill wants to be an "experientialist" but he does not want to be an "empiricist". He wants, that is to say, to derive all knowledge from experience, but he also wants to hold that there are various ways of deriving it, some of which are scientific and safe. And the general question that arises concerning Mill's philosophy is, How successful was he in combining these two tenets? This, however, is a question to which at first sight it seems very difficult to give a general answer. Mill's attempt to derive all universal propositions from experience and at the same time to characterise some of them as certain left him, as it left Bacon, with rocks and shoals on either hand. And the difficulty is not only that Mill steers an uncertain course between them, but that the course he holds in any particular case does not usually depend on the nature of the case. It depends rather on the way in which the views that have been adopted in that case have been associated with political opinions that Mill thinks it important either to support or to oppose. Mill was first and foremost a politician. And as war is sometimes said to be the extension of policy, so philosophy for Mill is the extension of politics. Hence the charges sometimes brought against him of unfair dealing in philosophical controversy. He was merely practicing in philosophy the usual and necessary reticences of the politician.

Now empiricism was associated in Mill's mind with the political theories of such men as Burke, Mackintosh and Macaulay; intuitionism with those of Coleridge, Carlyle and Whewell. The first group were Whigs, the second Tories. But there was also another difference between them. The strength of the first group lay in political theory and political theory alone. The strength of the second group was derived from all sorts of other studies whose findings had been represented as relevant to political theory. In particular, Whewell had written extensively on mathematics and science. And the tendency if not the intention of his efforts, Mill was convinced, was "to shape the whole of philosophy, physical as well as moral, into a form adapted to serve as a support and a justification to any opinions which happened to be established". It is this difference in the spread of Mill's two groups of opponents that determined which parts of the *Logic* should be predominantly anti-intuitionist and which parts anti-empiricist. As the strength of the Whig group was confined to politics the anti-empiricist polemic in the *Logic* is mainly to be found in Book VI, "Of the Logic of the Moral Sciences", and to those parts of Book III which lay the foundation for Book VI. On the other hand, having come to the conclusion that the chief strength of intuitionism lay "in the appeal which it is accustomed to make to the evidence of mathematics and of the cognate branches of physical science", Mill was primarily concerned in the *Logic* to meet them on this ground. Hence he pursued his attack on intuitionism in Book II, "Of Reasoning", and in those parts of the other Books which support or extend the argument of Book II. And, indeed, he pressed this attack so far and with so little fear of the consequences, that his position here is generally (and not unreasonably, if we neglect certain parts of it) regarded as a standard exposition of empiricism.[19]

Nevertheless it is not, I think, impossible to arrive at a general conclusion regarding the success of Mill's attempt to combine experientialism with a repudiation of empiricism. Notwithstanding the extent to which he trims the sails of his logic to suit his political purposes, a fairly definite pattern is discernible in his treatment of most logical topics—provided account is taken of all the elements in his treatment and not merely of those which for some reason or other have been stressed by Mill himself or his commentators. And considering the sort of position he was trying to maintain, it is not difficult to understand why he adhered to this pattern, as I propose to show, in regard to his treatment of the syllogism.

VIII

Logic, according to Mill, is the theory of proof, but proof supposes something provable and this is always a proposition. Hence it is necessary to enquire into the import or meaning of propositions, and Mill opens the enquiry by accepting the traditional analysis into subject, predicate and copula. A proposition, he says, is "discourse in which something is affirmed or denied of something". Thus in the proposition, 'Gold is yellow', the quality yellow is affirmed of the substance gold; in the proposition, 'Franklin was not born in England', the fact expressed by the words 'born in England' is denied of the man Franklin. The predicate is the name of that which is affirmed or denied; the subject is the name

---

[19] *Dissertations*, Vol. II, p. 453; *Autobiography*, p. 191.

of the person or thing of which something is affirmed or denied; the copula is the sign indicating that there is an affirmation or denial. And while this analysis applies in the first instance only to categorical propositions, Mill also holds that all propositions may be stated in the categorical form, disjunctive propositions being reducible to hypotheticals and hypotheticals to categoricals. The disjunctive proposition, 'Either A is B or C is D', for example, is equivalent to the hypothetical, 'If A is not B, then C is D'; and this is equivalent to the categorical proposition, 'All cases of A not being B are cases of C being D', or in other words, 'The proposition C is D is a legitimate inference from the proposition A is not B'. Thus Mill does not regard the distinctions between disjunctive, hypothetical and categorical propositions as of much importance, except in so far as the hypothetical form points more clearly than the categorical to the use that may be made of propositions in inference. And his further discussion of the import of propositions, assuming that all propositions may be regarded as categorical and that all categorical propositions may be stated in the subject-predicate form, turns on the interpretation to be made of the subject and the predicate, more particularly when they are general names like 'man' or 'snow' or 'white'.[20]

He is here concerned with the ancient problem of universals and in his time, as in the Middle Ages, three possible solutions of the problem are recognised—the realist, the nominalist and the conceptualist.[21] Accord-

---

[20] *Logic*, I. 3, 1, I. 4, 1 and 3. Mill actually reduces the disjunctive, 'Either A is B or C is D', to the two hypotheticals, 'If A is not B, C is D', and 'If C is not D, A is B'. But the latter is of course implied by the former.

[21] It was Reid who re-acquainted British philosophers with these doctrines. His usage, which is followed here, became the standard practice for the next hundred years, and he also cited the various passages by which they were generally illustrated. See Reid, *Essays on the Intellectual Powers* (1785), Essay V, ch. 6. Compare Jevons, *Elementary Lessons in Logic* (1870).

ing to the realists, like Plato, universals are things similar in some respects to the particular things denoted by singular names but differing from them in having an immutable existence which renders them the only possible objects of science. According to the nominalists, represented in modern times by Hobbes and Berkeley, there is nothing universal but names and they are universal because they stand for classes of particular things. According to the conceptualists, like Locke, universality attaches only to our ideas or conceptions and the possibility of using general names depends therefore upon our ability to form abstract ideas. And Mill's position regarding most topics in the *Logic* can be defined by reference to these doctrines.

In the first place he rejects conceptualism in order to provide the foundations for an objective treatment of logic which will enable him to join hands with the scientists and repudiate the intuitionists. In the second place he wavers between realism and nominalism. He is a realist (for all his disclaimers) so long as he is concerned with providing a basis for the dogmatic side of Utilitarianism; but he becomes a nominalist as soon as he has to allow for its critical and destructive side. His realism finds expression in the attributive view of propositions which implies and is implied by his doctrine of scientific explanation; his nominalism in the class view of propositions which implies the theory of the syllogism usually associated with his name. But in point of fact there is no topic in the *Logic* regarding which he does not at some time or other endorse both the realist and the nominalist views. Thus he not only holds that syllogistic reasoning must be interpreted as inference from particulars to particulars; he also holds that it must be regarded as indicating the applicability to a particular case of a universal connexion (or disconnexion) of attributes. In regard to explanation he holds that this is always effected by means of causal laws. But while these are sometimes said to describe the sequences that obtain among phenomena, they are also said to state the ultimate tendencies which operate beneath the surface of experience.

IX

The full title of Mill's *Logic* is, *A System of Logic—Ratiocinative and Inductive*. And according to the Preface, "It is an attempt not to supersede but to embody and systematize, the best ideas which have been either promulgated on its subject by speculative writers, or conformed to by accurate thinkers in their scientific enquiries". Thus Mill makes no pretence of giving to the world a new theory of the intellectual operations and indeed he considers that in the existing state of the sciences there would be a strong presumption against anyone who did. But he does admit that a certain amount of original speculation was required "to cement together the detached fragments of a subject never yet treated as a whole". And in doing so he hints at an important characteristic of his book. As he was concerned to give a connected view of logic he attempts to provide a foundation for ratiocination which will serve also for induction. And the difficulty is that the ideas on ratiocination and induction which he attempted to systematise were derived from fundamentally different traditions.

The logic of ratiocination had developed out of Aristotle's attempt to regularise the sort of disputations that are recorded in Plato's dialogues. And in this context the syllogism had a determinate meaning and an intelligible function, as a way of settling a difference of opinion about some proposition by discovering other propositions to which both parties can agree and from which the disputed proposition (or its contradictory) can be inferred.[22] If however logic is regarded as a means not of

---

[22] The assumption here is that it is the dialectical syllogism which is fundamental in Aristotle's logic and that the scientific syllogism was added as an afterthought. This is an assumption which was made by most seventeenth-century philosophers and

securing agreement among disputants but of discovering
the truth about things, then it is not at all easy to see
what purpose can be served by the syllogism. Thus it is
not surprising that when Bacon contemplated the possibility of such a logic he should have rejected its help. As
the conclusiveness of a syllogism depends upon agreement about propositions, so agreement about propositions
depends upon agreement about the concepts used in
propositions. But concepts refer to things and the great
need from Bacon's point of view is that they should correctly refer to things. If they are confused or rashly abstracted there is no firm foundation upon which to build a
logic concerned with "the discovery not of arguments
but of arts; not of what agrees with principles but on
principles themselves". And so Bacon called upon men to
renounce the terms they were accustomed to use in order
to "make acquaintance with things themselves".

In other words, Bacon was engaged in a quest for certainty which required him, as it required Descartes, to
make a completely fresh start, unhelped but also unhindered, by the efforts of previous thinkers. And where
Descartes sought within his own reason for propositions
(like the *Cogito ergo sum*) which asserted and hence
guaranteed themselves, Bacon called rather for the discovery of brute facts completely untainted by human
reason. But Aristotle did not pretend to dig so deep in
his logic. He was concerned rather that men should
make the best use of the knowledge they already had
without enquiring into its ultimate evidence. Hence Bacon was unable to make any use of his teaching. Nevertheless he did not deny the validity of the Aristotelian
logic within its own sphere, nor did he propose, like
Mill, to incorporate it into his new logic. He suggested
rather that as their aims were different—the one attempting "to subdue an opponent in disputation, the other to

it has been revived by some recent commentators on Aristotle's
logic. See Ernst Kapp, *Greek Foundations of Traditional Logic*
(Columbia).

command nature in action"—the two logics should be recognised as two independent "streams and dispensations of knowledge". And to all appearances he says this as much from conviction as from policy.[23]

Mill, however, pursued a different course. The principal reason, in his opinion, why logic had made such inconsiderable progress in the previous two centuries was the notion, "that what is of primary importance to the logician in a proposition is the relation between the two *ideas* corresponding to the subject and predicate". The consequence was that what had been done for the advancement of logic since this view came into vogue had been the work not of professed logicians but of scientists, "in whose methods of investigation many principles of logic not previously thought of, have successively come forth into light". In order, then, to bridge the gap between logic and science so as to make the methodological discoveries of science available in logic, he considered it necessary to insist that the logician is only interested in propositions so far as they assert facts. He admits indeed that propositions also involve ideas of facts and acts of believing or judging. But an act of judging, he argues, is a state of mind whose consideration belongs not to logic but to "another science", meaning psychology. And ideas, again, are "mental representations" or "mental conceptions"—"facts in my mental history"—which are essential to judging but form no part of what is judged. "In order to believe that gold is yellow", for example, "I must indeed have the idea of gold and the idea of yellow; and something having reference to these ideas must take place in my mind; but my belief has not reference to the ideas, it has reference to the things."

The decisive point for Mill is that when the logician enquires about the meaning or import of any proposition he is really asking what there is in it, "the conformity of which to fact constitutes the truth of the proposition".

---

[23] Bacon, *Instauratio Magna*, Distributio Operis; *Novum Organum*, Aph. 14, 36; Praefatio.

He must answer, Mill considers, that it is the matter of fact asserted by the proposition and not the ideas involved in the asserting of the proposition. And the general soundness of this answer, he argues, only becomes more apparent when we consider the exceptional case in which ideas actually form part of the matter of fact asserted by the proposition. "When I say", he says, "that fire causes heat, I mean that the natural phenomenon fire causes the natural phenomenon heat. When I mean to assert anything respecting ideas I give them their proper name, I call them ideas; as when I say that a child's idea of a battle is unlike the reality, or that the ideas entertained by the Deity have a great effect on the characters of mankind."[24]

X

These considerations, however, are not, I think, the only ones which moved Mill to attempt to incorporate the syllogistic logic within the inductive. No doubt systemisation was in the air and in his blood; but his enthusiasm for the new logic was also animated, it is suggested, by zeal for political reform. For the last two centuries political reformers in Europe had been impressed, and indeed obsessed, by the extent to which a ruling class was able to pervert the minds of a people by slogans disseminated from the pulpit and echoed in the nursery. It appeared to them that people were bound to behave more reasonably if they were taught to see things as they really are instead of (in Locke's phrase) "through other men's spectacles". Thus it became one of their first objects to destroy those spectacles and it was in the pursuance of this object that Mill attempts to restate the Aristotelian logic on the same basis as the Baconian. He does so by arguing that while logic must be regarded as concerned with propositions yet the whole meaning or import of propositions is to be found in the things

---

[24] *Logic*, I. 5, 1.

referred to and not in the conceptions we have of them. And it is on this argument that he mainly relies in his attacks on intuitionism. Thus when Whewell claims that there are some propositions which are not only true but necessarily true because their negation is inconceivable, Mill replies "that inconceivableness is an accidental thing not inherent in the phenomenon itself but dependent on the mental history of the person who has to conceive it".[25] And that, he seems to think, settles the matter.

It should be noted, however, that the position of other philosophers was not quite as Mill represented it. No doubt there were philosophers—Mansel was one, and Locke, unfortunately, had been another—who actually maintained that both the subject and predicate of propositions refer to ideas in our minds and not to facts beyond them. But that was not the contention of those who adhered to what Mill calls the Germano-Coleridgian doctrine. For them it was not a question of deciding whether propositions referred to ideas or to facts. Every proposition they held necessarily involved both and it was consequently impossible to draw any "definite and stable distinction" between them. And this contention may be supported by a strong argument. The distinction between the facts asserted in any proposition and the conceptions by means of which they are asserted can only be made in another proposition. It would seem, then, that we can only arrive at the facts, uncontaminated by *any* conceptions, at the end of an infinite regress in which each succeeding proposition distinguishes between the facts and the conceptions of the preceding one.

Another point also arises here. Although Mill's purpose in the *Logic* was to cement together the detached fragments of the subject, the immediate consequence of his theory of the import of propositions is to exclude from it some topics which have always been regarded as belonging to it. This is most obvious in connexion with

---

[25] *Logic*, II. 5, 6.

inference. An inference, it is generally held, has two characteristics—the conclusion must follow from the premises and it must be different from them. But according to Mill the import of any proposition is to be found exclusively in the matters of fact asserted by it. If then, notwithstanding a difference of form, the conclusion may be regarded as repeating the matters of fact asserted in the premises, there is no inference. And accordingly Mill holds that there is no inference in immediate inference or in perfect induction. Regarding such a process as the conversion of propositions he says, for example, that "there is in the conclusion, no new truth, nothing but what was originally asserted in the premises, and obvious to whoever apprehends them". And he uses similar language regarding perfect induction. It may be argued, for instance, that, All the apostles were Jews, because this is true of Peter, Paul, John and every other apostle. But this again, according to Mill, "is not an inference from facts known to facts unknown but a mere shorthand registration of facts known".[26]

Thus, so far as immediate inference and perfect induction are concerned, Mill apparently finds no difficulty in accepting the fact that his view of the import of propositions entails some revision of the meaning usually attached to the term inference. But on the face of it, his view would also seem to entail other consequences. Indeed it might seem to entail a complete denial of the existence of such a process as inference at all since, as Venn puts it, "inference turns mainly upon the distinction between what is known and what is unknown, and this distinction does not lie in the facts but in our appreciation of them."[27] This however is a point which

---

26 *Logic*, II. 1, 2; III. 2, 1.

27 Venn, *Empirical Logic*, Second Edition, pp. 22 f. Venn's views on this point are worth noticing because he was constantly concerned with it. In the Second Edition of his *Logic of Chance* (1876) he has an instructive chapter on what he calls the Materialist and Conceptualist views of logic in which with some

we are not yet in a position to decide. Although Mill has asserted that the logician is exclusively concerned with the matters of fact asserted in propositions, he has not yet discussed the nature of these matters of fact. He can still recognise the syllogism, for example, as a process of inference by drawing a sharp distinction, along Platonic lines, between universals (or at least some universals) and particulars. And indeed this is precisely what he does do, immediately before he does the opposite.

XI

Two alternative views are commonly recognised regarding the nature of the matters of fact asserted in propositions. According to the nominalists they are always in the last resort particulars, and any universals which appear to be asserted are reducible in some way to particulars. According to the realists, it is impossible to get behind the references to universals, and it can be shown that even the references to particulars also involve references to universals. These doctrines are sometimes called the class and attributive theories of propositions respectively. And they are associated with the fact that the terms of propositions, or at least the general terms, have two sorts of meaning or make two sorts of reference. The term 'man', for instance, *denotes* the class of men to which it applies, *connotes* the attributes which all men have in common. Similarly the term 'mortal' denotes everything that has died or is going to die, connotes the attribute mortality or liability to death. And generally speaking the connotation of a concrete general term is indicated by the corresponding abstract term—as 'humanity' corresponds to 'man', and 'mortality' to 'mortal'; its

---

qualifications he declares for the former. By the time, however, that he came to write his *Empirical Logic* (1889) he found that it was necessary to allow both for "an external element and an internal" and logic, he says, "is concerned with the judgments of the latter about the former".

denotation by the plural of the concrete term—'men' and 'mortals'.[28]

Now if the terms of the proposition, 'All men are mortal', are read in denotation, it will mean that the class of men is included in the class of mortals. If the terms are read in connotation, it will mean that the attribute humanity is always associated with the attribute mortality. Thus the decision between the class and the attributive views of the import of propositions depends upon whether classes are regarded as prior to attributes or *vice versa*. And it is remarkably easy to argue on either side. Classes, it may be held, depend on attributes because it is only by means of attributes that the various members of classes can be identified. On the other hand, it may be held that attributes are nothing but resemblances between the various members of classes and hence that they can be defined only by references to the classes.

But although the decision between the class and the attributive views of propositions turns on so fine a point the consequences of the decision are far-reaching. According to the class view a general truth is but an aggregate of particular truths, and therefore the singular proposition, 'Socrates is mortal' is included in the universal proposition, 'All men are mortal'. It follows that we cannot without arguing in a circle adduce the universal proposition as evidence for the singular proposition. And since this obtains quite generally the syllogism on this view must be condemned as involving a *petitio principii*. On the attributive view, however, the syllogism does not involve a *petitio principii* because the assertion of the universal proposition does not include the assertion of any singular proposition. It merely asserts a connexion or disconnexion of attributes. Hence it may be true even although there are no singular propositions to be subsumed under it. It may even be true if there cannot possibly be any such singular propositions.

On the attributive view, then, the widest possible lati-

28 *Logic*, I. 2, 5.

tude will be allowed to demonstrative reasoning. It will be quite as practicable to argue from assumed premises as from premises which are based on observation. Even although we know in point of fact that men never act in entire conformity with the principle that a greater gain is preferable to a smaller, we may trace the consequences of the assumption that they do in the science of political economy. And even although we know that all the lines we shall ever come across will have breadth as well as length, we may trace the consequence of the assumption that they have not in the science of geometry. Indeed on the attributive view it is only when we trace the consequences of universal propositions in this sort of way, abstracting entirely from any consideration of their applicability to particular cases, that we shall ever attain to anything worthy of the name of science, since there must always be some doubt about the existence and nature of particular cases. On the class view, on the other hand, there must always be an element of fiction about a demonstrative science in which the applicability of the premises to particular cases has not been made out, since universal propositions have no meaning apart from the particulars which may be subsumed under them.

XII

Now as between the class and attributive views of the proposition, Mill begins by declaring unhesitatingly for the latter. The "real meaning" of the name 'man', he holds, consists in the attributes connoted and not in the individuals denoted by it; and similarly with the name 'mortal'. Hence when we say, *All men are mortal*, we are saying that "the latter set of attributes constantly accompany the former set" and it is only "as a consequence" of this fact that the class of men is included in the class of mortals. Mill supports this view by arguing, with Plato, that "if by the *meaning* of a general name are to be understood the things which it is the name of, no general name, except by accident, has a fixed meaning at

all, or ever long retains the same meaning". And coming
to the syllogism he proposes an interpretation of it in
line with this view. Every syllogism, he says, comes
within the general formula—"Attribute A is a mark of
attribute B; The given object has the mark A; Therefore
it has the attribute B"; for example—The attributes of
man are a mark of the attribute mortality; Socrates has
the attributes of man; Therefore he has the attribute
mortality. And the general axiom of the syllogism is then,
"Whatever has any mark, has that which it is a mark of",
or in other words, *Nota notae est nota rei ipsius*.[29]

The amazing thing is, however, that having put forward this account of the syllogism, Mill immediately re-
opens the whole enquiry by asking how it must be interpreted in order that it may avoid the charge of begging
the question. On the face of it he has already met this
charge by saying that the propositions composing it are
to be read attributively; since the truth of the major premise, *The attributes of man are a mark of the attribute
mortality*, on this interpretation is quite independent of
the truth of the conclusion, *Socrates has the attribute
mortality*. Why, then, does not Mill meet the charge of
petitio principii in the obvious way by drawing attention
to this? Why, instead, does he think it necessary to propose the revolutionary doctrine that in the last resort all
inference is from particulars to particulars, and never,
as the theory of the syllogism assumes, from universals to
particulars?

The answer is, I think, that, as on so many other occasions, Mill wants to have it both ways. The attributive
view of propositions fits very well with the "abstract and
metaphysical" account of science commonly given by the
Utilitarians, and it is completely in line with the theory
of scientific explanation that Mill gives in Book III and
assumes in Book VI of the *Logic*. But at the same time
that he wishes to hold that everything that happens in
the universe is explicable by reference to underlying laws

29 *Logic*, I. 5, 2 to 4; II. 2, 3.

of nature which state connexions between attributes that hold independently of the occurrence of particular things, he also wishes to deny that there is anything in the universe which does not appear on the surface of experience. Thus the realist theory of universals which is the proper correlative of the attributive theory of propositions is condemned on the ground that it personifies abstractions and leads to mysticism.[30] With the rejection of realism comes the assumption of nominalism and consequently of the class theory of propositions. This implies that "from a general principle we cannot infer any particulars, but those which the principle itself assumes as known". And then having reached this point, Mill has no alternative but to assert the theory of the syllogism which is usually associated with his name. That is—"All inference is from particulars to particulars: General propositions are merely registers of such inferences already made, and short formulae for making more: The major premise of the syllogism, consequently, is a formula of this description: and the conclusion is not an inference drawn *from* the formula, but an inference drawn *according to* the formula: the real logical antecedent or premise being the particular facts from which the general proposition was collected by induction."[31]

XIII

There are three possible interpretations of the syllogism to be illustrated by the three readings that may be given of the Socrates argument. According to the first it runs—All men are mortal, Socrates is a man, Therefore Socrates is mortal. And although this may not seem a very convincing argument, torn out of any context, it is

---

[30] *Ibid.*, V. 3, 4. It is possible, however, that a more serious defect of realism in Mill's eyes was that it was "out of vogue" (*Ibid.*, I. 7, 1) and "no longer extant" (*Examination of Hamilton*, p. 382).

[31] *Logic*, II. 3, 2 and 4.

not difficult to imagine circumstances in which it may,
and should, produce conviction, provided we can imagine
a person genuinely in doubt about Socrates' mortality
and another anxious to convince him of it. The argument will then take the form of an examination—Well,
Socrates is a man, isn't he? And all men are mortal,
aren't they? Hence he must be mortal. And so far as we
are all open to conviction, and are right to be open to
conviction, in this sort of way we are, I take it, admitting
the validity of syllogistic argument in its original dialectical form. If, however, an attempt is made to represent
the syllogism as a means of securing knowledge about
things rather than agreement among disputants, it will
be necessary to add that there are some propositions about
which all men are agreed and that these propositions are
necessarily true. It is by means of these assumptions that
Aristotle attempted to turn the dialectical syllogism into
the scientific syllogism. And neither is at all easy to maintain, for while it is doubtful whether there are any propositions which have been believed by all men, it is certain
that some of the most widely believed propositions have
been false.

There is also a further difficulty. Even if the respond-
ent is doubtful about the mortality of Socrates, it may be
put to him in the dialectical syllogism that all men are
mortal. And if he agrees, the admission may be used
against him. But the solitary scientist is scarcely entitled
to assume that all men are mortal while he is doubtful
whether any particular man is mortal. Thus in effecting
the transition from the dialectical to the scientific syllogism, Aristotle is exposing it to the charge of begging the
question. And at the same time he is also exposing the
Dictum, which is the general axiom of the syllogism in
this form, to a parallel charge. This axiom asserts, that
whatever can be affirmed (or denied) of a class may be
affirmed (or denied) of everything included in the class.
And the obvious difficulty is, as Mill puts it, that "the
class *is* nothing but the objects contained in it; and the
dictum de omni merely amounts to the identical proposi-

tion, that whatever is true of certain objects is true of each of these objects".[32] If then the syllogism is to be represented as good for anything but dialectic, it would appear that it must be radically reformulated. And there would appear to be only two possible reformulations. In both an attempt is made to restrict the import of the propositions concerned to the facts of the case; but while one works upon the assumption that a distinction may be drawn between universals and particulars, the other denies the distinction.

According to the former, which provides the second interpretation of the syllogism, it reads—The attributes of man are a mark of the attribute mortality; Socrates has the attributes of a man; Therefore he has the attribute mortality. The axiom of the syllogism in this form is, Whatever has any mark has that which it is a mark of. And this according to Mill, at one stage, expresses with precision and force "what is aimed at, and actually accomplished in every case of the ascertainment of a truth by ratiocination".[33] The great advantage of this form is that it avoids the charge of *petitio principii* by stating the major premise of the syllogism in such a way that its truth is independent of any singular proposition that may be subsumed under it. But it labours under a corresponding disadvantage in that it is difficult to understand how the connexion of attributes asserted in the major premise can be arrived at independently of these singular propositions. And although Mill came to consider that he had in Book III of the *Logic* found a way round this difficulty, it led him in Book II to endorse the third interpretation.

According to this, the syllogism, "cut down to as much as is really known by direct evidence", runs—My father and my father's father and an indefinite number of other persons have died; Socrates resembles these persons in certain respects; Therefore he will also resemble them in

---

[32] *Logic*, II. 2, 2.
[33] *Ibid.*, II. 2, 4.

this. The general form of the argument on this reading will be, "Certain individuals have a given attribute; an individual or individuals resemble the former in certain other attributes; therefore they resemble them also in the given attribute."[34] And while this form of the syllogism, along with the preceding, has the advantage of not begging the question, it suffers from the disadvantage of being inconclusive. It can only be conclusive if it is assumed, and truly assumed, that there is a constant connexion between the given attribute of certain individuals and the other attribute in which another individual resembles them, that is, between mortality and humanity. And while it is interesting and important, in psychology, to distinguish between facts *from which* and the principles *according to which* people reason, that distinction can have no standing in logic. It is quite immaterial to the logician whether the proposition, Humanity is a mark of mortality, is "expressly adverted to" by the reasoner. The only material point is whether its truth is a necessary condition of the truth of his conclusion. Seeing that it is, it has to be regarded as a premise of his reasoning. And the third reading of the syllogism will then be reduced to the second.

There is, however, an alternative. And it is this which Mill chooses to countenance in Book II, although it involves the denial of the possibility of any such system of logic as he is attempting to formulate. The representation of the syllogism as an inference from particulars to particulars is, we have seen, the inevitable consequence of the two contentions that the import of propositions consists in the facts they assert and that these facts consist entirely of particulars. Since this sort of inference is necessarily inconclusive, it may be concluded, then, not that there is something wrong with these contentions, but rather that there is something wrong with the traditional idea of inference. And in fact Mill now proceeds to admit that he is unable, while he stands by these con-

---

[34] *Logic*, II. 3, 6.

tentions, to recognise any sense in which one proposition, different from one or more other propositions, can be said to follow from them.

"This type of ratiocination", he says, "does not claim, like the syllogism, to be conclusive from the mere form of the expression; nor can it possibly be so. That one proposition does or does not assert the very fact which was already asserted in another, may appear from the very form of the expression, that is, from the comparison of the language; but when the two propositions assert facts which are *bona fide* different, whether the one fact proves the other fact or not can never appear from the language but must depend on other considerations." And in another passage he goes even further and simply reduces inference, so far as it conforms to this third interpretation, to the free play of association where there can be no question of validity at all. "If reasoning be from particulars to particulars", he says, "nothing is required to render reasoning possible, except senses and association: senses to perceive that two facts are conjoined; association as the law by which one of those two facts raises up the idea of the other." It would, however, be a great mistake to regard these statements as representative of Mill's real opinions. Although he never repudiates this third interpretation of the syllogism, he constantly assumes that it is the second that is correct. And when he comes to deal with induction his purpose, he says, is to "provide rules and models (such as the syllogism and its rules are for ratiocination) to which if inductive arguments conform these arguments are conclusive and not otherwise".[35]

XIV

It is submitted, then, that Mill was mistaken in thinking that the philosophical controversies of the early nineteenth century, epitomised in his *Logic*, are reducible to

[35] *Logic*, II. 3, 7; III. 9, 6; IV, 3, 2.

a debate between the two schools of thought which he
describes in his essays on Bentham and Coleridge.
Whichever way we turn we are confronted not by two
but by three alternatives. There are three interpretations
of the syllogism. Closely connected with them and with
each other there are three theories of the import of propositions and three doctrines of universals. And behind
these again, although they do not, to be sure, stand in a
one-one relation with them, there are three theories of
politics. It is tempting to connect this situation with that
which had arisen in the eighteenth century. The new
way of ideas, initiated by Locke, had been succeeded by
the philosophies of Hume, of Reid and the Scottish
school, and of Hartley and Priestley. Hume traced and
enjoyed the sceptical implications of Locke's principles
and he may be regarded as the forerunner of the positive
philosophy of Comte. Reid found that he could neither
accept Hume's conclusions nor deny that they followed
from Locke's premises. And so he attempted to formulate
a new position, leaning heavily upon self-evident propositions, which anticipates in many respects that of Kant.
Hartley and Priestley, however, continued to stand by
Locke. They either ignored the difficulties raised by
Hume or they assumed, without going into the matter
very deeply, that these difficulties could be met without
any radical revision of his premises. And it was from
Hartley and Priestley, as they frequently assert, that the
Mills derived the main features of their philosophy.

Now in some respects this account of his origins does
give a true impression of the position of J. S. Mill. He
was attempting to steer a middle course between Hume
and Reid, and he was indebted to Locke for a good many
of his leading principles. But there was also another
strain in Mill, quite foreign to Locke, which connects
him rather with Bacon and even with Plato. The incep-
tion of the way of ideas was closely connected with the
rise of science in many ways. In an age, consequently,
that had produced a Boyle, a Sydenham, the great Huy-
genius and the incomparable Mr. Newton, Locke re-

garded it as "ambition enough to be employed as an under-labourer in clearing the ground a little and removing some of the rubbish that lies in the way to knowledge". But for all that he was remarkably open-minded about the achievements and the possibilities of science. And he concludes that, "as to a *perfect* science of natural bodies (not to mention spiritual beings) we are, I think, so far from being capable of any such thing, that I conclude it lost labour to seek after it".[36] Mill's position is, however, quite different. "On the subject of Induction", he says in the Preface to the *Logic*, "the task to be performed was that of generalizing the modes of investigating truth and estimating evidence, by which so many important and recondite laws of nature have, in the various sciences, been aggregated to the stock of human knowledge." And a little later he goes even further and speaks of the methods "by which so many of the laws of the physical world have been numbered among truths irrevocably acquired and universally assented to". Evidently then Mill is far from sharing Locke's suspicion that in accepting the findings of science regarding the original basis of knowledge he may find it difficult to understand how we come to have any knowledge of science. Thus although he accepts Locke's contention that the objects of the understanding are all *in the last resort* ideas, he also regards himself as free to assert with Bacon that they are not ideas but things. And then again although he wishes to say, and mostly does say, that the only things that exist are the particular things we know in sense experience, he is also tempted to say, and frequently does say, that the behaviour of these things is only explicable by laws of nature which hold independently of them.

---

[36] Locke, *Essay*, Epistle to the Reader, IV. 3, 29.

MILL'S TREATMENT OF
GEOMETRY—
A REPLY TO JEVONS

BY
Reginald Jackson

Within five years of the death of John Stuart Mill, the *Contemporary Review* accepted a series of articles by W. Stanley Jevons. The series was entitled "John Stuart Mill's Philosophy Tested", and its purpose was to expose "the disconnected and worthless character of his philosophy".[1] In pursuit of this purpose Jevons decided "to select a certain number of his more prominent and peculiar doctrines, and to show that, in their treatment, he is illogical".[2] The first article selected "Mill's doctrines concerning geometrical reasoning".[3]

Published in December, 1877, it drew a rebuke from the Editor of *Mind* as early as January, 1878. So prompt an intervention could do little to vindicate Mill's reputa-

From *Mind*, 50, January 1941. Reprinted by permission of the Editor of *Mind*.

[1] *Pure Logic and other Minor Works*, p. 202.

[2] *Ibid.*, p. 204.

[3] *Ibid.*

tion. Indeed, after questioning the utility of Jevons' project on the ground that "those who think most highly of Mill" were "perfectly familiar with all the inconsistencies that Prof. Jevons would now laboriously bring to light",[4] Croom Robertson was hardly at liberty to contest the substance of Jevons' indictment. It is true that Croom Robertson soon grew restive under this self-imposed restraint. But his belief that there was "no need to spend many words on the objections brought by Prof. Jevons against Mill's view of geometrical science"[5] prepared an easy triumph for Jevons in the ensuing number of *Mind*.

Croom Robertson did detect a major error. He declared the proposition that 'if these imaginary lines are not perfectly straight they will not enable us to prove the truths of geometry' to be "a premiss for which Mill is not in the least responsible"; and he protested that "of course Mill would allow nothing of the sort". His declaration and his protest are justifiable. But his attempt to justify them is ill considered: "In denying (with whatever reason) that straight lines really exist, Mill never says that we have no perception of things as apparently straight. So, when he comes to deal with the imaginary lines by which he supposes the geometer able to increase his experience indefinitely, he may very well say that these exactly resemble the lines that are perceptibly (without being really) straight".[6] To this Jevons was able to retort triumphantly: "That is to say, Mill after having made geometrical reasoning the crucial test of his philosophy, having written several laborious chapters on the subject, and having had seven opportunities of revising those chapters in new editions, leaves us still to judge of his doctrine, not by what he has so abundantly said, but by what he has left unsaid".[7]

A further suggestion was more fortunate only in es-

---

[4] *Mind*, 1878, p. 142.
[5] *Ibid.*, p. 143.
[6] *Ibid.*, p. 143.
[7] *Ibid.*, p. 285.

caping the eye of Jevons: "Did he not from the first declare, with Dugald Stewart, that there is a purely hypothetical element in the definition of geometrical figures,
and that it is this, and not anything we can actually see
or imagine, that enables us to prove the truths of geometry?"[8] This suggestion ignores Mill's divergence from
Stewart. Having completed his defence of Stewart
against Whewell, Mill proceeds: "But though Dr. Whewell has not shaken Stewart's doctrine as to the hypothetical character of that portion of the first principles of
geometry which are involved in the so-called definitions,
he has, I conceive, greatly the advantage of Stewart on
another important point in the theory of geometrical reasoning; the necessity of admitting, among those first principles, axioms as well as definitions". The relevance of
this divergence is shattering: "The axioms . . . differ
from that other class of fundamental principles which
are involved in the definitions, in this, that they are true
without any mixture of hypothesis".[9] What, then, enables us to prove *these* truths of geometry? "It remains to
inquire, what is the ground of our belief in axioms—
what is the evidence on which they rest? I answer, they
are experimental truths; generalizations from observation. The proposition, Two straight lines cannot inclose
a space . . . is an induction from the evidence of our
senses".[10] Mill's answer is precisely what Croom Robertson says it is not.

Those, then, "who think most highly of Mill" must
dissociate themselves from Croom Robertson's precipitate
intervention. Others are only too likely to find, in these
desperate expedients of counsel for the defence, an involuntary confirmation of the substance of Jevons' indictment. In 1890 Jevons' articles were republished in the
volume, *Pure Logic and other Minor Works*. They have
been widely read; and they have persuaded many that

---

8 *Mind*, 1878, p. 143.

9 *System of Logic*, Book II, chap. v, § 3.

10 *Ibid.*, § 4.

"Mill's mind was essentially illogical".[11] The charge is plausible. Just because Mill writes so very intelligibly, his inconsistency is easily detected and is never mistaken, as is the inconsistency of other philosophers, for profundity. Moreover, partly because of his capacity for sympathising with conflicting doctrines, partly because of his lack of leisure for revision, Mill's work is full of inconsistencies. Those "who think most highly of Mill" can admit this without admitting that "Mill's mind was essentially illogical". But they must beware of professing to be "perfectly familiar with all the inconsistencies that Prof. Jevons would now laboriously bring to light". For to admit the presence of the inconsistency which Jevons thought he had found in "Mill's doctrines concerning geometrical reasoning" *would* involve the admission that "Mill's mind was essentially illogical". The presence of *this* inconsistency I shall try not to *explain* but to *disprove*. Jevons thought he had found it only because his own mind was *essentially uncritical*. In seeking the hospitality of *Mind* for an article which can advance philosophy only by inducing philosophers to read Mill less censoriously, I am fortified by the pretext that I am trying to finish what its first Editor began.

What is the inconsistency imputed to "Mill's doctrines concerning geometrical reasoning"? Jevons formulates the indictment as follows:

"As a first test of Mill's philosophy I propose this simple question of fact—Are there in the material universe such things as perfectly straight lines? We shall find that Mill returns to this question a categorical negative answer. There exist no such things as perfectly straight lines. How then can geometry exist, if the things about which it is conversant do not exist? Mill's ingenuity seldom fails him. Geometry, in his opinion, treats not of things as they are in reality, but as we suppose them to be. Though straight lines do not exist, we can experiment in our minds upon straight lines, as if they did exist. It

---

[11] *Pure Logic, etc.,* p. 201.

is a peculiarity of geometrical science, he thinks, thus to
allow of *mental experimentation*. Moreover, these mental experiments are just as good as real experiments, because we know that the imaginary lines exactly resemble
real ones, and that we can conclude from them to real
ones with quite as much certainty as we conclude from
one real line to another. If such be Mill's doctrines, we
are brought into the following position:—

"1. Perfectly straight lines do not exist.

"2. We experiment in our minds upon imaginary
straight lines.

"3. These imaginary straight lines exactly resemble
the real ones.

"4. If these imaginary straight lines are not perfectly
straight, they will not enable us to prove the truths of
geometry.

"5. If they are perfectly straight, then the real ones,
which *exactly* resemble them, must be perfectly straight:
ergo, perfectly straight lines do exist."[12]

In recognition of the gravity of this indictment Jevons
remarks: "It would not be right to attribute such reasoning to Mill without fully substantiating the statements. I
must therefore ask the reader to bear with me while I give
somewhat full extracts from the fifth chapter of the second book of the *System of Logic*." And by copious quotation Jevons contrives that Mill shall seem, given a fair
hearing, to convict himself. But quotation can be copious
without being liberal. Mill is not given a fair hearing.
Jevons so selects his extracts as to suppress whatever is in-
conveniently relevant, including the key to the extracts
themselves.

Jevons is, moreover, confused about the nature of the
reasoning attributed to Mill, confused both about Mill's
problem and about Mill's solution. "How then can geometry exist, if the things about which it is conversant
do not exist?" There are more ways than one in which

---

12 *Pure Logic, etc.*, p. 205.

the possibility of geometry might seem to be endangered. How can geometrical propositions be *meaningful*? How can they be *true*? How can they be *evident*? The problem demands specification. More immediately relevant to the imputation of inconsistency is the nature of Mill's solution. "Mill's ingenuity seldom fails him." But the ingenuity is not Mill's. Mill merely inherits the device to which he has recourse. And Jevons' imputation of inconsistency is the immediate consequence of a complete misunderstanding of this device.

If no real things exactly conform to geometrical definitions, how can geometrical propositions be meaningful? Of this problem a solution has been sought in the doctrine that some imaginary things exactly conform to geometrical definitions and that geometrical propositions are about these. This solution is both popular and plausible. But nobody would attempt to combine this solution with the claim that imaginary things must resemble real things in those respects in which real things fail exactly to conform to geometrical definitions. Anyone who thought that Mill adopted this solution would have to suppose that Mill's claim that "we know that the imaginary lines exactly resemble real ones" is to be understood with an implicit reservation. But Mill formulates this solution only in order to reject it. From the second paragraph of § 1[13] Jevons quotes:

"It is acknowledged that the conclusions of geometry are deduced, partly at least, from the so-called Definitions, and that those definitions are assumed to be correct descriptions, as far as they go, of the objects with which geometry is conversant. Now we have pointed out that, from a definition as such, no proposition, unless it be one concerning the meaning of a word, can ever follow; and that what apparently follows from a definition, follows in reality from an implied assumption that there exists a real thing conformable thereto. This assumption,

---

[13] *System of Logic*, Book II, chap. v.

in the case of the definitions of geometry, is false:[14]
there exist no real things exactly conformable to the
definitions. There exist no points without magnitude;
no lines without breadth, nor perfectly straight; no circles
with all their radii exactly equal, nor squares with all
their angles perfectly right. It will perhaps be said that
the assumption does not extend to the actual, but only
to the possible, existence of such things. I answer that,
according to any test we have of possibility, they are not
even possible. Their existence, so far as we can form
any judgment, would seem to be inconsistent with the
physical constitution of our planet at least, if not of the
universe." At this point Jevons breaks off the quotation.
Fortunately, he cannot prevent others from hearing Mill
out:

"To get rid of this difficulty, and at the same time to
save the credit of the supposed system of necessary truth,
it is customary to say that the points, lines, circles, and
squares which are the subject of geometry, exist in our
conceptions merely, and are part of our minds; which
minds, by working on their own materials, construct an
a priori science, the evidence of which is purely mental,

---

14 Jevons observes (p. 206, note 2) that in the later editions
Mill substitutes for the word *'false'* the words *'not strictly true'*.
Later, Jevons calls this (p. 213) a "curious substitution" and says
that "a good many remarks might be made upon this little change
of words, were there not other matters claiming prior attention".
One shudders at the thought of the remarks which Jevons, had his
attention been free, might have made. Holding that a condition
is not exactly fulfilled, Mill describes the assumption that this
condition is fulfilled as *'false'*. On revision, he thinks that the
assumption is less misleadingly, because more specifically, described as *'not strictly true'*. Is this change "curious"? And is it
indicative of anything but a wholesome desire to be understood?

Jevons also insists (p. 212): "Any one who has the least knowledge of geometry must know that a straight line means a *perfectly*
straight line". Had Jevons faced the implication that, if 'straight'
always means 'perfectly straight', then 'perfectly straight' must
mean 'perfectly perfectly straight'?

and has nothing whatever to do with outward experience. By howsoever high authorities this doctrine may have been sanctioned, it appears to me psychologically incorrect. The points, lines, circles, and squares which anyone has in his mind, are (I apprehend) simply copies of the points, lines, circles, and squares which he has known in his experience. Our idea of a point, I apprehend to be simply our idea of the *minimum visibile*, the smallest portion of surface which we can see. A line, as defined by geometers, is wholly inconceivable. We can reason about a line as if it had no breadth; because we have a power, which is the foundation of all the control we can exercise over the operations of our minds; the power, when a perception is present to our senses, or a conception to our intellects, of *attending* to a part only of that perception or conception, instead of the whole. But we cannot *conceive* a line without breadth; we can form no mental picture of such a line: all the lines which we have in our minds are lines possessing breadth."

That in this passage Mill rejects the imaginary object solution will hardly be questioned. But it might be urged that, since Jevons is mainly concerned to prove that "Mill's mind was essentially illogical", he need not be disconcerted by Mill's rejection of the imaginary object solution in this passage, provided that he can establish Mill's adoption of this solution in other passages. Even so, Jevons' failure to discuss this passage would not be explained. Either this passage must shake his conviction that Mill elsewhere adopts the imaginary object solution, or he ought to adduce this passage as direct evidence of Mill's incoherence instead of contenting himself with the indirect evidence which he finds in Mill's claim about the resemblance between imaginary and real lines.

How did Jevons become convinced that Mill adopts the imaginary object solution? The passage which Jevons offers in evidence I do not yet examine. For I cannot imagine how that passage could be interpreted as Jevons interprets it by anyone not already independently convinced. The origin of Jevons' conviction must be sought elsewhere and is, I think, to be found in a complete misunderstanding of the very passage whose discussion he evades.

Mill's rejection of the view, that imaginary things come nearer than do real things to satisfying geometrical definitions, is accompanied by a concession:

"We can reason about a line as if it had no breadth; because we have a power, which is the foundation of all the control we can exercise over the operations of our minds; the power, when a perception is present to our senses, or a conception to our intellects, of *attending* to a part only of that perception or conception, instead of the whole." Mill is at pains explicitly to deny that what he concedes implies what he withholds:

"But it is an error to suppose, because we resolve to confine our attention to a certain number of the properties of an object, that we therefore conceive, or have an idea of, the object, denuded of its other properties. We are thinking, all the time, of precisely such objects as we have seen and touched, and with all the properties which naturally belong to them; but, for scientific convenience, we feign them to be divested of all properties, except those which are material to our purpose, and in regard to which we design to consider them."[15]

To say this is only to occupy the well-known stronghold designed by Berkeley[16] for the defence of Nominal-

---

[15] End of third paragraph of § 1.

[16] *Principles of Human Knowledge* (Third Edition), Introduction, § 16: "And here it must be acknowledged that a man may consider a figure merely as triangular, without attending to the particular qualities of the angles, or relations of the sides. So far he may abstract; but this will never prove that he can frame an abstract, general, inconsistent idea of a triangle. In like manner we may consider Peter so far forth as man, or so far forth as animal, without framing the forementioned abstract idea, either of man or of animal, inasmuch as all that is perceived is not considered." Cf. Hume, *Treatise*, Bk. I, Pt. I, sect. vii, especially the last paragraph.

ism against the Conceptualism of Locke. Abstraction is conceded; abstract ideas are rejected. Nothing, whether real or imaginary, need have (or lack) the properties which things may be thought of as having (or lacking).

On this concession of the possibility of abstraction Mill bases his solution of the problem of the meaningfulness of geometrical propositions. Those who are unable to distinguish the possibility of abstraction from the possibility of abstract ideas will be unable to distinguish Mill's solution from the imaginary object solution. But Mill at least clearly seeks a different solution:

"Since, then, neither in nature, nor in the human mind, do there exist any objects exactly corresponding to the definitions of geometry, while yet that science cannot be supposed to be conversant about non-entities; nothing remains but to consider geometry as conversant with such lines, angles, and figures, as really exist."[17]

Since nothing, whether real or imaginary, exactly conforms to the definitions, there is, Mill thinks, no escaping the admission that the objects of geometry do not exactly conform to the definitions. But the imaginary object solution is an attempt to escape this admission.

What solution of the problem does this admission leave open? A solution based on the possibility of abstraction. By feigning the objects of geometry "to be divested of all properties, except those which are material to our purpose", we feign the objects of geometry exactly to conform to the definitions.

To anyone who adopts this solution of the problem of the *meaningfulness* of geometrical propositions the further problem of the *truth* of geometrical propositions should present no difficulty. Geometrical propositions are hypothetical. Because nothing exactly conforms to the definitions, the antecedents of these propositions are not true. But just because geometrical propositions are hypothetical this does not matter. Neither the antecedents nor the consequents are *asserted*. Both antecedents and con-

---

[17] Beginning of third paragraph of § 1.

sequents are *entertained*. But the problem of their entertainment is only the problem of meaningfulness.

To Mill, however, the further problem of the *truth* of geometrical propositions *does* present a difficulty. In his anxiety to explain away "the peculiar certainty always ascribed to the sciences which are entirely, or almost entirely, deductive",[18] Mill *makes* the problem of the *truth* of geometrical propositions present a difficulty. He confuses *hypothetical judgment* with *inference*. The confusion has perhaps already appeared in Mill's assumption that geometry "cannot be supposed to be conversant about non-entities". Must we not protest that no hypothetical proposition is *about* anything? A hypothetical proposition may be *true of something*. In other words, its antecedent, and so (if the hypothetical proposition is true) its consequent, may be true. But a hypothetical proposition need not, in order to be true, be *true of anything*.

The confusion appears unmistakably in Mill's footnote on the remark that geometry "is built on hypotheses":[19]

"An hypothesis, in science, usually means a supposition not proved to be true, but surmised to be so, because if true it would account for certain known facts; and the final result of the speculation may be to prove its truth. The hypotheses spoken of in the text are of a different character; they are known not to be literally true, while as much of them as is true is not hypothetical, but certain. The two cases, however, resemble each other in the circumstance that in both *we reason, not from a truth, but from an assumption, and the truth therefore of the conclusions is conditional, not categorical.*" What would Mill say of the hypothesis of a *reductio ad absurdum*?[20]

---

[18] First paragraph of § 1.

[19] Fourth paragraph of § 1. My italics.

[20] From this confusion Mill perhaps partially extricates himself when he claims: "The axioms . . . differ from that other class of fundamental principles which are involved in the definitions, in this, that they are true without any mixture of hypothe-

The failure of real things exactly to conform to geometrical definitions has been seen to present two problems. How can geometrical propositions be *meaningful?* Mill rejects the solution that geometrical propositions are about imaginary things exactly conforming to the definitions, and adopts the solution that geometrical propositions are about real things feigned exactly to conform to the definitions. How can geometrical propositions be *true?* Instead of giving the obvious answer that geometrical propositions are hypothetical and that the truth of a hypothetical proposition does not require the truth of its antecedent, Mill insists that geometry is infected with the falsity of the hypotheses on which it is "built". But the failure of real things exactly to conform to geometrical definitions presents yet a third problem, a problem which for epistemological empiricism is formidable if not insoluble. How can geometrical propositions be *evident?*

---

sis". Does Mill here recognise that axioms, just because they are hypothetical propositions, are "true without any mixture of hypothesis"? He proceeds: "That things which are equal to the same thing are equal to one another, is as true of the lines and figures in nature, as it would be of the imaginary ones assumed in the definitions". By "the imaginary ones assumed in the definitions", Mill must mean, not the imaginary things which come no nearer than do real things to satisfying the definitions, but the things (neither real nor imaginary) which real things are feigned to be. The proposition, he must be claiming, is as true of things which do not, as it would be of things which did, exactly conform to the definitions. I think the explanation is only this: A definition of 'equal' is not among "the definitions", and "the lines and figures in nature" can, Mill thinks, be exactly "equal to the same thing". Yet the axiom which Mill selects for special study is "the proposition that two straight lines cannot inclose a space". Now Mill does not think *either* that "the lines and figures in nature" are "perfectly straight" *or* that their failure exactly to conform to the definition of 'straight' leaves unaffected the incapacity of any two of them to "inclose a space". How then can Mill claim of axioms in general that they are "true without any mixture of hypothesis"?

Neither Croom Robertson nor Jevons sufficiently distinguishes this problem from the others. Robertson, we saw, attributes to Mill the position "that there is a purely hypothetical element in the definition of geometrical figures, and that it is this, and not anything we can actually see or imagine, that enables us to prove the truths of geometry". Jevons, we saw, attributes to Mill the position that "if these imaginary straight lines are not perfectly straight, they will not enable us to prove the truths of geometry".

Mill, however, as an epistemological empiricist, is curiously unconcerned about this problem of evidence, and nowhere notices the problem except in a footnote introduced[21] into the later editions:

"Those who employ this argument to show that geometrical axioms cannot be proved by induction, show themselves unfamiliar with a common and perfectly valid mode of inductive proof; proof by approximation. Though experience furnishes us with no lines so unimpeachably straight that two of them are incapable of inclosing the smallest space, it presents us with gradations of lines possessing less and less either of breadth or of flexure, of which series the straight line of the definition is the ideal limit. And observation shows that just as much, and as nearly, as the straight lines of experience approximate to having no breadth or flexure, so much and so nearly does the space-inclosing power of any two of them approach to zero. The inference that if they had no breadth or flexure at all, they would inclose no space at all, is a correct inductive inference from these facts, conformable to one of the four Inductive Methods hereinafter characterized, the Method of Concomitant Variations; of which the mathematical Doctrine of Limits presents the extreme case." I cannot believe that either observation or inference can do the work to which Mill here calls them. And I quote this passage not for its merits but for its relevance. On the one

---

[21] At the end of the penultimate paragraph of § 4.

occasion on which Mill notices the problem of evidence which the failure of real things exactly to conform to geometrical definitions presents to the epistemological empiricist, Mill displays no inclination to seek exactly conformable objects among imaginary things.

Thus, neither in solving the problem of *meaningfulness* nor in solving the problem of *truth* nor in solving the problem of *evidence* have we found Mill qualifying his rejection of the view that imaginary things come nearer than do real things to satisfying geometrical definitions. Jevons' failure sufficiently to distinguish the three problems may have helped to prevent him from grasping Mill's solutions. But what convinced Jevons that Mill adopted an imaginary object solution of *any* problem? Sheer confusion of the possibility of abstraction with the possibility of abstract ideas. Sheer incapacity to distinguish the Nominalism of Berkeley and Hume from the Conceptualism of Locke.

Let us look once more at the indictment:

"Mill's ingenuity seldom fails him. Geometry, in his opinion, treats not of things as they are in reality, but as we suppose them to be. Though straight lines do not exist, we can experiment in our minds upon straight lines, as if they did exist. It is a peculiarity of geometrical science, he thinks, thus to allow of *mental experimentation*. Moreover, these mental experiments are just as good as real experiments, because we know that the imaginary lines exactly resemble real ones."

What imaginary lines? Those which Jevons tacitly presupposes to be involved in supposing lines to be other than "as they are in reality". Whether this tacit presupposition is true or false is irrelevant. What is relevant is Mill's plain statement that it is false. This alone is relevant since it is "Mill's ingenuity", "Mill's doctrines", that Jevons is avowedly engaged in expounding. But Mill's plain statement that "it is an error to suppose, because we resolve to confine our attention to a certain number of the properties of an object, that we therefore conceive, or have an idea of, the object, denuded of its other properties", finds no place in the "somewhat full extracts" to which Jevons restricts us. If, however, Jevons fails to appreciate the relevance of this statement, the only possible explanation is that Jevons can make nothing of the statement.

The truth of this explanation can be confirmed by an examination of the following passage: "In fact, Mill tells us that 'we can reason about a line as if it had no breadth', because we have 'the power, when a perception is present to our senses, or a conception to our intellects, of *attending* to a part only of that perception or conception, instead of the whole'. I believe that this sentence supplies a good instance of a *non sequitur*, being in conflict with the sentence which immediately follows. Mill holds that we learn the properties of lines by experimentation on ideas in the mind; these ideas must surely be conceived, and they cannot be conceived without thickness. Unless, then, the *reasoning* about a line is quite a different process from *experimenting*, I fail to make the sentences hold together at all. If, on the other hand, we can reason about lines without breadth, but can only experiment on thick lines, would it not be much better to stick to the reasoning process, whatever it may be, and drop the mental experimentation altogether?"[22]

The sentences which Jevons believes to be "in conflict" are these: '*we can reason about a line as if it had no breadth*' and '*we cannot conceive a line without breadth*'. He declares his inability "to make the sentences hold together" unless on the supposition that "the *reasoning* about a line is quite a different process from *experimenting*". Clearly, the supposition intended is the absurdity that reasoning about a line does not involve conceiving it. But why does Jevons believe the two sentences to be "in conflict"? Because he treats the sentence '*we can reason about a line as if it had no breadth*' as only verbally different from the sentence '*we can reason about lines without breadth*'. Jevons' mistaken belief that

---

[22] *Pure Logic, etc.*, p. 217.

Mill concedes to *reasoning* what he denies to *conceiving* is, therefore, the product of inability to understand the attempt to reconcile *a capacity to abstract* with *an incapacity to form abstract ideas*.

So much for the probable origin of Jevons' conviction that Mill adopted an imaginary object solution. I turn now to the passage which Jevons offers in evidence. Taken from § 5, this passage consists of the second paragraph, bereft of its first sentence, followed by the third paragraph, bereft of its last sentence. Jevons remarks: "I have been obliged to give this long extract in full, because, unless the reader has it all freshly before him, he will scarcely accept my analysis".[23] The truth is that the extract is not long enough. Jevons' analysis owes such plausibility as it achieves to his suppression of the context. This was pointed out by Arthur Strachey,[24] who, by supplying the opening sentence of the second paragraph and italicising the opening words of the third paragraph, established the important fact that what Jevons treats as an inconsistent admission is really the formulation of a possible objection to which Mill presently replies. Strachey fairly condemned Jevons' analysis as "a mistake which a moment's glance at the context . . . ought to have prevented". And he pertinently commented: "No doubt, if the 'essential illogicality' of Mill's mind can be proved by ascribing to him a statement which he represents as that of an opponent, Prof. Jevons will succeed in his undertaking".

Right so far, Strachey did not go far enough. The first paragraph of § 5 formulates one objection; the second paragraph formulates another objection; the third paragraph formulates Mill's reply to the objection formulated in the first; the fourth paragraph formulates Mill's reply to the objection formulated in the second. If, then, we can be persuaded to isolate the second and the third paragraph from the first and the fourth paragraph, we

23 *Ibid.*, p. 210.
24 *Mind*, 1878, pp. 283-4.

may easily acquiesce in the judgment that "Mill's mind was essentially illogical". Jevons' extract withholds the reply to the objection which it gives and withholds the objection the reply to which it gives. Such is the extract concerning which he says that "unless the reader has it all freshly before him, he will scarcely accept my analysis".[25]

In so far grasping the structure of § 5 there is no difficulty. There is difficulty only in seeing how Jevons could have failed so far to grasp its structure. And this difficulty I cannot overcome, though I should be reluctant to contemplate the implications of an admission that the difficulty is insuperable.

In order so far to grasp the structure of § 5 it is necessary to read what Mill says. Nothing else is necessary. The last two sentences of § 4 are: "The advocates of the *a priori* theory are obliged to have recourse to other arguments. These are reducible to two, which I shall endeavour to state as clearly and as forcibly as possible." The first sentence of the *first* paragraph of § 5 is: "In the first place it is said, that if our assent to the proposition that two straight lines cannot inclose a space, were derived from the senses, we could only be convinced of its truth by actual trial, that is, by seeing or feeling the straight lines; whereas in fact it is seen to be true by merely thinking of them". The first sentence of the *second* paragraph is: "To this argument it might be added in the case of this particular axiom, (for the assertion would not be true of all axioms,) that the evidence of

---

[25] In his preface to *Pure Logic and other Minor Works* (p. xxiii), Adamson wrote: "Whatever opinion may be formed of the value of the general objections taken to Mill's logical and philosophical doctrines, or of the appropriateness of the limits imposed by the author on his criticism, it must be acknowledged that he took every precaution against oversight or hasty judgment, and that his every utterance was supported by the fullest evidence attainable". In *The Metaphysics of John Stuart Mill* (pp. 124-127), W. L. Courtney swallows Jevons whole, remarking (p. 127, note): "His summing up of Mill's position is clear, and is adequately supported by his references".

it from actual ocular inspection is not only unnecessary, but unattainable". The first sentence of the *third* paragraph is: "To these arguments, which I trust I cannot be accused of understating, a satisfactory answer will, I conceive, be found, if we advert to one of the characteristic properties of geometrical forms—their capacity of being painted in the imagination with a distinctness equal to reality: in other words, the exact resemblance of our ideas of form to the sensations which suggest them". The first sentence of the *fourth* paragraph is: "These considerations also remove the objection arising from the impossibility of ocularly following the lines in their prolongation to infinity".

Never was a passage more amply or more unmistakably charted. Only those who disregard Mill's plain directions can lose their way. And it is because Jevons disregards these directions that he offers in evidence the extract which he quotes. We must concede to Jevons that in this extract Mill maintains both the possibility and the relevance of geometrical experimentation upon "imaginary lines". If, then, Mill is not here qualifying his rejection of the doctrine that imaginary things come nearer than do real things to satisfying geometrical definitions, what, in Mill's opinion, is the purpose of experimentation upon "imaginary lines"? I conjecture that Mill thinks its main purpose a very humble one. The geometer may find himself without chalk or pencil. But Mill does not here tell us. And anyone who supposes that Mill is here *advocating* experimentation upon "imaginary lines" will construe Mill's silence about the purpose of such experimentation as an omission. What I hope to show, however, is that Mill, although he maintains the possibility and the relevance of such experimentation, does not, in Jevons' extract, advocate such experimentation. His silence is, therefore, an omission only of the irrelevant. He is under no obligation to represent experimentation upon "imaginary lines" as serving any special purpose.

Mill sets himself the task of replying to the objection "that if our assent to the proposition that two straight

lines cannot inclose a space, were derived from the
senses", as Mill has in § 4 contended that it is, then
"we could only be convinced of its truth by actual trial,
that is, by seeing or feeling the straight lines; whereas in
fact it is seen to be true by merely thinking of them".
The objection is variously formulated, and among the
various formulæ is this: "if we see a property of straight
lines to be true by merely fancying ourselves to be looking at them, the ground of our belief cannot be the
senses, or experience; it must be something mental". Concerning this formula Carveth Read, in his critical notice
of *Pure Logic and other Minor Works*, says: "Oddly
enough Mr. Strachey himself, in correcting Jevons,
makes a precisely similar error. He says of Mill: 'His
theory being that we see a property of straight lines to be
true by merely fancying ourselves to be looking at them,
etc.'. But this Mill gives as an opponent's view."[26] The
proposition, that "we see a property of straight lines to
be true by merely fancying ourselves to be looking at
them", is indeed very wrongly described by Strachey[27]
as Mill's theory. But it is also inadequately described by
Carveth Read as "an opponent's view". For Mill does
not challenge it. He treats it as an obvious fact. What
he does challenge is only the claim that it conflicts with
his theory.

Admitting rather than claiming that we may "see a
property of straight lines to be true by merely fancying
ourselves to be looking at them", admitting rather than
claiming "the possibility of satisfying ourselves that two
straight lines cannot inclose a space, by merely thinking
of straight lines without actually looking at them", Mill
undertakes to reconcile this admission with his theory.
Formulated in general terms, the admission is that a geometrical axiom can be established without experimentation upon "real lines". The reconciliation can, Mill
thinks, be effected by a defence of the position that a

---

26 *Mind*, 1891, p. 108, note.
27 *Ibid.*, 1878, p. 283.

geometrical axiom can be established by experimentation upon "imaginary lines". This position requires the possibility and the relevance of such experimentation. But it does not require such experimentation to have any advantage over experimentation upon "real lines".

What Mill here contrasts under the unhappily chosen adjectives *"imaginary"*[28] and *"real"* are what Hume contrasts under the names *"idea"* and *"impression"* and what recent philosophers contrast under the names *"image"* and *"sensum"*. The distinction is, not between *realities and unrealities*, but between *realities of different kinds*. Mill holds that the part played by *sensa*, when, looking at straight lines, we think of them, is played by *images*, when, without looking at straight lines, we think of them. And he holds that the part played, whether by *sensum* or by *image*, is not that of a mere aid to attention but that of an object of attention. Geometrical axioms are, Mill thinks, established by observing the properties of sensa or of images and generalising what observation ascertains.

Geometrical experimentation upon images is, Mill thinks, possible because of "one of the characteristic properties of geometrical forms—their capacity of being painted in the imagination with a distinctness equal to reality". And he thinks it relevant "inasmuch as pictures, if sufficiently accurate, exhibit of course all the properties which would be manifested by the realities at one given instant, and on simple inspection: and in geometry we are concerned only with such properties, and not with that which pictures could not exhibit, the mutual action

---

[28] Mill's choice of the expression "object existing only in our fancy" is not less unhappy. But Mill also uses the expressions "mental image" and "idea". In Book I, chap. iii, § 3, Mill says: "Even imaginary objects (which are said to exist only in our ideas) are to be distinguished from our ideas of them". And in chap. ii, § 3, he says: "All names are names of something, real or imaginary". In these passages his distinction *is* between realities and unrealities.

of bodies one upon another". It is because images could not exhibit the mutual action of bodies one upon another that *physical* experimentation upon images is irrelevant. "That a stone thrown into water goes to the bottom, may be perceived by our senses, but mere thinking of a stone thrown into the water would never have led us to that conclusion."

It is easy to see how, by maintaining the possibility and the relevance of geometrical experimentation upon images, Mill hopes to *explain* "the possibility of satisfying ourselves that two straight lines cannot inclose a space, by merely thinking of straight lines without actually looking at them". But how does Mill hope by this explanation to *reconcile* his admission with his theory? He contends "that we do not believe this truth on the ground of the imaginary intuition simply, but because we know that the imaginary lines exactly resemble real ones, and that we may conclude from them to real ones with quite as much certainty as we could conclude from one real line to another". But this path leads nowhere. Mill finds himself compelled to admit that "we should not be authorized to substitute observation of the image in our mind, for observation of the reality, if we had not learnt by long-continued experience that the properties of the reality are faithfully represented in the image". Now from what kind of experience could we have learnt this? Obviously not from experience merely of sensa. In supporting the comparison of images with sensa, observation of images would be no less indispensable and no less ultimate than observation of sensa. Thus, while Mill can delay, he cannot escape, the admission of images among the *ultimate* data. Mill would perhaps have been wiser to admit them boldly and to qualify his theory accordingly. Geometrical axioms, he could still insist, are "experimental truths; generalizations from observation". But alongside "the evidence of our senses" must be recognised the evidence of our imaginations, both sense and imagination being faculties by which ultimate data may be experienced.

Whatever may be thought of Mill's attempt to reconcile his admission with his theory, there is no justification for thinking that Mill either *does* repent or *should* repent of his declaration that "neither in nature, nor in the human mind, do there exist any objects exactly corresponding to the definitions of geometry". He maintains the possibility and the relevance of geometrical experimentation upon images, because he thinks that such experimentation is involved in "satisfying ourselves that two straight lines cannot inclose a space, by merely thinking of straight lines without actually looking at them". He is no more advocating such experimentation than he is advocating "merely thinking of straight lines without actually looking at them". The straight lines of which we "merely think" need, therefore, be no straighter than the straight lines at which we "actually look". Images need come no nearer than sensa to satisfying geometrical definitions. It suffices that they come as near.

There is some confusion, however, in the passage in which Mill expresses his recognition that this suffices: The capacity of geometrical forms "of being painted in the imagination with a distinctness equal to reality . . . enables us to make . . . mental pictures of all possible combinations of lines and angles, which resemble the realities quite as well as any which we could make on paper; and . . . makes[29] those pictures just as fit subjects of geometrical experimentation as the realities themselves; inasmuch as pictures, if sufficiently accurate, exhibit of course all the properties which would be manifested by the realities at one given instant, and on simple inspection". Jevons characteristically comments: "Such pictures, Mill admits, must be *sufficiently accurate*; but what, in geometry, is sufficient accuracy? The expression is, to my mind, a new and puzzling one".[30] It is hard to believe that even to the mind of Jevons the expression

---

[29] In the later editions "makes" has been carelessly changed into "make".

[30] *Pure Logic, etc.*, p. 210.

"sufficiently accurate" could be either new or puzzling. But Mill's use of the expression here does present some difficulty.

The "mental pictures", Mill says, "resemble the realities quite as well as any which we could make on paper". But "any which we could make on paper" would *be* "the realities". They would be lines at which we could "actually look". And their fitness as "subjects of geometrical experimentation" would depend on the degree, not of their resemblance to any realities, but of their conformity to the definitions. Sufficient accuracy, whether of images or of sensa, would be sufficient approximation to the definitions to enable us to infer what complete satisfaction of the definitions would involve. The inadequacy of Mill's treatment of the nature of such inference has already been noted. But of any inclination to evade the need for such inference by recourse to the doctrine, that images come nearer than sensa to satisfying the definitions, there is no trace.

So far Mill has neither told us nor incurred an obligation to tell us of any purpose subserved by geometrical experimentation upon "imaginary lines". For so far Mill has not advocated such experimentation. But, having, in reply to one objection, maintained the possibility and the relevance of such experimentation, Mill, in reply to another objection, advocates such experimentation. And it is here that he for the first and last time finds a special purpose for such experimentation.

This purpose is very different from the purpose with which Jevons is obsessed. It is made clear even in Mill's formulation of the objection to which he is replying: Of the axiom "that two straight lines cannot inclose a space" the evidence "from actual ocular inspection is not only unnecessary, but unattainable". And the purpose is again made clear in Mill's reply: "These considerations also remove the objection arising from the impossibility of ocularly following the lines in their prolongation to infinity. For though, in order actually to see that two given lines never meet, it would be necessary to follow them to infinity; yet without doing so we may know that if they ever do meet, or if, after diverging from one another, they begin again to approach, this must take place not at an infinite, but at a finite distance. Supposing, therefore, such to be the case, we can transport ourselves thither in imagination, and can frame a mental image of the appearance which one or both of the lines must present at that point, which we may rely on as being precisely similar to the reality."

The futility of this reply is painfully evident. Why may we rely on the image "as being precisely similar to the reality"? Granted that the image must be precisely similar to some possible sensum, why may we rely on it as being precisely similar to the sensum which we should experience if we could "ocularly follow" the lines to that point? We might as well draw a picture on paper of the appearance which the lines must present. And we might as well take the portions of the lines which we can "ocularly follow" as a fair sample of the portions which lie beyond. The procedure prescribed clearly presupposes the knowledge which it is intended to acquire.

While Mill has no justification for claiming that we may rely on the image as being precisely similar to the unattainable relevant sensum, Jevons has no justification for supposing Mill to claim that the image comes any nearer than would the unattainable sensum to satisfying the relevant definition. Why need we "transport ourselves thither in imagination"? Only because we can transport ourselves in no other way. Not because, if we could "ocularly follow" the lines so far, the sensum which we should then experience would be in any way inferior to the image on which Mill thinks we must, only because the sensum is unattainable, rely.

In support of his general thesis that "Mill's mind was essentially illogical", Jevons builds his special case against "Mill's doctrines concerning geometrical reasoning" on his ascription to Mill of the doctrine, that the possibility of geometry is saved by imaginary lines exactly conforming to geometrical definitions. I have tried to show that

Jevons ascribed this doctrine to Mill only because his
own mind was essentially uncritical. Mill explicitly rejects the doctrine. And he nowhere, whether explicitly
or implicitly, accepts it. There are three ways in which
the possibility of geometry may seem to be endangered
by the failure of real lines exactly to conform to geometrical definitions. How can geometrical propositions
be *meaningful?* How can they be *true?* How can they be
evident? Mill's answers to these questions nowhere imply
that imaginary lines exactly conform to geometrical
definitions. What, then, is the explanation of Jevons' mistake? It originates in a complete misunderstanding of the
very passage in which Mill explicitly rejects the doctrine
ascribed to him. With his rejection of the doctrine, that
the objects of geometry are imaginary things exactly conforming to the definitions, Mill couples an acceptance of
the doctrine, that the objects of geometry are real things
feigned exactly to conform to the definitions. Jevons,
treating the sentence '*we can reason about a line as if
it had no breadth*' as only verbally different from the
sentence '*we can reason about lines without breadth*', is
unable to distinguish what Mill affirms from what Mill
denies. But what does Jevons offer in evidence? A passage
whose structure he grossly misrepresents. Mill maintains
the possibility and the relevance of geometrical experimentation upon what he unhappily calls "*imaginary
lines*" and under this description unhappily contrasts
with "*real lines*". The distinction intended is that between *images* and *sensa*. Mill is replying to objections.
To the objection that it is possible to establish a geometrical axiom without experimentation upon *sensa*, he
replies that this is made possible only by experimentation
upon *images*. So far he is not *advocating* experimentation
upon images. To the objection that the relevant sensa
may be unattainable Mill does indeed reply by advocating experimentation upon images. But he advocates such
experimentation only because he thinks that the relevant
sensa are unattainable and not because he thinks that
the images come any nearer than would the unattainable
sensa to satisfying geometrical definitions.

Note.

In Mill's chapter, "Of the Import of Propositions", Jevons thinks he finds a (p. 214) "denunciation of the handling of ideas" which is "in distinct conflict with Mill's subsequent advocacy of mental experimentation".[31] From Book I, chap. i, § 1 Jevons quotes: "The notion that what is of primary importance to the logician in a proposition, is the relation between the two *ideas* corresponding to the subject and predicate (instead of the relation between the two *phenomena* which they respectively express), seems to me one of the most fatal errors ever introduced into the philosophy of Logic, and the principal cause why the theory of the science has made such inconsiderable progress during the last two centuries. The treatises on Logic, and on the branches of Mental Philosophy connected with Logic, which have been produced since the intrusion of this cardinal error, though sometimes written by men of extraordinary abilities and attainments, almost always tacitly imply a theory that the investigation of truth consists in contemplating and handling our ideas, or conceptions of things, instead of the things themselves: a doctrine tantamount to the assertion, that the only mode of acquiring knowledge of nature is to study it at second hand, as represented in our own minds." Having thus quoted Mill, Jevons says (p. 214), "Mill here denounces the *cardinal error* of investigating nature at second hand, as represented in our own minds". But what Mill represents as an error is, not the investigation of nature at second hand, but (and even this is represented, not as the cardinal error, but as an erroneous implicate thereof) the assertion that this is "the only mode of acquiring knowledge of nature". So far from denying, Mill thereby suggests, that to study nature at second hand is among the modes of acquiring knowledge of nature. Jevons adds (p. 214) that "Mill's

---

[31] Again Courtney follows Jevons, *The Metaphysics of John Stuart Mill*, p. 125.

denunciation of the handling of ideas is not limited by any exceptions; it is applied in the most general way, and arises upon the general question of the Import of Propositions". Yet the sentence immediately preceding the passage quoted by Jevons runs: "When I mean to assert anything respecting the ideas, I give them their proper name, I call them ideas: as when I say, that a child's idea of a battle is unlike the reality, or that the ideas entertained of the Deity have had a great effect on the characters of mankind". Mill's position is (Book II, chap. vi, § 1) "that, though propositions may be made both respecting names and respecting ideas, neither the one nor the other are the subject-matter of Propositions considered generally". Clearly, then, Mill's answer to "the general question of the Import of Propositions" does not queer the pitch for "mental experimentation". Moreover, in place of the last clause of the passage quoted by Jevons, Mill had in the first two editions written: "a process by which, I will venture to affirm, not a single truth ever was arrived at, except truths of psychology, a science of which Ideas or Conceptions are avowedly (along with other mental phenomena) the subject-matter". Here an exception in favour of the value of some mental experimentation is explicitly admitted. Of the suppression of this clause Jevons says (p. 215, note 2): "The striking out of these words seems to indicate that he had perceived the absolute conflict of his two doctrines; yet he maintains his opinion about *the cardinal error* of handling ideas, and merely deletes a too glaring inconsistency which results from it". The probable explanation is that Mill became aware that further exceptions in favour of the value of mental experimentation would have to be admitted. Either because he felt diffident about the complete list, or because he felt unwilling to complicate what was already a digression, Mill preferred to withdraw his delimitation of the value of the investigation of nature at second hand and to content himself with a denial that this is "the only mode of acquiring knowledge of nature".

SENSATIONS OF COLOUR

BY

G. N. A. Vesey

I

What does it mean to say that something is white?
This is an odd question. If it had been 'What does it
mean to say that something is beautiful?', it would have
been more understandable. People often discuss what it
means to say that something is beautiful. But unless one
is blind, or does not know the language, surely one would
not be likely to ask what it means to say that something
is white.

And yet some philosophers have taken questions like
this one about whiteness very seriously. What is more,
they have said that there is a good deal more to noticing
that things are white, and calling them 'white', than one
would suppose. Some such philosophers say that one notices that something is white through noticing its resemblance to other things. Others say that the resemblance
one notices is between sensations, and that what one
means when one says something is white is that a sensation one has on looking at it resembles a sensation one
has had before and to which one gave the name 'sensation of white'. This is what John Stuart Mill says.

Why do philosophers talk of 'resemblances' and 'sensations' in this connexion?

Some philosophers talk of 'resemblances', I suppose, because they think of the question 'What does it mean to say that something is white?' as involving the question 'What reason has a person, on looking at something white, to call it white?' The theory seems to be (1) that some act—noticing a resemblance—must precede uttering the word 'white' for the person who utters the word genuinely to be describing the object, and not merely coming out with the words 'It's white' as might a parrot no matter what it was shown; and (2) that the resemblance the theory requires one to have noticed, which is one's reason for calling the thing 'white', and which is supposed to justify one's calling it white as opposed, say, to blue, is what one is referring to when one calls the object 'white'.

And philosophers talk of 'sensations' in this connexion because of views they hold about perception. They may hold these views about perception because of views they hold about our nature and the nature of the things we look at. Thus if it is held that really we are substances (Descartes), then, it would seem, it must also be held that all we can be aware of in perception are modifications of ourselves, which are, at most, the representations in us of modifications of other substances. If these modifications are called 'sensations', and if it is allowed that different substances can be related causally, then on this view something's looking white to someone is his having certain sensations which are excited in him by what we would ordinarily say was the object he saw to be white.

Mill's answer to the question 'What does it mean to say that something is white?' arises out of his reflections on the representative theory of perception. Making use of quotations from Mill, the argument of Book I, Chapter 3, Sections 3, 4, 7 and 9 of his *System of Logic* (1843) may be summarised as follows:

On a representative theory of perception, something's looking white to us consists in our having sensations of white which are excited in us by the object. We attribute the quality, whiteness, to the object in virtue of its exciting the sensations. Moreover, 'we know not, and cannot know, anything of bodies but the sensations which they excite in us'. It follows that 'those sensations must be all that we can, at bottom, mean by their attributes; and the distinction which we verbally make between the properties of things and the sensations we receive from them, must originate in the convenience of discourse rather than in the nature of what is signified by the terms'. However, 'it may be said that . . . because one thing may be the sole evidence of the existence of another thing, it does not follow that the two are one and the same. The attribute whiteness (it may be said) is not the fact of receiving the sensation, but something in the object itself; a *power* inherent in it; something *in virtue* of which the object produces the sensation.' But the only foundation for this view is 'the disposition, wherever we meet with two names which are not precisely synonymous, to suppose that they must be the names of two different things'. The reasonable conclusion is that one and the same thing is 'called a sensation when considered merely in itself, and a quality when looked at in relation to any one of the numerous objects, the presence of which to our organs excites in our minds that among various other sensations or feelings'.

The last sentence of this repays careful study. Compare it with the sentence: 'That sensation is excited in our minds by the presence to our organs of any one of numerous objects'. What is the logic of the expression 'that among various other sensations or feelings' in Mill's sentence, and of 'that sensation' in mine? Is the concept of sensation involved in these sentences such that it makes sense to say that the *same* sensation is excited by the presence to our organs of *numerous* objects, or is it such that *numerous* objects (and, indeed, the same object at different times) cannot but excite *different*, though possibly exactly similar, sensations? Have the 'sensations' to which Mill refers the character of universals, or the character of particulars? It is as if Mill was in two minds about it. In so far as sensations are 'things excited in our minds', they seem to have the character of particulars; but in so far as the same sensation can be excited by any one of numerous objects, they (the sensations) seem to have the character of universals.

We can see how Mill resolves the issue if we turn to his editorial footnote (on pp. 260–61) to his father's *Analysis of the Phenomena of the Human Mind* (1869). In the text James Mill writes that it is 'obvious, and certain, that men were led to class solely for the purpose of economizing in the use of names':

> Could the processes of naming and discourse have been as conveniently managed by a name for every individual, the names of classes, and the idea of classification, would never have existed. But as the limits of the human memory did not enable men to retain beyond a very limited number of names; and even if it had, as it would have required a most inconvenient portion of time, to run over in discourse, as many names of individuals, and of individual qualities, as there is occasion to refer to in discourse, it was necessary to have contrivances of abridgment.

In his footnote John Stuart Mill objects that economizing in the use of names is not the sole purpose of classification: 'We could not have dispensed with names to mark the points in which different individuals resemble one another: and these are class-names.' In other words, we need class-names to predicate qualities of individuals.

From the passage quoted from James Mill, it might seem that he would reply that names can be given to 'individual qualities' without classification; that is, that names of 'individual qualities' are not class-names.

John Stuart Mill notices this (he quotes the sentence in question, italicizing 'and of individual qualities'), and proceeds (i) to ask what is meant by an 'individual quality', (ii) as if he knows the answer to this question (namely, the individual qualities of an object are 'the individual and instantaneous impressions which it produces in us'), to deny that predicating a quality of an object is predicating of it one of its individual qualities, and (iii) to say what it is to predicate a quality of an object (namely, 'to assert that the object affects us in a manner similar to that in which we are affected by a known class of objects'). He writes:

But what is meant by an individual quality? It is not *individual* qualities that we ever have occasion to predicate. It is true that the qualities of an object are only the various ways in which we or other minds are affected by it, and these affections are not the same in different objects, except in the sense in which the word same stands for exact similarity. But we never have occasion to predicate of an object the individual and instantaneous impressions which it produces in us. The only meaning of predicating a quality at all, is to affirm a resemblance. When we ascribe a quality to an object we intend to assert that the object affects us in a manner similar to that in which we are affected by a known class of objects. A quality, indeed, in the custom of language, does not admit of individuality: it is supposed to be one thing common to many; which, being explained, means that it is the name of a resemblance among our sensations, and not a name of the individual sensations which resemble. Qualities, therefore, cannot be predicated without general names; nor, consequently, without classification.

In this passage Mill resolutely turns his back on allowing sensations to have a universal character. 'These affections are not the same in different objects, except in the sense in which the word same stands for exact similarity.' This being so, he has to locate the universality elsewhere. He locates it in the resemblance of a sensation to other sensations. He holds what might be called 'the resemblance doctrine'.

Mill's version of the resemblance doctrine, however, differs from that of some other, more recent, holders of it —and not merely in that for him it is a matter of the resemblance of sensations, not objects.

His version can be introduced by asking: What is classification? To find out whether an element is a metal, a metal being defined as an element whose oxide dissolved in water yields an alkaline solution, I have to find out whether the element has this peculiarity in common with other metals. Is this process of finding out (performing tests indicated by the definition) classification? Or is only pronouncing the element to be a metal (or a non-metal) classification? The point is that not all general names have definitions. The names for what Mill calls 'simple feelings' have not. Consequently, there is no test I can perform, comparable to dissolving oxides in water, etc., to give me the right to say something looks white. All I can do is look. Things do not look white in virtue of something analytically involved in their looking white, something which they have in common—as metals have in common that their oxides dissolved in water yield an alkaline solution—with other things that look white.[1] If we say that they do have something in common with other things that look white we must remember that *their having something in common simply is their looking white*. It makes sense to say 'Ah, now I see what metals have in common'; but it makes no sense to say 'Ah, now I see what things that look white have in common'. They do not look white in virtue of having something in common; they have something in common (their whiteness) in virtue of looking white. Their resemblance is a consequence, not a pre-condition, of their looking white.

---

[1] Cf. Anthony Manser, 'Games and Family Resemblance', *Philosophy*, 1967, pp. 210–25, esp. pp. 220–25.

There are several ways in which this difference between names like 'metal' and those like 'white' can be marked. One would be to say that the predicating of names like 'white' does not involve classification (taking classification to be the performing of tests indicated by the definition of the general name). Another would be to say that whereas some classes (e.g. the class metal) are grounded on resemblance in some respect, others (e.g. the class sensation of white) are not grounded on resemblance at all. (This is not to deny that the members of the class resemble one another—they must—but only that the resemblance comes first, and so can be the 'ground' of the class.) To say this would be to deny the universality of what Professor A. J. Ayer says it is natural for us to assume, namely that we use the same word in different situations because we have noticed a distinctive common feature.[2]

Mill adopts neither of these ways of marking the difference. He marks it by distinguishing between resemblance in a given particular, resemblance which consists in the possession of certain common peculiarities, on the one hand, and what he calls 'mere general resemblance', 'general unanalysable resemblance', or 'simple likeness', on the other. Sensations of white are not alike in some respect; they are alike 'altogether'. In his *System of Logic* (Book I, Chapter 5, Section 6), he writes:

It is sometimes said, that all propositions whatever, of which the predicate is a general name, do, in point of

---

[2] A. J. Ayer, *The Problem of Knowledge*, 1956, Ch. 1, Section 2: 'Except when a word is patently ambiguous, it is natural for us to assume that the different situations, or types of situation, to which it applies have a distinctive common feature. For otherwise why should we use the same word to refer to them?'
Cf. R. M. Hare, *Freedom and Reason*, 1963, Ch. 2, Section 3: 'Descriptive meaning . . . relies upon the concept of similarity. . . . A descriptive meaning-rule is one which lays it down that we may apply an expression to objects which are similar to each other in certain respects.'

fact, affirm or deny resemblance. . . . There is some slight degree of foundation for this remark, but no more than a slight degree. The arrangement of things into classes, such as the class *metal*, or the class *man*, is grounded indeed on a resemblance among the things which are placed in the same class, but not on a mere general resemblance; the resemblance it is grounded on consists in the possession by all those things of certain common peculiarities; and those peculiarities it is which the terms connote, and which the propositions consequently assert; not the resemblance. For though when I say Gold is a metal, I say by implication that if there be any other metals it must resemble them, yet if there were no other metals I might still assert the proposition with the same meaning as at present, namely, that gold has the various properties implied in the word metal. . . . Propositions, therefore, in which objects are referred to a class, because they possess the attributes constituting the class, are so far from asserting nothing but resemblance, that they do not, properly speaking, assert resemblance at all. . . . [There is an] exceptional case, in which, though the predicate is the name of a class, yet in predicating it we affirm nothing but resemblance, the class being founded not on resemblance in any given particular, but on general unanalysable resemblance. The classes in question are those into which our simple sensations, or rather simple feelings, are divided. Sensations of white, for instance, are classed together, not because we can take them to pieces, and say they are alike in this, and not alike in that, but because we feel them to be alike altogether, though in different degrees. When, therefore, I say The colour I saw yesterday was a white colour, or, The sensation I feel is one of tightness, in both cases the attribute I affirm of the colour or of the other sensation is mere resemblance —simple *likeness* to sensations I have had before, and which have had those names bestowed upon them. The names of feelings, like other concrete general names, are connotative; but they connote a mere resemblance. When predicated of any individual feeling, the information they

convey is that of its likeness to the other feelings which we
have been accustomed to call by the same name.

To understand this we have to see that Mill is basing
his answer to one question on his answer to another.
There is the Ayer-Hare question 'Why do we use the
same colour-word in different situations?' to which Mill
gives the non-Ayer-Hare answer 'Not because of resemblance in some respect, but because of *mere* resemblance';
and there is the question 'What does the colour-word
connote?' to which Mill gives the answer 'The mere resemblance'. He is stuck with this answer to the second
question because he holds (as does Hare, but not Ayer[3])
that what one is saying about something when one calls
it *x* is identical with one's reason for calling it *x*.

In short, his argument is of the form:

1. Sensations of white are not alike *in some respect*; they
   are alike *altogether*.

---

[3] Hare, *ibid.*, writes: 'Suppose that I say that X is red; I am
committed to holding that anything which is like X in the relevant respect is also red. But suppose that I am asked What *is* the
relevant respect. I shall be able to answer this question only by
giving an indication, vague or precise, of what it was about X
that made me call it red; i.e. by explaining what I meant by calling it red.' Ayer ('Basic Propositions', *Philosophical Analysis*, ed.
Max Black, 1950, p. 69), on the other hand, writes: 'Allowing,
what is undoubtedly true, that I learned the use of the English
word "green" by being shown certain objects which resembled
each other in respect of being green, it is suggested that what I
now assert when I say, for example, that the blotting paper in
front of me is green is that it resembles these objects in the way
that they resembled one another. But this suggestion is false; and
to see that it is false we have only to reflect that from the statement that this piece of blotting paper is green it cannot be deduced that anything else exists at all. No doubt what justifies me
in calling it green, as opposed, say, to blue, is the fact that it
resembles one set of objects rather than another; but this does not
mean that in calling it green I am saying that it resembles any
other objects.'

Therefore

2. My reason for calling a sensation 'a sensation of white' is not its resemblance *in some respect* to other sensations called by the same name, but its *mere* resemblance to them.

But

3. What I *mean* by calling a sensation 'a sensation of white' is the same as my *reason* for calling it 'a sensation of white'.

Therefore

4. What I *mean* by calling a sensation 'a sensation of white' is its *mere* resemblance to other sensations called by the same name.

In the footnote to *Analysis of the Phenomena of the Human Mind* Mill says that it is not 'the individual and instantaneous impressions' that an object produces in us that we predicate of the object. How does he conceive of these 'impressions'?

In Book I, Chapter 3, Section 3 of his *System of Logic* (written before he had decided that a quality is simply a sensation regarded in a certain relation) he distinguishes between a sensation and a quality, a distinction which, he feels, may be missed because we can seldom refer to the sensation otherwise than by a circumlocution, e.g. by reference to the quality, as when we call a sensation 'the sensation of white'. This suggests that he thinks of the impression as being something that *could* have a name of its own. He regrets that 'language, which adapts itself for the most part only to the common uses of life, has provided us with no single-worded or immediate designation' for the impression. This suggestion is combined with his version of the resemblance doctrine in the following passage from Book I, Chapter 8, Section 2:

The only names which are unsusceptible of definition, because their meaning is unsusceptible of analysis, are the names of the simple feelings themselves. These are in the same condition as proper names. They are not indeed, like proper names, unmeaning; for the words sensation of white signify, that the sensation which I so denominate resembles other sensations which I remember to have had before, and to have called by that name. But as we have no words by which to recall those former sensations except the very word which we seek to define, or some other which, being exactly synonymous with it, requires definition as much, words cannot unfold the signification of this class of names; and we are obliged to make a direct appeal to the personal experience of the individual whom we address.

The implication of this passage is that the words 'sensation of white' *denote* the sensation, but *connote* its resemblance to other sensations called by the same name. The words 'sensation of white' are *unlike* a proper name in that they have connotation. They differ from connotative terms like 'metal'—and to this extent 'are in the same condition as proper names'—in that whereas to the question 'What are the things the resemblance to which you mark by calling this thing a "metal"'? the answer 'Things of which it is true that their oxide dissolved in water yields an alkaline solution' can be given, to the question 'What are the things the resemblance to which you mark by calling this sensation "a sensation of white"'? the only answer that can be given is 'Sensations to which I have given the name "a sensation of white"', an answer that does not 'unfold the signification of this class of names'. The signification is private to the user, and he can only hope that resemblances in his own experience have their counterpart in the experience of others, so that they can attach a meaning of their own to what he says.

II

Are there conditions which have to be satisfied for a colour-word to be used meaningfully?

The implications of Mill's answer to the question

'What does it mean to say that something is white?' for
this question, are clear. If I had not had a sensation
which resembles my present sensation I could not assert
'My sensation is a sensation of white' with the same
meaning as it would have if I had had a sensation re-
sembling it. The only meaning it could have would be:
'I bestow the name "sensation of white" on the sensation
I am now having'. In other words, having had a previous
similar sensation is a logically necessary condition of my
apprehending a sensation of white as such, on Mill's
version of the resemblance doctrine. On a version such as
Hare's, which does not incorporate a representative theory of perception, there will be a comparable implication:
if things had not, in the past, looked to me as this now
looks, I could not mean by 'This looks white' what I do
mean.

Mill does not explicitly assert this implication of his
holding the resemblance doctrine. The closest he comes
to it is, I think, in the passage quoted earlier in which he
says that 'though when I say Gold is a metal, I say by
implication that if there be any other metals it must resemble them, yet if there were no other metals I might
still assert the proposition with the same meaning as at
present, namely that gold has the various properties implied in the word metal'. This remark, occurring as it
does in a passage in which he is distinguishing between
the grounds of the class *metal* ('the possession of certain
common peculiarities') and those of the class *sensation
of white* ('nothing but resemblance') clearly implies that
if I had had no other sensations of white I could *not*
assert the proposition 'This is a sensation of white' with
the meaning it has when I have had such sensations.

Even if one rejected Mill's answer to the question
'What does it mean to say something is white?' one might
still hold there to be conditions which have to be satisfied
for a colour-word to be used meaningfully. According
to Wittgenstein, for instance, it is a condition of a colour-
word, such as 'blue', being used meaningfully by a per-

son, that he should have learnt (been trained) to react
to the things other people call 'blue' in the same way as
they do.[4] Without this agreement communication would
not be possible.

There is a difference, however, between what Mill
says about the conditions of a colour-word being used
meaningfully, and what Wittgenstein says. What one
means when one calls something 'white', according to
Mill, is that one's present sensation resembles a past one.
The condition of what one says being meaningful is part
of what one means. For Wittgenstein, on the other hand,
the condition is *not* part of what one means. In *Zettel*
(1967) Section 430, he explicitly denies that the agreement between colour-word-users is part of what is communicated.

III

I want, now, to turn to another question, which is
not, or not obviously, about the *meaning* of, or the conditions of the meaningful employment of, colour-words,
but about our *experience* of colours. It is a question
which may be introduced by quoting something Wittgenstein says about experiencing first one, and then another,
side of a triangle as its base.

Writing about 'aspects of organization' in his *Philosophical Investigations* (1953, II, xi, p. 208e), Wittgenstein says:

> One *kind* of aspect might be called 'aspects of organiza-
> tion'. When the aspect changes parts of the picture go to-
> gether which before did not.
>
> In the triangle I can see now *this* as apex, *that* as
> base—now *this* as apex, *that* as base.—Clearly the words
> 'Now I am seeing *this* as the apex' cannot so far mean

---

[4] This requires qualification so as not to exclude the blind from
all understanding of colour-words. The qualification, however,
would not affect the point being made.

anything to a learner who has only just met the concepts of apex, base, and so on.—But I do not mean this as an empirical proposition.

'Now he's seeing it like *this*', 'now like *that*' would only be said of someone capable of making certain applications of the figure quite freely.

The substratum of this experience is the mastery of a technique.

But how queer for this to be the logical condition of someone's having such-and-such an *experience!* After all, you don't say that one only 'has toothache' if one is capable of doing such-and-such.—From this it follows that we cannot be dealing with the same concept of experience here. It is a different though related concept.

It is only if someone *can do,* has learnt, is master of, such-and-such, that it makes sense to say he has had *this* experience.

And if this sounds crazy, you need to reflect that the *concept* of seeing is modified here.

Formulated in words suggested by this quotation, the question I want to find an answer to is: Are there logical conditions of someone's having the experience of seeing something as, say, blue? I prefer the formulation: Are there logical conditions of something's looking blue to someone?

It is clear what Mill's answer would have to be: 'Yes, since to see that something is a certain colour is to be aware of the mere resemblance between a present sensation and a remembered past one'.

For a number of reasons I cannot accept Mill's answer to the question 'What does it mean to say that something is white?' In the first place I do not accept the representative theory of perception. Secondly, I do not accept any version of the resemblance doctrine. (I am persuaded of the untenability of Hare's version by what Wittgenstein says in Part II of the 'Brown Book' [*The Blue and Brown Books*, 1958]. In Section 2 he rejects the suggestion, conveyed by the exclamation 'Surely a similarity must strike us, or we shouldn't be moved to use the same word', that some act must precede the act of using the word; and in Sections 5 and 10 he talks about the 'mistake' labelled by the word 'to make' as it occurs in the question 'What made you call this "red"?') Thirdly, I do not accept the principle that the meaning of utterances is the same as a person's (alleged) reasons for saying what he says.

This being so, I cannot accept what would be Mill's reason for giving an affirmative answer to the question 'Are there logical conditions of something's looking blue to someone?'

Are there reasons for giving an affirmative answer to it to be found in what Wittgenstein says?

If there are, they are not obvious to me. At the beginning of the section from which I have just quoted he distinguishes two 'objects' of sight, between which, he says, there is a *categorial* difference. The first 'object' is what is there to be seen; the second is what it looks like. There are logical conditions of experiencing objects of the second category, but colour always figures as an object of the first category, as in the following passage (pp. 196e–97e):

> If I saw the duck-rabbit as a rabbit, then I saw: these shapes and colours (I give them in detail)—and I saw besides something like this: and here I point to a number of different pictures of rabbits. This shows the difference between the concepts.

It might be said that what Wittgenstein says about the criteria of someone having understood a colour-word provides a reason for answering the question affirmatively.

If I said 'It looks blue' but otherwise seemed incapable of colour discrimination, of being able to respond differently, verbally and in other ways, to differently coloured things, and, particularly, of being able to tell when other blue things were present and when absent, then people would rightly suspect that I did not know what I was talking about, that my experience could not really be of its looking blue.

The nagging doubt remains, however, that the thing might have looked blue to me, and that I had simply not realised that it was to the thing's colour that I was expected to respond. Not to admit this doubt is to embrace behaviourism. Wittgenstein is not a behaviourist.

In spite of not being able to find support for an affirmative answer to the question 'Are there logical conditions of something's looking blue to someone?' in what Wittgenstein says, and not accepting what would be Mill's reasons for an affirmative answer, I think an affirmative answer is the right answer. I must now try to show that it is.

The first step is to distinguish between two senses of 'something's looking blue'. One sense is an obvious one, but the other is not obvious, and possibly for that reason, although they are radically different senses, their difference is not recognised and people suppose they are dealing with an unambiguous expression.

Perhaps the distinction I want to draw can be seen more clearly if we start with an example involving size rather than colour. Berkeley, in his *New Theory of Vision*, Section LXVII, remarks that 'the apparent magnitude of the moon, when placed in the horizon, is much greater than when placed in the meridian'. One can ask: Does he mean that the horizontal moon, perhaps owing to some magnifying effect of the earth's atmosphere, actually presents a larger appearance than the meridian moon, or does he mean merely that it looks bigger, perhaps because it is seen in a context of trees and houses? Leaving aside the question as to which Berkeley meant, let us consider the alternatives. How could we settle whether or not the horizontal moon actually does present a larger appearance? One way would be to hold up a pencil at arm's length and measure their relative sizes as an artist might. Another would be to take photographs of the moon on the horizon, and in the meridian, without altering the camera settings, and compare the size of the moon on the two prints. It might be found that there was no difference.[5] And yet the horizontal moon might look bigger than the meridian moon in the other, non-objective, sense of 'looks'.

The terms 'objective' and 'subjective' being over-worked, I shall refer to the 'presentation appearance' and the 'perceived-as appearance'. One can talk of an object presenting an appearance to an unoccupied point in space, and of the presentation appearance of an object itself being larger or smaller than the presentation appearance of another to that point. Whether it is larger or smaller will depend entirely on such factors as the relative size of the objects, their distance from the point, magnifying effects of the media, etc.

Suppose there is a piece of green material on a yellow background. It will be perceived as blue (phenomenon of colour contrast). But human sensory physiology, which mediates the colour contrast phenomenon, does not have anything to do with the presentation appearance of the material to the point at which the observer is. In 'white' light this will be the colour of the material, green. An artist, to convey the scene as it presents itself, would have to paint his representation of the green material, not as he sees it, blue, but as it is, green.

One difference between perceived-as appearances and presentation appearances is that whereas it does not make sense to talk of being mistaken about the former it does make sense to talk of being mistaken about the latter. In fact, one frequently is mistaken. A person may falsely believe that the horizontal moon, because it is perceived as being larger, must be presenting a larger appearance. He may falsely believe that the difference between something's looking blue and its looking green cannot be merely a perceived-as appearance difference, but that

---

[5] See I. Rock and L. Kaufman, 'The Moon Illusion, II', *Science*, 1962, Vol. 136, pp. 1023–31.

there must be a difference in the presentation appearance. As Thouless' classical experiments on 'Phenomenal Regression to the "Real" Object'[6] have shown, we can be wrong about the presentation appearance even when, short of holding a pencil at arm's length and measuring, we are doing our best to be right about it. The constancy effects Thouless demonstrated are built into our perceptual mechanism. We can conjure them away only by observing things under conditions in which the cues to three-dimensional perception are inoperative. Asked to see things *as if* they were inoperative when they are not inoperative, one no more knows what to do than one does if asked to see things as if the phenomena of colour contrast were absent when they are present.

I said that whereas it does make sense to talk of being mistaken about presentation appearances it does not make sense to talk of being mistaken about perceived-as appearances. This is because in saying what something looks like to me I am not saying something about something other than the thing I am looking at, its look. To talk of the presentation appearance, on the other hand, is to talk of something that can, itself, properly be said to be large, round, blue, etc.[7] The presentation appearance of the horizontal moon, for instance, can properly, though falsely, be said to be larger than the presentation appearance of the meridian moon. There is something for me to be mistaken about. I cannot be mistaken about perceiving something as, say, a cigarette case, because in saying 'It looks like a cigarette case' I am not saying that there is an appearance which is a cigarette case. Professor R. M. Chisholm has expressed this well in Chapter 8, Section 1, of his *Perceiving: A Philosophical Study* (1957):

---

[6] R. H. Thouless, *British Journal of Psychology*, XXI, 1931, pp. 339–59, and XXII, 1932, pp. 1–30.

[7] Presentation appearances correspond to sensations conceived as having the character of particulars; perceived-as appearances, to sensations conceived as having the character of universals.

'The pail feels empty' and 'The woods sound inhabited' do not imply that there is an appearance which is empty or one which is inhabited; 'The curtains appear green' does not imply that there is an appearance—or way of appearing—which is green. And, more generally, the locution

x appears . . . to S

does not imply

There is something which is . . .

The second step in my attempt to show that an affirmative answer to the question 'Are there logical conditions of something's looking blue to someone?' is warranted, is to identify perceived-as appearances with would-be beliefs.

In a paper 'Seeing and Seeing As'[8] I wrote:

A stick half in water looks bent both to the man who says 'It's bent' and to the man who says 'It looks bent'. But the man who says 'It looks bent' thereby exhibits his sophistication in the matter of how an object's being half in water leads to his seeing it otherwise than as it is. What an object looks like to somebody is what, on looking at it, that person would take it to be, if he had no reason to think otherwise. If he has a reason to think otherwise then he says, not 'It is . . .', but 'It looks . . .'.

I now say: that to talk about perceived-as appearances, and to talk about what, on looking at things, listening to them, etc., we would believe about them if we had no reason to think otherwise, are to talk about one and the same thing. In other words, to give, to the question 'Why, on looking at the horizontal moon, would you believe it to be larger than the meridian moon if you had no reason to think otherwise?' the answer 'Because it appears larger', is, if it means 'Because I perceive it as

[8] *Proceedings of the Aristotelian Society*, Vol. LVI, 1955–56, reprinted in *Perceiving, Sensing, and Knowing*, ed. R. J. Swartz, 1965.

larger', to give no answer at all. Only if it means 'Because it is presenting a larger appearance' is it to give an answer, one which happens to be wrong. We can explain, correctly or incorrectly, our would-be beliefs on looking at things by reference to presentation appearances, but to try to explain them by reference to perceived-as appearances is to try to explain them by reference to themselves.

Now, one cannot have what I have called a 'would-be belief' that something is x unless there is at least the possibility of taking the thing to be x. And one cannot take something to be x unless one can distinguish between things which are x and things which are not x, as such. And so the experience of seeing something as blue has logical conditions in that one logically cannot have it unless one can discriminate between objects in respect of their being or not being blue. To someone without this discriminative capacity, either congenitally or because it has not been developed, a thing can present a blue appearance, but he cannot see it as blue. He can see it as blue (i.e. it can be the case that, on looking at it, he would take it to be blue if he had no reason to think otherwise) only if he can discriminate between objects in respect of their being or not being blue. He can be trained to discriminate as the rest of us do, between things that are blue and things that are not, just as people can be trained to discriminate between harmonies and discords. His discriminating as the rest of us do is, in Wittgenstein's phrase, 'the substratum of the experience' of seeing something as blue.

To this it might be objected that one learns the meaning of 'blue' through seeing blue things and being told they are blue;[9] learning the meaning of the word is a

---

[9] In the passage quoted from his paper 'Basic Propositions' in footnote 2 above, Ayer says that it is 'undoubtedly true' that he learnt the use of the English word 'green' by being shown certain objects which resembled each other in respect of being green. What makes him so sure?

matter of attaching a word to the look of something; the look is basic.

This objection relies for its persuasiveness partly on an ambiguity in 'seeing blue things'. Does this mean 'there being things one sees that are in fact blue' or does it mean 'one's seeing things as blue'?

Compare 'One learns what it is for something to be absent through things being absent' and 'One learns what it is for something to be absent through noticing the absence of things'. Neither will do. If one can notice the absence of something one must already know what it is for things to be absent. Similarly if one can see things as blue one must already have the concept of blueness. On the other hand, that something is in fact absent, or in fact blue, does not help. Empiricism, as a theory of how we acquire concepts, requires there to be something which is *both* a 'state of consciousness' *and* such that it does not have logical conditions, i.e. is unlike a would-be belief. What it requires it posits: a 'feeling' or 'sensation'. 'What I am conscious of when I see the colour blue', says Mill (*System of Logic*, Book I, Chapter 3, Section 4), 'is a feeling of blue colour'—a feeling excited in my mind by the outward object. Once posited, to be what the colour-word is the name of, this 'feeling' or 'sensation' becomes an element, in our thought about these matters, of which it is almost impossible to rid ourselves.

MILL ON MATTER

BY

J. P. Day

Mill holds a metaphysical theory about the nature of things which is of the sensationalist or phenomenalist variety, and which he derives admittedly from the idealism of Berkeley. This metaphysical theory is introduced into a discussion in which he is attempting something different, namely, to offer a rival psychological account to Hamilton's intuitionist one of how it is that men possess that familiar but complex conception, Nature or the external world. It will be convenient to consider his psychological theory first.

Mill describes the belief, the origin of which is to be explained, as follows. The terms 'the external world', 'body', and 'matter', are collective expressions for the sum of things, a typical item of which is the orange on my sideboard. In our conception of this orange, and of things like it, Mill discerns three main features. First, we regard its existence as permanent, 'real' or 'external'. In this, it differs radically from the sensations that we

From *Philosophy*, 38, 1963. Reprinted by permission of the author and the Editor of *Philosophy*.

have when we perceive it, for the existence of these is fugacious, 'ideal' or 'in the mind'. I.e., the orange does not cease to exist when no one perceives it, unlike sensations which do not exist unless they are experienced. Second, we conceive the orange to be the cause of our having the sensations that we have when we perceive it. Third, whereas the sensations that A has when he perceives the orange are private to A, in the sense that only A can logically have A's sensations, the orange is a common or public object, in the sense that it can be perceived by anyone.

According to Hamilton, our belief in the existence of an external world of things possessing the properties just specified is intuitive. Mill, on the other hand, maintains that it is acquired. His view derives in part from his general opposition to intuitionism; in this respect, his criticism of Hamilton's theory of the external world parallels his criticism of Whewell's philosophy of mathematics. Mill aims to show that the belief may have resulted from the operation of known laws upon known facts, and that if it had so resulted it would naturally appear intuitive.

The known laws and facts in terms of which Mill couches his explanation are partly psychological and partly physical. The psychological ones are these. First, the fact that men can conceive of possible sensations. When they have experienced a sensation of a certain sort under conditions of a certain kind, they can anticipate or expect that they would have a sensation of that sort if conditions of that kind were to recur. Second, the laws of association of ideas. Third, the existence of minds possessing the powers of having sensations, of remembering having sensations of certain sorts under conditions of certain kinds, and of expecting that they would have sensations of those sorts if conditions of those kinds were to recur.

Each of these three factors requires comment. As to the first, Mill observes that his possible sensations are 'contingent sensations' or 'conditional certainties' and not

'mere vague possibilities'. To say that a (tactual) sensation of a certain sort (namely, of the sort that one has
when one touches an orange) is now feelable by A, is to
say that, if some necessary condition were satisfied (say,
A's having first a [kinaesthetic] sensation of the sort that
one has when one extends one's hand), then A would
certainly have a (tactual) sensation of the sort in question. Thus, Mill equates 'possible sensation' with 'sensation which anyone would have if some necessary condition were satisfied'. (See below, however.) Viewed in the
light of recent discussions of the meanings of 'can' and
'if', this point will be seen to be not trivial.[1]

As to the second factor, inferences by association are
not conscious inferences *from* a general rule and some
other premiss, but unconscious inferences from particulars to particulars *in accordance with* a rule. Hence,
when I infer from the existence of a group of simultaneous possibilities of sensation the existence of a permanent, public, etc. object (say, a mountain), I am doing
the same kind of thing as I do when I infer from its
faintness that the mountain is several miles distant, and
say (what is strictly speaking false) that I see that it is
so. For another point in which Mill agrees with Berkeley
is the doctrine of the 'acquired perceptions of sight'.[2]

As to the third factor, Mill, again like Berkeley but
unlike Hume, holds that a phenomenalist account of
minds or persons will not do. For he considers that that

---

[1] See J. L. Austin, "Ifs and Cans," *Proceedings of the British
Academy*, London, 1956.

[2] Stereoscopic vision is a controversial subject, but the view of
most psychologists today seems to be that, though what Berkeley
and Mill say is true, it is not the whole truth. Thus, most psychologists do not dispute that our perception of distance and depth
depends largely on automatic and unconscious inferences from
such 'cues' as the degree of faintness of the object seen. But they
point out that this is not the whole story, since in ordinary bi-
nocular vision we should still perceive distance to some extent if
all such cues were absent, because of the operation of, notably,
retinal disparity.

which can remember actual sensations and anticipate possible ones cannot itself be no more than a set of possible sensations. He propounds no alternative theory about the nature of mind.

The physical factors on which Mill bases his explanation are two. First, the fact that sensations occur. Second, the fact that they occur in order. For sensations succeed one another and sometimes co-exist. But more, certain sorts of sensations regularly co-exist in stable groups, and certain sorts of stable groups regularly succeed certain other sorts of stable groups in stable sequences.

The stable groups are composed predominantly, and sometimes exclusively, of possible sensations, not actual ones. The reason for this has been indicated above. That which a certain sort of actual sensation (say, the sort of visual sensation one has on seeing an orange) regularly co-exists with is not another sort of actual sensation (say, the sort of tactual sensation one has on touching an orange). For a sensation of the latter sort does not occur until a third sort of actual sensation has occurred first (namely, the sort of kinaesthetic sensation one has on extending one's hand). Hence, that which the first sort of actual (visual) sensation regularly co-exists with is, not the second sort of actual (tactual) sensation, but a sort of possible (tactual) sensation. 'This is what is meant by saying that a Body is a group of simultaneous possibilities of sensation, not of simultaneous sensations.'

Similarly, the stable sequences are composed predominantly, and usually exclusively, of groups of possible sensations, not of groups of actual ones. Only a small minority of causal laws, namely, some physiological ones, state that one sort of actual sensation is the unconditional invariable antecedent of some other sort of actual sensation. The great majority of them, such as 'Fire melts ice', state that one sort of group of possible sensations is the unconditional invariable antecedent of some other sort of group of possible sensations.

According to Mill, there are two stages in the genesis of the belief in the external world. The first is the formation of the conception of a group of simultaneous possibilities of sensation. This arises from experience. It is by experience that A learns that, if he were to have a visual sensation of a certain sort, then, if he first had a kinaesthetic sensation of a certain sort, he would have a tactual sensation of a certain sort. The second is the formation of the conception of a thing or body. This arises from the operation of the laws of association upon the conception of a group of simultaneous possibilities of sensation, and Mill accounts for the properties we impute to bodies as follows.

The reason why we attribute permanent or real existence to things is this. Permanence is a property of possible sensations, though not of actual ones. But the conception of a group of possible sensations is that which we transform into the conception of a real thing. And by association we simply transfer the permanence that characterises the former to the latter. We think of things as common or public for a similar reason. Possible sensations, unlike actual ones, are public; for a possible sensation is a sensation that anyone would experience in certain conditions. Here again, by association, we transfer to our conception of bodies the publicity that attaches to the groups of possible sensations in the conception of which the conception of bodies originates. The notion of things being the causes of sensation originates as follows. We have seen that groups of possible sensations succeed one another regularly, so that each sort of group has some other sort of group for its unconditional invariable antecedent. Hence, by association, we come to think of sensation itself as having an unconditional invariable antecedent in the same way as do groups of possible sensations, and of matter as that which exercises this causal function.

From these psychological considerations, Mill turns abruptly to metaphysics, and propounds his own theory on the nature of things in the following words: 'Matter, then, may be defined, a Permanent Possibility of Sensation. If I am asked, whether I believe in matter, I ask whether the questioner accepts this definition of it. If he does, I believe in matter: and so do all Berkeleians. In any other sense than this, I do not. But I affirm with confidence, that this conception of matter includes the whole meaning attached to it by the common world, apart from philosophical, and sometimes from theological, theories.'

Since Mill thus admits his indebtedness to Berkeley in his theory of the external world, it will be instructive to notice his criticism of Berkeley's theory. He disposes shortly of Berkeley's psychological theory in the same way as Hume does. According to Berkeley, the reason why we attribute real or external existence to the sensations which we obtain by the five senses, and not to others, is that the former are involuntary. Mill points out that this will not do, for sometimes the latter are involuntary too, e.g., the pain that one feels when he puts his hand close to the fire; yet we do not attribute real or external existence to pains.

But Mill's main difference from Berkeley is over the metaphysical point about the nature of matter. According to Berkeley, things are groups of actual sensations, whereas according to Mill they are (conceptions of) groups of possible sensations. Not but what, Mill remarks, Berkeley sometimes comes close to his own view, as when he writes: 'The table I write on, I say, exists, that is, I see and feel it; and if I were out of my study I should say it existed—*meaning thereby that if I was in my study I might perceive it*, or that some other spirit actually does perceive it.'[3] (My italics.) But his main position is undoubtedly the 'actual sensations' one, for on this hinges his favourite proof of the existence of God. This runs: Since bodies exist really or continuously, and bodies are groups of actual sensations, but these actual sensations do not exist continuously in finite

---

[3] *Principles of Human Knowledge*, pt. 1, sec. 3.

minds since bodies are not observed continuously by men; there must exist an infinite mind in which these sensations exist when they are not in finite minds.

Mill attributes Berkeley's mistaken view principally to his confusion over the word 'same'. As Mill interprets Berkeley, what happens when A looks at the orange, then looks away, and then looks at it again, is this. God detaches a particular visual sensation from His mind and impresses it on A's, then detaches it from A's mind and puts it back in His, and then again detaches it from His mind and impresses it on A's. So that the sensation which A has when he sees the orange the second time is numerically the same as the sensation which he had when he saw it the first time. But this is false, for the sensation which he has the second time is in fact at best qualitatively the same as the sensation which he had the first time and numerically different from it. Berkeley goes wrong through failing to distinguish between numerical and qualitative identity.[4]

Mill might have added that the doctrine he attributes to Berkeley is untrue for the further reason that it involves that numerically the same sensation can be (successively) both in God's mind and in A's. Which, however, is also false, since sensations are private, so that A cannot, logically, have God's sensations any more than He can, logically, have A's.

The most conspicuous defect in Mill's psychological theory is perhaps his omission of a feature of the order of our sensations which, as Hume points out, is of great influence in inducing us to form the conception of things or bodies that exist externally or really; namely, what he calls the 'constancy' and 'coherence' of some of them. At times, indeed, Mill comes close to making the point, as when he writes: 'We find that the modifications which

---

[4] Mill refers in particular to Berkeley's failure to make this distinction in his discussion of *same* in the *Third Dialogue between Hylas and Philonous*. See A. A. Luce and T. E. Jessop (eds.), *Works of George Berkeley*, Vol. 2, pp. 247 f.

are taking place more or less regularly in our possibilities of sensation, are mostly quite independent of our consciousness, and of our presence or absence. Whether we are asleep or awake the fire goes out, and puts an end to one particular possibility of warmth and light.' But he is not explicit or circumstantial on the question as Hume is, and his neglect of this valuable clue provided by his great predecessor in the empiricist tradition is surprising.

Mill's metaphysical theory comprises two assertions. The first is that his definition of 'matter' as 'a permanent possibility of sensation' agrees with the common conception of the nature of things if not with the philosophical one. Mill's claim to be with the vulgar in this matter of matter and against the philosophers is the same as Berkeley's, and it is equally unacceptable in the case of both philosophers. For there are in fact radical differences between things as ordinarily conceived and things as defined by Mill.

Thus, the former exist actually whereas the latter exist potentially. This difference tends to be obscured in Mill's discussion for two reasons. First, it may be thought that we have actual existence in both cases, that which exists actually being in the former case a thing and in the latter case a possibility or set of possibilities. But the last contention is misleading. For to say that there is a possibility of snow is simply to say in other words that snow exists potentially: it is not to say that a possibility, or anything whatever, exists actually. Second, Mill's practice of prefixing 'permanent' and 'simultaneous' to 'possibilities of sensation' strongly suggests that these possibilities exist actually, for these adjectives are usually applied to actual, not to potential, existents, as when we speak of 'simultaneous shots' or 'the permanent way'.

There is a possible reply to this objection which turns on an ambiguity in Mill's definition of 'matter'. He usually writes as if a thing, say the orange, were the (set of) *sensations* which anyone would have if he first had certain other sensations. However, he also says explicitly

that contingent sensations are conceptions which men
form because they are capable of expectation. So that his
real account of the nature of the orange is, not the one
just given, but that it is anyone's *conception* of the sensations which he would have if he first had certain other
sensations. On this account, the objection just made does
not hold, since conceptions exist actually. However, it is
open to other, equally decisive, objections. Thus, conceptions exist only in the minds of their conceivers,
whereas things (are said to) exist 'without the mind'.
Again, whereas things are permanent, the conceptions in
question are short-lived; for no-one dwells in imagination for long on such thoughts as that of the tactual
sensation which he would have if he were first to have
the sort of kinaesthetic sensation that goes with extending one's hand.

Another objection holds against both of Mill's definitions of 'matter'. Namely that, whereas things are common, both possible sensations and conceptions of possible
sensations are private. As to the latter, it is clear that A
cannot have B's conception or anticipation, or conversely.
But the privacy of possible sensations is perhaps less evident, and we have seen that Mill himself insists on the
publicity of possible sensations as contrasted with the privacy of actual ones. He is nonetheless mistaken in this,
for it is no less logically true that any particular sensation
which is feelable by A is feelable only by A than it is
that any particular sensation which is felt by A is felt
only by A.

I suggest that Mill was led astray here by ambiguities
in 'sensation' and 'feel'. As to the first, 'sensation' is ambiguous as between 'particular sensation' and 'sort of
sensation'. Now, the latter is indeed common in the sense
that the same sort of sensation is feelable by both A and
B. But it seems pretty clear, though not perhaps so clear
as to settle the question conclusively, that Mill holds that
the orange on my side-board is (anyone's conception of)
the *particular* sensations which he would have if certain
conditions were satisfied, not (anyone's conception of)

the *sort* of sensations which . . . etc. And possible particular sensations, to repeat it, are no less private than are actual particular sensations. It is to be noticed that this is the right form in which to express Mill's doctrine. For he is in the main, like Berkeley, a factual and not a linguistic idealist or phenomenalist. Formulated linguistically, Mill's doctrine would be: any statement about the orange means the same as a conjunction of statements about (anyone's conception of) the sensations which . . . etc.

As to the second ambiguity, 'feel' is in one use a verb of perception taking a common object, but in another use a verb of sensation taking a private object. Thus, cp. (i) 'the orange which anyone would feel if he first extended his hand' with (ii) 'the sensation which anyone would feel if he first had another sensation'. In (i), 'the orange' means 'the particular orange', and 'feel' is a verb of perception. In this sense of 'feel', numerically the same object (i.e. one and the same orange) is feelable by both A and B. But in (ii) 'the sensation' means 'the sort of sensation', 'another sensation' means 'another sort of sensation', and 'feel' is a verb of sensation. In this sense of 'feel' only qualitatively and not numerically the same object (i.e. the same sort of sensation) is feelable by both A and B. It seems likely that Mill was misled into believing in the publicity of contingent sensations by his unconsciously misassimilating (ii) to (i).

But, in any case, the fact is that Mill himself, in his psychological theory, insists on the difference between the conception of a set of contingent sensations and the conception of a physical object. For the aim and upshot of that theory is to show how the laws of association so operate upon the former conception as to transform it into a different conception, namely, that of a thing. And if this is so, Mill cannot be right in asserting, in his metaphysical theory, that the two conceptions are the same. In fact, it is the metaphysical thesis which is the false one, as Mill sometimes shows himself to be dimly but uneasily aware: 'We may infer, therefore, that both

philosophers and the world at large, when they think of
matter, conceive it really as a Permanent Possibility of
Sensation. But the majority of philosophers fancy that it
is something more; and the world at large, though they
have really, as I conceive, nothing in their minds but a
Permanent Possibility of Sensation, would, if asked the
question, undoubtedly agree with the philosophers. . . .'

As to the cause of his mistake, I surmise that it is simply the genetic fallacy. For, as I have just said, his psychological theory represents the conception of a possible
sensation as that in which the conception of a thing
originates. But saying that the latter therefore *is* (really
only) the former is like saying that a man is (really
only) so much carbon, hydrogen, oxygen and nitrogen.

The second assertion comprised in Mill's metaphysical
theory is that 'matter exists' is true if 'matter' is taken to
mean '(conceptions of) sets of contingent sensations',
but false if it is taken to mean anything else, such as and
more particularly 'external existents'.

If 'matter' is taken to mean 'external existents', the
question 'Does matter exist?' may be interpreted in different ways. First, as a factual question. On this interpretation, it is like 'Do moas (still) exist?' Second, as a
theoretical question. Here, the existence of the external
world is regarded as an hypothesis designed to explain
the occurrence and order of sensations. On this interpretation, the question is like 'Does ether exist?' Third, as a
philosophical question. Here, the real existence of things
is regarded as a commonsense belief which is implicit in
our common ways of speech. The question 'Does matter
exist or not?' is the question 'Do we, or do we not, attribute to e.g. the orange on the sideboard an existence
without the mind, i.e. do men, or do they not, *speak* of
it as being still there when no one is perceiving it?' On
this interpretation, the question is like 'Does mind exist?'

In his metaphysical theory, Mill takes the question in
the factual way. It is clear from the context that he does
not interpret it in the theoretical way. It is also clear
that he cannot be interpreting it in the philosophical

way, since his own psychological theory shows that, taken in *this* sense, he holds the answer to the question to be affirmative: this, he agrees, is what men think and say, and the object of his psychological theory is to account for the existence of the belief.

Now, if the question 'Does matter exist?' is taken to be factual, the first part of Mill's second assertion (namely, that the answer to the question is affirmative if 'matter' is taken to mean '[conceptions of] contingent sensations') is warranted and true. For we are all directly aware of the existence of our own expectations of sensations. But, on the same interpretation of the question, the second part of Mill's second assertion (namely, that the answer to the question is negative if 'matter' is taken to mean 'external existents') is not warranted. For though it may *be* false that matter, in this sense of 'matter', exists, it is logically impossible to *establish* that it is false or true. For the only way to establish that a thing of a certain sort does or does not exist is to observe it or fail to observe it; but it is self-contradictory to speak of observing or failing to observe a thing to which is imputed the property of existing when no-one observes it. Hence, the second part of Mill's second assertion is pointless. It is not competent in him to 'attack the belief in Matter as an entity *per se*'. At times, indeed, he appears to realise this. As when he says 'I do not believe that the real externality to us of anything, except other minds, is capable of proof'; though even here he seems not to see that, for the same reason that it is not capable of proof, it is not capable of disproof either. Or when he admits that, of course, Malebranche *may* be right in asserting that the external world does in fact exist, since God says so in the Bible, even though it performs no function in his system.

The source of Mill's error lies in his taking the question 'Does matter exist?' in an illegitimate, i.e. the factual, way. It is strange that he should slip into doing this in his metaphysical theory because, as I have said above, in his psychological theory he interprets it in a legitimate way, namely the philosophical one. So that, in his psychological moments, if not, unfortunately, in his philosophical ones, he agrees with Hume that 'We may well ask, *What causes induce us to believe in the existence of body?*, but it is in vain to ask, *Whether there be body or not?* That is a point which we must take for granted in all our reasonings',[5]—it being understood that the interpretation in which the question 'Does body exist?' is vain is that in which it is taken to be a question about a matter of fact.

References

J. S. Mill, *Bailey on Berkeley's Theory of Vision, Dissertations and Discussions*, Vol. 2 (London, 1859); *Examination of Sir W. Hamilton's Philosophy*, ch. 11, appendix to chs. 11 and 12 (3rd ed., London, 1867); *Berkeley's Life and Writings, Dissertations and Discussions*, Vol. 4 (London, 1875); R. P. Anschutz, *Philosophy of J. S. Mill*, ch. 10, secs. 7-10 (Oxford, 1953); A. J. Ayer, *Foundations of Empirical Knowledge*, ch. 5 (London, 1940); "Phenomenalism," *Philosophical Essays* (London, 1959); I. Berlin, "Empirical Propositions and Hypothetical Statements," *Mind*, Vol. 49 (Edinburgh, 1950); K. Britton, *J. S. Mill*, ch. 6, secs. 3-5 (London, 1953); R. J. Hirst, *Problems of Perception*, ch. 4, ch. 9, sec. 2 (London, 1959); D. G. C. MacNabb, *David Hume*, ch. 8 (London, 1951); H. H. Price, *Perception*, pp. 260 ff., 282 ff. (London, 1932); G. Ryle, *Concept of Mind*, ch. 7 (London, 1949); L. Stephen, *The English Utilitarians*, Vol. 3, ch. 6, sec. 3 (London, 1900); H. H. Price, "Mill's View of the External World," *Aristotelian Society Proceedings*, Vol. XXVII, 1927.

---

[5] *Treatise of Human Nature*, Bk. 1, Pt. 4, Sec. 2.

THE "PROOF" OF UTILITY IN BENTHAM AND MILL

BY

Everett W. Hall

The ostensible object of the present paper is to correct an interpretation that, in the author's estimation, involves a grave historical injustice. Frankly, however, this would never have been undertaken had there not been a supporting motivation—the desire to bring to the attention of contemporary ethicists a basic, yet simple, methodological distinction, a distinction imbedded, so it will be contended, in the writings of Bentham and Mill but almost completely neglected up to the present.

One need not be a worshiper at the shrine of one's intellectual ancestors to feel a slight sense of distaste at the sight of every author of an elementary textbook in logic or ethics scurrying to chapter iv of Mill's *Utilitarianism*, "Of What Sort of Proof the Principle of Utility Is Susceptible," for examples of fallacies sufficiently blatant to be grasped at a glance by the untrained mind. It is just too obvious that the relation of "desirable" to "de-

Reprinted from *Ethics*, 60, October 1949, by permission of The University of Chicago Press.

sired" is only suffixally similar to the relation of "audible" to "heard" ("audited"). And who cannot spot the error of deriving "everyone desires the general happiness" from "each desires his own happiness"? And so we might go down through the traditional list. But were we to try to understand Mill's argument as a whole and in the simple and obvious sense in which, when viewed as a whole, it seems only fair to take it, we might find a core worth serious consideration.

We must charge this tendency to force Mill's proof of the principle of utility into a set of the most patent fallacies to really first-line philosophers. For example, F. H. Bradley, in *Ethical Studies*,[1] excuses himself for taking time to point out the tissue of inconsistencies that, so he claims, is Mill's argument. "I am ashamed," he writes, "to have to examine such reasoning, but it is necessary to do so, since it is common enough."[2] I shall, however, be mainly concerned to scrutinize the criticisms of another first-line philosopher, partly because I think he is probably the most influential source of the traditional disparagement of Mill's argument and partly because he has stated the supposed case against Mill's proof most clearly and cogently. I refer to G. E. Moore, and specifically to chapter iii of *Principia Ethica*. Moore here admits, candidly enough, that his analysis derives from Sidgwick. This is entirely true, but the tone is quite different, for Sidgwick believed he was simply explicating certain hidden, but necessary, intuitionistic assumptions in utilitarianism, whereas Moore is an avowed, even an aggressive, opponent of that position.

Let us see what Moore's criticism is. For purposes of analysis it is well to have Mill's argument before us, familiar as that argument is. For the moment we shall note only what Moore calls the "first step" and, in fact, only the first half of the first step, which I shall designate "1A":

[1] (2d ed.; Oxford, 1927), pp. 113–24.
[2] *Ibid.*, p. 115 n.

1A. "The only proof capable of being given that a thing is visible, is that people actually see it. The only proof that a sound is audible, is that people hear it; and so of the other sources of our experience. In like manner, I apprehend, the sole evidence it is possible to produce that anything is desirable, is that people do actually desire it. If the end which the utilitarian doctrine proposes to itself were not, in theory and in practice, acknowledged to be an end, nothing could ever convince any person that it was so."[3]

Of this, Moore says: "Well, the fallacy in this step is so obvious, that it is quite wonderful how Mill failed to see it."[4] What fallacy? A fallacy Moore calls "the naturalistic fallacy." "Mill has made as naïve and artless a use of the naturalistic fallacy as anybody could desire. 'Good,' he tells us, means 'desirable,' and you can only find out what is desirable by seeking to find out what is actually desired. . . . The important step for Ethics is this one just taken, the step which pretends to prove that 'good' means 'desired.'"[5]

And just what is this naturalistic fallacy that Mill committed so naïvely and artlessly? Let me quote one or two passages, as I fear I cannot find a single straightforward answer:

It may be true that all things which are good are *also* something else, just as it is true that all things which are yellow produce a certain kind of vibration in the light. And it is a fact, that Ethics aims at discovering what are those other properties belonging to all things which are good. But far too many philosophers have thought that when they named those other properties they were actually defining good; that these properties, in fact, were simply not "other," but absolutely and entirely the same

---

[3] Quoted by Moore, *Principia Ethica*, p. 66.
[4] *Ibid.*, p. 67.
[5] *Ibid.*, p. 66.

with goodness. This view I propose to call the "naturalistic fallacy" and of it I shall now endeavour to dispose.[6]

If I were to imagine that when I said "I am pleased," I meant that I was exactly the same thing as "pleased," I should not indeed call that a naturalistic fallacy, although it would be the same fallacy as I have called naturalistic with reference to Ethics.[7]

It is a very simple fallacy indeed. When we say that an orange is yellow, we do not think our statement binds us to hold that "orange" means nothing else than "yellow," or that nothing can be yellow but an orange. Supposing the orange is also sweet! Does that bind us to say that "sweet" is exactly the same thing as "yellow," that "sweet" must be defined as "yellow"?[8]

. . . There is no meaning in saying that pleasure is good, unless good is something different from pleasure.[9]

Professor Frankena, in an article on "The Naturalistic Fallacy,"[10] has taken these and similar passages in *Principia Ethica* to mean that the naturalistic fallacy is a species of the definist fallacy, which "is the process of confusing or identifying two properties."[11] Mr. Frankena rightly points out that this fallacy can occur only within a system that distinguishes the properties said (by him who claims a commission of the naturalistic fallacy) to be confused or identified. Thus a naturalist who denies any property of goodness or desirableness as different from desiredness has not committed the definist fallacy in saying, "The desirable just is the desired." This

---

[6] *Ibid.*, p. 10.
[7] *Ibid.*, p. 13.
[8] *Ibid.*, p. 14.
[9] *Ibid.*, p. 14.
[10] *Mind*, XLVIII (new ser., 1939), 464-77.
[11] *Ibid.*, p. 471.

seems so obviously correct that one wonders how Moore could have failed to see it or how he could have made the equivalent error, "that 'good is indefinable,' and that to deny this involves a fallacy, is a point capable of strict proof: for to deny it involves contradictions."[12]

I think the truth is that Moore had in mind, as well as the definist fallacy, and confused therewith, two others, which *are* strictly fallacies and which, if committed, would involve one in the commission of the definist fallacy or would easily lead to it. The passages already quoted seem to bear this out. First, there is the confusion of the predicative with the identity "is." Let us call this the "predicative fallacy." To go from "the orange is yellow" to "the orange is nothing but yellow," or from "I am pleased" to "I am identical with having pleasure" would be to commit the predicative fallacy. Second, there is what, for lack of a recognized name, I might call the "extensionalist fallacy." This goes from the extensional equivalence of two predicate terms (whenever either is truly predicated of a particular, the other is also) to their identity (they designate the same property). Of course, an extensional language could be set up such that this implication holds. But it does not hold in ordinary language. Moore makes frequent appeal to its invalidity. To go from "Properties A and B always accompany goodness" to "Goodness just is A and B" would be to commit the extensionalist fallacy.

Now to return to the issue. When Moore says that Mill, in step 1A, has committed the naturalistic fallacy, what does he accuse him of? I think it is the definist fallacy. In any case, he does nothing to show that Mill committed the extensionalist fallacy. For example, he does not accuse Mill of going from "Whatever is desirable is desired and *vice versa*" to "'Desirableness' and 'desiredness' designate the same property." And, were he to do so, Mill's actual statement would not bear him out; for that statement simply is that the *sole evidence* that

---

12 Moore, *op. cit.*, p. 77.

anything is desirable is that it is desired. This does not
claim extensional equivalence of "x is desirable" and "x
is desired," nor does it go from this to an identification of
the two predicates. Nor does Moore show that Mill has
committed the predicative fallacy, that, for example, he
has gone from "Desirableness is desired" to "Desirableness
just is desiredness." So I think that Moore simply means
to accuse Mill of identifying two properties that are different, viz., desirableness and desiredness, and this,
perhaps, as a step toward identifying goodness with
pleasure.

Now we have seen that the definist fallacy is no fallacy
unless the predicates definitionally identified are also
taken to refer to different properties. So here, if Mill is
saying that there is no property of desirableness or goodness different from the property of desiredness, that it is
consonant with common usage to suppose that the word
"desirableness" just refers to desiredness, he has committed no fallacy whatsoever. I happen to believe, however, that Mill does mean to accept desirableness and
desiredness as different properties and that his argument
makes this clear and that he does not commit the definist
fallacy.

Turning back to step $1A$, we find Mill saying: "The
sole evidence it is possible to produce that anything is
desirable is that people actually do desire it." Moore
himself correctly paraphrases this in one place: ". . . you
can only find out what is desirable by seeking to find out
what is actually desired." But then, later, he makes the
astounding assertion, without any foundation, that Mill
has pretended "to prove that 'good' means 'desired'"! I
can only account for this flagrant reading into Mill of
the definist fallacy by supposing Moore could not grasp
any other sense to Mill's argument and so thought that
Mill *must* have committed this fallacy. But *there is* another and an obvious sense to any interpreter not de-
bauched with verbal casuistry, as I hope to show.

To proceed: Moore continues his attack as follows:

The fact is that "desirable" does not mean "able to be desired" as "visible" means "able to be seen." The desirable means simply what *ought* to be desired or *deserves* to be desired; just as the detestable means not what can be but what ought to be detested and the damnable what deserves to be damned. Mill has, then, smuggled in, under cover of the word "desirable," the very notion about which he ought to be quite clear. "Desirable" does indeed mean "what it is good to desire"; but when this is understood, it is no longer plausible to say that our only test of *that,* is what is actually desired.[13]

This passage is a classic. Does it not show the complete bankruptcy of Mill's proof of utility? But there is one small question. What reason is there to suppose that Mill was not perfectly aware that "desirable" does not mean "able to be desired" and so, in *this* respect, was not at all analogous to "visible"? Could there be no other way in which the evidence for desirability must be like the evidence for visibility than in the suffixes of the adjectival designations? I think a glance at the whole argument shows that there is. And on what grounds does Moore so peremptorily continue: " 'Desirable' does indeed mean 'what it is good to desire'; but when this is understood, it is no longer plausible to say that our only test of *that* is what is actually desired"? Does he mean to make the astounding assertion which he seems to make, that anyone who says that the only test of the occurrence of A is the occurrence of B must be identifying A with B? This would force everyone who admits the extensional equivalence of two properties into a commission of the extensionalist fallacy!

Let us continue with Moore's criticism:

Is it merely a tautology when the Prayer Book talks of *good* desires? Are not *bad* desires also possible? Nay, we find Mill himself talking of a "better and nobler object

---

13 *Ibid.,* p. 67.

of desire," . . . as if, after all, what is desired were not *ipso facto* good, and good in proportion to the amount it is desired.[14]

Heaven forbid that any English philosopher should espouse a position that makes anything in the prayer-book a trivial tautology! I shall not undertake to defend Mill in general against such a serious charge, but on the particular point at issue I think I can clear his name. Apparently Moore's argument (which is here mostly suppressed, which perhaps accounts for its mounting vehemence) is that, since the desirable just is the desired for Mill, every desire must be good (desirable). Note, first, that this again assumes that Mill has committed the definist fallacy. Now, even supposing that he had, Moore's argument breaks down; for this fallacy would identify the desirable with the desired, not with desire. A desirable desire would be a desired desire, and not every desire is desired (in fact, even if it were, to state this would require a synthetic sentence). And, still on the assumption that the definist fallacy has been committed, it would be appropriate to define "bad" as "being the object of an aversion," so that it could be plausibly held that there are bad desires. However, all this is out of the whole utilitarian framework of ideas. That framework requires that a motive be judged good or bad not by the goodness or badness of its object but by the goodness or badness of its tendency, that is, of its total probable consequences if its object be realized. It is true that Mill rejects the hedonic calculus of Bentham (if that means that the morally good man must calculate the probable effects of every alternative in every choice-situation) in favor of living by traditional moral rules in most situations, but this is only a concession as to a tool for ascertaining probable consequences and does not entail giving up the position that desires can be judged good or bad only by the test of their total probable consequences.

---

[14] *Ibid.*

This leads immediately into a consideration of Moore's next thrust:

> Moreover, if the desired is *ipso facto* the good; then the good is *ipso facto* the motive of our actions, and there can be no question of finding motives for doing it, as Mill is at such pains to do. If Mill's explanation of "desirable" be *true*, then his statement . . . that the rule of action may be *confounded* with the motive of it is untrue: for the motive of action will then be according to him *ipso facto* its rule; there can be no distinction between the two, and therefore no confusion, and thus he has contradicted himself flatly.[15]

The reference here is to the following passage from chapter ii of *Utilitarianism:* Some objectors to utilitarianism

> . . . say it is exacting too much to require that people shall always act from the inducement of promoting the general interests of society. But this is to mistake the very meaning of a standard of morals, and confound the rule of action with the motive of it. It is the business of ethics to tell us what are our duties, or by what test we may know them; but no system of ethics requires that the sole motive of all we do shall be a feeling of duty; on the contrary, ninety-nine hundredths of all our actions are done from other motives, and rightly so done, if the rule of duty does not condemn them.[16]

This is in manifest contradiction with the definist fallacy of identifying good with desired (on the assumption, probably correct, that "motive of action" refers to the object desired)—so much so, in fact, that it should have at least raised the suspicion that Mill's argument for the principle of utility does not reduce to a commission of that fallacy.

---

[15] *Ibid.*
[16] *Utilitarianism* (Everyman's ed.), p. 17.

Finally, Moore formulates his criticism of Mill's step 1*A* in the form of an accusation that Mill has committed the fallacy of ambiguous middle:

> Well, then, the first step by which Mill has attempted to establish his Hedonism is simply fallacious. He has attempted to establish the identity of the good with the desired, by confusing the proper sense of "desirable," in which it denotes that which it is good to desire, with the sense which it would bear if it were analogous to such words as "visible." If "desirable" is to be identical with "good," then it must bear one sense; and if it is to be identical with "desired," then it must bear quite another sense. And yet to Mill's contention that the desired is necessarily good, it is quite essential that these two senses of "desirable" should be the same.[17]

I take it Moore is saying that Mill's argument can be formulated as a syllogism in *Barbara:*

> The good is identical with the desirable.
> The desirable is identical with the desired.
> Therefore, the good is identical with the desired.

And in this syllogism, says Moore, the middle term, "desirable," is ambiguous. Here the definist fallacy would appear as the conclusion of a fallacious line of proof. But what evidence is there that Mill meant to use such a syllogism? I find none. Of the whole syllogism, it is clear only that Mill would accept the minor premise, that the desirable and the good are identical.

It is now time to turn to the second half of Mill's first step, which I shall name "1*B*":

> 1*B.* "No reason can be given why the general happiness is desirable, except that each person, so far as he believes it to be attainable, desires his own happiness. This,

17 Moore, *op. cit.*, pp. 67–68.

however, being the fact, we have not only all the proof which the case admits of, but all which it is possible to require, that happiness is a good: that each person's happiness is a good to that person, and the general happiness, therefore, a good to the aggregate of all persons. Happiness has made out its title as *one* of the ends of conduct, and consequently one of the criteria of morality."[18]

Moore does not specifically criticize this passage, though it is easy to guess how he would criticize it by reference to his method of dealing with step 1A and his discussion (without special reference to this passage) of egoistic hedonism.[19] But there is no need to construct a hypothetical criticism; we can fill in the lacuna in Moore by turning to Bradley, who, in this particular conflict, is clearly an ally. Referring to step 1B, Bradley writes:

Whether our "great modern logician" thought that by this he had proved that the happiness of all was desirable for each, I will not undertake to say. He either meant to prove this, or has proved what he started with, viz. that each desires his own pleasure. And yet there is a certain plausibility about it. If many pigs are fed at one trough, each desires his own food, and somehow as a consequence does seem to desire the food of all; and by parity of reasoning it should follow that each pig, desiring his own pleasure, desires also the pleasure of all.[20]

And in a footnote he adds:

Either Mill meant to argue, "*Because* everybody desires his own pleasure, *therefore* everybody desires his own pleasure"; or "Because everybody desires his own

---

[18] Quoted by Moore (*ibid.*, p. 66).
[19] Cf. *ibid.*, pp. 96, 105. His object of condemnation here is Sidgwick.
[20] *Ethical Studies* (2d ed., 1927), p. 113.

pleasure, *therefore* everybody desires the pleasure of everybody else." Disciples may take their choice.[21]

Somehow the warning that Mill put right into step 1*B*—
"all the proof that the case admits of"—did not make any
impression. Bradley, like Moore, is assuming that our
"great modern logician," as he derisively characterizes
Mill, *must* be presenting in his "proof" of the principle
of utility a strict logical deduction. It is high time that
this whole interpretation be fundamentally and deci-
sively challenged.

If we turn back to chapter i of *Utilitarianism*, we find
Mill unequivocally rejecting any such interpretation:

> On the present occasion, I shall, without further discus-
> sion of the other theories, attempt to contribute something
> towards the understanding and appreciation of the Utilitar-
> ian or Happiness theory, and towards such proof as it is
> susceptible of. It is evident that this cannot be proof in the
> ordinary and popular meaning of the term. Questions of
> ultimate ends are not amenable to direct proof. Whatever
> can be proved to be good, must be so by being shown to be
> a means to something admitted to be good without proof.
> . . . If, then, it is asserted that there is a comprehensive
> formula, including all things which are in themselves
> good, and that whatever else is good, is not so as an end,
> but as a mean, the formula may be accepted or rejected,
> but is not a subject of what is commonly understood by
> proof.[22]

And the very first sentence of chapter iv reverts to this
disavowal of any strict proof of the principle of utility:
"It has already been remarked, that questions of ultimate
ends do not admit of strict proof, in the ordinary acceptation of the term."[23] Not only does Mill thus explicitly

---

[21] *Ibid.*, pp. 113–14 n.
[22] *Op. cit.*, p. 4.
[23] *Ibid.*, p. 32.

disavow any attempt to give a strict proof of the principle of utility, but he makes it clear that the "proof" which he offers is quite another sort of thing. Returning to chapter i, we find him continuing:

> We are not, however, to infer that its acceptance or rejection must depend on blind impulse, or arbitrary choice. There is a larger meaning of the word proof, in which this question is as amenable to it as any other of the disputed questions of philosophy. The subject is within the cognisance of the rational faculty; and neither does that faculty deal with it solely in the way of intuition. Considerations may be presented capable of determining the intellect either to give or withhold its assent to the doctrine; and this is equivalent to proof.
>
> We shall examine presently of what nature are these considerations; in what manner they apply to the case, and what rational grounds, therefore, can be given for accepting or rejecting the utilitarian formula.[24]

The very title of chapter iv is illuminating, "Of What Sort of Proof the Principle of Utility Is Susceptible." Apparently, Mill considered that he was not so much giving a proof of the principle of utility as discussing the question of the meaning of "proof" when applied to an ethical first principle. So we find him asking, concerning the principle of utility, "What ought to be required of this doctrine—what conditions is it requisite that the doctrine should fulfil—to make good its claim to be believed?"[25]

So much, then, is obvious. Mill utterly disavows any attempt to give a strict proof of the principle of utility. Thus steps $1A$ and $1B$ cannot be interpreted as Moore and Bradley have interpreted them; for then they would be simply attempted strict deductions that, unfortunately,

---

[24] *Ibid.*, p. 4.
[25] *Ibid.*, p. 32.

are failures because of the commission of fallacies that any schoolboy can detect.[26]

This result is final and quite unassailable. We now come to the more interesting and hazardous task of trying to ascertain just what is the nature of those considerations which, Mill thinks, are capable of determining the intellect to give assent to the principle of utility. And first let us call to mind the well-known, but not on that account wholly irrelevant, fact that Mill was an empiricist, an opponent of all forms of intuitionism and a priorism. That Mill himself thought this relevant is clear from chapter i of *Utilitarianism*, which is devoted precisely to its reiteration in application to ethics:

> According to the one opinion, the principles of morals are evident *a priori*, requiring nothing to command assent, except that the meaning of the terms be understood. According to the other doctrine, right and wrong, as well as truth and falsehood, are questions of observation and experience.[27]

Yet Mill is clear that a peculiar problem marks off ethical questions from factual. It is not possible to determine what is right or wrong in individual cases by direct perception. It is necessary, in making ethical judgments, to apply general principles that go back to an ethical first principle: ". . . the morality of an individual action is not a question of direct perception, but of the application of a law to an individual case."[28] Thus this serious ques-

---

[26] It would do no good were the critic of Mill to say that Mill's disavowal of strict proof applies only to his whole proof, that this latter includes step 2, which is inductive, and that therefore it is permissible to treat steps 1A and 1B as attempts at strict deduction. First, Mill would call such a combination of deduction and induction a strict proof "in the ordinary acceptation of the term." Second, his disavowal of strict proof is re-emphasized within both step 1A and step 1B.

[27] P. 2.

[28] *Ibid.*

tion faces the ethical empiricist: How can one's ethical
first principle (such as the principle of utility) be established? Self-evidence is not available, for appeal to it
would be an embracing of intuitionism; nor is inductive
generalization, since the rightness or wrongness of individual acts is not open to direct perception.

In this situation Mill makes use of two considerations,
both of which he got from Bentham, not to *prove* the
principle of utility but to *make it acceptable* to reasonable men. One of these is essentially an appeal to men's
honesty. When ordinary men try to justify their moral
judgments rationally, they do so by the tacit use of the
principle of utility. When an ethicist attempts to show
why his ethical first principle (if it differs from that of
utility) should be accepted, he does so by utilitarian arguments.[29] This is not, I am convinced, the old *consensus
gentium* argument, nor does it rest on a social-agreement
theory of truth. If it were, a strict proof of utility would
be possible. It is rather, as I have said, an appeal to intellectual honesty. It says: "My dear ethicist, whenever
you are caught off guard, either in everyday situations or
in arguing for some ethical principle, you find your
reasons go back to a tacit assumption of utility as the
first principle of ethics. What more does the utilitarian
need to do than to bring this clearly to your attention?"

I do not, however, think that this was the main consideration that Mill wished to present in developing a
favorable attitude toward the principle of utility. In the
first place, it is not in any special sense empirical. In the
second place, he adverts to it briefly in chapter i, but not
at all in chapter iv, which, as we have seen, is devoted
to the task of showing "of what sort of proof the principle of utility is susceptible." Chapter iv is, I wish to
urge, simply an explication of a certain sort of consideration that an empiricist can use to gain acceptance for an
ethical first principle, the first principle in this instance
(though it is not used as a mere illustration, for Mill

---

[29] Cf. *ibid.*, pp. 3–4.

does wish to get his readers to accept it) being, of course, that of utility.

Let us recall that an empiricist cannot hold that we directly perceive ethical attributes of particular actions. Thus he cannot establish his ethical first principle by an inductive generalization. This, however, is true of any first principle.[30]

> To be incapable of proof by reasoning is common to all first principles; to the first premises of our knowledge, as well as to those of our conduct. But the former, being matters of fact, may be the subject of a direct appeal to the faculties which judge of fact—namely, our senses, and our internal consciousness. Can an appeal be made to the same faculties on questions of practical ends? Or by what other faculty is cognisance taken of them?[31]

It is in answer to this question that Mill gives us step 1A. Now just what is the analogy that he wishes to urge upon us between visible and seen, on the one hand, and desirable and desired, on the other? I submit the following as an interpretation that at least makes sense of Mill's argument as a whole.

In the area of knowledge the empiricist cannot strictly prove his first principle. He cannot prove, by induction or by deduction from any more ultimate principle, that there are no unobserved entities, that there are no visible things never seen, audible occurrences never heard, and so on. But he can set it up as a plausible principle (as a "meaning criterion," as a later positivist put it) that any epistemological theory that requires visible or audible entities that are never seen or heard is talking nonsense. The only test anyone can seriously propose that a thing

---

[30] The critic can rightly urge that this does not square with the traditional interpretation of Mill's justification of induction (by the use of induction). On this point the critic has, I fear, firmer ground to stand on.

[31] *Op. cit.*, p. 32.

is visible is that it actually is seen. A theory that conflicts with this requirement will just not be accepted by reasonable people. Similarly in ethical theory. A theory that sets up, as ends desirable in themselves (i.e., good, *not* simply capable of being desired), states of affairs that nobody ever desires is just being academic and unrealistic. "If the end which the utilitarian doctrine proposes to itself were not, in theory and practice, acknowledged to be an end, nothing could ever convince any person that it was so." That is, if no one appealed to the greatest happiness to justify ethical judgments or ever in practice desired the greatest happiness, no considerations capable of getting reasonable people to accept that principle as ethically ultimate could be presented. Let us call this the requirement, directed toward any ethical first principle, of "psychological realism." Since a first principle is incapable of proof, anyone could arbitrarily set up any ethical first principle he chose, and there would be no basis for deciding between this and any other (if we eschew the intuitionist's self-evidence) unless some such requirement as that of psychological realism were set up.

Step 1*B* is to be interpreted in similar fashion, with the addition that Mill is here assuming the truth of psychological hedonism. Now, whatever one's opinion as to this latter doctrine (I believe it to be false), the design of Mill's argument is not affected. "No reason can be given why the general happiness is desirable, except that each person, so far as he believes it to be attainable, desires his own happiness." Let us remember that, for Mill, the desirability of the general happiness is a first principle that cannot be proved. The sentence just quoted, therefore, sets down no requirement as to strict proof. It rather shows what sort of consideration must be presented to lead to the acceptance of this first principle. One cannot sensibly present general happiness as desirable if it is completely unrelated to what individual people actually desire. Mill cannot and does not argue that each seeks the general happiness or that society as a whole somehow has its own motives, over and above those of its members, and that these are directed toward the general happiness. Rather, Mill simply says (anticipating the outcome of step 2 and the acceptance of the pleasure of each individual as a good) that, since the pleasure of each is a good, the sum of these must be a good: "each person's happiness is a good to that person, and the general happiness, therefore, a good to the aggregate of all persons."[32] Or, as he explains in a letter: "I merely meant in this particular sentence to argue that, since A's happiness is a good, B's a good, C's a good, &c., the sum of all these goods must be a good."[33] This may be incorrect; it may be that goods cannot be added, though surely it is not just obvious that Mill is mistaken in this matter. However that may be, Mill is clearly *not* trying to prove that "*because* everybody desired his own pleasure, *therefore* everybody desires the pleasure of everybody else."[34] He is not (if the reader will tolerate another reiteration) trying to *prove* anything. He is attempting simply to present the general-happiness principle in a way that will make it seem acceptable as an ethical first principle to people who, rejecting self-evidence in this matter, still wish to be intelligent.

The test of psychological realism condemns any ethical theory that would set up as good in themselves ends which no one actually ever seeks. The principle of utility comes through this test, in Mill's first step, unscathed. Now comes the second step as a clincher. No other ethical theory can pass this test successfully, since the only thing people ever desire is happiness. Suppose, now, for a moment, that Mill does make this out. Then, clearly, the principle of utility holds the field alone. Any acceptable ethical first principle must meet the test of psychological realism. Only the principle of utility can meet this

[32] *Ibid.*, p. 33.

[33] Hugh S. R. Elliot, *The Letters of John Stuart Mill* (1910), II, 116.

[34] Bradley, *op. cit.*, p. 114 n.

test. When and as this is shown, utilitarianism will, as a matter of fact, be accepted. No other kind of proof is required or possible.

Mill himself admits that people do desire as ends many things besides pleasure. He tries to square this with his contention that "there is in reality nothing desired except happiness" by appeal to the sort of associationist account that goes back to John Gay. Frequent association of these other things (e.g., money or moral virtue) with pleasures to which they give rise has set up an inseparable association. Whenever we think of these things, we think of them as pleasant, and so we seek *them*, not some pleasant effect. This line of thought bears different possible interpretations. It may mean simply that, though we do desire other things than pleasure, (associated) pleasure is the cause of our doing so. This is a plausible account of motivation, but it does not show that only pleasure is desired; it shows only that pleasure is the cause of our desiring whatever we do desire. Thus it is not to the point, for psychological realism does not require of an ethical theory that what it posits as good must be the cause of our desires but rather that it be something actually desired. And it is clear that Mill wants to show that only pleasure is desired for its own sake. Again Mill may mean to say that we are mistaken, we think we seek other things, but we really seek the pleasure so indissolubly associated with them that we do not, consciously, separate it. It seems, however, rather obvious that this is not what he means, as he reiterates that we do seek these other things than pleasure for their own sakes. Moreover, he says that we seek them as parts of happiness. Tentatively, then, I suggest the following: Only that which is experienced as pleasant is sought for its own sake. Many things originally not themselves experienced as pleasant come to be so through association with pleasant effects. Thus money or virtue really are desired as ends, but only so far as they are experienced as pleasant. This can then be expressed loosely by saying

only pleasure is desired, yet other things are also—as concrete parts of it. It would be better to say: Only things
experienced as pleasant are desired for their own sakes.
Now, if this be accepted, then what does it involve if we
are to suppose that the principle of utility successfully
passes the test of psychological realism? It requires that
that principle, when it says that happiness is the sole
good, mean not that pleasantness is good but that things
experienced as pleasant, and they alone, are good. Pleasure, as a property, is not good, and certainly not the sole
good. Is this a tenable interpretation? I think it is. But
this carries us away from the question of the proof of the
principle of utility to the nature of that principle, and
that will be dealt with at a later point in this paper and
only very briefly.

One last word, and I am done with my criticism of
the traditional way of disposing with Mill's argument.
Moore finishes off his criticism of Mill's step 2 as follows:

> Mill, then, has nothing better to say for himself than
> this. His two fundamental propositions are, in his own
> words, "that to think of an object as desirable (unless for
> the sake of its consequences), and to think of it as
> pleasant, are one and the same thing; and that to desire
> anything except in proportion as the idea of it is pleasant,
> is a physical and metaphysical impossibility." Both of
> these statements are, we have seen, merely supported by
> fallacies. The first seems to rest on the naturalistic fallacy;
> the second rests partly on this, partly on the fallacy of
> confusing ends and means, and partly on the fallacy of
> confusing a pleasant thought with the thought of a
> pleasure.[35]

It is clear again that Moore is thinking of Mill's argument as a strict proof. Had he read it in context, even
going back one paragraph, he would have had to give up

---

[35] *Op. cit.*, p. 72.

this whole interpretation. Let me set down the paragraph that immediately precedes the passage Moore quotes:

> We have now, then, an answer to the question, of what sort of proof the principle of utility is susceptible. If the opinion which I have now stated is psychologically true— if human nature is so constituted as to desire nothing which is not either a part of happiness or a means of happiness, we can have no other proof, and we require no other, that these are the only things desirable. If so, happiness is the sole end of human action, and the promotion of it the test by which to judge of all human conduct; from whence it necessarily follows that it must be the criterion of morality, since a part is included in the whole.[36]

This, so it seems to me, is just a summary of what step 2 purports to do. It says that, if there is only one sort of thing that is ever desired, then psychological realism requires one's ethical theory to square with this. This sort of plausibility is all that can be required of any ethical theory.

Turning, now, to the paragraph which is the immediate context of the passage that Moore quotes, we find that Mill simply summarizes his contention that there is only one sort of thing ever desired, that this is happiness, that utilitarianism alone, therefore, is acceptable to ethicists who are honestly realistic. However, he does fall into a loose manner of speaking, upon which a casuist is able to capitalize. He writes, "to think of an object as desirable," when the context makes clear that he meant "to desire an object." He has just written, in an earlier part of the same sentence, "desiring a thing and finding it pleasant . . . are phenomena entirely inseparable," which he then reiterates in different words, "to think of a thing as desirable . . . and to think of it as pleasant, are one and the same thing." All this means is that any

---

[36] Mill, *op. cit.*, p. 36.

object desired (for its own sake) is inseparably associated
with pleasure. I find no evidence that this commits the
naturalistic fallacy in any of its three senses. Mill does
use the infelicitous term "desirable" here. But he could
have used "good" in the same loose and colloquial sense;
i.e., he could have said, in accordance with frequent
popular usage, "to think of an object as good" when he
meant "to desire an object."

In summary, the argument of chapter iv of Mill's *Utilitarianism* is extremely simple and (in the main) sensible.
To an empiricist who eschews all intuitive self-evidence,
no ethical first principle can be strictly proved. All that
one can do is to present considerations that will lead
honest and reasonable people to accept such a principle.
These considerations, for an empiricist, must turn on
what people actually desire. Each person desires his own
happiness. Therefore, a first principle that makes happiness good will prove acceptable to honest men when they
consider it. And if the happiness of each is good, then
the sum of happiness of all is good. Thus the principle
of utility is something that men, constituted as they are,
can honestly accept. But no other ethical first principle
can meet this simple test of psychological realism; for
(and here the reasoning is not too clear) the only thing
people seek (for its own sake) is happiness. At least a
plausible interpretation of this last consideration is that
happiness is not a sum of pleasures in the sense of an
amount of sheer pleasantness but is a sum of things
experienced (whether by one's original nature or through
long association) as pleasant.

It must be admitted that this whole interpretation presupposes a fundamental distinction, a distinction which
intuitionists[37] like Moore and Sidgwick, thinking they

---

[37] Sometimes by "intuitionistic ethics" is meant not an ethics
whose first principles are taken to be self-evident but simply an
ethics that claims that there is some value term (such as "good")
whose reference is uniquely nondescriptive. In this sense, I claim,
both Bentham and Mill are intuitionists.

can rest their case on the self-evidence of their first principles, apparently ignore. I refer to the distinction between a statement in a theory and a statement about a theory, which here takes the form of the distinction between a proof within an ethical system and a proof of an ethical system. A first principle in an ethical system (or in an epistemological or ontological system) obviously cannot be proved in that system. It is possible to deal with an ethical system whose first principles are, within that system, self-evident, as a whole, and to ask, "Of what proof is it susceptible?" But this would put it on all fours with other systems and would lose for it the advantage of the supposed certainty which its self-evident first principles give it. In fact, to say that a principle is self-evident may mean just that it is a first principle; in *that* system in which it is self-evident it is not to be questioned; the possibility of its falsehood would just be the possibility of a contradiction in the system. In any other sense the self-evidence of a first principle takes us outside the system. But that brings up the serious question of how a whole ethical system can be established, a question that such an intuitionist as Moore never clearly faced just because he never saw this ambiguity in the concept of self-evidence.

It may, indeed, be contended that Moore meant by "self-evident" simply being a first principle in a system. In fact, Moore explicitly says: "When I call [propositions asserting that something is good in itself] 'intuitions' I mean *merely* to assert that they are incapable of proof; I imply nothing whatever as to the manner or origin of our cognition of them."[38] And again, he says:

> The expression "self-evident" means properly that the proposition so called is evident or true, *by itself* alone; that it is not an inference from some proposition other than *itself*. The expression does *not* mean that the proposition is true, because it is evident to you or me or all mankind,

---

[38] *Op. cit.*, p. x.

because in other words it appears to be true. That a proposition appears to be true can never be a valid argument that true it really is.[39]

I am not sure that in his later writings Moore so clearly distinguished self-evidence from psychological conviction. His frequent contention that he could be certain about the truth of such propositions as "This is a hand" and that philosophical analysis must start with such indubitable propositions seems to indicate that he did come to confuse first principles and propositions that are psychologically indubitable. But for the present purpose I need only point out that he was not aware in *Principia Ethica* that to be a first principle is always relative to a system. He assumes that self-evident propositions just are true. He does not see that the fact that they are not, in a given system, deduced from other propositions but serve as ultimate premises indicates nothing whatever as to their truth save as that is an intra-systemic matter. Whether the system in which their truth is fundamental to all else is as a whole true or is more acceptable than rival systems is a question he completely fails to see. That is, he fails to distinguish between the question of how a whole ethical system, with its first principles, can in any way be established, and the question of proof within such a system. Mill, in his loose, common-sensical way, is trying to state this distinction and to answer the question, "What kind of proof of an ethical system is possible?" He is saying that an ethical system as a whole cannot be established in any other way than by making it acceptable to reasonable men; and this is done just by showing that it and it alone (in its first principles, though not as theoretically elaborated) is actually accepted by men when outside the philosopher's closet. Mill simply asks ethicists to square their professionally elaborated ethics with the common-sense ethics of every man, including themselves. His statement of his problem and

---

[39] *Ibid.*, p. 143.

his answer are not too clear-cut; but what, in essentials, he was trying to do should be obvious to any sympathetic reader. All the more so because, in the main, he is just following Bentham, and Bentham did the same thing very clearly.

Having made a case that Mill is arguing *about* his system, not *in* it, and that his argument amounts to an appeal to the honesty of his readers in admitting that only utilitarianism squares with their actual motives, I need not take the space necessary to argue for a similar interpretation of Bentham. I need only point out some passages which show that, particularly in chapter i of *An Introduction to the Principles of Morals and Legislation*, Bentham was doing quite clearly what Mill did somewhat more blunderingly.

"Is the principle of utility susceptible of any direct proof?" asks Bentham. "It should seem not: for that which is used to prove everything else, cannot itself be proved: a chain of proofs must have their commencement somewhere. To give such proof is as impossible as it is needless."[40] However, there are those who do not accept utility as their ethical first principle. To such a one Bentham says: "If he thinks the settling of his opinions on such a subject worth the trouble, let him take the following steps, and at length, perhaps, he may reconcile himself to it."[41] If his alternative is the absence of all first principles whatever, then, in all consistency, he must admit that his ethical judgments are without foundation. If his first principle be merely an expression of some sentiment or approbation of his own, will not his whole system be founded on caprice? Can he claim objectivity for it? Does he give the like right to everyone else to found his ethics on an individual feeling? If so, let him ask himself

---

[40] *Introduction to the Principles of Morals and Legislation*, chap. i, § xi.

[41] *Ibid.*, § xiv.

whether it is not anarchial, and whether at this rate there
are not as many different standards of right and wrong
as there are men? and whether even to the same man, the
same thing, which is right today, may not (without the
least change in its nature) be wrong tomorrow? and
whether the same thing is not right and wrong in the
same place at the same time? and in either case, whether
all argument is not at an end? and whether, when two
men have said, "I like this" and "I don't like it," they can
(upon such a principle) have any thing more to say?"[42]

All this may sound highly rhetorical, but at least Bentham is not fooling himself or others—he is offering no
proof of his first principle, he is persuading people to
accept it by showing them that they would not consider
the alternatives to it to be sensible if they understood
them. And this can hardly be said of G. E. Moore's
famous elaboration (in his *Ethics* and in "The Nature of
Moral Philosophy") of this last passage from Bentham.
Moore thinks that the consequence of subjectivism
pointed out by Bentham, viz., that disagreement on moral
matters becomes impossible, *disproves* subjectivism, in
some strict sense.

But to resume. Bentham saves for the last his most
telling appeal—the need for psychological realism:

Admitting any other principle than the principle of
utility to be a right principle, a principle that it is
right for a man to pursue; admitting (what is not true)
that the word *right* can have a meaning without reference to utility, let him say whether there is any such
thing as a *motive* that a man can have to pursue the
dictates of it: if there is, let him say what that motive is,
and how it is to be distinguished from those which enforce
the dictates of utility: if not, then lastly let him say what it
is this other principle can be good for?[43]

---

42 *Ibid.*, § xiv.
43 *Ibid.*, § xiv, 10.

This rhetorical question is clearly meant to have a negative answer—no other first principle sets up as good anything that anyone has any motive to seek. Bentham is, of course, assuming the truth of psychological hedonism. Besides this list (which I have here shortened) of rhetorical questions, a serious consideration of which, Bentham believes, will lead any doubter to be reconciled to the principle of utility, Bentham has one other device for making that principle appear plausible. He points out that, "when a man attempts to combat the principle of utility, it is with reasons drawn, without his being aware of it, from that very principle itself."[44] Also, most men, without thinking of it, order their lives or at least found their judgments of people's actions by assuming this principle. Since this is the case, it is only being intellectually honest to accept that principle explicitly when our universal dependence upon it is pointed out to us.

But G. E. Moore, though not quite so vitriolic as he is against Mill, is inclined to believe that Bentham's case rests on a commission of the naturalistic fallacy. Here again he follows Sidgwick:

> "Bentham," says Sidgwick, "explains that his fundamental principle 'states the greatest happiness of all those whose interest is in question as being the right and proper end of human action'": and yet "his language in other passages of the same chapter would seem to imply" that he *means* by the word "right" "conducive to the general happiness." Prof. Sidgwick sees that, if you take these two statements together, you get the absurd result that "greatest happiness is the end of human action, which is conducive to the general happiness."[45]

This absurdity is due to "the naturalistic fallacy, which is implied in Bentham's statements."[46] Now, apparently

[44] *Ibid.*, § xiii.
[45] Moore, *op. cit.*, p. 17.
[46] *Ibid.*, p. 18.

Moore does not wish to condemn Bentham's definition (on Sidgwick's authority) of "right" as "conducive to general happiness." This alone would be no commission of the naturalistic fallacy. (It must be remembered that Moore himself at the time accepted a very similar definition of "right.") What he wishes to condemn is Bentham's use (still on Sidgwick's authority) of this definition to prove that the greatest happiness is the only right end of human action.

> [Bentham] applies the word "right," therefore, to the end, as such, not only to the means which are conducive to it; and, that being so, right can no longer be defined as "conducive to the general happiness," without involving the fallacy in question. For now it is obvious that the definition of right as conducive to general happiness can be used by him in support of the fundamental principle that general happiness is the right end; instead of being itself derived from that principle. . . . What I am maintaining is that the *reasons* which he actually gives for his ethical proposition are fallacious ones so far as they consist in a definition of right. What I suggest is that he did not perceive them to be fallacious; that, if he had done so, he would have been led to seek for other reasons in support of his Utilitarianism; and that, had he sought for other reasons, he *might* have found none which he thought to be sufficient. In that case he would have changed his whole system—a most important consequence.[47]

It is clear here that Moore is interpreting Bentham as trying to give a strict proof of the principle of utility, by means of a definition of "right" which commits the naturalistic fallacy (since, even though right is complex, it includes a nonnatural or value component and hence cannot be identified with the referent of "conducive to the general happiness," which embraces no nonnatural property). This, however, flies directly in the face of the

---

[47] *Ibid.*, pp. 18–19.

whole organization of chapter i, in which, as we have seen, Bentham not only disavows a strict proof of that principle but shows clearly what sort of proof is here possible.

But let us look more closely at the passages that, pulled out of their context, have led to this misinterpretation. It is quite correct that Bentham does specify the principle of utility as ". . . that principle which states the greatest happiness of all those whose interest is in question, as being the right and proper, and only right and proper and universally desirable, end of human action."[48] But where in this same chapter does he use language indicating that he means to *define* "right" as conducive to the greatest happiness? I find only two passages that could be construed in this way. The first is:

> Of an action that is conformable to the principle of utility, one may always say either that it is one that ought to be done, or at least that it is not one that ought not to be done. One may say also, that it is right it should be done; at least that it is not wrong it should be done: that it is a right action; at least that it is not a wrong action. When thus interpreted, the words *ought,* and *right* and *wrong,* and others of that stamp, have a meaning: when otherwise, they have none.[49]

The other, which I have already quoted, runs: ". . . admitting (what is not true) that the word *right* can have a meaning without reference to utility, let him say whether there is any such thing as a *motive* that a man can have to pursue the dictates of it. . . ."

If these passages are taken to mean that Bentham arbitrarily defines "right" as "conformity to general happiness," then the principle of utility follows immediately and tautologically. And Bentham is quite wrong in saying that it is an ethical first principle that cannot be

---

[48] Bentham, *op. cit.,* chap. i, § i n.
[49] *Ibid.,* § x.

proved and that all one can do is to get people to consider it honestly. But, if these passages are not to be taken
thus, how are they to be interpreted? Bentham, note,
does not say, "right" *means* "conformable to the greatest
happiness." He says we may say of an action conformable
to utility that it is right; that, when so used, "right" has a
meaning, otherwise not; and again that "right" can have
no meaning without reference to utility. Now this is
perfectly consonant with the view that, though "right"
does not refer to utility, what it does refer to is regularly
related to utility, is present only when utility is. Moreover, it squares with the use of psychological realism as a
test: that is, only when "right" is so used that it points
out acts that do have utility does it fit with people's actual motives; thus any other first principle than utility
would make "right" and other ethical terms meaningless,
in the sense that these terms would no longer agree with
people's actual motives and judgments. This is a perfectly plausible interpretation that has the merit of fitting
these passages into Bentham's thought rather than specu-
lating on them in isolation. But it has the consequence
that the principle of utility is no tautology and does not
involve the naturalistic fallacy in any of its forms. Can
this be made out? I think it can, and without any forcing.

In the first place, though Bentham embraces psychological hedonism, he does not confuse this with ethical
hedonism. The first three sentences of his *Principles*
make this unmistakable: "Nature has placed mankind
under the governance of two sovereign masters, *pain* and
pleasure. It is for them alone to point out what we ought
to do, as well as to determine what we shall do. On the
one hand the standard of right and wrong, on the other
the chain of causes and effects, are fastened to their
throne."[50] It is true, he goes on to say, that "the *principle
of utility* recognises the subjection, and assumes it for
the foundation of that system, the object of which is to
rear the fabric of felicity by the hands of reason and of

---

[50] *Ibid.*, § i.

law."[51] But here he is clearly speaking of his attempt to write a handbook for the judge and legislator that will square with actual human motives and thus deter from crime and encourage obedience to law. The twofold character of pleasure, as a test of what is desirable and as an object of desire, is made, as it were, the cornerstone of his whole attempt at legal codification and reform: "Pleasures then, and the avoidance of pains, are the *ends* which the legislator has in view [i.e., are the ends he should aim at]. . . . Pleasures and pains are the *instruments* he has to work with. . . ."[52] This distinction, between pleasure as marking the good and pleasure as controlling human action, is present throughout Bentham's whole discussion of principles of legislation: of cases unmeet for punishment, of rules governing the proper proportion between punishments and offenses, etc. His basic principle, that one is never justified in inflicting more pain (through punishment) than is necessary to deter from crime, would be meaningless without it.

Thus the principle of utility is definitely an ethical principle (a "standard of right and wrong," as he calls it). Though realistically geared to or paralleling a hedonistic law of human motivation, it is not that law, nor is it proved by that law. It is no identity statement, or definition, in nonethical terms, of basic ethical words, such as "right" or "desirable end." It is clearly a synthetic statement to the effect that the only situation desirable as an end in itself, and in terms of which human actions can be judged good or bad as they tend to promote or hinder its achievement, is that which exemplifies the greatest happiness of all concerned. This cannot be proved within the utilitarian system because that system is simply a development of it (plus an indefinite number of empirical laws connected directly or indirectly with the occurrence of happiness). But the utilitarian system

---

[51] *Ibid.*
[52] *Ibid.*, chap. iv, § i.

is capable of the sort of "proof" open to any ethical system. It can be made to appear plausible, it can be presented so that people who try honestly to be reasonable will be led to accept it. And this is done, so Bentham thinks, by showing that it, and it alone of all ethical theories, squares with our unsophisticated moral judgments and reasonings and sets up as morally good something which, by the basic law of human motivation, actually is sought by people.

Now I can imagine an objector arguing in the following vein: Granted that you have shown that the proof of the principle of utility as formulated in Bentham and Mill does not rest on the set of fallacies traditionally ascribed to it, haven't you, on the other hand, made of it little more than a farce? You point out that it is no proof at all, it is merely an appeal to people's belief. It is just an attempt to get people to accept utilitarianism. It is reduced to so much propaganda.

This is no place for an extended statement of method in ethics. But since, as indicated at the outset, this paper was written largely from a methodological rather than a historical interest, a few concluding words on this head may not be inappropriate.

First, it seems to me that Bentham and Mill are right in saying that any ethical theory must contain at least one first principle that cannot be proved; for to prove it would involve deriving it from some more basic principle, which latter would, then, be part of the theory. And, as Mill indicates, this is true of theories in other branches of philosophy. Examples would be the correspondence theory of truth in epistemology, the tautological theory of entailment in the philosophy of logic, the nominalistic theory of existence in ontology. Though I think it proper to demand that theories in different philosophic disciplines be harmoniously fitted together to make a categorically unified metaphysics, they are not derivable from anything more basic. This is their peculiarity as philosophical. They are self-contained.

Second, proofs, both inductive and deductive, are possible within a philosophical theory or system. In fact, however, a great deal of the development of such a theory is strictly neither deductive nor inductive but involves a sort of consistency that may perhaps be designated as "fittingness" or "appropriateness." Philosophic competence in developing a theory is a curious amalgam of technical logical and linguistic skill and philosophic insight and imagination.

Third, however competently developed, there still remains the question of the acceptability of a philosophic theory as a whole. This is in part just a matter of actual success or failure in getting people who turn their attention to such matters to accept the theory. But this is not quite all; for it must be admitted that there are good and bad ways of going about this. Appeal to authority—whether of a church, a great tradition in philosophy, the writings of a certain individual philosopher, or the tenets of a particular school of thought—is a bad way. Another bad way is through confusion as to what one is doing. An important instance is the confusion between talking within a system and about a system, which, no doubt, springs from the desire for certainty and seems to be the source of that curious delusion that there are self-evident first principles. A good way of going about gaining acceptance of a philosophic system is to show that, though clearer and more consistent, it yet squares in some overall large fashion with common sense, with those ways of organizing experience that we all adopt when not in the closet of philosophic speculation. Why is this a good way? In the first place, it is the way most likely to succeed in the long run. We humans are basically intellectually honest, I optimistically believe, and will not for long accept a philosophic theory that we cannot in any way integrate with our everyday fashion of looking at things. In the second place, common sense, so far as relevant in this matter, is itself metaphysics—only half-thought-out, full of confusions and even contradictions, yet the residue of attempts through the centuries of untold numbers of men to categorize experience. It is, then,

with all its need of clarification, a more reliable basis
than any one man's speculations for determining what
categorial systems can and what ones cannot be permanently successful in ordering experience.

Fourth, implicit in all of the third point is a metaphysics. There are people who do accept and reject philosophic systems. There is experience that can be categor-
ized in different ways. And so on. All this, of course, I
accept in my own metaphysics. And it is consonant
with my method of "proving" that metaphysics by appeal
to common sense. But what of another metaphysics that
might reject all this, and thus the whole method it embraces? What can I do with it? Nothing, except to say
it will not be accepted for long by many, which, of
course, is to bring it within my metaphysics. Yet this is
the peculiar situation a metaphysical system is in. And
so here we must stop.

This may seem a long way from Bentham and Mill,
but I am convinced that a sympathetic reading of the
"proof" of utilitarianism by these men shows that they
were trying to face, in ethics, the sort of peculiar difficulty that any philosophic theory is in when questions
about establishing it, as contrasted with proving things
within it and by means of it, are honestly faced. And,
though I do not wish to condone laxity of formulation, I
do wish to condemn that sort of casuistry which fastens
to another man's words and neglects his sentences or, in
reading a sentence, ignores the paragraphs and chapters.

THE INTERPRETATION OF
THE MORAL
PHILOSOPHY OF J. S. MILL

BY

J. O. Urmson

It is a matter which should be of great interest to those who study the psychology of philosophers that the theories of some great philosophers of the past are studied with the most patient and accurate scholarship, while those of others are so burlesqued and travestied by critics and commentators that it is hard to believe that their works are ever seriously read with a sympathetic interest, or even that they are read at all. Amongst those who suffer most in this way John Stuart Mill is an outstanding example. With the exception of a short book by Reginald Jackson,[1] there is no remotely accurate account of his views on deductive logic, so that, for example, the absurd view that the syllogism involves *petitio principii* is almost invariably fathered on him; and, as Von Wright says, 'A good systematic and critical monograph on Mill's

From *Philosophical Quarterly*, III, 1953. Reprinted by permission of the author and the Editor of the *Philosophical Quarterly*.

[1] *An Examination of the Deductive Logic of J. S. Mill* (1941).

Logic of Induction still remains to be written'.[2] But even
more perplexing is the almost universal misconstruction
placed upon Mill's ethical doctrines; for his *Utilitarianism* is a work which every undergraduate is set to read
and which one would therefore expect Mill's critics to
have read at least once. But this, apparently, is not so;
and instead of Mill's own doctrines a travesty is discussed, so that the most common criticisms of him are
simply irrelevant. It will not be the thesis of this paper
that Mill's views are immune to criticism, or that they
are of impeccable clarity and verbal consistency; it will
be maintained that, if interpreted with, say, half the
sympathy automatically accorded to Plato, Leibniz, and
Kant, an essentially consistent thesis can be discovered
which is very superior to that usually attributed to Mill
and immune to the common run of criticisms.

One further note must be made on the scope of this
paper. Mill, in his *Utilitarianism* attempts to do two
things; first, he attempts to state the place of the conception of a *summum bonum* in ethics, secondly, he attempts
to give an account of the nature of this ultimate end.
We shall be concerned only with the first of these two
parts of Mill's ethical theory; we shall not ask what Mill
thought the ultimate end was, and how he thought that
his view on this point could be substantiated, but only
what part Mill considered that the notion of an ultimate
end, whatever it be, must play in a sound ethical theory.
This part of Mill's doctrine is logically independent of
his account of happiness.

Two Mistaken Interpretations of Mill.

Some of Mill's expositors and critics have thought that
Mill was attempting to analyse or define the notion of
right in terms of the *summum bonum*. Thus Mill is
commonly adduced as an example of an ethical naturalist by those who interpret his account of happiness

---

[2] *A Treatise on Induction and Probability* (1951), p. 164.

naturalistically, as being one who defined rightness in terms of the natural consequences of actions. Moore, for example, while criticising Mill's account of the ultimate end says: 'In thus insisting that what is right must mean what produces the best possible results Utilitarianism is fully justified'.[3] Others have been less favourable in their estimation of this alleged view of Mill's. But right or wrong, it seems clear to me that Mill did not hold it. Mill's only reference to this analytic problem is on page 27 (of the Everyman edition, to which all references will be made), where he refers to a person 'who sees in moral obligation a transcendent fact, an objective reality belonging to the province of "Things in themselves"', and goes on to speak of this view as an irrelevant opinion 'on this point of Ontology', as though the analysis of ethical terms was not part of ethical philosophy at all as he conceived it, but part of ontology. It seems clear that when Mill speaks of his quest being for the 'criterion of right and wrong' (p. 1), 'concerning the foundation of morality' (p. 1), for a 'test of right and wrong' (p. 2), he is looking for a 'means of ascertaining what is right or wrong' (p. 2), not for a definition of these terms. We shall not, therefore, deal further with this interpretation of Mill; if a further refutation of it is required it should be sought in the agreement of the text with the alternative exposition shortly to be given.

The other mistaken view avoids the error of this first view, and indeed is incompatible with it. It is, probably, the received view. On this interpretation Mill is looking for a test of right or wrong as the ultimate test by which one can justify the ascription of rightness or wrongness to courses of action, rightness and wrongness being taken to be words which we understand. This test is taken to be whether the course of action does or does not tend to promote the ultimate end (which Mill no doubt says is the general happiness). So far there is no cause to quarrel with the received view, for it is surely correct.

---

[3] *Principia Ethica*, reprinted 1948, p. 106.

But in detail the view is wrong. For it is further suggested that for Mill this ultimate test is also the immediate test; the rightness or wrongness of any particular action is to be decided by considering whether it promotes the ultimate end. We may, it might be admitted, on Mill's view sometimes act, by rule of thumb or in a hurry, without actually raising this question; but the actual justification, if there is one, must be directly in terms of consequences, including the consequences of the example that we have set. On this view, then, Mill holds that an action, a particular action, is right if it promotes the ultimate end better than any alternative, and otherwise it is wrong. However we in fact make up our minds in moral situations, so far as justification goes no other factor enters into the matter. It is clear that on this interpretation Mill is immediately open to two shattering objections; first, it is obviously and correctly urged, if one has, for example, promised to do something it is one's duty to do it at least partly because one has promised to do it and not merely because of consequences even if these consequences are taken to include one's example in promise-breaking. Secondly, it is correctly pointed out that on this view a man who, *ceteris paribus*, chooses the inferior of two musical comedies for an evening's entertainment has done a moral wrong, and this is preposterous.[4] If this were in fact the view of Mill, he would indeed be fit for little more than the halting eristic of philosophical infants.

A Revised Interpretation of Mill.

I shall now set out in a set of propositions what I take to be in fact Mill's view and substantiate them afterwards from the text. This will obscure the subtleties but will make clearer the main lines of interpretation.

---

[4] For an example of this interpretation of Mill and the first and more important one, cf. Carritt, *The Theory of Morals*, Ch. IV.

A. A particular action is justified as being right by showing that it is in accord with some moral rule. It is shown to be wrong by showing that it transgresses some moral rule.

B. A moral rule is shown to be correct by showing that the recognition of that rule promotes the ultimate end.

C. Moral rules can be justified only in regard to matters in which the general welfare is more than negligibly affected.

D. Where no moral rule is applicable the question of the rightness or wrongness of particular acts does not arise, though the worth of the actions can be estimated in other ways.

As a terminological point it should be mentioned that where the phrase 'moral rule' occurs above Mill uses the phrase 'secondary principle' more generally, though he sometimes says 'moral law'. By these terms, whichever is preferred, Mill is referring to such precepts as 'Keep promises', 'Do no murder', or 'Tell no lies'. A list of which Mill approves is to be found in *On Liberty* (p. 135).

There is, no doubt, need of further explanation of these propositions; but that, and some caveats, can best be given in the process of establishing that these are in fact Mill's views. First, then, to establish from the text that in Mill's view particular actions are shown to be right or wrong by showing that they are or are not in accord with some moral rule. (i) He says with evident approbation on p. 2: 'The intuitive, no less than what may be termed the inductive, school of ethics, insists on the necessity of general laws. They both agree that the morality of an individual action is not a question of direct perception, but of the application of a law to an individual case. They recognise also, to a great extent, the same moral laws'. Mill reproaches these schools only with being unable to give a unifying rationale of these laws (as he will do in proposition B). (ii) He says on page 22: 'But to consider the rules of morality as improvable is one thing; to pass over the intermediate generalisations entirely, and endeavour to test each individual action directly by the first principle, is another. It is a strange notion that the acknowledgement of a first principle is inconsistent with the admission of secondary ones'. He adds, with feeling: 'Men really ought to leave off talking a kind of nonsense on this subject which they would neither talk nor listen to on other matters of practical concernment'. (iii) Having admitted on p. 23 that 'rules of conduct cannot be so framed as to require no exceptions', he adds (p. 24) 'We must remember that only in these cases of conflict between secondary principles is it requisite that first principles should be appealed to. There is no case of moral obligation in which some secondary principle is not involved; and if only one, there can seldom be any real doubt which one it is in the mind of any person by whom the principle itself is recognised'. This quotation supports both propositions A and D. It shows that for Mill moral rules are not merely rules of thumb which aid the unreflective man in making up his mind, but an essential part of moral reasoning. The relevance of a moral rule is the criterion of whether we are dealing with a case of right or wrong or some other moral or prudential situation. (iv) The last passage which we shall select to establish this interpretation of Mill (it would be easy to find more) is also a joint confirmation of propositions A and D, showing that our last was not an *obiter dictum* on which we have placed too much weight. In the chapter entitled 'On the connection between justice and utility', Mill has maintained that it is a distinguishing mark of a just act that it is one required by a specific rule or law, positive or moral, carrying also liability to penal sanctions. He then writes this important paragraph (p. 45), which in view of its importance and the neglect that it has suffered must be quoted at length: 'The above is, I think, a true account, as far as it goes, of the origin and progressive growth of the idea of justice. But we must observe, that it contains, as yet, nothing to distinguish that obligation from moral obligation in general. For the truth is, that the idea of penal sanction, which is the essence of law, enters not only into the conception of injustice, but into that of any kind of wrong. We do not call anything wrong, unless we mean to imply that a person ought to be punished in some way or other for doing it; if not by law, by the opinion of his fellow-creatures; if not by opinion, by the reproaches of his own conscience. This seems to be the real turning point of the distinction between morality and simple expediency. It is a part of the notion of Duty in every one of its forms, that a person may rightfully be compelled to fulfil it. Duty is a thing which may be exacted from a person, as one exacts a debt. Unless we think that it may be exacted from him, we do not call it his duty. . . . There are other things on the contrary, which we wish that people should do, which we like or admire them for doing, perhaps dislike or despise them for not doing, but yet admit that they are not bound to do; it is not a case of moral obligation; we do not blame them, that is, we do not think that they are proper objects of punishment. . . . I think there is no doubt that this distinction lies at the bottom of the notions of right and wrong; that we call any conduct wrong, or employ, instead, some other term of dislike or disparagement, according as we think that the person ought, or ought not, to be punished for it; and we say, it would be right to do so and so, or merely that it would be desirable or laudable, according as we would wish to see the person whom it concerns, compelled, or only persuaded and exhorted, to act in that manner'. How supporters of the received view have squared it with this passage I do not know; they do not mention it. If they have noticed it at all it is, presumably, regarded as an example of Mill's inconsistent eclecticism. Mill here makes it quite clear that in his view right and wrong are derived from moral rules; in other cases where the ultimate end is no doubt affected appraisal of conduct must be made in other ways. For example, if one's own participation in the ultimate end is impaired without breach of moral law, it is (*Liberty*, p. 135) imprudence or lack of self respect, it is not wrong-doing. So much for the establishment of this interpretation of Mill, in a positive way, as regards points A and D. We must now ask whether there is anything in Mill which is inconsistent with it and in favour of the received view.

It is impossible to show positively that there is nothing in Mill which favours the received view against the interpretation here given, for it would require a complete review of everything that Mill says. We shall have to be content with examining two points which might be thought to tell in favour of the received view.

(a) On p. 6 Mill says: 'The creed which accepts as the foundation of morals, Utility, or the Greatest Happiness Principle, holds that actions are right in proportion as they tend to promote happiness, wrong as they tend to promote the reverse of Happiness'. This seems to be the well-known sentence which is at the bottom of the received interpretation. Of course, it could be taken as a loose and inaccurate statement of the received view, if the general argument required it. But note that strictly one can say that a certain action tends to produce a certain result only if one is speaking of type rather than token-actions. Drinking alcohol may tend to promote exhilaration, but my drinking this particular glass either does or does not produce it. It seems, then, that Mill can well be interpreted here as regarding moral rules as forbidding or enjoining types of action, in fact as making the point that the right moral rules are the ones which promote the ultimate end (my proposition B), not as saying something contrary to proposition A. And this, or something like it, is the interpretation which consistency requires. Mill's reference to 'tendencies of actions' at the top of p. 22 supports the stress here laid on the word 'tend', and that context should be examined by those who require further conviction.

(b) Mill sometimes refers to moral rules as 'intermediate generalisations' (e.g., p. 22) from the supreme principle, or as 'corollaries' of it (also p. 22). These are probably the sort of phrases which lead people to think that they play a purely heuristic role in ethical thinking for Mill. As for the expression 'intermediate generalisation', Mill undoubtedly thinks that we should, and to some extent do, arrive at and improve our moral rules by such methods as observing that a certain type of action has had bad results of a social kind in such an overwhelming majority of cases that it ought to be banned. (But this is an over-simplification; see the note on p. 58 on how we ought to arrive at moral rules, and the pessimistic account of how we in fact arrive at them in *Liberty*, p. 69-70). But this account of the genesis of moral rules does not require us to interpret them as being anything but rules when once made. It really seems unnecessary to say much of the expression 'corollary'; Mill obviously cannot wish it to be taken literally; in fact it is hard to state the relation of moral rules to a justifying principle with exactitude and Mill, in a popular article in *Fraser*, did not try very hard to do so.

Moral Rules and the Ultimate End.

We have already been led in our examination of possible objections to proposition A to say something in defence of the view that Mill thought that a moral rule is shown to be correct by showing that the recognition of that rule promotes the ultimate end (proposition B). A little more may be added on this point, though it seems fairly obvious that if we are right in saying that the supreme principle is not to be evoked, in Mill's view, in the direct justification of particular right acts, it must thus come in in an indirect way in view of the importance that Mill attached to it. And it is hard to think what the indirect way is if not this. (i) On p. 3 Mill reproaches other moral philosophers with not giving a satisfactory account of moral rules in terms of a fundamental principle, though they have correctly placed moral rules as governing particular actions. It would be indeed the mark of an inconsistent philosopher if he did not try to repair the one serious omission which he

ascribes to others. (ii) Mill ascribes to Kant (p. 4) the
use of utilitarian arguments because, Mill alleges, he in
fact supports the rules of morality by showing the evil
consequences of not adopting them or adopting alternatives. Thus Mill is here regarding as distinctively utilitarian the justification or rejection of moral rules on the
ground of consequences. He could hardly have wished
to suggest that Kant would directly justify, even inad-
vertently, particular actions on such grounds. But it is
perhaps not to the point to argue this matter more elab-
orately. If anyone has been convinced by what has gone
before, he will not need much argument on this point;
with others it is superfluous to make the attempt.

In What Fields are Moral Rules of Right and Wrong Applicable?

The applicability of moral rules is, says Mill, 'the characteristic difference which marks off, not justice, but
morality in general, from the remaining provinces of Expediency and Worthiness' (p. 46). Mill says little or
nothing in *Utilitarianism* about the boundary between
morality and worthiness (surely it would be better to
have said the boundary between right and wrong on
the one hand and other forms of both moral and non-
moral appraisal on the other?). It seems reasonable to
suppose that he would have recognised that the use of
moral rules must be confined to matters in which the
kind of consequence is sufficiently invariable for there
not to be too many exceptions. But this is a pragmatic
limitation; Mill does have something to say about a limitation in principle in *Liberty* which I have crudely summarised in my proposition C—moral rules can be justifiably maintained in regard only to matters in which
the general welfare is more than negligibly affected.

It is important to note that Mill in *Liberty* is concerned with freedom from moral sanctions as well as
the sanctions of positive law. The distinction between
self-regarding and other actions is regarded by him as

relevant to moral as well as to political philosophy. The most noteworthy passage which bears on the scope of moral rules is on page 135. Here he mentions such things as encroachment on the rights of others as being 'fit objects of moral reprobation, and, in grave cases, of moral retribution and punishment'. But self-regarding faults (low tastes and the like) are 'not properly immoralities and to whatever pitch they are carried, do not constitute wickedness. . . . The term duty to oneself, when it means anything more than prudence, means self-respect or self-development'. Self-regarding faults render the culprit 'necessarily and properly a subject of distaste, or, in extreme cases, even of contempt', but this is in the sphere of worthiness not of right and wrong.

So much then for Mill's account of the logic of moral reasoning. It must be emphasised that no more has been attempted than a skeleton plan of Mill's answer, and that Mill puts the matter more richly and more subtly in his book. Even on the question of general interpretation more store must be laid on the effect of a continuous reading in the light of the skeleton plan than on the effect of the few leading quotations introduced in this paper. It is emphatically not the contention of this paper that Mill has given a finally correct account of these matters which is immune to all criticism; an attempt has been made only to give a sympathetic account without any criticism favourable or unfavourable. But I certainly do maintain that the current interpretations of Mill's *Utilitarianism* are so unsympathetic and so incorrect that the majority of criticisms which have in fact been based on them are irrelevant and worthless.

INTERPRETATIONS OF MILL'S UTILITARIANISM

BY

J. D. Mabbott

Professor Urmson's article 'The Interpretation of the Moral Philosophy of J. S. Mill' in *The Philosophical Quarterly* for January 1953 [Vol. 3, No. 10 (reprinted above)] is a most interesting and stimulating piece of work. The main point Urmson makes is that previous critics have interpreted Mill to hold, as G. E. Moore certainly did hold, that 'it is always the duty of every agent to do that one, among all the actions which he *can* do on any given occasion, whose *total consequence* will have the greatest intrinsic value' (Moore, *Ethics*, p. 232). But, on Urmson's view, Mill's real position was as follows. 'A. A particular action is justified as being right by showing that it is in accord with some moral rule. It is shown to be wrong by showing that it transgresses some moral rule. B. A moral rule is shown to be correct by showing that the recognition of that rule promotes the ultimate end (sc. the greatest happiness of the great-

From *Philosophical Quarterly*, VI, 1956. Reprinted by permission of the author and the Editor of the *Philosophical Quarterly*.

est number)' [p. 35 (p. 183 of this volume)]. I think
in the second clause there are two slight amendments
to be made. 'Recognition' is not enough; practice according to the rule is required. And 'promotes' suggests that
all defensible moral rules are in fact recognised or
obeyed; I should prefer 'would promote' (at least as an
elucidation of Mill).

Now from these two principles there follow two crucial differences between the orthodox interpretation of
utilitarianism and that of Urmson. (1) On the orthodox
interpretation it is never right to do an action when
some alternative action would produce more good (cf.
the Moore quotation above). But on Urmson's view it
may be right to do an action which is in accord with a
moral rule, even if that particular action does less good
than some alternative action—on the ground that the
general practice of the rule does more good than the
omission of such practice or the practice of an alternative
rule. (2) On the orthodox interpretation (again compare G. E. Moore) the rightness of an action is determined by its *actual* consequences; on Urmson's interpretation by *hypothetical* consequences, by what *would
happen if* the rule which the action follows were generally practised.

Now there is one passage in *Utilitarianism* (Everyman Edition—to which all other references will be given
—pp. 17-18) in which Mill explicitly accepts both these
important corollaries; though Urmson does not quote it,
it is one of the most striking pieces of evidence in favour
of his interpretation. 'In the case of abstinences indeed
—of things which people forbear to do from moral considerations, *though the consequences in the particular
case might be beneficial*—it would be unworthy of an intelligent agent not to be consciously aware that the action is of a kind which, *if practised generally, would be
generally injurious,* and that this is the ground of the
obligation to abstain from it'.

Re-reading Mill in the light of Urmson's comments
reveals many passages such as this in his support, pas-

sages whose significance certainly seems to have escaped previous critics. But it seems to me doubtful whether Mill is as clearly and consistently committed to the Urmson view as he suggests. Many passages fit the old ortho-dox interpretation and I doubt whether Mill himself realized the fundamental differences between the two views. The remainder of this paper is intended not only to show the difficulties which some passages in Mill pre-sent to Urmson's thesis but also to use these difficulties to bring out more sharply the differences between the two views.

The main point of the new interpretation is that the first principle is not relevant to determine the rightness of any particular act. Mill says there is only one excep-tion to this, namely the case in which two rules conflict. 'We must remember that only in these cases of conflict between secondary principles is it requisite that first principles should be appealed to. There is no case of moral obligation in which some secondary principle is not involved; and, if only one, there can seldom be any doubt which one it is' (p. 24). But when two rules con-flict what question do I ask? How do I apply the first principle to escape my dilemma? Do I ask whether keep-ing the one rule would *in general* do more good than keeping the other? This would seem, on Urmson's inter-pretation, to be the right question, but it would be very difficult to answer. Or do I ask whether keeping the one rule *on this particular occasion* will do more good than keeping the other? But then I might as well have left out all reference to the rules and just asked whether act A which happens to accord with rule X will do more good than act B which happens to accord with rule Y. Mill gives no guidance to the question which he would approve.

The passage quoted above maintains that the *only* ex-ception to the ban on deciding particular actions by reference to the first principle is that of conflict of sec-ondary principles. But there is another exception which Mill elsewhere allows. The 'chief exception' to the rule against lying is said to be where withholding the truth 'would save an individual from great and unmerited evil' (p. 21). The word 'unmerited' may seem to import a conflicting secondary principle—'to each his due'; but I do not think this is the main point. Mill is admitting what all would admit, that when the consequences of keeping a secondary rule are very bad indeed (or of breaking it very good) an exception may be made. Now this other exception (and it is called the 'chief exception') also produces a further difficulty in Urmson's interpretation. Mill also says, in the passage quoted above from p. 24, that there is no case of moral obligation in which a secondary principle is not involved. What of the case where no secondary principle is involved and yet some act open to me can produce very good results or avert very bad ones? Would not such an act be moral, right, my duty? Yet the only principle here is the first principle. It may be recalled that alongside his *prima facie* duties of keeping faith, etc., which correspond to Mill's secondary principles, Sir David Ross lists *prima facie* duties of beneficence and non-maleficence. One way of putting the two present difficulties is that on Urmson's interpretation of Mill the production of the greatest happiness would have to be (*a*) a *prima facie* obligation (i.e. relevant to determine the rightness of particular acts), (*b*) the basis of every other *prima facie* obligation (or secondary principle), (*c*) the arbiter between conflicting *prima facie* obligations.

The third difficulty, and one admitted by Urmson, is that Mill calls the secondary principles 'corollaries' of the first principle (p. 22). But they can hardly be corollaries if in a particular case they contradict the first principle when I abstain from a particular act in order to obey a rule 'though the consequences in the particular case might be beneficial' (p. 18, cited above). The term 'corollary' suggests, as Urmson agrees, that the value of secondary principles is purely heuristic; and this is borne out by Mill's metaphors. 'It is a strange notion that the acknowledgement of a first principle is inconsistent with the admission of secondary ones. . . . To inform the traveller of a destination is not to forbid the use of land-marks and direction-posts on the way' (pp. 22-3). But a land-mark or signpost may on a particular occasion fail to point the best way to a destination. I may be on foot and there is an obvious short-cut across the fields; or the signposted road may be visibly blocked by floods or drifts. We should then say 'neglect the signpost'. But what happens when we cash the metaphor? The destination is the greatest happiness of the greatest number; the signpost the secondary rule. What happens when a sign-post visibly fails to point the best route? Shall we neglect it? On Urmson's interpretation Mill must say 'No, there are occasions when, though you see another route leads to the general happiness, you must follow the signpost—the secondary rule'. Similarly with the comparison (p. 23) with an almanack (which saves the navigator from having to calculate on each occasion what course to set). No problem arises if the almanack is held to be infallible. But the almanack of secondary principles does not in every case provide sailing directions leading to the maxi-mum happiness. Yet even when it does not, Mill must maintain (on Urmson's interpretation) that we should follow it.

It might be suggested to meet that difficulty, as it is by Burke and by G. E. Moore (*Principia Ethica*, p. 162), that the reason why we should follow a rule even when breaking it will visibly produce better consequences is that the rule enshrines the stored wisdom of generations of men with their experience and traditions and that the individual is therefore likely to be mistaken in his judg-ment that better consequences will result from breaking it, especially as bias or prejudice may influence his judg-ment. But it is easy to find cases where bias and preju-dice are excluded, and such a view as Moore's would prescribe a rigid adherence to rules, which no one would defend.

A further difficulty closely related to the preceding one arises when Mill tries to explain away the case where we have a duty to follow a rule when more good would be done by some alternative action. 'It may be held that it is expedient for some immediate object, some temporary purpose, to violate a rule whose observation is expedient in a much higher degree'. Thus 'it would often be expedient to obtain some object useful to ourselves or others to tell a lie' (p. 21). But Mill then goes on to argue that in fact telling the lie in such a case would not have better results than telling the truth. He has already foreshadowed his argument by calling the good results of telling the lie 'temporary' and 'immediate'. He says telling the truth will do more good in the long run for two reasons 'inasmuch as the cultivation in ourselves of a sensitive feeling on the subject of veracity is one of the most useful, and the enfeeblement of that feeling one of the most hurtful, things to which our conduct can be instrumental; and inasmuch as any, even unintentional, deviation from truth does that much towards weakening the trustworthiness of human assertion' (p. 21). Now the crucial point to notice is that Mill is here relying on the consequences of telling this particular truth now and not on the consequences of truth-telling in general.

It is perhaps worth noticing that the two arguments themselves are inconclusive, since they are the arguments usually used by utilitarians of the orthodox or non-Urmson type to explain why a rule should be kept on some occasions when more good would be done to those directly concerned by breaking it. Keeping the rule will do indirect or long-term good in two ways: (1) by strengthening in the agent the habit of keeping the rule; (2) by fostering the reliance others will place in the keeping of it. I shall discuss these arguments in the reverse order for reasons which will appear in the discussion.

Ross raised the vital difficulty for the 'fostering-reliance' argument. If my breaking of the rule is not known to anyone else, general reliance on the rule will be unaffected. In *The Right and the Good* Ross illustrated this point by what Mr. Nowell-Smith has called an instance of 'desert-island morality' (*Ethics*, p. 240). This is unfair, for Ross in his later book, *Foundations of Ethics*, gives a simple real life example. It is important to see that real life examples are frequent and easy to find. I quoted two from my own experience in my article on 'Punishment' in *Mind* (April 1939), which turns throughout on this very distinction between orthodox and Urmson-type utilitarianism with which we are here concerned, and a third in 'Moral Rules' (*Proceedings of the British Academy*, 1953). As the point is vital, I offer yet another. An ex-pupil of mine was secretary to a very rich man. His employer had ordered him to put all begging letters in the wastepaper basket unanswered. He was liberal to his chosen causes and life was too short to verify the *bona fides* of every begging letter. His employer also had a habit of leaving bundles of notes in the pockets of his suits. These the secretary regularly extracted before sending suits to be cleaned, and returned them to his employer who at once put them into another pocket uncounted. One slack morning the secretary read the begging letters out of curiosity and found among them one which made a good case. A few minutes earlier he had found a bundle of notes in a blazer pocket. He told me that he had wondered whether to pick off five of the notes and send them to the writer of the letter. 'My boss would never have known'. I asked him whether he did, and he replied 'No, it wasn't my money'. This is not a utilitarian reason; and, in particular the fact that his boss would never have known removes the 'fostering-reliance' argument. But, it may be said, there is one person who would know and that is the secretary himself, and here the utilitarian will fall back on the other argument. The secretary, if he sent the money, would enfeeble his tendency not to take other people's property and on other occasions this enfeeblement would have bad results. But this argument also is no good. For a utilitarian secondary rules are not to be applied without exception and therefore rigid habits should not be acquired. The following dialogue at a bridge table will illustrate the fallacy. I am third player on the first trick; the second player has played the ace; I hold the King. I remember I have been told that third player should play high. I whisper to my mentor standing behind me 'What do I play?' He says 'The King'. 'But it will do no good; the ace has been played'. 'Never mind that. You must play your King; otherwise you will enfeeble your tendency to play high as third player'. 'But is this rule an absolute rule?' 'No, there are exceptions'. 'What are they?' 'When it will do no good to play high.' 'But this is such a case'. 'Never mind. You must not weaken your good habits'.

There is an interesting parallel to this last point in Mill's treatment of rights. In his essay *On Liberty* he argues that a man should not be prevented from publishing his scientific opinions. He argues this on the grounds that his opinion may be true or part of the truth, in which case it will be useful for it to become known. Even if it is false it will serve the useful purpose of keeping the holders of the true opinion alert and preventing the true opinion from becoming a dead dogma. The point of special interest here is that he recognizes that some might say that a man has a right to publish his scientific opinions even if publishing them will have none of these beneficial results. His comment is 'It is proper to state that I forego any advantage which could be derived to my argument from the idea of abstract right as a thing independent of utility'. It might be supposed that he is admitting there is such an advantage. But he goes on 'I regard utility as the ultimate appeal in all ethical questions, but it must be utility in the largest sense grounded in the permanent interests of man as an intelligent being' (Everyman Edition, p. 74). He is appealing here, as in the case of truth-telling, to the long-term results of publication in the particular case. Now I have come across a little periodical devoted to maintaining that the earth is flat. It can hardly be held that this is the whole truth. That part of the truth which it might be said to enshrine (that a small part of the earth's surface is very nearly

flat) has already been included in the orthodox view.
And it is difficult to believe that the publication of this
little periodical keeps the Astronomer Royal on his toes.
Yet most of us would reject the suppression of the periodical. But we need not call this an abstract right (or a
self-evident or natural right). We can say that it is *generally* useful to have this rule and to apply it in all cases,
even though in some cases no good will accrue from its
application. This would be the Urmson interpretation,
but it does not seem to be Mill's argument.

This paper is not concerned with the rival merits of
the two types of utilitarianism. I argued that issue in my
papers on 'Punishment' (1939) and 'Moral Rules' (1953)
cited above. I have taken Mill's text as a means of shar-
pening the distinctions between them.

It is interesting that in an article entitled 'Two Concepts of Rules' (*Philosophical Review,* Vol. LXIV, Jan.
1955) Mr. J. B. Rawls discusses the same issue and illustrates his points by reference to another great utilitarian,
John Austin. He shows convincingly that Austin in his
'Lectures on Jurisprudence' (Vol. I, p. 116) states very
clearly the Urmson interpretation of utilitarianism. But
when he goes on to discuss and defend it he slides away
from it into the orthodox interpretation, just as I have
tried to show Mill does in his essay.

ON MOORE'S CRITICISMS OF MILL'S "PROOF"

BY

Mary Warnock

. . . Moore's criticism of Mill's argument here has had a considerable effect upon the subsequent history of ethics, and therefore it is worth considering both what Mill's argument was in fact meant to show, and what precisely it was of which Moore accused him.

Mill started by saying that it is impossible to prove the truth of statements about ultimate ends. 'Whatever can be proved to be good, must be so by being shown to be a means to something admitted to be good without proof.' With this of course Moore does not disagree; for Mill is simply making the distinction which it is the purpose of Moore's book to establish, between the type of ethical statement for which evidence is required and the type for which there can be no evidence. But Mill goes on, just as Moore does, to attempt to show what things are as a matter of fact good as ends. His argument here,

From *Ethics Since 1900*, by Mary Warnock. Oxford University Press, London, 1960, Home University Library. Reprinted by permission of the Oxford University Press.

as we have seen, falls into two parts: first he argues that pleasure or happiness is good as an end, and secondly, more dubiously, that it is the only thing which is good as an end. Now though Moore admits that he agrees with Mill's initial distinction between propositions which are and those which are not susceptible of proof, he does not, I think, realize that his approval of Mill ought to go further. When Mill uses the argument from the analogy between 'visible' and 'desirable' he is attempting to establish what things are good, and this, Moore constantly assures us, is a perfectly legitimate undertaking. Mill is not, that is to say, going back on his contention that it is impossible to *prove* what is good as an end. He is saying rather that if people did not already regard some things as ends, and therefore desire them, it would be impossible to prove to them that these things really were ends. 'How is it possible to prove', he asks, 'that health is good?' The answer is that it is *not* possible to prove it; but the fact is that everybody knows that it is good, and shows this by desiring it. When he says 'the sole evidence it is possible to produce that anything is desirable, is that people actually do desire it' he is repeating the same point. 'The sole evidence' is not evidence in the sense of *proof* that something is good, but it is evidence simply that people already know, without waiting for proof, that it is good. In the very next sentence, Mill makes this clear: 'If the end which the utilitarian doctrine proposes to itself were not, in theory and practice, acknowledged to be an end, nothing could ever convince any person that it was so.' The question of proving what is an ultimate end does not arise; but you can find out what people recognize as ultimate ends by finding out what they desire. What they desire, Mill goes on to say, is happiness. I cannot see anything wrong or fallacious about this. . . . If Mill had first defined 'good' as 'desirable' and had then gone on to define 'desirable' as 'desired', he would no doubt have been open to criticism. But it was no part of his interest to define 'good' or 'desirable' at all. Indeed, if anything,

his remarks about the impossibility of proving propositions concerned with ultimate ends would suggest that
he agreed with Moore that 'good' was indefinable, though
it need not mean this. The fact is that the question of
definition was never raised by him at all. He was interested in discovering the underlying principles of ethical
conduct, and not in defining ethical terms. His introduction of the concept of 'what is desired' was, as I hope I
have shown, due to the very fact that you cannot prove
what is or is not good. All that you have to go on is what
people think is good, what, that is, they have always
thought worth desiring. What they have always thought
worth desiring is what they have in fact desired. Mill's
procedure here is like Hume's, who argues that the qualities which we have come to regard as virtuous are those
which we in fact find are desired for the sake of the
general well-being of society; and it is not so very unlike
Moore's own procedure when, in the last chapter of *Principia Ethica*, he turns to consider the question what
things are intrinsically good. In each case the question
at issue is: What is it that people value most highly?
Mill's perhaps unduly simple answer is, happiness. Mill
cannot, therefore, be rightly accused of trying to define
'good'; and this accusation must be at least part of what
Moore meant by his statement that the naturalistic fallacy had been committed, since we have been told over
and over again that the naturalistic fallacy consists in
just this. But, even if Mill had been trying to define
'good', and had therefore offered 'What is desired' as a
definition of 'desirable', which he did not, I think that
Moore would have been unduly hard on him. If the
argument comes down to a discussion of the meanings
of words, then, though the analogy between the meanings of 'desirable' and 'visible' is not close, still the distinction between 'desired' and 'desirable' is not so clear and
sharp as Moore suggests. When house agents speak of
houses as desirable they do not mean that these houses
are such that we ought to desire them. Very often 'de-

sirable' means something like 'What any sane person would desire', and if this is what it means, then the relevance of the consideration of what sane people do in fact desire is at once obvious. But this defence of Mill should not be taken very seriously, for I hope I have said enough to show why I do not believe that for Mill the question was one of the meanings of words at all. . . .

Mill had not only to establish that pleasure or happiness was desirable in itself, but also that it was the *only* thing desirable in itself. Mill admits that whether or not this second proposition is true is a psychological matter, and therefore his answer is supposed to be based on empirical evidence. But he concludes by saying that 'to desire anything except in proportion as the idea of it is pleasant, is a physical and metaphysical impossibility'. This is rather mysterious. 'Metaphysical impossibility' suggests that it is supposed to be necessarily true that we desire only pleasure. But if this is so, it is hard to see how the question whether we do or not could be said to be one of psychology. The trouble arises largely, it seems to me, because of the extreme difficulty of using expressions such as 'pleasure' or 'for the sake of pleasure' intelligibly. There is in fact no contradiction between saying that we desire something for its own sake and that we desire it for the sake of pleasure, in at least one possible meaning of that expression. Moore is very savage with Mill for saying just this.

> Pray consider a moment [he says (p. 72)] what this contemptible nonsense really means. 'Money', says Mill, 'is only desired as a means to happiness'. Perhaps so, but what then? 'Why,' says Mill, 'money is undoubtedly desired for its own sake.' 'Yes, go on,' say we. 'Well,' says Mill, 'if money is desired for its own sake, it must be desirable as an end-in-itself: I have said so myself.' 'Oh,' say we, 'but you also just now said that it was only desirable as a means.' 'I own I did,' says Mill, 'but I will try to patch up matters, by saying that what is only a

means to an end is the same thing as a part of that end. I daresay the public won't notice.' And the public haven't noticed.

Once again, I feel inclined to defend Mill. The language of means and ends would doubtless be better dropped, since it does suggest just the incompatibility which Moore finds. But there is no need to employ it. If Mill had instead talked about doing things 'for the sake of pleasure or happiness' and 'for their own sake' then I should find nothing ludicrous in his remarks. This, then, is one part of Moore's criticism of Mill's argument to show that only pleasure is desired. He argues that Mill confuses what is a means to an end with what is part of an end. I do not think this criticism is well founded. On the other hand, it is because one can speak of pleasure in these ways that it can be made to look plausible to say we desire nothing except pleasure. For whatever end anybody suggests as a possible object of desire it is always open to Mill to say that pleasure is part of that end, though the end *is* desired for its own sake. And because it is open to him in every case whatever to do this, he is really landed with an uninteresting tautology. Pleasure turns out to be 'whatever we desire', and therefore, necessarily, whatever we desire turns out to be pleasure. This necessity, which is the necessity of tautology, is, I suspect, what Mill was referring to, confusingly, as the *metaphysical* impossibility of desiring anything but pleasure.

ON PROVING UTILITARIANISM

BY

J. P. Day

Although Mill signally fails to prove the truth of the utility-principle, it may yet be true. But rather than investigate this question by seeking exceptions, I shall conclude by showing why his critics are dispensed from this trouble, and by simultaneously indicating a radical defect in *Utilitarianism*. Briefly, there is a far-reaching inconsistency between Mill's notion of the nature of ethical philosophy and his primary objective in the essay. According to Mill, the aim of the former, to repeat it, is "to *tell* us what are our duties, or by what test we may know them" (my italics). Mill, like Bentham, writes as a reformer and uses his standard of morality to criticize existing institutions and practices. The questions whether, or how far, his principle and its consequences square with "the morality of common sense" does not concern him. But in that case, the question of the *truth*

From *A Critical History of Western Philosophy*, edited by D. J. O'Connor, The Free Press, New York, Collier-Macmillan Limited, London. Copyright © 1964 by The Free Press of Glencoe, A Division of The Macmillan Company. Reprinted by permission.

of his principle cannot arise—though that of its goodness certainly does. Hence, Mill's main aim in *Utilitarianism*, which is to prove the truth of the utility-principle, is misconceived, and any attempt by a critic to establish its truth or falsity would be misconceived also.

TWO MOOT ISSUES IN MILL'S *UTILITARIANISM*

BY

Maurice Mandelbaum

In the present paper I shall be concerned with two points at which I believe Mill's *Utilitarianism* is frequently misinterpreted. The first, which is a relatively new issue, is whether Mill should be regarded as subscribing to a "rule-utilitarianism," rather than to that unrestricted form of utilitarianism which is presently termed "act-utilitarianism."[1] The second is whether Mill's proof of the hedonistic principle does in fact com-

---

[1] This issue was first raised in its present form by J. O. Urmson in "The Interpretation of the Moral Philosophy of J. S. Mill," *Philosophical Quarterly*, vol. 3 (1953), pp. 33–39 (reprinted above). Urmson's interpretation was discussed by J. D. Mabbott in "Interpretations of Mill's Utilitarianism," *Philosophical Quarterly*, vol. 6 (1956), pp. 115–20 (reprinted above). Another article on the same topic, but only incidentally concerned with Mill, was J. J. C. Smart's "Extreme and Restricted Utilitarianism," *Philosophical Quarterly*, vol. 6 (1956), pp. 344–54. In the many subsequent discussions of rule-utilitarianism there has been little attempt to deal with the issue of whether Urmson was in fact correct in attributing to Mill the position which he did.

mit the elementary blunder which most critics, following
G. E. Moore, have been ready to assume that it does.[2]
In discussing each of these points I shall make more extensive use of Mill's other writings than has been usual
among commentators. As I have elsewhere sought to establish, it is a mistake to attempt to interpret *Utilitarianism* apart from a consideration of Mill's less well known
ethical writings, and especially apart from his psychological theory and his explicit rejection of Bentham's
psychology.[3]

I

Mill and Rule-Utilitarianism

Whether or not Mill is to be interpreted as a rule-
utilitarian depends in part on how we are to characterize
rule-utilitarianism. As we shall finally see, our answers
may be different (though only in part) if we characterize
that theory as primarily concerned with "a method for
determining what acts are right," or if we characterize
it as a way of saying how, in a particular case, the use
of a moral predicate such as "right" is to be justified.[4] I

---

[2] There have been a number of recent re-examinations of this
issue; for example, Carl Wellman, "A Reinterpretation of Mill's
Proof," *Ethics*, vol. 49 (1958–59) and E. W. Hall's article reprinted above.

[3] Cf. "On Interpreting Mill's *Utilitarianism*," *Journal of the
History of Philosophy*, vol. VI, No. 1 (January 1968), pp.
35–46.

[4] According to R. B. Brandt, the primary purpose of rule-
utilitarianism is to offer "a method for determining what acts are
right" (*Ethical Theory* [Englewood Cliffs, 1959], p. 253). However, his formal definition of the position (p. 396 f.) would be
wholly compatible with the second interpretation of what rule-
utilitarianism aims to do. A considerable diversity in the definition
of rule-utilitarianism has in fact developed, but the consequent
differences in usage are not, I believe, directly relevant to my
present aim. I wish to establish what Mill's position actually was.
How one then labels that position is not of primary interest to me.

shall take its primary meaning to be the latter. In so doing I am (I believe) in agreement with the usage of J. O. Urmson, whose views I wish to discuss. This conformity with his usage can be seen in the first of the four propositions which he gives as characterizing rule-utilitarianism:

A particular action is justified as being right by showing that it is in accord with some moral rule. It is shown to be wrong by showing that it transgresses some moral rule.[5]

Taken alone, this proposition concerning the moral justification of particular actions would of course fail to characterize rule-utilitarianism. To constitute a species of utilitarianism at all, the notion of utility (that is, of the general welfare, or the maximization of good consequences) must be introduced. This Urmson does in the second of his propositions:

A moral rule is shown to be correct by showing that the recognition of that rule promotes the ultimate end.[6]

The ultimate end is, of course, utility.

That Mill did justify moral *rules* in terms of their utility, and held that there was no other way in which they could be justified, is a point on which there is agreement among all commentators. We may then take it for

---

[5] Urmson, p. 35 (p. 183, above). To be sure, Urmson also appeals to rule-utilitarianism as a method for determining what acts are right, but this (I take it) follows from the proposition quoted above.

[6] Urmson, p. 35 (p. 183, above). Mabbott points out in his rejoinder to this article (*op. cit.*, p. 115 [p. 190, above]) that two slight emendations must be made in this second proposition if it is to be accurate.

I shall not discuss the last two of Urmson's four propositions since I am here concerned only with Mill's position, and as we shall see that position is not in fact consonant with the first of the four propositions.

granted that Mill's thought conforms to Urmson's second proposition. Does it, however, conform to the first? Here the crucial question is whether it was Mill's view that moral predicates such as "right" and "wrong" are to be applied to particular actions *because* these actions were instances of what specific moral rules prescribed or proscribed. Formulating this question by means of a familiar technical term, one may ask whether, according to Mill, rule-conformity is in itself "a right-making characteristic" and rule-infringement "a wrong-making characteristic." While some ethical writers would surely accept a position of this sort (one thinks immediately of W. G. Sumner), I have found no passage in Mill that can be fairly interpreted as committing him to it.[7]

---

[7] Urmson challenges those who do not regard Mill as a rule-utilitarian to explain a passage in *Utilitarianism* in which it is held that the differentiating characteristic of moral acts, as distinct from expedient or inexpedient acts not regarded as "moral," is to be found in the notion of punishment. Cf. Ch. V, par. 14 (p. 45); cf. Urmson, pp. 36–37 (pp. 184–86, above).

In reply, I should like to point out that in this passage Mill never mentions specific moral rules. He says: "we do not call anything wrong unless we mean to imply that a person ought to be punished in some way or other for doing it." He then explicitly recognizes three classes of such punishments: punishment by law, by the opinions of one's fellows, and by one's own conscience. Now, in so far as punishment by law is concerned, it is natural enough to equate the justification of such punishment with the agent's breach of some specific rule. However, I see no reason to interpret Mill as holding that the sanctions of one's conscience *do* operate only when specific rules are broken, nor that they *should* operate only under these conditions. (Nor do I believe that he would hold this position with respect to the opinions of one's fellows.) Thus, this passage, taken by itself, does not (in my opinion) establish the fact that Mill should be regarded as a rule-utilitarian. My doubts on this score seem to me fortified by a letter that Mill had previously written to W. G. Ward (cf. *Letters of John Stuart Mill*, edited by Elliot, vol. I, pp. 229–31). In that letter he analyzes the meaning of "ought" and refers it to punish-

To be sure, one might use the term "justify" in a weaker sense than the above, when speaking of justifying moral judgments through moral rules. For example, if you ask me why I praise or condemn a particular action, I may, in my answer, tacitly appeal to some particular moral precept or maxim: I may say, "it was an unusually kind thing to have done," or I may say "it was practically stealing." A response of this sort might be taken as offering a justification of my original judgment; in that case the precept to which appeal was made would have been taken as serving as a justifying ground for my praise or condemnation. However, such a response would only be seen as a justification by those who not only accepted the precept as itself being a justified precept, but regarded it as a precept applicable to this case, and one which was not overridden by any other considerations. In thus limiting the conditions under which the precept or rule serves as a justification of the judgment, one is using "justification" in a much weaker sense than is usual in ethical theory. Used in this way, it does little more than provide a clue as to what particular aspect of the action led me to praise or condemn it.[8] Thus, if it is to count as a justification it does so only because it is linked with other premises relevant to the moral assessment of the act in question. Under these circumstances, the function which a general moral maxim or rule performs is to indicate the locus of one of the main right-making or wrong-making aspects of the action, our expectation being that this will suffice to evoke agreement on the part

---

ment. However, the punishment which he explicitly mentions is that of the "internal and disinterested feeling" of conscience.

Furthermore, exegesis of this passage aside, if one turns to Mill's lengthier discussion of precisely the same problem in his edition of his father's *Analysis of the Phenomena of the Human Mind,* one sees that his account does not in the least conform to rule-utilitarianism. (Cf. the last part of his note to his father's chapter on "The Acts of Our Fellow-Creatures," vol. II, pp. 324–26.)

[8] Cf. my article, "On the Use of Moral Principles," *Journal of Philosophy,* vol. 53 (1956), pp. 662–70.

of those who have asked us, or who might ask us, to justify our judgment. In this weaker sense of "justify," Mill
does hold that general maxims can be used to help justify
a particular moral judgment.[9] However, on his view, one
of the tacit premises which is involved in such a justification is the acceptance of the principle of utility: one
cannot, on that view, justify a judgment by appealing to
a rule unless at the same time one takes that rule to be
justified by its utility. To separate the justification of
particular moral judgments from the justification of the
precepts which they instantiate is not, so far as I can see,
a position which Mill ever adopted; though this is what
Urmson's argument demands.[10]

---

[9] Examples of this are frequently suggested in *Utilitarianism*,
and two of his general statements on the need for subsidiary principles provide evidence that such was his view. Cf. *Utilitarianism*,
Ch. II, the next to the last and the last paragraphs (pp. 22–23
and p. 24). (In citing Mill's *Utilitarianism*, I shall make use of
Mill's paragraphing, so that the reader may readily find the passage regardless of edition he uses. I add the pagination of the
Everyman edition.) However, the clearest expression of it comes
in his praise of Bentham in the essay devoted to attacking the
doctrines of Whewell. Mill says:

> Bentham was a moralist of another stamp. With him, the first
> use to be made of his ultimate principle, was to erect on it, as a
> foundation, secondary or middle principles, capable of serving
> as premises for a body of ethical doctrine not derived from
> existing opinions, but fitted to be their test. . . . He was the
> first who, keeping clear of the direct and indirect influences of
> all doctrines inconsistent with it, deduced a set of subordinate
> generalities from utility alone, and by these tested all particular
> questions. This great service, previous to which a scientific doc
> trine of ethics on the foundation of utility was impossible, has
> been performed by Bentham (though with a view to the exi
> gencies of legislation more than to those of morals) in a manner,
> as far as it goes, eminently meritorious, and so as to indicate
> the way to complete the scheme (*Dissertations and Discussions*,
> vol. III, p. 143).

[10] In "Two Concepts of Rules," *Philosophical Review*, vol. 64
(1955), pp. 3–32, John Rawls distinguishes between a "summary"

Mill's general position (which we shall shortly supplement with further details) can best be made clear through two major passages which Urmson fails to analyze. One is in the opening paragraphs of *Utilitarianism,* in which Mill contrasts the role of first principles in the sciences and their role in morals; the second is in the concluding chapter of the *Logic,* where Mill addresses himself to the differences between the sciences and the practical arts.

The point of the passage in *Utilitarianism* is clear, in spite of the fact that Mill uses qualifying phrases such as "one might think." After noting the lack of agreement concerning the ultimate principles of morality, he proceeds:

> It is true that similar confusion and uncertainty and, in some cases, similar discordance exist respecting the first principles of all the sciences, not excepting that which is deemed the most certain of them—mathematics, without much impairing, generally indeed without impairing at all, the trustworthiness of the conclusions of those sciences. An apparent anomaly, the explanation of which is that the detailed doctrines of a science are not usually deduced from, nor depend for their evidence upon, what are called its first principles. . . . The truths which are ultimately accepted as the first principles of a science are really the last results of metaphysical analysis practiced on the elementary notions with which the science is conversant; and their relation to the science is not that of foundations to an edifice, but of roots to a tree, which may perform their office equally well though they be never dug down to

---

conception of rules, and a "practice" conception. In terms of this distinction, Urmson's interpretation of Mill makes him an upholder of the practice conception, whereas my interpretation (with one qualification, to be explained below) makes him an upholder of the summary conception. Rawls, it may be noted, interprets Mill as an upholder of the summary view (cf. p. 21 of his article).

and exposed to the light. But though in science the particular truths precede the general theory, the contrary might be expected to be the case with a practical art such as morals or legislation. All action is for the sake of some end, and rules of action, it seems natural to suppose, must take their whole character and color from the end to which they are subservient. When we engage in a pursuit, a clear and precise conception of what we are pursuing would seem to be the first thing we need, instead of the last we are to look forward to. A test of right and wrong must be the means, one would think, of ascertaining what is right or wrong, and not a consequence of having already ascertained it.

That the qualifying phrases in this passage are not to be taken as indicating reservations or a disclaimer on Mill's part, can be seen from the next paragraph, which must be read as a continuation of the same argument. Mill there refers to those who appeal to a native faculty of conscience as the arbiter of right and wrong in specific cases, and he argues against them that morals must be a matter not of direct perception, but of reasoning and general rules.[11] However, he remains dissatisfied with the appeal to a series of rules unless they be shown to be exhaustive, and unless they be shown to have a fixed order, or to derive from one first principle. Thus, he argues for the necessity of one fundamental moral standard as the basis for our concrete judgments of right and wrong.

If it should be doubted that this is the point which he is seeking to make in these paragraphs, one need merely turn to the following paragraph in which Mill raises

---

[11] It is at this point in the argument that Mill makes the statements cited by Urmson (p. 35 [above, p. 183]) as the first of his four illustrations of rule-utilitarianism in Mill. However, as the context makes clear (as I am about to suggest), Mill immediately goes on to attack any attempt to rest our moral justification of actions on an unco-ordinated set of moral rules.

the question of why, if a single principle must serve as the basis for our judgments of conduct, the absence of any clear recognition of such a standard has not had more deleterious effects than it apparently has. To this he answers: "whatever steadiness or consistency these moral beliefs have attained has been mainly due to the tacit influence of a standard not recognized."[12] Bearing this statement in mind, the fact that we often find that a particular moral judgment in a concrete case is ostensibly being justified through the appeal to some moral rule, should not preclude us from saying that justification by such a rule only carries conviction where, behind it, there is a tacit appeal to the standard without which the rule itself would lack justification.

The second passage in which there is a general discussion of the same subject is, as I have said, in the concluding chapter of the *System of Logic*, a chapter entitled "Of the Logic of Practice, or Art; Including Morality and Policy." In this place Mill explicitly says:

In all branches of practical business, there are cases in which individuals are bound to conform their practice to a pre-established rule, while there are others in which it is part of their task to find or construct the rule by which they are to govern their conduct. The first, for example, is the case of a judge, under a definite written code. The judge is not called upon to determine what course would be intrinsically the most advisable in the particular case in hand, but only within what rule of law it falls.[13]

---

12 *Utilitarianism*, Ch. I, par. 4 (p. 3). This statement must, I believe, be taken as Mill's explanation of the fact (which was acknowledged by him in the preceding paragraph) that utilitarians and apriorists agree to a significant extent concerning specific moral rules. Thus, Urmson's use of Mill's recognition of this agreement is misleading.

For another passage in which Mill cites this agreement, cf. *Dissertations and Discussions*, vol. I, pp. 409–10.

13 *System of Logic*, Bk. VI, Ch. XII, Sect. 2. [This passage is to be found in all editions of the *Logic*, and appears as Section 2

In contrast to the judge, Mill cites the legislator:

> As the judge has laws for his guidance, so the legislator has rules, and maxims of policy; but it would be a manifest error to suppose that the legislator is bound by these maxims in the same manner as the judge is bound by the laws, and that all he has to do is argue down from them to the particular case, as the judge does from the laws. The legislator is bound to take into consideration the reasons or grounds of the maxim.

And it is clear that for Mill the proper function of the legislator can only be fulfilled by reasoning in terms of the ultimate end which legislation is to serve:

> To the judge, the rule, once positively ascertained, is final; but the legislator, or other practitioner, who goes by rules rather than by their reasons, like the old-fashioned German tacticians who were vanquished by Napoleon, or the physician who preferred that his patients should die by rule rather than recover contrary to it, is rightly judged to be a mere pedant, and the slave of his formulas.[14]

This contrast between the judge and the legislator should be borne in mind when one reads the contrast which Mill later drew (1863) between Austin and Bentham. In his essay "Austin on Jurisprudence," Mill says:

> Mr. Austin's subject was Jurisprudence, Bentham's was Legislation.

---

of the concluding chapter. However, Book VI originally had only eleven chapters, the chapter on the Science of History having been added in the fifth edition (1862).]

In the passage quoted above, Mill is saying that the judge must adopt what Rawls referred to as the "practice" conception of rules. However, as Rawls points out, this is not Mill's own view of the place of rules in *moral* justification. (Cf. above, note 10.)

14 *System of Logic*, Bk. VI, Ch. XII, Sect. 2.

The purpose of Bentham was to investigate principles from which to decide what laws ought to exist—what legal rights, and legal duties or obligations, are fit to be established among mankind. This was also the ultimate end of Mr. Austin's speculations; but the subject of his special labors was theoretically distinct, though subsidiary, and practically indispensable, to the former. It was what may be called the logic of law, as distinguished from its morality or expediency (*Dissertations and Discussions*, vol. IV, p. 160).

This surely in part explains why it is so much easier to find clear cases of the "practice" conception of rules in Austin. However, as Rawls points out (pp. 19–21), even Austin is probably not to be characterized as having rejected the "summary" conception.

Originally, in the first edition of the *Logic*, Mill explicitly discussed how the problem of moral decision was to be construed in terms of the contrast between judge and legislator. He said:

Questions of practical morality are partly similar to those which are to be decided by a judge, and partly to those which have to be solved by a legislator or administrator. In some things our conduct ought to conform itself to a prescribed rule; in others, it is to be guided by the best judgment which can be formed by the merits of the particular case.

He then proceeded to state in what kinds of cases morality consists in the simple observance of a rule:

The cases in question are those in which, although any rule which can be formed is probably . . . more or less imperfectly adapted to a portion of the cases which it comprises, there is still a necessity that some rule, of a nature simple enough to be easily understood and remembered, should not only be laid down for guidance, but universally observed, in order that the various persons concerned may know what they have to expect: the inconvenience of uncertainty on their part being a greater evil than that which may possibly arise, in a minority of cases, from the imperfect adaptation of the rule to those cases.

Such, for example, is the rule of veracity; that of not infringing the legal rights of others; and so forth.[15]

And in this connection we may note that in *Utilitarianism* Mill cites breach of friendship and breach of promises (two types of case in which, as he points out, expectations count heavily) as cases in which a species of conduct is generally reprehensible apart from its specific consequences.[16]

Now, it is to be noted that in his discussion Mill explicitly limits to a single type those cases in which rules are to be followed without considering the specific circumstances under which the action is to be done. In this exceptional type of case, rules are made necessary

---

[15] This quotation, and that immediately preceding it, appear in Section 6 of the same chapter. Cf. first edition (London, 1843), vol. II, pp. 621–22.

There is no reason to suppose that Mill suppressed this passage in later editions of the *Logic* because he disagreed with it. It is wholly consistent with the other passages which I have cited from the same chapter, and which Mill allowed to remain in all editions of the *Logic*. And, as I am claiming, it is wholly consistent with *Utilitarianism* as well. Rather, its deletion is correlated with an enlarged discussion of the relations of science and art, which constitute the theme of the chapter as a whole. Furthermore, one may note that, in the first edition, Section 5 ended with fulsome praise of Comte, whereas the changed version of Section 6 (including a new Section 7) are to be read as critical of Comte. It is their theme that "ought" cannot be reduced to "is," "should be" to "will be," and that there is "a Philosophia Prima peculiar to Art, as there is one which belongs to Science." This contention is clearly to be taken as a rectification of Mill's former praise of Comte. However, Mill's discussion of the role of first principles in Art, and (more specifically) in Morality, in no wise contradicts the views on *this* topic which he had earlier expressed.

[16] Cf. *Utilitarianism*, Ch. V, fifth paragraph from the end (p. 56 f.).

in order that individuals may be clear as to what sort of conduct they may expect of others. Bearing this in mind, it would surely be false to interpret him as holding, *tout court*, that in these cases a judgment of rightness or wrongness was justified *because* the action fell under a rule. To capture his meaning we should surely have to say that abiding by a rule, rather than consulting circumstances, was justified only because the action was one of a special class of actions in which it was *for the general good* that all persons act in accordance with set rules. Thus, as justification of the use of the predicates "right" and "wrong" it is not sufficient, even in these special cases, only to cite the relevance of the rule to the action: the rule must be understood to be a socially necessary rule. And it is to be noted that Mill does not shrink from saying that there are exceptional cases in which even *such* rules may be abrogated.[17]

With respect to all cases in which the foregoing condition does not obtain, Mill is quite explicit in advocating the view that it is the general principle of utility, not the specific rule, which serves as the morally justifying factor with respect to particular actions. He says:

> In cases, however, in which there does not exist a necessity for a common rule, to be acknowledged and relied upon as the basis of social life; where we are at liberty

---

[17] Immediately after the passage last quoted from the *Logic*, Mill admits the possibility that it might be permitted to deviate from the rule in cases "of a very peculiar and extreme nature." And in *Utilitarianism* he points out that even with respect to cases in which we should normally say that justice was at stake, it is in some cases morally justifiable to abrogate a person's rights (cf. Ch. V, next to last paragraph [p. 59]). Finally, it is to be noted that in a letter in which Mill argues that the obligation of veracity depends upon the social utility of their being such a rule, he nonetheless cites the fact that we must, in particular cases, look to the particular results which are to be achieved. (This letter—which is not entirely clear, since we do not have the objections to which it is an answer—is to be found in Elliot's edition of the *Letters of John Stuart Mill*, vol. II, p. 73.)

to inquire what is the most moral course under the particular circumstances of the case, without reference to the authorized expectations of other people; there the Method of Ethics cannot differ materially from the method of every other department of practice. Like other arts, it sets out from a general principle, or original major premiss, enunciative of its particular end.[18]

And this end is, for Mill, that which is defined by the principle of utility.

In the light of these passages it is hard to find grounds for saying that there is any type of case in which Mill would hold that rule-conformity is, by itself, a justifying ground of obligation. Why then can one find passages in *Utilitarianism* which seem to provide justification for attempting to ascribe rule-utilitarianism to Mill? The answer to this query is, I believe, to be found in the same chapter of the *Logic* from which our other evidence has been taken. There Mill says that *as a practical matter* in actual deliberations, a particular rule or maxim may sometimes be helpful in the following way:

> [It] may very properly serve as an admonition that a certain mode of action has been found by ourselves and others to be well adapted to the cases of most common occurrence; so that if it be unsuitable to the case in hand, the reason of its being so will be likely to arise from some unusual circumstances.[19]

However, this admission of the usefulness of rules in practice is in effect a concession on the part of Mill, for it is introduced only after he has said:

> By a wise practitioner . . . rules of conduct will only be considered provisional. Being made for the most numerous

---

[18] This is also from Section 6 of the early editions of the last chapter of the *Logic*.

[19] From Section 3 of the concluding chapter of the *Logic*. (This section is to be found in the same form in all editions.)

cases, or for those of most ordinary occurrence, they point out the manner in which it will be least perilous to act, where time or means do not exist for analysing the actual circumstances of the case, or where we cannot trust our judgment in estimating them. But they do not at all supersede the propriety of going through (when circumstances permit) the scientific process for framing a rule from the data of the particular case before us.

This passage makes it clear that Mill should not be classed as a rule-utilitarian, even if one were to characterize rule-utilitarianism as a theory primarily concerned with a method of saying what acts are right. Nonetheless, the content of these passages serves to suggest why, in the second chapter of *Utilitarianism,* there are a number of places in which Mill emphasizes the usefulness of secondary principles in morality. In that chapter, it will be recalled, he was replying to those who had criticized the principle of utility. Among their criticisms were charges that the utilitarian standard was not (for various reasons) practically applicable. It is in this connection that Mill would obviously feel himself justified in pointing to the practical use which can be made of ordinary moral rules. However, the utility of secondary principles in affording rule-of-thumb guidance does not suggest that the use of such rules is a necessary condition for deciding which acts are morally right acts. Nor did Mill hold that there is any case in which knowing that an act conforms to a specific rule is a sufficient condition for knowing it to be a right act—we must first know that the rule is itself a justified rule, as is true in the case of justice. Thus, even if we were to follow R. B. Brandt in his characterization of rule-utilitarianism as a theory which "consists primarily of the proposal of a method for determining what acts are right,"[20] Mill should not be classified as a rule-utilitarian. And if rule-

---

[20] *Ethical Theory,* p. 253.

utilitarianism holds that "a particular action is *justified* as being right by showing that it is in accord with some moral rule," then Mill cannot, on any grounds whatever, be identified with that position.

II

The Proof of Hedonism

In Mill's critical examination of Bentham's ethical theory, he found it a major weakness that Bentham had failed to offer any positive argument for his utilitarianism, relying instead on a rejection of alternative principles.[21] Furthermore, Mill criticized Bentham for an inability to treat opposed positions with adequate sympathy and understanding.[22] Such a charge cannot with justice be leveled against Mill, who was generally able to appreciate why the theories of his opponents seemed convincing to honest and enlightened men. Nonetheless, he was no more inclined than was Bentham to test a moral theory through its conformity with judgments and practices which were widely accepted: he wished to find a standard, criterion, or test—the terms were

---

[21] Cf. "Remarks on Bentham's Philosophy" in J. B. Schneewind (ed.): *Mill's Ethical Writings,* New York, 1965, pp. 46–47.

It is usually overlooked that Mill wrote two essays on Bentham. The first, "Remarks on Bentham's Philosophy," was anonymous (but is mentioned in Mill's *Autobiography*); it was published in 1833 as an appendix to E. L. Bulwer's *England and the English*. Fortunately, it is now readily available in the collection cited above. Mill's second essay, which was simply entitled "Bentham" is the well-known companion piece to his essay on Coleridge; it will be cited as it appears in Mill's *Dissertations and Discussions,* published in five volumes in 1874.

For a discussion of the relation of Mill's thought to Bentham's, see my recent article in the *Journal of the History of Philosophy,* as cited in note 3.

[22] Cf. "Bentham," *Dissertations and Discussions,* vol. I, p. 370 and p. 375.

equivalent for him[23]—by means of which those judgments and practices which were morally right could be shown to be so, and those which were wrong could be legitimately condemned. It was to such a standard that he referred when he used phrases such as "the foundation of morality" or "the fundamental principle of morality and the source of moral obligation."[24] This standard or test was the principle of utility, and it is with Mill's attempt to establish that principle—or, rather, the hedonistic aspect of that principle—that we are now concerned.[25]

Mill had one basic *negative* argument which he frequently used when he was arguing for the principle of utility. It consisted in the charge that those who rejected the principle would be forced to rely upon a theory of knowledge which was erroneous. In most instances, Mill identified this erroneous theory as the a priori view, but it was not only the rationalist appeal to a priori insights that was the object of his attacks. In a passage to which

---

[23] Among the instances in which he uses "standard" in *Utilitarianism,* cf. Ch. II, par. 10 (p. 11) and par. 19 (p. 17); for his use of "criterion," cf. Ch. I, par. 1 (p. 1) and Ch. IV, par. 9 (p. 36); in the latter passage he also uses the term "test," as he does in Ch. II, par. 19 (p. 17). All three are also used as equivalent terms in his other works.

[24] For these phrases, cf. *Utilitarianism,* Ch. I, par. 1 (p. 1) and par. 4 (p. 3), respectively.

[25] In the present article I shall not deal with Mill's attempted proof of the *universalistic* aspect of the principle of utility. His attempt in Ch. IV, par. 3 (p. 32 f.) to establish the desirability of the general happiness seems to me to fail, as he has formulated it. Nor do I believe that his later explication of his argument (*Letters of John Stuart Mill,* ed. by Elliot, vol. II, p. 116) extricates him from the difficulty.

If the purpose of the present article were to defend Mill's moral theory, I should of course have to deal with this question. However, it does not seem to me to affect the main issues with respect to which Mill has been misinterpreted, and I shall not discuss it here.

we have already called attention in criticizing Urmson,[26] Mill linked any appeal to a native faculty of conscience (that is, any belief in a moral sense) with the apriorist's claim that certain rules of conduct are self-evidently correct. The connection between these two dissimilar doctrines, and the sense in which they may be said to form a single philosophic school, is that both are "nativistic": both appeal to some sort of native, inborn capacity to distinguish moral truths, whereas utilitarianism holds that moral discriminations are to be accounted for through the effects of experience.[27] One of the discussions in which it is clear that Mill is concerned to attack nativism as such, and not merely one or another of its variant forms, is to be found in his article on Sedgwick's *Discourse*:

> It is a fact in human nature, that we have moral judgments and moral feelings. . . . Concerning their reality there is no dispute. But there are two theories respecting the origin of these phenomena, which have divided philosophers from the earliest ages of philosophy. One is,

[26] *Utilitarianism,* Ch. I, par. 3 (p. 2).

[27] From the point of view of ethical theory the two schools also form one class, which is to be differentiated from utilitarianism: neither appeals to the *consequences* of actions in determining the rightness or wrongness of those actions.

It is to be noted that Mill not infrequently conflated this specifically ethical characterization of his opponents with his epistemological charges against them. Although the two sets of objections do not actually have any necessary connection with one another (as one can see if one calls to mind various forms of noncognitivism), Mill failed to see that it was possible to abandon nativism and *not* hold that actions are designated as right or wrong on the basis of their consequences. We shall, I think, better understand Mill's failure in this respect if we recall that he assumed (as the opening paragraph of *Utilitarianism* clearly shows) that there *must be* some universally valid standard or test of morality, and that it is the business of ethical thought to determine the nature of that standard.

that the distinction between right and wrong is an ultimate
and inexplicable fact; that we perceive this distinction, as
we perceive the distinction of colors, by a peculiar faculty;
and that the pleasures and pains, the desires and aversions, consequent upon this perception, are all ultimate
facts in our nature, as much so as the pleasures and pains,
or desires and aversions, of which sweet or bitter tastes,
pleasing or grating sounds are the object. This is called
the theory of the moral sense, or of moral instincts, or of
eternal and immutable morality, or of intuitive principles
of morality, or by many other names; to the differences
between which, those who adopt the theory often attach
great importance, but which, for our present purpose, may
all be considered as equivalent.[28]

In discussing what sort of theory stands opposed to these
unsatisfactory beliefs, Mill cites only one example: the
theory of utility. And time and again he returns to this
contrast, in which only utilitarianism is cited as an alternative to the various forms of nativism.[29] Since it
was Mill's most basic epistemological conviction that
nativism was fundamentally mistaken even in those
areas, such as mathematics and logic, in which it appeared to have its greatest strength,[30] the fact that his
opponents were committed to that theory provided him
with what he took to be a strong negative argument in
favor of his own position.

In addition to using this very general argument that
ethical theories other than utilitarianism rest on false
epistemological assumptions, Mill attacked these theories
by claiming that whatever acceptability their principles

---

[28] *Dissertations and Discussions,* vol. I, p. 148.

[29] As examples, see "Remarks on Bentham," p. 316; in Schneewind, p. 47. Also, *Dissertations and Discussions,* vol. III, pp.
137–39, and vol. IV, pp. 106–7; and *Utilitarianism,* Ch. III, par.
7 and par. 8 (p. 28).

[30] Cf. *Autobiography,* Ch. VII, par. 4; (*Early Draft,* pp.
168–69).

possessed was dependent upon a tacit and unrecognized use of the utilitarian standard. This form of argument appears in his brief criticism of Kant's first formulation of the categorical imperative;[31] it is also present in his criticism of Whewell.[32] Furthermore, Mill brought forward what was essentially the same argument, but put in a more concrete form, when he suggested that the standards upheld by his opponents provided no guidance where practical questions were in dispute. For example, he held that if one is to adjudicate among the conflicting claims as to what is just with respect to punishment, one cannot try to do so by a direct appeal to one's conscience or to self-evident maxims: one must turn for guidance to the utilitarian standard.[33] Mill also used an analogous argument with respect to questions of moral motivation. Like most of his predecessors (and like his opponents), Mill assumed that moral philosophy must provide an answer to the question of what motives can lead men to act in accord with that which the moral standard demands.[34] What he was able to point out against his opponents was that they—no less than the utilitarians—appealed to pleasure and pain as fundamental motives in so far as the *external* sanctions of morality were concerned:[35] thus, what they were inclined to regard as ignoble motives played precisely the same role in their own systems as was the case in the utilitarian system. (And whatever noble motives were connected with the external sanctions were, he claimed, also the same.) Furthermore, Mill's argument that a person's sense of duty, which is the inner sanction of morality, is itself a *feeling* to the mind, can be interpreted as an attempt to

---

[31] *Utilitarianism*, Ch. I, par. 4 (p. 4).

[32] *Dissertations and Discussions*, vol. III, pp. 177–79.

[33] *Utilitarianism*, Ch. V, par. 27 and 28 (p. 51 f.), and following.

[34] Cf. *Utilitarianism*, Ch. III, par. 1 (p. 24).

[35] *Utilitarianism*, Ch. III, par. 3 (p. 25 f.).

show that his opponents are able to explain the efficacy of this noblest of human motives only by themselves appealing to a hedonistic psychology: to be moved by a feeling of duty is to respond to the immediate pleasure or pain of the ideas to which that feeling attaches.[36] Thus, once again, what his opponents claim turns out to be in accord with the very principles which they criticize utilitarians for upholding.

Mill makes such points only in passing, for he explicitly states that in *Utilitarianism* he is not concerned to discuss other theories, but to "attempt to contribute something toward the understanding and appreciation of the 'utilitarian' or 'happiness' theory, and toward such proof as it is susceptible of."[37] We turn, therefore, from his negative arguments to his attempted positive proof.

Mill's proof of hedonism, which he offers in Chapter IV, is often claimed to involve a confusion between normative and non-normative propositions, since he apparently attempts to show that happiness is *desirable* by showing that it is in fact *desired*. Now, regardless of how we are to interpret this famous passage in which Mill draws an analogy between proving that something is desirable and proving that a thing is either visible or audible,[38] it is necessary to note that he is *usually* very insistent on the need to distinguish between normative and factual propositions. For example, time and again one finds him distinguishing between *can* and *should*,[39]

---

[36] It is often overlooked that the theory of motivation which Mill espoused was what is usually termed "a psychological hedonism of the present moment": that it is the pleasantness-unpleasantness of present ideas, and not that of future consequences, which moves us to action. (Cf. his "Remarks on Bentham's Philosophy," and my own discussion of his psychology in the article already cited.)

[37] *Utilitarianism*, Ch. I, par. 5 (p. 4).

[38] Cf. Ch. IV, par. 3 (p. 32 f.).

[39] For example, in *Utilitarianism* he does so explicitly in Ch. II, at the end of paragraph 15 (p. 15), and implicitly in dis-

between *is* and *ought*,[40] and between the *origin* of something and its *validity* (to which he usually refers as its *binding force*).[41] Furthermore, in the fourth chapter, which is the chapter devoted to the proof of the principle of utility, the very first paragraph contains an explicit acknowledgment that the way in which one can establish a first principle of *conduct* may be different from the way in which one establishes a first principle of *knowledge*. If, then, we are not to do violence to the actual text of *Utilitarianism*, we must admit that Mill was fully aware of the distinction to be drawn between normative and factual questions. It would therefore seem necessary to interpret his proof in such a way that one is not forced to find him guilty of a wholly naïve confusion between that which is actually desired and that which is truly desirable.

It must be admitted that the charge that his proof contains such a confusion is made somewhat more plausible by his use of the analogy between the visible and the audible on the one hand, and the desirable on the other. Although (as we shall see) I do not believe this analogy

---

tinguishing between a rule of action and the motive of the action (Ch. II, par. 19 [p. 17]). He again does so implicitly when he separates the existence of habits from questions concerning the moral standard (Ch. IV, next to last paragraph [p. 38]).

[40] For example, in the later editions of the *Logic*, Bk. VI, Ch. XII, Sect. 6. It should also be noted that such a distinction is at least implicit in every criticism of a social custom, and it comes out very strongly throughout Mill's criticism of Whewell (cf. *Dissertations and Discussions*, vol. III, p. 154 f.).

[41] A clear and explicit example is to be found in his treatment of the sentiment attaching to our idea of justice (cf. *Utilitarianism*, Ch. V, par. 2 [p. 38 f.], *et pass.*). The same distinction is equally sharply drawn in a letter to Thornton (*Letters of John Stuart Mill*, ed. by Elliot, vol. I, pp. 291–92), and in his review of Blakey (*Monthly Repository*, vol. 7 [1833], p. 666). (The latter passage is also to be found in Schneewind, *Mill's Ethical Writings*, p. 70.)

to be misleading in every respect, there is certainly at least one respect in which the desirable is not to be compared with the visible or the audible. This can be seen in noting that it is *not* a sufficient proof of the desirability of an object to show that the object is sometimes actually desired, although it is regarded as a sufficient proof of the visibility of an object that it is sometimes actually seen. However, I do not believe that the point which Mill may be assumed to have been making is really damaged by this flaw in the analogy. To show this, I need merely point out that in speaking of what men desire, Mill is *not* here speaking of particular, specific objects of their desires, but of what they desire as an ultimate end, as the *summum bonum*. Considering the context of the passage, it would not be unnatural for Mill to take it for granted that this would be understood by his readers. Interpreting the offending passage on the basis of this assumption, and adding in italics the phrases which would be necessary to make this meaning unambiguous even when the passage is torn out of context, what we should understand Mill to be saying is the following:

> The only proof capable of being given that an object is visible is that people actually see it. The only proof that a sound is audible is that people hear it; and so of the other sources of our experience. In like manner, I apprehend, the sole evidence it is possible to produce that anything is desirable *as an ultimate end* is that people do actually desire it *as such an end*.

And this, I submit, is precisely the way in which Mill's much maligned sentence is to be interpreted when one also takes into account the sentence which immediately follows it:

> If the end which the utilitarian doctrine proposes to itself were not, in theory and in practice, acknowledged

to be an end, nothing could ever convince any person that it was so.[42]

Now, it is to be borne in mind that Mill specifically says that in this passage he has only proved that happiness is *one* of the ends of conduct. "It has not," Mill says, "by this alone proved itself to be the sole criterion."[43] Therefore, Mill immediately proceeded to ask whether there were any other ends which men desired as ultimate ends; if there were, then his argument would also involve holding these ends to be intrinsically desirable. Now, in making this examination of other possible ultimate ends, Mill apparently thought it sufficient to consider the case of virtue. That he should take virtue to be a possible end in itself, and an end which might be independent of happiness, was not surprising: as he himself pointed out, in common language virtue and the absence of vice are regarded as being quite different ends

---

[42] It is not essential to my interpretation to do so, but I should like to point out that it is not difficult to see how Mill came to draw the analogy between the visible and the desirable, even though this analogy is bound to be misleading in various respects.

In the first place we may note that if men did not have the capacity to see certain objects, one could scarcely argue them into acknowledging that these objects *are* visible. Similarly, Mill wishes to hold that if men did not have the capacity to find certain ends good in themselves, it would be futile to try to argue them into believing that these ends *really* were so. What Mill is concerned to show (as his own words should serve to make clear) is that there must be some form of experience with which we are directly acquainted which can serve as the source of our notion of what is desirable. This form of experience, Mill holds, is provided by our consciousness of the ends that we seek, and the ends sought by others. As he says in another place, the court of appeal in this matter is "practiced self-consciousness and self-observation, assisted by the observation of others" (*Utilitarianism*, Ch. IV, par. 10 [p. 36]).

[43] *Utilitarianism*, Ch. IV, par. 4 (p. 33), referring back to paragraph 3.

from pleasure and the absence of pain. It is at this point, therefore, that Mill was led into his discussion of virtue as an end in itself, and until he had completed that discussion he could not be regarded as having established the principle of utility.[44]

With respect to virtue, Mill argued that it—like money, power, or fame—is a specific end which men do seek, and which they may be said to seek disinterestedly, for its own sake.[45] However, he also argued that such ends are sought only because there is a direct connection between pursuing them and experiencing pleasure. Thus Mill believed that he had shown it to be a fact of human nature that all human desires are either desires for happiness or are derivative from that desire, being desires for ends which have come to constitute what a person considers to be a part of his happiness. Having proved this, he concludes:

> We have now, then, an answer to the question, of what sort of proof the principle of utility is susceptible. If the opinion which I have now stated is psychologically true —if human nature is so constituted as to desire nothing which is not either a part of happiness or a means to happiness—we can have no other proof, and we require no other, that these are the only things desirable.[46]

If it be doubted that this constitutes a proof of what is desirable, consider the alternative. Let some one say: "This goal, X, is desirable in itself; it is the goal which

---

[44] How Mill uses the term "virtue," and what relation it bears to happiness as an end in itself, is the subject of one section of my article, "On Interpreting Mill's *Utilitarianism*."

[45] For other instances in which Mill compares the disinterestedness of virtue and the pursuit of wealth and power, cf. his notes to his father's *Analysis of the Phenomena of the Human Mind,* which he edited, 2nd ed., vol. II, p. 233 f. and p. 307 f.

[46] *Utilitarianism,* Ch. IV, par. 9 (p. 36). Cf. also the paragraph which follows (p. 36).

all human beings *should* desire." Now, suppose that, upon inquiry, it turns out that X is something which, as a matter of psychological fact, no human being is *capable* of desiring. Could it still be held that X is desirable? Is it not a necessary condition—though not a sufficient condition—of the desirability of something that it should be capable of being desired?[47] I know of no one who has sought to uphold the contrary position. And if we are speaking of human goals, it follows that it is a necessary condition of the desirability of such a goal that human beings should be capable of desiring it. However, Mill has argued that, as a matter of fact, there is no goal other than happiness which human beings *are* capable of desiring. Should this psychological point

---

[47] In this context we may quote a statement from R. B. Brandt, made in connection with Mill's proof:

> I think we may take it as uncontested that attitudes are at least relevant guides, reliable at some points. Take the case of desires and the desirable. Will anybody in fact deny that a certain kind of thing is desirable, if in fact everybody would desire it in all circumstances? Or will anybody in fact deny that a thing is not desirable, if nobody would desire it under any circumstances whatever? We may doubt whether anybody would in fact deny either of these things (*Ethical Theory,* p. 262).

I might add that it seems to me that most contemporary philosophers have erred in thinking that the term "desirable" must be taken to mean "worthy of desire," and that this phrase must, in its turn, mean "ought to be desired." If one consults dictionaries (including those current in Mill's time), one finds this pair of assumptions to be unfounded. In this connection, we may quote Sidgwick on the meaning of "desirable," remembering that few philosophers have been more scrupulous in attempting to distinguish "ought" from "is." In the following passage he explains his use of "desirable":

> —meaning by 'desirable' not necessarily 'what *ought* to be desired' but what would be desired, with strength proportioned to the degree of desirability, if it were judged attainable by voluntary action, supposing the desirer to possess a perfect forecast, emotional as well as intellectual, of the state of attainment or fruition (*Methods of Ethics,* p. 111).

be granted, then I see no escape from his conclusion.
Since we cannot desire any end but happiness, no other
end is capable of fulfilling what is a necessary condition
of desirability. Thus—by default—what is desired turns
out in Mill's system to be both a necessary *and* a sufficient
condition of desirability.[48]

The foregoing discussion shows that Mill's proof of
hedonism is not to be identified with the brief passage in
which he draws an analogy between the visible and the
desirable. The contention on which his positive proof
rests is not merely that men do desire happiness, nor that
they do desire it as an end in itself, but that this is in
fact the *only* end which they do so desire. And Mill's
proof of this last point, as should now be abundantly
clear, rests on a particular set of psychological principles.
If one is to overthrow his proof, I should contend, one
cannot merely attack the logical form in which his argument is cast; one must be prepared to show that he is
mistaken in adopting the principles by means of which
he explains the specific ends which men actually seek.

Perhaps recent trends in ethical theory will have
cleared the way for a more sympathetic treatment of Mill
with respect to his argument for hedonism, once that
argument is understood. It has been my aim in the foregoing discussion to place Mill's proof in the context in

---

[48] My interpretation of Mill's proof may be challenged on the
ground that in the introductory chapter of *Utilitarianism* Mill
himself said that "questions of ultimate ends are not amenable to
direct proof" (Ch. I, par. 5; p. 4). However, as that paragraph
makes clear, Mill was only speaking of "what is commonly accepted as proof"; he proceeds to say that "considerations may be
presented capable of determining the intellect either to give or
withhold its assent to the doctrine; and this is equivalent to proof."
In short, if by "proof" be meant a chain of deductive argument
which depended upon some more ultimate premise, then it is obvious that no proof of the ultimate moral principle could be given.
However, the argument which the foregoing exposition has attempted to reconstruct is not of that nature: it consists in a set of
considerations which are "equivalent to proof."

which it properly belongs; and I have attempted a similar task with respect to the question of whether Mill is to be interpreted as a rule-utilitarian. If I am not mistaken, his theory—whatever its difficulties—is at once more coherent, and less open to reinterpretation or to easy objection, than it is now frequently taken to be.

PLEASURE AND HAPPINESS

BY

Jean Austin

First a word about my title: 'Happiness' is ground upon which so many angels have feared to tread that it seemed not inappropriate for me to rush in. It is a subject to which we all do give thought, not only with the force majeure of professional philosophising, but in our personal lives; however, in trying to sort the subject out a little, and it is one about which both our literature and our thinking are notoriously muddled, I fear I may rather have generated confusion than diminished it. In attempting by a somewhat roundabout method to clarify a little the sort of question, though scarcely, I am afraid, the sort of answer, that is appropriate to such thought, it has, perhaps inevitably, seemed necessary to consider in almost as much detail the more fashionable subject of Pleasure; and here too, with less excuse, the points I wish to make are abbreviated and unashamedly over-simplified. An Aunt Sally, however, has its uses, and my

Reprinted by kind permission of the author and the Editor from *Philosophy*, Vol. XLIII No. 163 (John Stuart Mill number), January 1968, with minor emendations by the author.

neck is not so precious that it cannot afford to be stuck out.

I must begin by pointing out that I shall not consider *feeling* happy, in so far as it is to be distinguished from *being* happy: euphoria may be produced by drugs, and however interesting or relevant to morality this may be, it is not my concern here. I shall confine myself to 'happy' as predicated of a person, or of the life of a person, or a portion of that life. My paper will fall roughly into two parts, each part itself being divided into sections. I shall first try to show the seductiveness, and the dangers (they often go together) of taking it as a psychological fact, as Mill did, 'that each person desires his own happiness'. I shall then go on to examine the two favoured quasi-specific 'ingredients' of happiness, pleasure and virtue. In doing so I shall have to discuss what seems to be the real villain of the piece, the verb *to want*, which appears disguised in the statement 'that each person desires his own happiness' and wriggles its way through the most subtle expositions of the case for either ingredient, wriggles its way in such a fashion that the case for each ingredient is shown to be inextricable from the other. The second, shorter, part will start in a negative way and I hope will reach, though very tentatively and certainly contentiously, a more positive denouement. Here I shall discuss certain predicates which seem logically incompatible with the predicate happy, and, by a somewhat contrapositive method, I shall try to sketch very briefly the way that to me happiness seems to lie.

Mill states as a 'fact', and in a later passage implies, given his analysis of the word 'happiness', that it is a *psychological* fact that each person desires his own happiness. In this he might seem to have Aristotle's support in his statement that there is agreement as to the 'name' at least of what he calls the *'general'* aim (each activity according to him having its own particular aim), viz. 'happiness'. There is indeed a plausibility about the statement that we do all want to be happy; perhaps too much plausibility: the suspicion that it has the ring not of truth, but of necessary truth. And this of course would entail that it was not a statement of fact at all. 'Want' is scarcely an unequivocal verb, but for the moment allowing it to stand for what both these philosophers and many others have intended to claim, why should 'happiness' be, as it is, the generally favoured candidate for what we all want? Aristotle suggests that on a different plane its general philosophical grammar is parallel to that of the word 'health'. None of us, nor, I suspect, any physiologist, would like to offer any positive definition of what it is to be healthy. A man cannot be called 'healthy' if his body is suffering from any specific disorder, though it is not so certain that the removal of a limb or perhaps of a more vital organ would be clearly incompatible with health. One could not be jaundiced but healthy, or tuberculous but healthy, though one might be without a leg but healthy, or even without a lung but healthy. That it should be healthy is perhaps the highest assessment that could be given of a man's bodily condition (of his body's condition: scarcely of his body itself which could be assessed more highly in other dimensions, such as that of beauty or strength). That he should be happy, not content but happy, is similarly the highest assessment of his total condition: and here again it is an assessment leaving room for possible surprise, in the same way that it may surprise us that a man may be healthy without a lung. He may be crippled but happy, in pain but happy, unsuccessful but happy, poor but happy, unscrupulous but happy, a victim or a martyr but happy. These cases vary very widely, and I shall be returning to some of them in more detail in the later part of this paper. My point here is that though, as the word 'but' suggests, the achievement in the particular circumstances may surprise us, the total assessment is satisfactory. The parallel that Aristotle draws may safely be pressed so far: it is obviously vulnerable in other respects, but perhaps less so than it may appear to be. A man's physician is the best authority on his bodily health: it might be natural to think that the man would himself be the best authority on his happiness. This is true in that it would be absurd (except where the word has become clinical, and equivalent indeed to mental health), to assess a man as happy in the face of his own denial of this assessment; but it would on the other hand be equally absurd to allow his own assertion as sufficient grounds for such an assessment. To do so would not only be to let in again cases of euphoria, but to allow an idiosyncratic assessment which might be in place where the question was one of pleasure or enjoyment, but not where it is one of happiness. If this is indeed an assessment of man's total condition the assessment must be in accordance with the standards accepted by the society in which he lives and precludes outrages to these.

I hope this point will be made clearer in what I have to say about pleasure, and more explicit in the second part of this paper. To state that a man is happy is to assess his total condition, of which of course his own reactions to his situation are a part. Since it is of his total condition it is inevitably a temporal assessment, an assessment over a period, and an assessment of which the man or his life is an equally proper subject. As subjects, a man and his life differ only to the extent that his life or life history will include all his experiences and accordingly statements about the latter cannot be made until it is complete. But this does not matter very much. It is an indifference which is reflected in our verbal habits, and is itself illuminating as to the nature of the assessment. We speak of a happy life, a happy childhood, a happy month in New York, a happy week or hour in someone's society: equally of a happy man, or being happy while one was a child or for the ten minutes between his making his proposal and his taking it back again. In each set of cases a period of time is implicitly or explicitly judged. Unlike bliss or ecstasy or, significantly, pleasure, happiness cannot be momentary, and, though in fact it may not endure, it cannot be seen as essentially transitory. Again, and perhaps this follows at

least in part from my previous discussion, it is an assessment that we are more inclined to make about other
people or about our past than about our own present
condition. For an assessment of happiness to be in place,
as for an assessment of health, nothing essential must be
wrong or be seen to be wrong, and it is this negative
force that gives the word its power: it is non-specific.
What in fact will determine whether things will go right
or wrong we are unable to specify in advance. If there
were a simple recipe it would scarcely remain a philosophical problem. It is not, however, only a philosophical difficulty, but perhaps in this case really a psychological fact, and one of which we are deeply aware, that
though we may very much want some specific object or
to bring about some specific state of affairs, we may not
at all like it when we have done so. This is the moral of
many legends: we may have to use the last of our three
wishes to wish away the sausages that landed on our nose
as the result of the granting of the first; if we are allowed
only one wish we may not be able to end the tragedy of
Hippolytus' death. We simply cannot tell in advance
what may go bad on us. Wealth, celebrity, devotion, all
have their attractions and, as notoriously, their hazards.
It seems that to be happy is something it is safe to want,
but *too* safe: safe just because it is sufficiently non-
specific to be non-significant as an object of wanting.

I have obviously cheated in the brief list I gave just
now of possible happiness-producing objects of wanting;
I omitted the two most favoured, most sophisticated and
significantly least specific candidates: pleasure and virtue. These have always had their adherents, among them
the two authors whose names I have already mentioned:
Mill, who claimed that 'by happiness is intended a balance of pleasure over pain', and Aristotle, who, though
he was careful to stress that in order for the word to be
in place, certain external conditions must be fulfilled,
defined happiness essentially as 'an activity of the soul
in accordance with virtue'. I shall take each of these as
a protagonist of the ingredient upon which he places

most stress. I choose them partly because even the briefest
outline of their views, all that I can give here, should be
enough to show, on the one hand, the need each felt to
accommodate within the total picture the other's candidate, and, on the other, what perhaps lies behind this
need, the difficulty to which I have already alluded, the
equivocation, ambiguity, open texture, what you will, of
the verb *to want*—a verb at least as much in need of
clarification as its object in the original dictum that *what
we all want is to be happy*. Pleasure and virtue then are
the favoured candidates, but they are not quite parallel
candidates. That pleasure is what we want might itself
look like a necessary truth: Mill not only defines happiness in terms of pleasure, but seems at times to use the
words interchangeably. That we want to be virtuous
might be taken by many to be plain false: the relationship between virtue and happiness has no such specious
simplicity. That virtue will cater for what we want has
to be shown. The use of the verb *to want* is not a simple
one, and it is consequently about this that I must first
make a few fairly obvious points.

The verb Mill himself most commonly uses is 'desire',
but 'desire' is a verb which apart from its use in philosophical discussion naturally takes only a specific object,
and that object, usually among those classes of things
Mill would not have had us 'desire'; he has simply extended its use to cover the normal range of the verb
'want.' His choice, however, of the verb 'desire' is not
quite irrelevant. It might well have been influenced by
the fact that 'desire' is the standard translation of the
Greek verb *epithumein*. This certainly was used in such
a way that *hedone,* pleasure, does seem to have been an
internal accusative, comparable for instance to the English construction according to which it follows that if we
smell, it is a smell we smell. Or perhaps more nearly
parallel to the Greek—if we have a craving, and if this
craving is satisfied, satisfaction is logically inescapable.
If we desire it might seem *eo ipso* that it is pleasure
we desire—pleasure or what in Greek were the natural

external accusatives to *epithumein,* food, drink and sexual satisfaction: to these I shall be returning in considering pleasure. Given for the present this internal accusative construction, if we desire (and it is worth noting
the verb is not so very unlike the verb to crave: desire
as such is uncomfortable), and if our desire were satisfied, it would be logically necessary that pleasure should
follow. The converse, however, was not true; *hedone*
could be the object of other verbs, just as it is in order to
choose pleasure rather than duty, or indeed the reverse.

Mill uses the verb *to desire,* but uses it to cover the
range of the verb *to want*—a range which includes significantly the range also of the verb *to choose.* It is not
therefore unfair to claim that it is an analysis of the verb
to want that is relevant to Mill's thesis. That its range is
very wide is indeed undisputed, and I shall not here
enter the controversy as to whether it may significantly
take anything as its object: it is enough that such a controversy can exist. We can undoubtedly want an apple
or a drink, to listen to music or to go for a walk, to
enjoy ourselves or to fulfil our obligations. A case has
been made that everything we do as 'free agents', not
under duress, we must in some sense have 'really' wanted
to do. This thesis in its turn may be relevant to Aristotle's
case for virtue; I shall accordingly be alluding to it under
that heading. Meanwhile I should like first to distinguish
it from the verb *to wish,* and then to compare it with the
artificial verb *to will,* or the natural verb *to choose.* The
grammar of the verb *to wish* allows us to use it of any
state of affairs that our imagination can compass. We
can wish we were wealthy, that we had been alive in
the sixteenth century, that we were children again, or
at the moment that we could visit the moon. The verb
to want, on the other hand, commits us to a state of affairs which is at least seen as theoretically possible. It
would be in place to want to be wealthy, but not to want
to be alive in the sixteenth century or to be a child again,
and to want to visit the moon would be to project oneself
forward to the time when tickets will be available. There

is, however, unfortunately a difference between theoretical possibility and realisation. It is in place, logically and psychologically, to want to spend the only capital one possesses on a new car, and to want to spend it on a holiday abroad, but it is not possible to spend the same capital twice. Though x, y, and z may each be independently realisable the realisation of one may be incompatible with the realisation of one or more of the others; wanting incompatibles is the human predicament. We may have to choose between incompatibles: choose what we 'really' want, and in describing our position, the 'having chosen' may be suppressed: we should correctly describe the result of a choice as 'wanting' x, y, or z alone. Our choice or our will commits us to what is seen as realisable by us, given our particular situation: we cannot will incompatibles. The sort of objects the verb *to want* may take may be here and now incompatible with each other, they may be long-term or short-term, they may be specific or general. There is a difference between wanting to play baseball, and wanting pleasure, since though for one man the first might be a specific substitute for the second, this would not be true for us all: there is also a difference between wanting to fulfil our obligations and wanting, say, to read five hundred examination papers—two differences which again I hope will be made more clear in my discussion of pleasure. At every level there may be a conflict between what we 'really' (suspect word) want to do or have; and we may be forced to choose, the choice not always being between what appear to be commensurables. It may not be difficult to choose between drinking and not drinking, or even between pleasure and duty, but alternatives do not always present themselves so neatly categorised. It is very possible to choose to do what in many senses we do not want to do, and not to choose what we do want to do. To add a little more confusion it must be remembered that though 'choose' does not cover the range of 'want', 'want' importantly does cover the range of 'choose', and so may well be substituted here where I have used the latter verb. This logical

slipperiness of the word *want* reflects, I think, the psychological impossibility of predicting whether when we have
got what we *want*, and perhaps its consequences, we
shall in fact *like* it. And to like what one has got, rather
than to get what one wants, is a necessary, though not
perhaps a sufficient, condition of happiness.

I may want something but not like it when I have got
it. If something gives me pleasure, that is, to that extent,
that. The difficulties about prediction reflected in the
verb *to want* do not *as such* reappear in discussing pleasure, though of course we may be mistaken as to what
in fact will give us pleasure. *These* difficulties may not
be there, but many, as I have already suggested, do reappear; and there are others at least as germane to the
subject—of these I cannot do more than indicate, or raise
without answering, those that seem relevant to my central topic. To start with, the word may be used in a
specific and narrow sense as a contrary of pain. That is
to say that if we agree to there being a group of sensations identifiable, as such, as being painful, we must
equally agree to there being a group of sensations identifiable as those of pleasure: here pleasure would be
equivalent to the Greek *hedone* used as an internal accusative of *epithumein* and take as its specific substitutes
the appropriate external accusatives I mentioned earlier.
In this sense, which, though historically it was taken as
basic, is in fact not the most usual, just as it is in order to
speak of 'degrees' of pain, it would be possible, as the
Utilitarians did, to speak of 'degrees' of pleasure.

A more common use covers roughly the range of the
verb *to enjoy*. If we find pleasure in deep-sea diving or
in playing billiards or in listening to Mozart, we would
naturally describe ourselves as enjoying these activities.
The grammar of this is assimilated to that of enjoyment,
in that just as there are not two separately identifiable
activities involved in enjoying playing billiards, playing
billiards and enjoying oneself, there is no separately identifiable 'pleasure' to be found in the pleasure we take in
playing billiards. But whereas the verb *to enjoy* has a

subjective and autobiographical ring about it—I could never safely assume that what I enjoy anyone else would necessarily enjoy—the noun *pleasure* sounds dangerously objective and impersonal, as though pleasure was an identifiable characteristic that certain activities had, or might have, in common. It is in place to speak of *enjoying* listening to Mozart *more* than playing billiards, and consequently of *finding more pleasure* in the former than in the latter: this in its turn sounds as though *degrees* of pleasure were in place again here, as they might be in the first use I mentioned. If one enjoys x more than y it is a matter of *preference*, and a scale of preferences is a much more complicated affair than a calculus of degrees. It is here that part of the early Utilitarian confusion lay. One may in fact *prefer* many things to pleasure itself, or enjoyment, just as one may *choose* other things than these, however much one may want them. One may prefer to those activities it would be natural to claim to find pleasure in or to enjoy, fulfilling one's obligations, sacrificing one's standard of living to one's children's education, dying for one's faith or one's country, activities which under their specific descriptions it would be most unnatural to *find pleasure in* or to enjoy. The martyr may *choose* to go to the stake and perhaps find *happiness* in doing so, but unless he is also a masochist he will not *find pleasure in* the flames.

This leads to a third shift in the use of the word 'pleasure', again tied to the link between pleasure and wanting. This I think comes about through first identifying pleasure, in the first, 'sensation', sense with the second, 'enjoyment', sense, in which preference but not degree is in place, and then indulging in something like the fallacy of the illicit converse. It does not follow that because we *prefer* x to y we necessarily take more pleasure in x than in y in the sense that we *enjoy* x more than y. If we prefer x to y it may be said that we *want* to do x, and do x *gladly*, or even *take pleasure* in doing x, but pleasure here has become a comparatively empty, formal word, far from its significance either as a 'sensation-word' or an 'enjoyment-word'. It was with this last shift that Aristotle, in his defence (if it was such) of morality, made most play.

Now for the protagonists themselves, Mill for pleasure, Aristotle for virtue, and the need each felt to accommodate the other's candidate. Mill states that 'to think of an object as desirable . . . and to think of it as pleasant are one and the same thing, and to desire anything except in proportion as the idea of it is pleasant is a physical and metaphysical impossibility'. He defines the will as an 'offshoot of desire', and suggests that this may be conditioned into desiring not only the 'higher' intellectual pleasures but, more generally, virtuous activity. First then he takes *pleasure* as an internal accusative to *desire* which as I have said may be legitimate in the Greek, but is dubious in English, and certainly mistaken when he extends, as he does, the range of the verb *to desire* to cover the range of the verb *to want*. By so doing he elevates, or reduces, the statement that we desire pleasure to a necessary truth. But he felt the need to accommodate not only the plausible candidates as substitutes for the internal accusative, the pleasures of sensation, but also the intellectual pleasures, and the virtues, within the general picture in order to justify his original dictum that 'happiness consists in a balance of pleasure over pain', and so committed himself to a reduction of morality in terms of pleasure. He saw that 'amount', whatever that means, of pleasure experienced will not alone do to determine an assessment of happiness, or some, such as the Marquis de Sade, or Hitler, whom he would not have liked to do so, would have qualified to be so assessed; but he cheated in his attempt to reduce to terms of pleasure the moral element normally present in such an assessment. The experiencing of pleasure, the capacity for enjoyment may well again be a necessary but not a sufficient condition of happiness. For *what* we enjoy does rather matter; it makes a difference *in what* we find pleasure. He was aware of the shortcomings of his own candidate. Aristotle, who though he was careful to stress that external circumstances could rule out the possibility of assessing anyone as happy, stressed, as many others have, the moral element. It is perhaps a necessary truth that it is socially desirable that morality should flourish, and, though, whether or not it is a necessary truth that we desire pleasure, people do not generally require to be persuaded of the delights of pleasure, they may well need to be convinced that there *are* delights in being virtuous: there have consequently always been plenty of advocates of virtue as a necessary ingredient of happiness. It obviously would not be fair to place Aristotle simply among these any more than it would be fair to place Mill simply among the advocates of pleasure. Starting at the other end from Mill, Aristotle defined happiness essentially as an activity of the soul in accordance with virtue. He took as the test of a virtuous man, as distinct from the man who happened to perform a virtuous activity, the pleasure taken in its performance. Aristotle was perfectly well aware of the use of the word, or its Greek equivalent *hedone* (it does seem to be curiously equivalent)—which I have suggested covers the range of enjoyment. If a man consistently indulges himself in doing what he enjoys doing, our assessment of his happiness may depend to a large extent upon our approval or disapproval of what he enjoys doing. This I think is the claim he makes in the last book of the *Nicomachean Ethics*, and is an admission of the important part that enjoyment must play in any assessment of happiness. But, and it is quite clear in the context, it is not in *this* sense that he is using the word as a test of the virtuous man: it is in the third and emptier sense. To state that one *will enjoy* doing x is to make a *prediction*, and perhaps a risky one: to state (truly) that one *will gladly* do x is not to make a prediction at all. Aristotle's virtuous man acts gladly, not with enjoyment. He is concerned, and properly concerned, with the man who *gladly* hangs on to his shield or returns upon it, rather than throwing it away, or *chooses* or *wants* to do so, rather than with the man who *enjoys* such a situation in itself. Some people may, but most do not, enjoy exposing themselves to probable wounding or death in battle: many have *chosen* to do this when other real possibilities have been open to them, have *opted for* it and have done so *gladly*: they have *taken pleasure* in it. Bravery, physical bravery, was a virtue that played a larger part in the lives of Aristotle's contemporaries than it does in our own, but it would not be hard to find parallels among the virtues with which we are now more concerned: for instance, kindness. There is a distinction between *enjoying* a wearisome journey on someone else's behalf and doing it *gladly*: between *finding* pleasure in the struggle and *taking* pleasure in the service we are doing. To claim that the more virtuous activities a man can *gladly* do, the greater his share of *happiness*, may well be in order, but it is not to claim that his share of *pleasure* in its 'fuller' sense is the greater. Mill would like the most virtuous man to have the largest share of the *right* kind of pleasure and therefore to be the happiest. Neither pleasure alone, nor virtue, is satisfactory as an ingredient of happiness: but perhaps this is because happiness is not to be analysed at all, at least not in terms of *wanting and getting what one wants*, but within the general framework of a society as consisting of *liking and enjoying what one has got*; and that is a different matter.

My second and much shorter part will be diffident, contentious and probably obscure. I intend only to sketch a line of discussion that might prove more fruitful than comparatively straightforward analysis. I mentioned before that there are certain conditions which, though in general we do not expect them to be compatible with happiness, are in fact sometimes found to be so. Though perhaps it is not common for the poor, for those in pain, or those deprived of companionship, to be happy there is no logical nor presumably any psychological absurdity in describing anyone as 'in pain but happy', 'poor but happy', or 'alone but happy'. Such examples are logically in order. The relationship between logic and psychology is obviously too complex for me to discuss here: perhaps it is enough to say that since in this area at least we learn psychology at its most elementary level through learning the use of those words which embody traditional and no doubt superficial psychological distinctions, there are good enough grounds for allowing logic to be our guide as to what, at the same level, is, or is not, psychologically in order. It is worth, therefore, considering such examples as: 'mean, unkind, malevolent, evil, wicked, malicious, frustrated, lonely, anxious, remorseful, bored, resentful, but happy'. A mixed bag to start with, but they seem to fall into groups. The first, 'mean', 'unkind', 'malevolent' and 'evil', are all morally pejorative and heavily so: they all strike one as logically incompatible with the predicate 'happy', and in their case this incompatibility arises from the impossibility of a combination of moral condemnation with a favourable overall assessment. They may be compared with the following pair, 'malicious' and 'wicked', which may seem odd but are not so quickly to be dismissed as out of order. 'Malicious', by contrast with 'malevolent', is a term of trivial condemnation, perhaps not of condemnation at all. 'Wicked', on the other hand, by contrast with 'evil', is an attribute typically of actions, and in so far as it is applied to people, it is to people whom we see as outside our own moral system: we may condemn their actions but they themselves escape our condemnation to the extent that the morality they outraged was not shared by them. The oddness of these last two expressions illuminates the absurdity of the first group which I might invoke to support my original thesis that the predicate 'happy' implies an assessment of a man's total condition, a part of which is his moral environment.

The second group, 'lonely', 'frustrated', 'anxious' and 'remorseful', seem to be interesting in another way, and a way that I hope is relevant to my central thesis that happiness is not so much a question of getting what one wants, but of enjoying what one has got. There is for each of these four predicates a near parallel which does, as they do not, seem to be compatible with the predicate 'happy'. 'Alone but happy' is in order, 'lonely but happy' is not.

'Unsuccessful but happy' is in order, 'frustrated but happy' is not. 'Aware of peril but happy' is in order, 'anxious but happy' is not. 'Guilty but happy' is in order, 'remorseful but happy' is not. How precisely being alone differs from being lonely, how being unsuccessful differs from being frustrated, how being aware of peril differs from being anxious or how being guilty differs from being remorseful would be difficult to say, and whether the pairs are indeed parallel is itself contentious. All I can say here is that there seems to be some sort of objectivity about each of the first predicates which the second lacks. To put it more positively, and to stress again my earlier point, it is not our situation as such, but our general feelings about, and reactions to, such situations which will determine whether or not we are happy. Feelings and reactions are notoriously, perhaps as a matter of logic, not within our control, but the identification of a situation and the disentangling of this from our reactions will itself depend upon our viewpoint: and a viewpoint is as notoriously something it *is* possible to change. It may be a fact that one is *alone*, in an empty house or in a crowd, but *that* one is *alone* is not in either case the only relevant fact to be taken account of in assessing or describing one's situation: it would be open to us to concentrate upon an infinite number of its other aspects, and the mere attempt to do so would constitute an escape from the unhappy condition of *loneliness* and its essential egocentricity. Similarly, however many projects or ambitions we may have had and may have failed in, there must always be—unless we confine our view to our own failure, or more dangerously to the unfairness of our lot— some further attempt, perhaps at another level, to be made. *That* one has failed, or had an unfair deal, may be of immense importance to *oneself*, but its importance can be diminished by bearing in mind that that importance is usually *confined* to oneself. There are people who enjoy and seek out situations involving peril, but, whether we enjoy them or not, most of us are at some time or another faced with them. It is inevitable that we

should be faced with situations the outcome of which
should cause us anxiety, but the constitutionally anxious
man is not usually so much distressed by the possibility
of a specific disaster as by a fear of *he knows not what*.
It is this element of *knowing not what*, whether it is a
matter of the inherent difficulty of predicting and specifying consequences, or whether of assessing the impact
upon oneself of an identified hazard, that is the painful
element in *reasonable* anxiety: in *reasonless* anxiety, the
absence of reason makes this element the stronger. To
objectify and specify as exactly as possible what it is one
fears, is itself to relieve one's anxiety. Finally, we all make
mistakes and we most of us do things we know we ought
not to have done. It is laudable to feel distress at the
consequences of such acts, but wrongly egocentric to
dwell upon the fact it should be *oneself* who was responsible for these. The disaster, if it was one, must be *re-
gretted in itself*, but *remorse*, though it may function as
a useful deterrent to future wrong doing, contains an
element of self-indulgence that if again one can sufficiently objectify, one can to that extent rightly diminish.

The last two of my examples, boredom and resentment,
differ from the previous group in that I have been unable
in their cases to find any objective neutral predicates
which look even speciously parallel. If one is resentful
one may or may not be suffering from an injury, one
may or may not be imagining one. If we nurse resentment or foster it, and these are the natural metaphors, it
is upon our own grievance that we concentrate. The
field of possible resentment is the field of interpersonal
relationships, and within this field anything may be a
cause of resentment, since, where we are most vulnerable,
and for most of us it is here, anything may wound. We
may not be able to do much about the wound, but imagination may help us to avoid its festering, by enabling
us to eliminate or at least explain, which can be to excuse,
the intentional element which is the most dangerous, in
its infliction. To nurse resentment is to allow egocentricity
to exclude anything else. Again one can be idle and

bored or over-busy and bored. If one is bored one is not liking what one is doing, and one can be bored in such a way that nothing one could be offered would be what one could conceivably enjoy doing. One is by definition excluded from any interest or involvement in what is going on around one: these conditions being precisely those that might save us in any of the four more specific predicaments I have discussed above. These two words, then, and I am very far from suggesting that they are alone in this, do seem to refer primarily to those characteristics which distinguish those predicates which are incompatible with the predicate, 'happy', from their 'neutral' parallel predicates. They both entail undue egocentricity and suggest at least a refusal to use the imagination. They are both essentially subjective and *'feelings'* seem to have re-entered the picture in a big way. As a conclusion I can only suggest, as I did to begin with, that though happiness as an assessment of a man's overall condition must depend ultimately upon his feelings, this is *not* to equate *feeling* happy with *being* happy. Our feelings may not be within our control but they in their turn depend upon what is at least to some extent a matter of choice: what *viewpoint* we in general adopt. Not to see oneself as the victim of fortune may be to force her to bestow upon one her most precious gift: to see oneself as happy.

J. S. MILL'S THEORY OF POETRY

BY

John M. Robson

John Stuart Mill is often held up to scorn as a cold, mechanical thinker for whom ethics is no more than logic, and politics no more than political economy. Swathed in mournful black, hard-visaged and ice-veined, Mill stands for the Victorian virtues to which we (thank heaven) cannot pretend. The picture is patently a caricature, failing to do justice to the man or to his thought, but correcting it seems difficult. Mill is himself mainly responsible for the difficulty, his *Autobiography* being little more than the history of his education and opinions. His first biographer, Bain, was *plus royalist que le roi*, and recent biographers (most notably Packe), while reopening important evidence, appear strangely unable to relate his personal experience to his thought. Actually, though most of Mill's work seems to hide rather than to reveal the man, and most of his correspondence is public

From the *University of Toronto Quarterly*, 39, 1960. Reprinted by permission of the author and the University of Toronto Press, with revisions by the author.

rather than private, even in his *System of Logic* there is material to show more than a superficial relation between his life and his thought. What the evidence shows, in fact, is that Mill not only had emotions and was motivated by them, but recognized their place in a complete moral and social theory.

Some of the evidence, of course, has not been ignored. Mill's early letters to Carlyle and Sterling, his criticisms of Benthamism in the 1830's, and his *Autobiography* have been seen as indicating emotional tensions, and his praise of Wordsworth and Coleridge has been often recognized as awareness of these tensions. But almost always this material has been seen as yet more evidence of Mill's inconsistency, best explained as a relatively harmless Utilitarian sowing of wild oats. While it is usual now to see that Mill's life falls into three parts (up to about 1828, from 1828 to 1840, and after 1840), not enough credence has been given to Mill's own account of these periods in the *Autobiography*. Clearly it is his opinion that if any part of his life is distinct from the rest, it is the early years when he was a logic-machine, not the years following his mental distress. In these latter years he judges that by growing in appreciation of all facets of life he laid a firm base for his mature opinions. As a result of his experience, he was able about 1840 to accept a general framework of opinion for the rest of his life. Just a framework, however, was accepted; his thought was fixed in direction, not in place, for his was an open, fact-hungry philosophy.

Although studies of Mill's ethics, politics, or economics could be used to substantiate his account, the best support for it is to be found in his theory of poetry, which is commonly seen as an aberration, at best curious, but certainly jejune. To defend it as a complete literary theory is no part of my purpose; its place in the total purview of Mill's thought, however, is important, and the burden of my song. Mill at sixty years of age is indebted to Mill at twenty-six; "What is Poetry?" is echoed in the footnotes to James Mill's *Analysis of the Phenomena of the Human Mind*; the early critic of Tennyson's poems is clearly seen in the author of *Utilitarianism*.

Mill's early reading and writing of poetry[1] was directed by his father's tastes and purposes. The reading was mostly in the eighteenth-century poets, the only later poets being Scott and Campbell. The writing was purely academic, as the "Ode to Diana"[2] shows; probably its main effect was to convince Mill that he was not a poet. So although, as he says in the *Autobiography*, he was passively susceptible from the first to all poetry or oratory "which appealed to the feelings on any basis of reason" (p. 50), he was really open to a new experience, his own and not his father's, when he read the great Romantics in his early twenties. Although the memory is recorded and analysed by the mature Mill, there seems to be no reason to question its truth to his early experience. The key to his response is in the clause just quoted: an appeal to feeling on the basis of reason remained for him the essential task of poetry, essential in two ways, as defining the "essence" of the poet (or of poetry), and as answering to individual and social necessities. The poet, for Mill, is peculiarly useful in bringing closer the greatest happiness of the greatest number.

Like so much else in Mill, his poetic theory resulted from the fusion of old and new ideas, with the initial heat being supplied by personal experience. The old in this case are the theories of the association of ideas; the new, the poetry and poetic theories of the Romantics; the personal experience, the collapse of motivation in the years 1826–7.

First the old ideas: Mill read Hartley's *Observations on Man* in 1822, and studied it carefully and intensively with a group of friends again in 1829. His father began writing his *Analysis of the Phenomena of the Human*

---

[1] J. S. Mill, *Autobiography* (New York: Columbia University Press, 1924), pp. 10–2.
[2] British Museum Add. MSS. 33, 230.

Mind in 1822, and between then and its publication in
1829, John Stuart read and re-read it in manuscript.
When it was published, he studied it with the same group
of friends. The study was thorough and searching:

> Our rule was to discuss thoroughly every point raised,
> whether great or small, prolonging the discussion until all
> who took part were satisfied with the conclusion they had
> individually arrived at; and to follow up every topic of
> collateral speculation which the chapter or the conversa-
> tion suggested, never leaving it until we had untied every
> knot which we found. (*Autobiography*, p. 84.)

This systematic controversy led not only to assimilation
of association theory, but also to comprehension of it.
There is little doubt that many of Mill's footnotes to the
edition of 1869 of the *Analysis* found their origin and
perhaps even wording in the discussions of forty years
earlier.

The new ideas about poetry came mainly to Mill initially through the London Debating Society. Becoming
acquainted there with disciples of the Lake Poets, he
first read, and then met Wordsworth, Coleridge, and
Southey. Of these, only Wordsworth is here significant.
Mill first read his poetry in 1828; soon afterwards he
defended it against Byron's; and, probably most significantly, he called upon Wordsworth during his tour of
the Lake District in 1831. Although Mill contributed
three short notices on artistic matters to the *Examiner*
previous to this tour, only in the next two years can one
see the formation of a theory of art in his writings. It is
likely that he first learned from Wordsworth the possibility and value of such a theory. Writing to John Sterling
(September 20-2, 1831), Mill remarks, after praising
the largeness and comprehensiveness of Wordsworth's
thought, feeling, and spirit, that he is the "first person
who ever combined, with such eminent success in the
practice of the art, such high powers of generalization &

habits of meditation on its principles."[3] Again, in a foot-note to his article, "The Use and Abuse of Political Terms" (1832), Mill expresses his regret that a poet like Wordsworth, who has

> meditated so profoundly on the theory of his art, as he has laboured assiduously in its practice, should have put forth nothing which can convey any adequate notion to pos-terity of his merits in this department; and that philosophi-cal speculations on the subject of poetry, with which it would be folly to compare any others existing in our lan-guage, have profited only to a few private friends.[4]

Mill's nervous attack came just before his first reading of Wordsworth, and not long before his renewed study of association theory. In simplified (and non-psychologi-cal) terms, his depression revealed to him a major inade-quacy in utilitarian theory: the happiness therein de-scribed seemed to have nothing to do with his own happiness. The analysis of man's "moral" (as opposed to "physical") nature drained away motivation, leaving only the dregs of selfish desire. But Mill accepted the accuracy of the analysis; had he not, there would have been no despair. How did he escape? Of the many explanations that have been offered, Levi's psychoanalytic account, which cannot be overlooked but need not be here re-peated, and Mill's own theoretical account in terms of an "anti-self-conscious" habit, are the most interesting. Un-fortunately Mill's account is so incomplete that it can be interpreted as a contradictory element in his ethics be-cause, *inter alia*, it does not explain why certain courses of action would be chosen by individuals, and why de-cisions to follow these courses would be moral. A third explanation, one related to both those already mentioned,

---

[3] *Earlier Letters*, ed. Francis E. Mineka, in Collected Works, XII (Toronto: University of Toronto Press, 1963), 81–2.

[4] *Tait's Edinburgh Magazine*, I, 165n.

and stronger because more complete, can be derived from his remarks on poetry.

One of Mill's releases from depression came from a reading of Wordsworth in 1828. On later examination he found two reasons: (*a*) the poetry appealed to "one of the strongest of [his] pleasurable susceptibilities, the love of rural objects and natural scenery," especially of mountains, his "ideal of natural beauty," and (*b*) it was also, and more importantly, "a medicine for [his] state of mind . . . [expressing] not mere outward beauty, but states of feeling, and of thought coloured by feeling, under the excitement of beauty."[5] It was medicinal for Mill because it aroused in him feelings which he thought he had lost. Wordsworth's poetry, then, coming after his depression, showed Mill that his education had ignored the affective for the intellectual. In it he found the "very culture of the feelings" for which he was searching, as well as "a source of inward joy, of sympathetic and imaginative pleasure. . . ." Without feeling there was no desire, without desire no motivation, without motivation no action, without action no morality. For Bentham and James Mill morality depended on selfish feelings, because only these, in their view, were strong and constant enough to make a science of morality possible. But John Mill had found that the science thus arrived at had no power to motivate his actions; he turned his attention to the unselfish feelings, and to the "art" or practice of morality rather than to the "science" or theory. Eventually he found that although the selfish feelings may be used by the legislator, only the unselfish feelings are moral. So, as will become clear, when he talks of the poet, he talks of the moralist-poet, the poet who portrays other-regarding affections, and he avoids, ignores, or condemns in passing the pseudo-poet who treats immoral or amoral affections.

The discovery in poetry of a perpetual source of ethical joy was particularly valuable to Mill, who had worried

---

[5] *Autobiography*, pp. 103–4.

about the diminution of motivation in a progressive world. He had wondered whether, "if the reformers of society and government could succeed in their objects, and every person in the community were free and in a state of physical comfort, the pleasures of life, being no longer kept up by struggle and privation, would cease to be pleasures."[6] This peculiarly nineteenth-century attitude (open to religious, philosophical, and psychological interpretations) held no more terrors for him once the perennial and universally available source of affective culture was revealed to him.

So personal experience brought together and made meaningful the old and new doctrines. The further experience of the early 1830's, the opening ceremonies of the life-long devotional service to Harriet Taylor, is so obviously important as to need no comment. Worthy of note, however, is Mill's continued conviction, in spite of his love, and in spite of his enthusiasm for the insipid verses of Harriet and of Sarah Flower, that he himself is no poet. In the previously mentioned letter to Sterling he makes a point to which he returns time and again in his letters to Carlyle during the next few years:

> The only thing which I can usefully do at present, & which I am doing more & more every day, is to work out *principles*: which are of use for all times, though to be applied cautiously & circumspectly to any: principles of morals, government, law, education, above all self-education. I am here much more in my element: the only thing that I believe I am really fit for, is the investigation of abstract truth, & the more abstract the better. If there is any science which I am capable of promoting, I think it is the science of science itself, the science of investigation—of method. (*Earlier Letters*, XII, 78–9.)

This germ bore most obvious fruit in the publication twelve years later of the *System of Logic*, but the leaves

---

[6] *Ibid.*, p. 102.

and buds, in the form of poetic theory, began to appear within a year.[7]

The task of the poet will be clear from the preceding discussion: he is to make available to the public a source of moral feeling. What sort of a man is the poet, and how does he perform his task? Various suggestions are made by Mill: (I) The poet has a fine and quick susceptibility to pleasure and pain, especially to pleasure; (II) He has a unique method of mental association—between ideas, and between idea and sensation, the link is emotional; (III) Unlike other benefactors of mankind, therefore, his appeal is not primarily to the intellect; (IV) But to be truly great, the poet must have a cultivated intellect; (V) Imagination is also necessary. Although Mill uses the word in many senses, one is here especially significant: the poet, by using "imagination," feels in himself the emotions appropriate to the situation he is treating, whether or not he has actually experienced those emotions in that situation. These qualities of the poet (discussed at greater length in the following paragraphs) are not treated in one place by Mill, but their interconnections indicate that they are all part of one definition.

---

[7] I do not here trace the development of Mill's poetic theory in detail, choosing rather to make clear the importance of the theory to Mill's ethical thought. Therefore (and also in the interests of brevity) I treat together the principal articles of the early 1830's: "On Genius," *Monthly Repository*, VI (Oct., 1832); "What is Poetry?" *Monthly Repository*, VII (Jan., 1833); "Writings of Junius Redivivus," *Monthly Repository*, VII (Apr., 1833); "Writings of Junius Redivivus," *Tait's Edinburgh Magazine*, III (June, 1833); "The Two Kinds of Poetry," *Monthly Repository*, VII (Nov., 1833); and "Tennyson's Poems," *London and Westminster Review*, XXX (July, 1835). (Those articles reprinted in *Early Essays*, ed. J. W. Gibbs [London, 1897], are quoted from that source.) Corroborating and explanatory material is found mostly in the contemporary letters to Carlyle, and in articles in the *Examiner*.

(I) When discussing Shelley, his type of the "natural" poet, possessed of an "original fineness of organization," Mill remarks that the "poetic temperament is usually, perhaps always, accompanied by exquisite senses."[8] The power of producing poetical compositions is not brought into the world at birth with the poet; however,

> there is poetry which could not emanate but from a mental and physical constitution peculiar, not in the *kind*, but in the *degree* of its susceptibility: a constitution which makes its possessor capable of greater happiness than mankind in general, and also of greater unhappiness; and because greater, so also more various. And such poetry, to all who know enough of nature to own it as being *in* nature, is much *more* poetry, is poetry in a far higher sense, than any other; since the common element of all poetry, that which constitutes poetry, human feeling, enters far more largely into this than into the poetry of culture. Not only because the natures which we have called poetical, really feel more, and consequently have more feeling to express; but because, the capacity of feeling being so great, feeling, when excited and not voluntarily resisted, seizes the helm of their thoughts, and the succession of ideas and images becomes the mere utterance of an emotion; not, as in other natures, the emotion a mere ornamental colouring of the thought. ("The Two Kinds of Poetry," pp. 230–1.)

Here "human feeling" is revealed to be the basic element in poetry; the poet is more open to human feeling than any other type of man, and this susceptibility forces him to display examples of powerful emotion in his works. He thus not only feels exquisitely but also makes exquisite feeling available to the reader.

(II) The extreme sensibility of the poet points to a peculiarity in his habitual associations. Mill, although a confirmed associationist, diverges from both his father

---

[8] "The Two Kinds of Poetry," *Early Essays*, p. 229.

and Hartley in describing the associations of the poet.
James Mill scorns the notion that poetic "trains" are organized differently from those of any other men:

> The trains of poets . . . do not differ from the trains of
> other men, but perfectly agree with them, in this, that
> they are composed of ideas, and that those ideas succeed
> one another, according to the same laws, in their, and in
> other minds. They are ideas, however, of very different
> things. The ideas of the poet are ideas of all that is most
> lovely and striking in the visible appearances of nature,
> and of all that is most interesting in the actions and af-
> fections of human beings.[9]

Hartley is more analytic, but argues for no peculiar
organization in the poet apart from that explicable by
"the differences of [men's] situations in life, and of the
consequent associations formed in them."[10] His further
remarks[11] defining the poet in terms of mechanical attainments could not have satisfied the younger Mill, who
argues that a man may pass a life "in writing unquestionable poetry," and earn a place in "the table of contents
of a collection of 'British Poets,'" yet not be a poet. Only
those are true poets who "are so constituted, that emotions are the links of association by which their ideas,
both sensuous and spiritual [i.e., mental], are connected
together."[12] The prevailing associations of the poet "will
be those which connect objects and ideas with emotions,
and with each other through the intervention of emotions."[13] Although the link is changed, Mill sticks to
the usual associationist descriptions of the operation,

---

[9] James Mill, *Analysis of the Phenomena of the Human Mind*,
ed. J. S. Mill (London, 1869), I, 241–2.

[10] David Hartley, *Observations on Man, His Frame, His Duty,
and His Expectations* (London, 1810), I, 434.

[11] *Ibid.*, 441, 447–8.

[12] "The Two Kinds of Poetry," p. 223.

[13] *Ibid.*, p. 225.

without clearing up the confusion often attached to some terms. At times he talks of "synchronous" and "successive" associations as opposite types; at other times he opposes "contiguous" and "similar" associations. The facile assumption that "contiguous" includes "synchronous" and "successive" is not always satisfactory, nor is the sometimes helpful assumption that the first pair refers to initial sensation while the second pair refers to mental perception and recall. In spite of this confusion, Mill's meaning can be made out. The untrained mind in a dull body, Mill contends, thinks, as it experiences, chronologically. Sensations are reflected in ideas in the order in which they occur, that is, successively. The trained mind, on the other hand, learns to associate through learned patterns and recognized similarities. It can, unfortunately, have habitual "trains" forced upon it by bad educational practices, and so lose its originality and vitality. The natural poet, untrained in mind but strong in feeling, is a third case: in him sensations call up emotions immediately, so that the ideas connected with the sensations are welded to the ideas connected with the emotions. The chronological "trains" have no chance to form, and so the succession of ideas bears no resemblance to the succession of external events. In his *Logic*, referring to his earlier remarks in "The Two Kinds of Poetry," and to the speculations of James Martineau, Mill argues that since the effect of pleasurable and painful impressions is more marked in cases of synchronous association, therefore,

in minds of strong organic sensibility synchronous associations will be likely to predominate, producing a tendency to conceive things in pictures and in the concrete, richly clothed in attributes and circumstances, a mental habit which is commonly called Imagination, and is one of the peculiarities of the painter and the poet; while persons of more moderate susceptibility to pleasure and pain will have a tendency to associate facts chiefly in the order of their succession, and such persons, if they possess mental superiority, will addict themselves to history or science rather than to creative art.[14]

An even later passage should be seen with this; in reviewing Bain's psychological works in 1859, Mill says:

> The two kinds of association [by resemblance or similarity, and by contiguity] are indeed so different, that the predominance of each gives rise to a different type of intellectual character; an eminent degree of the former constituting the inductive philosopher, the poet and artist, and the inventor and originator generally; while adhesive association gives memory, mechanical skill, facility of acquisition in science or business, and practical talent so far as unconnected with invention.[15]

The second passage (in which Mill is expressing agreement with Bain) could be taken to cancel the first, or at least to correct it, but in fact the two can be reconciled. Mill believed with Bain, against his father, that resemblance is more basic than contiguity, and so associations even when synchronous need not be casual. In "The Two Kinds of Poetry" he implies the primacy of resemblance in poetic associations: "Thoughts and images will be linked together [in the poet's mind], according to the similarity of the feelings which cling to them. A thought will introduce a thought by first introducing a feeling which is allied with it." (p. 225.)

When he turns to composition, then, the "natural" poet, starting with a sensation, throws off a series of images connected emotionally with the sensation. In a short poem, the only sort proper to the uncultivated poet, these images will cluster around the emotion, which will give a centre to the experience portrayed and thus

---

[14] J. S. Mill, *System of Logic* (London: Longmans, Green, 1906), 317 (III, xiii, 6).

[15] "Bain's Psychology," *Dissertations and Discussions* (London, 1859–75), III, 131.

a unity to the poem. In longer poems and with complex emotions or situations, the poet without intellectual training will prove weak. The uncultivated mind, Mill says, forms "casual" associations. Knowing no governor, it plunges ahead, repeating, when called upon, accidental experiences, of interest only to the naïve, of immediate use to no one.

(III) While the purposes are shared with other men, the poetic powers are special. And just because special, they are not universally effective. In describing his own skills, Mill does much to clarify the poet's function, although here again the possibility of confusion exists because he offers several distinctions. Writing to Carlyle (July 17, 1832), he says he is called to logic rather than art ("a higher vocation") like Carlyle, and adds that only in the artist's hands does "Truth" become "impressive, and a living principle of action."[16] In this age, however, when only the understanding is cultivated and trusted, people are influenced by lessons in logical garb, and so, he says in a later letter:

> *my* word again is partly intelligible to many more persons than yours is, because mine is presented in the logical and mechanical form which partakes most of this age and country, yours in the artistical and poetical (at least in one sense of those words though not the sense I have been recently giving them [presumably in "What is Poetry?"]) which finds *least* entrance into any minds now, except when it comes before them as mere dilettantism and pretends not to make any serious call upon them to change their lives.[17]

Like the "logical and mechanical" word, then, the "artistic and poetical" word makes a serious call upon men. After mentioning to Fox (May 19, 1833) a "growing want of interest in all the subjects which [he] under-

---

16 *Earlier Letters*, XII, 113.
17 *Ibid.*, 155–6 (May 18, 1833).

stand[s], and a growing sense of incapacity *ever* to have real knowledge of or insight into the subjects in which alone [he will] ever again feel a strong interest,"[18] Mill tries to explain to Carlyle what he meant by calling him Poet and Artist:

> I conceive that most of the highest truths are, to persons endowed by nature in certain ways which I think I could state, intuitive; that is, they need neither explanation nor proof, but if not known before, are assented to as soon as stated. Now it appears to me that the poet or artist is conversant chiefly with *such* truths and that his office in respect to truth is to declare *them*, and to make them *impressive*. This, however, supposes that the reader, hearer, or spectator is a person of the kind to whom those truths *are* intuitive. Such will of course receive them at once, and will lay them to heart in proportion to the impressiveness with which the artist delivers and embodies them. But the other and more numerous kind of people will consider them as nothing but dreaming or madness: and the more so, certainly, the more powerful the artist, *as* an artist: because the means which are good for rendering the truth impressive to those who know it, are not the same and are often absolutely incompatible with those which render it intelligible to those who know it not. Now this last I think is the proper office of the logician or I might say the metaphysician, in truth he must be both. The same person may be poet and logician, but he cannot be both in the same composition: and as heroes have been frustrated of glory '*carent quia vate sacro,*' so I think the *vates* himself has often been misunderstood and successfully cried down for want of a Logician in Ordinary, to supply a logical commentary on his intuitive truths. The artist's is the highest part, for by him alone is real *knowledge* of such truths conveyed: but it is possible to convince him who never could *know* the intuitive truths, that they are not inconsistent with anything he *does* know; that they

---

[18] *Ibid.,* 157.

are even very *probable*, and that he may have faith in them when higher natures than his own affirm that they are truths.

His own task, he says again, is the humbler one of the man of speculation:

> I am not in the least a poet, in any sense; but I can do homage to poetry. I can to a very considerable extent feel it and understand it, and can make others who are my inferiors understand it in proportion to the measure of their capacity. I believe that such a person is more wanted than even the poet himself; that there are more persons living who approximate to the latter character than to the former. . . . Now one thing not useless to do would be to exemplify this difference by enlarging in my logical fashion upon the difference itself: to make those who are not poets, understand that poetry is higher than Logic, and that the union of the two is Philosophy.[19]

Carlyle being still not satisfied with the explanation (or perhaps the praise), Mill writes again (August 2, 1833):

> By logic . . . I meant the antithesis of Poetry or Art: in which distinction I am learning to perceive a twofold contrast: the *literal* as opposed to the *symbolical*, and *reasoning* as opposed to *intuition*. Not the *theory* of reasoning but the *practice*. In reasoning I include all processes of thought which are *processes* at all, that is, which proceed by a series of steps or links.[20]

This distinction is clear—the speaker of the Word as against the weaver of arguments—and clearly leaves the Artist in the position of preaching to the converted. It would appear that the weight of conversion rests on the thin shoulders of the Logician. Insight is translated into

---

[19] *Ibid.*, 163 (July 5, 1833). Cf. *ibid.*, 219 (March 2, 1834).
[20] *Ibid.*, 173.

syllogism, for comprehension must precede belief. With belief (in Newman's terms) certainty can give way to certitude, and then action can follow. The argument in these letters foreshadows the pregnant passage in Book VI of Mill's *Logic*, where he sets forth the proper relation between the work of the Artist and the Scientist in all social endeavour:

> the imperative mood is the characteristic of art, as distinguished from science. Whatever speaks in rules or precepts, not in assertions respecting matters of fact, is art; and ethics or morality is properly a portion of the art corresponding to the sciences of human nature and society. (VI, xii, 1, p. 616.)

The distinction is roughly that between theoretical and practical, but art has a twofold role, coming both before and after the operations of science. Art, in Mill's meaning, is prior to science, for it decides upon and defines the end to be pursued in a particular area. It then hands this end over to science, as an effect to be studied; science inquires into the causes of the effect, and then turns the problem back to art with a description of the circumstances by which the end can be reached. Art now examines these circumstances and, if they are practicable and moral, proclaims the end as the object of action, and makes the theorem of its attainment, formulated by science, into a rule or precept for practical guidance. In the end, the artist tries to induce a current of morality into the community.

Such apparently dry speculations as these (forecast in the letter to Carlyle of July 5, 1833) seem to drive the poor poet into the market place, with zeal in his heart and text in his hand. Actually the artist is for Mill protean, and the poet is only one shape. One must look at the earlier of his two articles on poetry to see how he distinguishes the poet from the other isotopes of the artist. In "What is Poetry?" he argues that poetry, "the better part of all art whatever, and of life too," is distinguished from its logical opposite, matter of fact or science, by its attempt to move its audience rather than convince it. It offers interesting objects of contemplation to the "sensibilities," not propositions to the understanding. The coincidence with the later argument is obvious, but just at this point Mill indicates that further distinctions are necessary. The novelist, for instance, is also concerned with emotion; is he, then, a poet? No, says Mill, for mere narratives depend for their interest on outward circumstances as opposed to inner sensibility. The truth of narrative is not the truth of poetry:

> The truth of poetry is to paint the human soul truly: the truth of fiction is to give a true picture of *life*. The two kinds of knowledge are different, and come by different ways, come mostly to different persons. Great poets are often proverbially ignorant of life. What they know has come by observation of themselves; they have found *there* one highly delicate, and sensitive, and refined specimen of human nature, on which the laws of emotion are written in large characters, such as can be read off without much study: and other knowledge of mankind, such as comes to men of the world by outward experience, is not indispensable to them as poets: but to the novelist such knowledge is all in all; he has to describe outward things, not the inward man. . . .[21]

A further distinction remains, that between the poet and the orator—and here are found the most often quoted, and most perceptive, of Mill's remarks on poetry.

> Poetry and eloquence are both alike the expression or uttering forth of feeling. But if we may be excused the antithesis, we should say that eloquence is *heard*, poetry is *over*heard. Eloquence supposes an audience; the peculiarity of poetry appears to us to lie in the poet's utter uncon-

---

[21] "What is Poetry?" *Early Essays*, p. 205 ("refine" corrected to "refined").

sciousness of a listener. Poetry is feeling, confessing itself to itself in moments of solitude, and embodying itself in symbols, which are the nearest possible representations of the feeling in the exact shape in which it exists in the poet's mind. Eloquence is feeling pouring itself out to other minds, courting their sympathy, or endeavouring to influence their belief, or move them to passion or to action.[22]

But even in this description the poet is not morally useless; he pursues a genuine end for its own sake, but the personal end becomes a social means. "All poetry is of the nature of soliloquy . . . , [but what] we have said to ourselves, we may tell to others afterwards; what we have said or done in solitude, we may voluntarily reproduce when we know that other eyes are upon us."[23] And the cultivated poet will here be most effective.

(IV) Without resigning his special strengths the poet should cultivate his intellect by retiring at times from the world of strong feeling to meditate upon experience in the manner of the philosopher.[24] Emotional links cast aside, the poet then reasons like other men, connecting ideas logically, forming associations on the basis of his own and others' experience, testing—the point is not made by Mill in this connection, but is clear from his *Logic*—mental against physical experience, checking apparent against actual resemblances, associations between

---

[22] *Ibid.*, pp. 208–9 ("appear" corrected to "appears").

[23] *Ibid.*, p. 209.

[24] The Wordsworthian influence is seldom far below the surface—and it remained. In a letter to his wife from Naples (Feb. 9, 1855) he writes: "Nothing can be more beautiful than this place. You can I dare say imagine now I enjoy the beauty when I am *not* looking at it—now in this bedroom by candlelight I am in a complete nervous state from the sensation of the beauty I am living among—while I look at it I only seem to be gathering honey which I savour the whole time afterwards." (F. A. Hayek, *John Stuart Mill and Harriet Taylor* [London, 1951].)

ideas against associations between their parent sensations. In short, bringing objectivity as far as possible into
his subjective world. (The question of the appropriateness of a belief in right reason in Mill is admittedly
begged.) A beneficial result is sure:

> Where . . . a poetic nature has been united with logical
> and scientific culture, the peculiarity of association arising
> from the finer nature so perpetually alternates with the as-
> sociations attainable by commoner natures trained to high
> perfection, that its own particular law is not so conspicu-
> ously characteristic of the result produced. . . . Whether
> the superiority will naturally be on the side of the logician-
> poet or of the mere poet—whether the writings of the one
> ought, as a whole, to be truer, and their influence more
> beneficent, than those of the other—is too obvious in prin-
> ciple to need statement: it would be absurd to doubt
> whether two endowments are better than one; whether
> truth is more certainly arrived at by two processes, verify-
> ing and correcting each other, than by one alone. ("The
> Two Kinds of Poetry," p. 235.)

When experience and reason combine, the poet is unlikely to repeat Browning's failure in *Pauline:*

> With considerable poetic powers, the writer seems to me
> possessed with a more intense and morbid self-conscious-
> ness than I ever knew in any sane human being. . . .
> [Browning] should not attempt to show how a person
> may be *recovered* from this morbid state,—for *he* [on the
> evidence of the poem] is hardly convalescent, and 'what
> should we speak of but that which we know?'[25]

Images supplied spontaneously through the fineness of
the poet's perceptions are not enough; he must also be
supplied through "the vigour and richness of his intel-

---

[25] Note in copy of *Pauline* sent by Fox to Mill. Quoted in
Griffin and Minchin, *Life of Robert Browning*, pp. 59–60.

lect" with an "abundance of moving thoughts."[26] Only
when the poet becomes, as he may, a poet-philosopher,
can his works conduce fully to the betterment of mankind. Mill makes the point at length in his review of
Tennyson's poems:

> Every great poet, every poet who has extensively or per-
> manently influenced mankind, has been a great thinker;
> —has had a philosophy though perhaps he did not call it
> by that name;—has had his mind full of thoughts derived
> not merely from passive sensibility, but from trains of re-
> flection, from observation, analysis, and generalization;
> however remote the sphere of his observation and medita-
> tion may have lain from the studies of the schools. Where
> the poetic temperament exists in its greatest degree, while
> the systematic culture of the intellect has been neglected,
> we may expect to find, what we do find in the best poems
> of Shelley—vivid representations of states of passive and
> dreamy emotion, fitted to give extreme pleasure to persons
> of similar organization to the poet, but not likely to be
> sympathized in, because not understood, by any other per-
> sons; and scarcely conducing at all to the noblest end of
> poetry as an intellectual pursuit, that of acting upon the
> desires and characters of mankind through their emotions,
> to raise them towards the perfection of their nature. This,
> like every other adaptation of means to ends, is the work
> of cultivated reason; and the poet's success in it will be in
> proportion to the intrinsic value of his thoughts, and to the
> command which he has acquired over the materials of his
> imagination, for placing those thoughts in a strong light
> before the intellect, and impressing them on the feelings.[27]

(V) Mill's uses of the word "imagination" are as loose
as most people's. Sometimes he accepts the meaning given
to it by his father, "train of ideas." Sometimes, again,
he uses it in a very common way, as signifying a train

---

[26] "The Two Kinds of Poetry," p. 231.
[27] "Tennyson's Poems," *Early Essays*, pp. 260–1.

of ideas in which the person having the train does not believe. When Mill applies the term to the poet, however, it obviously describes a *power*. He refers, for example, to "that kind of self-observation which is called imagination," and which, like "simple observation and a more complicated process of analysis and induction" is a method of extracting "the knowledge of general truth . . . from our own consciousness."[28] A similar meaning is indicated in a passage already quoted from "What is Poetry?" (p. 205): "What [poets] know has come by observation of themselves; they have found *there* one highly delicate, and sensitive, and refined specimen of human nature, on which the laws of emotion are written in large characters, such as can be read off without much study. . . ." But beneath this power of observation must lie another power if the poet is to avoid narrowness; this more basic power needs the information gathered by a cultivated intellect, but, being active, is not limited by such information. Mill, in his earliest remarks on artistic matters, calls this latter power also imagination. He is discussing acting, but the passages have an obvious relevance to his theory of poetry.

> A great actor must possess imagination, in the higher and more extensive meaning of the word: that is, he must be able to conceive correctly, and paint vividly within himself, states of external circumstances, and of the human mind, into which it has not happened to himself to be thrown.[29]

He agrees with Pemberton, an actor,

> that in acting, as in everything else, genius does not consist in being a copyist; even from nature: That the actor of genius is not he who observes and imitates what men of

---

[28] "On Genius," p. 652.
[29] *Examiner*, pp. 325–6 (May 22, 1831).

particular characters, and in particular situations, *do*, but
he who can, by an act of imagination, actually *be* what
they *are*: who can so completely understand, and so viv-
idly conceive, the state of their minds, that the conception
shall call up in his own the very emotions, and thereby
draw from him the very sounds and gestures, which would
have been exhibited by the imaginary being whom he is
personifying. Such a man's representation of nature will
have a consistency and keeping in it, and will reach depths
in the human heart, which no man's opportunities and
powers of mere outward observation could ever have enabled him to attain to.[30]

Here again Mill sets off imagination from "outward observation," but obviously without some outward observation the portrayal of other men by the actor or the poet
would be impossible. He is suggesting, actually, that passive copying or reporting is not art; art lies in the active
sharing in the feelings of the imitated or described persons; and this sharing is imagination. Pemberton has the
"faculty" or "power," says Mill,

to call up by a voluntary effort of imagination, what he
not unhappily terms *secondary* feelings, that is, feelings
suggested by a vivid conception of similar feelings in
others: and by thus *realizing* for the time being, an imaginary character, to give a profoundly true dramatic presentation of it.[31]

Elsewhere Mill even introduces the crucial term "creative imagination," but adds little to his previous definition:

The faculty of thus bringing home to us a coherent conception of beings unknown to our experience, not by logically *characterizing* them, but by a living *representation*

---

[30] *Ibid.*, p. 226 (June 3, 1832).
[31] *Ibid.* Cf. "Bentham," *Dissertations and Discussions,* I, 353.

of them, such as they would, in fact, *be*, if the hypothesis of their possibility could be realized—is what is meant, when anything is meant, by the words creative imagination.[32]

The reader, Mill indicates in his discussion of Tennyson, must cooperate with the poet by suspending his "critical understanding" and giving his "spontaneous feelings" full play, surrendering his "imagination [i.e., trains] to the guidance of the poet."[33] He will then feel with the characters in the portrayed situation to the extent that the poet is able to recreate the feelings in his readers by first creating them in himself.

Although, as has been seen, unity of conception and execution is necessary for the greatest art, Mill does not see imagination as the controlling, unifying power; the intellect, governing the essential, but essentially random, emotional associations, selects, discards, and adds. As always in Mill's discussions of man, feeling is the horse, but intellect the rider. So Tennyson is warned by Mill not to accept "poetical" conclusions when unsupported by evidence, especially when philosophical systems are in question. No philosophy should deny the validity of poetry, for philosophic systems are properly "comprehensive" and "commanding":

Let our philosophical system be what it may, human feelings exist: human nature, with all its enjoyments and sufferings, its strugglings, its victories and defeats, still remains to us; and these are the materials of all poetry. Whoever, in the greatest concerns of human life, pursues truth with unbiased feelings, and an intellect adequate to discern it, will not find that the resources of poetry are lost to him because he has learnt to use and not to abuse them. They are as open to him as they are to the sentimental weakling, who has no test of the true but the orna-

---

[32] "Tennyson's Poems," p. 263n.
[33] *Ibid.*, p. 248.

mental. And when he once has them under his command,
he can wield them for purposes, and with a power, of
which neither the dilettante nor the visionary have the
slightest conception.[34]

The purposes come from the philosophy (intellect); the
power from the poetry (feeling).

This attempt to define the nature and function of the
poet leads outwards into other areas of Mill's thought.
The poet is one who speaks *truth*, who deals in *realities*
(in his later years Mill was more chary of these Carlyl-
ianisms). He presents a scene and characters so representative of valid human feelings as to be a moral lesson
to all who hear him. He teaches men to share the feelings
of others. True sympathy, the ground of morality, can
result only from empathy with others. The importance
of this sharing is touched on in a passage in which Mill
praises Bain for separating "Tender Affections" from
"Sympathy," and for treating the latter not "as an emotion, but as the capacity of taking on the emotions, or
mental states generally, of others. A character may possess tenderness without being at all sympathetic, as is the
case with many selfish sentimentalists; and the converse,
though not equally common, is equally in human nature."[35] Ideally, the audience does not stop with mere
identification, but goes further into a contemplation of
perfection beyond that portrayed. In an interesting comment upon Beauty in a footnote to his father's *Analysis*,
Mill commends Ruskin's discussion in *Modern Paint-
ers*, saying that all the elements which Ruskin finds in
the idea of Beauty, except those like Moderation,

represent to us some valuable or delightful attribute, in a
completeness and perfection of which our experience presents us with no example, and which therefore stimulates

[34] *Ibid.*, pp. 266–7 ("remain" corrected to "remains").
[35] "Bain's Psychology," p. 134.

the active power of the imagination to rise above known reality, into a more attractive or a more majestic world. This does not happen with what we call our lower pleasures. To them there is a fixed limit at which they stop: or if, in any particular case, they do acquire, by association, a power of stirring up ideas greater than themselves, and stimulate the imagination to enlarge its conceptions to the dimensions of those ideas, we then feel that the lower pleasure has, exceptionally, risen into the region of the aesthetic, and has superadded to itself an element of pleasure of a character and quality not belonging to its own nature. (*Analysis*, II, 255n.)

The highest pleasures for Mill, of course, are those mental pleasures of sympathy which guide the actions of the good man. So the poet, speaking "the word . . . with truthful intent," lets his audience "know one human soul"; the greatest poets, living in accord with their word, reveal nobility through beauty, and lead the audience to emulation. So Milton[36] and Plato have given us works which are evidence of their lives; more important, the Gospel is the record of the life of Christ as much as of his doctrines.[37] The usual attitude to Jesus is typically mistaken: he has been

> likened to a logician, framing a rule to meet all cases, and provide against all possible evasions, instead of a poet, orator, and *vates*, whose object was to purify and spiritualize the mind, so that, under the guidance of its purity, its own lights might suffice to find the law of which he

---

[36] Later, in a letter to Lalor (*c.* June 20, 1852), Mill, probably having heard Harriet on the subject, says: ". . . it is not agreeable to me to be praised in the words of a man whom I so wholly disrespect as Milton, who with all his republicanism had the soul of a fanatic, a despot and a tyrant." British Library of Political and Economic Science, Mill-Taylor Collection, I, #22, 64r.

[37] "Writings of Junius Redivivus," *Monthly Repository*, VII, 269.

only supplied the spirit, and suggested the general scope. ("On Genius," p. 657.)

At this point Mill's theory seems to be complete, and no one has bothered to consider whether he retained it throughout life. He would appear, from most accounts, to have forgotten, misplaced, or discarded it. But in fact it remained with him, and was altered only by being made more complete as it was brought into closer conjunction with the rest of his thought. Documentation is difficult, but a few references in Bain's *Autobiography* and Caroline Fox's *Memories of Old Friends* indicate a constant interest in poetic and artistic matters throughout the 1840's and into the 1850's. For the bulk of the 1850's, Mill's decade of marriage and mourning, there is very little record of any sort, but even here the remarks in "Bain's Psychology" already quoted show that his concern is still present. (*On Liberty*, while its argument is consonant with that outlined here, is not an obvious source.) In 1867 and 1869, however, appeared two documents which establish not only his continued interest but also his continued belief in the importance of poetry. The latter document, *The Analysis of the Phenomena of the Human Mind*, with John Mill's footnotes, has already been discussed in the account of association. The former, Mill's *Rectorial Address at St. Andrews*, a much neglected work, contains as good a summary of Mill's thought as that in the *Autobiography*, including a lengthy passage on the importance of poetry.

In this *Address* Mill argues, in terms reminiscent of both his "Bentham" and his *Logic*,[38] that while the two most important parts of education are the intellectual and the moral, the third part, the aesthetic, is also essential. Aesthetic education involves the education of the feelings and the cultivation of the beautiful. The moderns, inferior in poetic control to the ancients, are superior in their choice of subject because they pay more heed

---

[38] "Bentham," p. 387; *Logic*, 620 (VI, xii, 6).

to the depths of human experience, having the habit of "meditative self-consciousness" and "brooding and self-conscious minds." Because the proper study of mankind is man, the modern concentration upon inner feelings rather than outer circumstances produces more interesting, more useful, and more moral literature.

In this context the important modification (really no more than an intensification) of one aspect of his theory becomes significant. The cultivation of the beautiful which Mill desiderates is in truth for him a cultivation of beautiful character; the most beautiful nature is worthy human nature. His passion for Wordsworth, continued throughout his life, is most easily explained by the poet's belief in the power of nature to moralize man as it moralizes the poet's song. Now the ethical aim of the poet becomes apparent: he presents scenes and characters which play upon the feelings of his readers in such a way as to pattern out for them a standard of beautiful conduct. If fully communicated, the standard becomes a model permitting of imitation. And imitation is at the root of Mill's ethic. Lacking the supernatural sanctions, he accepts a Religion of Humanity which bolsters moral conduct with natural sanctions. The test of action, ultimately utilitarian, practically and immediately is the imagined approbation of some revered figure. The "passion for ideal excellence," as he remarks in "The Utility of Religion,"[39] can be made into a powerful motive; the individual must ask himself whether Socrates, Howard, Washington, Antonius, or Christ (p. 109), or even "ideal perfection embodied in a Divine Being"[40] would approve his conduct, and then model his conduct according to the answer of his conscience.

The literary presentation of great men dedicated to altruism and duty supports and aids conscience, which

---

[39] *Three Essays on Religion* (London, 1874), p. 108.
[40] *Rectorial Address*, in *James and John Stuart Mill on Education*, ed. F. A. Cavenagh (Cambridge University Press, 1931), p. 193.

is cultivated in other ways. As conscience is a restraining force, preventing evil actions, so cultivated sentiment is active, leading a man to dedicate himself to love of his country, human improvement, freedom, and virtue. The self must be felt to be insignificant; devotion to others must be all. And the great source of this "elevated tone of mind . . . is poetry, and all literature so far as it is poetical and artistic." All other arts, as their content too is "feeling," tend to the same end, as does natural beauty, especially of the sublime order, for there is a natural affinity between goodness and the cultivation of the beautiful. The virtuous man who has learned to appreciate beauty will try to realize it in his own life, "will keep before himself a type of perfect beauty in human character, to light his attempts at self-culture."[41] Mill even goes so far as to say that there is truth in Goethe's remark that the Beautiful is greater than the Good, for it includes the Good, and adds perfection to it. As always with him, then, art centres upon humanity and is dedicated to morality.

The species poet is neither last nor least of the genus moralist; often, indeed, in Mill's writings the genus seems only to have one species. The poet's "word" becomes "message" when assimilated by individuals in the audience. As poetry speaks to individuals and transmits human motive power, that is, feeling, it is moral—if the poet has so cultivated his whole being as to escape idiosyncratic (if powerful) emotional displays. Even the immature poet (Shelley) can create great poems on occasion, as can the poet of unpoetic natures (Wordsworth). Parnassus has visitors as well as dwellers, and visitors too can bring guests.

Mill's theory of poetry is no aberration. After 1840 he seldom wrote on poetry, but the almost casual remarks herein mentioned (by no means an exhaustive list) indicate his continued interest and continued convictions.

---

[41] The preceding account is drawn from the *Rectorial Address, passim*, especially pp. 191–6.

The *Autobiography*, written and revised in his maturity, is evidence enough, but one brief glance at the sober Mill of 1870 gives life to the contention:

> After dinner Mr. Mill read us Shelley's Ode to Liberty & he got quite excited & moved over it rocking backwards & forwards & nearly choking with emotion; he said himself: 'it is almost too much for one.' Miss Taylor read the Hymn to Intellectual Beauty but in rather a theatrical voice not as pleasant as Mill's, he also read some of his favourite bits of Wordsworth whom he admires very much.[42]

---

[42] *The Amberley Papers*, ed. Bertrand and Patricia Russell (London, 1937), II, 375 ("Kate's Journal," Sept. 28, 1870).

J. S. MILL AND DEMOCRACY, 1829–61[1]

BY

J. H. Burns

In the preface to his *Considerations on Representative Government*, Mill warns those who have read his earlier writings that they

> will probably receive no strong impression of novelty from the present volume; for the principles are those to which I have been working up during the greater part of my

From *Political Studies*, 5, 1957. Originally published in two parts. Reprinted by permission of the Clarendon Press, Oxford.

[1] I have to thank the authorities of the following libraries for permission to quote from MSS. in their possession, and their librarians and staffs for the courteous assistance I have received: National Library of Scotland; King's College, Cambridge; British Library of Political and Economic Science. The following abbreviations are used in subsequent footnotes:

Considerations: *Utilitarianism, Liberty, and Representative Government*, by John Stuart Mill (Everyman's Library edn.).

DD: *Dissertations and Discussions* . . . , by John Stuart Mill (4 vols.), 2nd edn., London, 1867, 1875.

ER: *Edinburgh Review*.

life, and most of the practical suggestions have been anticipated by others or by myself.[2]

It is proposed here to survey this life-long process of 'working up', in which, it is submitted, the nature of Mill's political thought can be better appreciated than in the *Representative Government* itself. Justice to Mill as a political thinker cannot be done without close observation of the several strands which he endeavoured to weave into a coherent theory of representative government.

The process to be studied falls into three main phases, roughly equal in length, though unequal in importance and in abundance of evidence for Mill's changing views. The first phase runs from 1829 (a point of departure to be explained presently) to 1840, when Mill gave up his ownership of the *London and Westminster Review*; the second from 1840 to 1849, when he published his defence of the French Revolution of 1848; and the third from 1849 to the publication of the *Considerations* in 1861.

I

By 1829 Mill was emerging from the worst after-effects of the 'mental crisis' of 1826. He was making new con-

---

Elliot: *The Letters of John Stuart Mill*, ed. Hugh S. R. Elliot (2 vols.), London, 1910.

Hayek: *John Stuart Mill and Harriet Taylor . . .*, by F. A. Hayek, London, 1951.

LR: *London Review*.

LWR: *London and Westminster Review*.

M–T Coll.: Mill–Taylor Collection in British Library of Political and Economic Science (Roman numerals refer to volumes, Arabic to items).

OPC vi (1): *Œuvres, papiers et correspondances d'Alexis de Tocqueville*, ed. J.-P. Mayer, tome vi, vol. 1, Paris, 1954.

WR: *Westminster Review*.

[2] *Considerations*, p. 173.

tacts and assimilating new ways of thought. Coleridge, the St. Simonians, and even the despised Macaulay's attack on his father's *Essay on Government* in the *Edinburgh Review* conspired to induce a gradual revaluation of the political orthodoxy he had taken for granted since boyhood. Only slowly, however, did he diverge from accepted Radical principles and policies so far as representation was concerned. In the debate on Montesquieu in which he opposed John Sterling shortly before the latter's resignation from the London Debating Society, he defended as 'a universal principle in politics' the requirement

> that that body which, like the House of Commons in this country, holds substantially in its own hands the governing power should be chosen by, and accountable to, some portion or other of the people whose interest is not materially different from that of the whole,[3]

treating such matters as universal suffrage and short parliaments as being dependent on varying circumstances. When the July Revolution of the following year inaugurated a decade of intensive political activity for Mill, his earliest appearances were in the role of a defender of the Radical position. Thus in the *Examiner* in November and December 1830, he put forward a straightforward defence of a central plank in the Radical platform—the ballot. Both in his defence and in his discrimination between cases (such as the election of representatives 'under a really popular system') where 'the ballot is indispensable' and cases (such as voting by representatives in the assembly) where secrecy would destroy the essential responsibility of elected to electors, Mill was following his

---

[3] Appendix to *Autobiography* by John Stuart Mill, World's Classics edn., p. 308. For approximate date of this speech, cf. Elliot, i. 1–3: Mill to Sterling, 15 Apr. 1829.

father, whose *History of British India* he quotes at length in support.[4]

Only six weeks later, however, the first of a series of essays on 'The Spirit of the Age' indicated the direction in which Mill's mind was moving. One sentence from the third of these will serve to suggest how Mill's general frame of mind at this time affected his attitude to politics:

> Society may be said to be in its natural state, when worldly power, and moral influence, are habitually and undisputably exercised by the fittest persons whom the existing state of Society affords.[5]

For the rest of Mill's life, it may be said, the central problem in politics was for him to establish how best a democratic order of society could achieve this 'natural state'. His quest for a solution was to take him at times far away from the orthodox Radical theory of representative government.

Mill's first public clash with at least one powerful section of Radical opinion came in the summer of 1832. In two articles on 'Pledges' Mill attacked a doctrine which had wide support and could be plausibly represented as the logical consequence of a democratic theory of government—the doctrine that an elected representative should be bound by specific pledges to his constituents to act in certain ways. Subsequently Mill told de Tocqueville that he had his father's support in opposing this doctrine, but that his views caused considerable offence in Radical circles:[6] his second article was a lengthy reply to criticisms in the *Morning Chronicle*. Some quotations will make clear the nature of Mill's argument and its close connexion with the position adopted in 'The Spirit of the Age':

---

[4] Cf. *Examiner*, 28 Nov. 1830, pp. 754–5; also 5 Dec. 1830, p. 769, and 12 Dec. 1830, pp. 786–7.

[5] *The Spirit of the Age*, ed. F. A. Hayek, Chicago, 1942, p. 35.

[6] *OPC* vi (1), 305: Mill to de Tocqueville, 11 Dec. 1835.

The true idea of popular representation is not that the people govern in their own persons, but that they choose their governors. In a good government public questions are not referred to the suffrages of the people themselves, but to those of the most judicious persons whom the people can find. The sovereignty of the people is essentially a delegated sovereignty. Government must be performed by the few, for the benefit of the many: and the security of the many consists in being governed by those who possess the largest share of their confidence, and no longer than while that confidence lasts.

. . . If the House of Commons were constituted in the most perfect manner, whom would it consist of? Surely of the wisest and best men in the nation, or those whom the people believe to be such. Now, if I vote for a person because I think him the wisest man I know, am I afterwards to set myself up as his instructor, as if I were wiser than him? . . .

'Wisdom cometh by opportunity of leisure.' . . . We shall never have wise legislators, until legislation is a profession . . . when the value of knowledge is adequately felt, a man will choose his legislator as he chooses his physician. No man pretends to instruct his physician. No man exacts a pledge from his physician that he shall prescribe for him a particular treatment. . . .[7]

This and similarly Platonic parallels are developed at length by Mill in both articles. There is implicit here a conception of representative government very different from that of James Mill's *Essay*, with its single-minded concentration on the tendency of *any* governing minority to make a bad use of its power and the consequent need to check and limit that power. Yet John Mill is as clear as his father about the need for checks: so much so that in the circumstances of 1832 he feels bound to admit substantial exceptions to the general principle that

---

[7] *Examiner*, 4 July 1832, p. 417.

'no pledges ought in any case whatever to be exacted from representatives'. But the most important exceptions arose in regard to the shortening of parliaments and the introduction of the ballot; and here, in Mill's view, another general principle is involved—the principle that

> Of the propriety of changes in the constitution, the only proper judges are the people themselves. The trustee is to judge how he can best discharge his trust, but not upon what terms it is to be confided to him.[8]

None of this, in any case, affected Mill's conviction of the validity and importance of his conception of the true nature of representation. He summed up his argument in the second article thus:

> . . . We know that the will of the people, even of the numerical majority, must be supreme . . . but in spite of that the test of what is right in politics is not the *will* of the people, but the *good* of the people, and our object is, not to compel but to persuade the people to impose, for the sake of their own good, some restraint on the immediate and unlimited exercise of their own will. . . .
>
> It was for this reason; it was because we knew the formidable array of human weaknesses and passions which would be at work to make a Representative Democracy (what it has so often been asserted to be in its own essence) a mere mob-government; that we deemed it necessary to call thus early upon the intelligent leaders of the people that they might join in stemming the threat before it becomes irresistible.[9]

In this endeavour Mill evidently believed he had some success; for, writing to Carlyle two months later, he said (without mentioning his own share in the matter):

---

[8] Ibid., p. 418.
[9] Ibid., 15 July 1832, pp. 450–1.

If coincidence were proof of causation, I should say that the pledge-mania has been abated by the tone which his [Fonblanque's] paper has taken respecting it. What may be true is, that the *Examiner* has furnished arguments to those who were not disposed to give pledges, and has shown that a person may refuse them without being a Tory and all that is wicked. . . .[10]

The next few years form a period when Mill's views on the topics we are concerned with must be collected not only from discursive articles on the principles of politics but from his comments on the politics of the day; for this is perhaps of all his life (apart from the years of his own parliamentary career) the period when he was most intensely interested in the day-to-day political struggle. Great and beneficent as he believed the change wrought by the Reform Bill to be, he fully realized its limitations. Here is his assessment of the situation in July 1833:

The cause of the evil is one which I foresaw and predicted long before—the anomaly of a democratic constitution in a predominantly plutocratically constituted society. Till changes have taken place which can only be remotely promoted by any Reform Bill, the people will continue from necessity to select their representatives from the same class as before, avoiding only those who are *committed* to principles which the people abhor. The consequence is they must take the *feebles*. . . .

Nothing better than piecemeal reform can be expected

till the real waking minds of the country renounce money-getting, and till they are paid for devoting their time to legislation.[11]

---

[10] National Library of Scotland, MS. 618: Mill to Carlyle, 17 Sept. 1832.

[11] W. Knight, 'Unpublished Letters from J. S. Mill to Prof. Nichol', *Fortnightly Review*, lxi, Jan.–June 1897, p. 665: Mill to Nichol, 10 July 1833.

But there were immediate improvements in political machinery which Mill thought worth pressing for as urgently as possible. In the *London Review* for October 1835 he said that the Reform Bill

> gave us an instrument of government which wanted only two things to make it adequate to most of the purposes for which Reform in Parliament was sought: the protection of the ballot, for electors in dependent circumstances; and to be freed from a House of Lords determined to render the Reform of the House of Commons a nullity.[12]

A passage written two years later, however, perhaps puts the case in truer perspective: the Radicals, Mill now says,

> had faith in the Ballot, even without the Reform Bill. We had no faith in the Reform Bill without the Ballot. The foundation of our hope in the Reform Bill was that it would bring the Ballot.[13]

It is, then, on the ballot, together with the elimination of the hereditary second chamber (and with surprisingly little reference to the need for shorter Parliaments) that Mill concentrates during the middle 1830's. When the Whigs returned to office in April 1835, Mill wrote eagerly to Fonblanque:

> How do you like the new Cabinet? All things considered I am very well satisfied with it,—but I hope you will *push* them to the ballot and a few other things— they can't stand without.[14]

And when the Whigs reaffirmed their opposition to the ballot Mill's comment was:

---

[12] LR ii [WR xxxi], 271.

[13] LWR vi [WR xxviii], Oct. 1837, p. 2.

[14] M–T Coll. xlix/5: Mill to Fonblanque, 20 Apr. 1835.

A government which is determined to oppose the ballot must end by a coalition with the Tories. Without the ballot there will, in two or three years more, be a Tory parliament. . . .[15]

By the end of the 1835 session, while Mill believed that events had brought the ballot 'several years nearer', he thought that interest was for the moment shifting to the problem of the Lords: he anticipated the introduction of a 'House of Lords Amendment Bill' in 1836.[16] These hopes were, of course, disappointed, and Mill's interest swung back to the ballot again. When one of Grote's repeated motions on the subject was pending in the spring of 1837, Mill wrote an urgent appeal to Fonblanque:

Unless you and a few others bestir yourselves, and give the word to the people to meet and petition for the ballot during the next three weeks, Grote's motion will go off as flatly as it did last year, and if so, the consequences will be unspeakably mischievous.[17]

---

[15] LR i [WR xxx], July 1835, p. 514. On p. 515 Mill refers to Lord John Russell's unshaken opposition to the ballot despite his own electoral defeat as a result of 'intimidation beyond all former precedent'. Mill had forecast this in a letter to Aristide Guilbert on 8 May 1835: '. . . you will see that even Lord John Russell's defeat in Devonshire by the intimidation practised by the Tory squires and parsons will not make him an advocate of the ballot' (King's College, Cambridge, MS. K.169).

[16] Cf. LR ii [WR xxxi], Oct. 1835, pp. 270–7, especially 272, 277. In the same month Mill published two articles in the Globe attacking the view that a reformed House of Lords should have a hereditary basis and advancing the suggestion that the upper house should be elected by the lower (cf. McMinn and others, Bibliography of the Published Writings of John Stuart Mill, Evanston, Ill., 1945, pp. 45, 46).

[17] M–T Coll. xlix/12: Mill to Fonblanque, 13 Feb. 1837 (?). Grote's motion can be identified as that of 1837 by Mill's reference to his delight in the three volumes of Fonblanque's England under Seven Administrations, published early that year and reviewed

And as yet another session closed with no progress to record, urgency turned to impatience. Writing for the October 1837 number of his *Review*, Mill conceded that there were many Radical objects which the Whig government could not be expected to support:

> But there is one which can no longer be trifled with. If they can *now* persist in refusing the Ballot, they are not worth supporting any longer; they will fall, and fall unregretted.[18]

The important article just cited, on 'Parties and the Ministry', also throws some interesting light on Mill's conception of the social basis of successful radicalism. First, Mill says, the Radicals are seriously wrong in

> not putting themselves at the head of the working classes. A Radical party which does not rest upon the masses is no better than a nonentity;[19]

and he argues that the true Radical principle of government is

> until Universal Suffrage shall be possible, to do everything for the good of the working classes, which it would be necessary to do if there were Universal Suffrage.[20]

It is apposite to recall here that in an article on the 'State of Society in America' published in January 1836 Mill had said:

---

by Mill in the April *London and Westminster Review*. Grote moved his motion on Tuesday, 7 Mar., and if we assume that the 'Monday' of Mill's letter was three weeks earlier, we arrive at 13 Feb. as its probable date.

18 *LWR* vi/xxviii. 7.
19 Ibid., p. 16.
20 Ibid., p. 18.

High wages and universal reading are the two elements
of democracy; where they co-exist, all government, except the government of public opinion, is impossible.[21]

But there is for Mill a second essential element in the
social basis of Radicalism—the support of

> a class, now greatly multiplying in this country, and gen-
> erally overlooked by politicians in their calculations; those
> men of talent and instruction, who are just below the rank
> of society which would of itself entitle them to associate
> with gentlemen. Persons of this class have the activity and
> energy which the higher classes in our state of civilization
> and education almost universally want. They have
> hitherto exerted that activity in other spheres. It is but of
> yesterday that they have begun to read and think. . . .
> They are, as it is natural they should be, Radicals to a
> man, and generally Radicals of a deep shade. . . . It is
> among them that men fit to head a Radical party will be
> found, if they cannot be found among the Radicals of
> the higher classes.[22]

So much has to be said, in analysing Mill's thought at
this period, about the growing influence upon it of conservative forces, that it is important to bear in mind this
governing conception in his approach to politics: the
conception of a Radical party broadly based upon the
proletarian masses and drawing its energy and leadership more and more from the self-made men of the
under-privileged middle classes.

Meanwhile, the deeper foundations of Mill's political
thought were undergoing a gradual change. The progress of this development down to the middle of the 1830's
can be inferred from a group of articles written between
the middle of 1835 and the beginning of 1836. The first
was a review of Bailey's *Rationale of Political Represen-*

[21] *LR* ii [*WR* xxxi], 372.
[22] *LWR* vi/xxviii. 24–25.

tation.[23] This article (which incidentally includes Mill's first public reference to de Tocqueville)[24] is remarkable chiefly for clarifying Mill's conception of the essential requisites of good government. These he takes to be two in number. The first is the orthodox Utilitarian principle of identification of interests (so far as possible) between rulers and ruled; this to be achieved by a properly organized representative system. The second requisite is

> the only other condition requisite to good government . . . : That it be government by a select body, not by the people collectively: That political questions be not decided by an appeal, either direct or indirect, to the judgment or will of an uninstructed mass, whether of gentlemen or of clowns; but by the deliberately-formed opinions of a comparatively few, specially educated for the task.[25]

Mill naturally links this with the rejection of the theory of instructions or pledges, quoting his own earlier discussion of the problem in the *Examiner*.[26] Similarly, he agrees with Bailey in advocating the payment of members of the legislature, as a result of which

> legislation would become—what, to be well discharged it must become—a profession: the study and the occupation of a laborious life.[27]

---

[23] *LR* i [*WR* xxx], July 1835, pp. 341–71. Some salient passages from this and from the article next examined are reprinted as an Appendix in *DD* i. 467–74.

[24] *LR* i [*WR* xxx], 342n.: 'The most important contribution which has been made for many years to the Philosophy of Government . . . is the recent work of M. Alexis de Tocqueville, "De la Démocratie en Amérique", a book, the publication of which constitutes an epoch in the kind of writing to which it belongs. . . .'

[25] Ibid., pp. 347–8; *DD* i. 468.

[26] *LR* i [*WR* xxx], 366n.

[27] Ibid., p. 360.

But the examples by which Mill illustrates the conception of 'government by a select body' strongly suggest something more. These are, first, 'the government of Prussia—a most powerfully and skilfully organised aristocracy of all the most highly educated men in the kingdom'; and second, 'the British government in India'.[28] This is an early indication of a point it is most important not to overlook in assessing Mill's theory of representative government—the crucial role he ascribes to a professional Civil Service.

For the rest, this article shows Mill reiterating his endorsement of accepted Radical doctrines, the ballot, shorter parliaments, and a gradual approach to universal suffrage, limited, if at all, only by tests of education and, perhaps, of morality. His approach to the suffrage problem is cautious; and he concludes:

> Happily there is no necessity for a speedy decision of the question. Many important things are yet to be done, before universal suffrage can even be brought seriously into discussion.[29]

Similarly, in respect of women's suffrage: Mill agrees with Bailey that the exclusion of women is indefensible, but adds that

> the subject . . . is not one which, in the present state of the public mind, could be made a topic of popular discussion with any prospect of practical advantage.[30]

This circumspection drew adverse comment from Mill's friend W. J. Fox in the *Monthly Repository*, to which Mill replied in a footnote to his review of de Tocqueville in the October number of the *Review*, insisting that all he had meant was that no advantage was to be expected

[28] *LR* i [*WR* xxx], 348; *DD* i. 469.

[29] *LR* i [*WR* xxx], 357.

[30] Ibid., p. 353n.

from discussing the political question apart from the general problem of 'the faulty social position and consequent bad education of women', and acknowledging that for discussion of *this*, 'the time is most completely come'.[31] Mill links the question of the suffrage with the problem of reconciling the two requisites of good government. This problem, he thinks,

> is a smaller matter than might at first be supposed. It is not necessary that the many should themselves be perfectly wise. . . . It is sufficient if they be aware, that the majority of political questions turn upon considerations of which they, and all persons not trained for the purpose, must necessarily be very imperfect judges; and that their judgment must in general be exercised rather upon the characters and talents of the persons whom they appoint to decide these questions, than upon the questions themselves. . . . This implies no greater wisdom in the people than the very ordinary wisdom of knowing what things they are and are not sufficient judges of. If the bulk of any nation possess a fair share of this wisdom, the argument for universal suffrage, so far as respects that people, is irresistible. . . .[32]

The only point of substance for which Mill censures Bailey's book is one which shows how firmly entrenched in orthodox Radicalism much of his thought still was: it is the book's failure to deal with

> the master fallacy of all, the theory of *class-representation*. . . . The ready answer to the doctrine of the representation of interests is, that representation of separate and sinister interests we do not want. The only interest which we wish to be consulted is the general interest, and that, therefore, is the only one which we desire to see represented.[33]

[31] Cf. *LR* ii [*WR* xxxi], 92n.

[32] *LR* i [*WR* xxx], 348–9; *DD* i. 470.

[33] *LR* i [*WR* xxx], pp. 369–70.

Thus it was from the standpoint of democratic Radicalism, cautious in practical approach and tempered in principle by a distrust of 'direct democracy' and a belief in
the virtue of expert professionalism in politics that Mill
read the first part of de Tocqueville's *Democracy in
America* in the spring of 1835.[34] And when he reviewed
it in the October *London Review*,[35] he concentrated on
the distinction between true and false democracy:

> . . . we may remark, that the evils which M. de Tocque-
> ville represents as incident to democracy, can only exist in
> so far as the people entertain an erroneous idea of what
> democracy ought to be. . . .
>
> The idea of a rational democracy is, not that the people
> themselves govern, but that they have security for good
> government. This security they cannot have, by any other
> means than by retaining in their own hands the ultimate
> control. . . . In no government will the interests of the
> people be the object, except where the people are able
> to dismiss their rulers as soon as the devotion of those
> rulers to the interests of the people becomes questionable.
> But this is the only purpose for which it is good to intrust
> power to the people. Provided good intentions can be se-
> cured, the best government (need it be said?) must be the
> government of the wisest, and these must always be a few.
> The people ought to be the masters, but they are masters
> who must employ servants more skilful than themselves.[36]

Mill goes on to admit the danger that the people may
abuse even this ultimate power; they may interfere by its

---

[34] He had read it by 8 May, when he wrote to Aristide Guilbert: 'Tocqueville's book "De la démocratie en amérique [*sic*]"
is an admirable book. Can you tell me anything of Tocqueville?
What is his history? and in what estimation is he held in France?'
(King's College, Cambridge, MS. K.169). Mill met de Tocqueville, who was then in England, sometime before 11 June (cf.
OPC vi (1), 291).

[35] *LR* ii [*WR* xxxi], 85–129.

[36] Ibid., p. 109–10; *DD* i. 470–1.

means in government and make their representatives 'mere delegates for carrying into execution the preconceived judgment of the majority'. 'This', he says, 'rests with the good sense of the people themselves.'[37] But he does not share all de Tocqueville's fears on this score. He points out that many qualifications are to be found in de Tocqueville's own pages so far as America itself is concerned; and on the general question Mill is inclined to be optimistic:

> When there shall exist as near an approach to unanimity among the instructed, on all the great points of moral and political knowledge, we have no fear but that the many will not only defer to their authority, but cheerfully acknowledge them as their superiors in wisdom, and the fittest to rule.[38]

Similarly, when Mill considers the problem of 'the omnipotence of the majority', he does not go all the way with de Tocqueville. So far as concerns Europe, at least, there is, he believes, a safeguard against the tyranny of mass opinion which is unlikely soon to disappear—'the existence of a leisured class'.[39] And his general summing-up is again optimistic:

> . . . we see nothing in any of these tendencies, from which any serious evil need be apprehended, if the superior spirits would but join with each other in considering the instruction of the democracy, and not the patching of the old worn-out machinery of aristocracy, the proper object henceforth of all rational exertion. No doubt, the

---

[37] Cf. *LR* ii [*WR* xxxi], 111; *DD* i. 472–3.

[38] *LR* ii [*WR* xxxi], 112n. This passage brings out the close connexion in Mill's mind between the practical problem of organizing representative democracy and the theoretical problem of discovering the proper method for achieving progress in moral and political science.

[39] Cf. ibid., pp. 122–5.

government which will be achieved will long be extremely imperfect, for mankind are as yet in a very early stage of improvement. But if half the exertions were made to pre-pare the minds of the majority for the place they are about to take in their own government, which are made for the chimerical purpose of preventing them from as-suming that place, mankind would purchase at a cheap price safety from incalculable evils, and the benefit of a government indefinitely improveable.[40]

None the less, the reading of de Tocqueville's book seems to have acted as a catalyst in the development of some of Mill's own ideas. These he expressed in the ar-ticle on 'Civilization' in the first number of the combined *London and Westminster Review* (April 1836).[41] With the (highly debatable) postulates on which Mill bases his thesis—that, with the advance of civilization, 'power passes more and more from individuals and small knots of individuals, to masses; that the importance of the masses becomes constantly greater, that of individuals less'[42]—we are not concerned. We need merely note, before going on to the political consequences of this thesis, that in formulating it Mill was consciously gen-eralizing more broadly and trying to penetrate more deeply than de Tocqueville. The rise of democracy, on this view, becomes only one aspect of the broad move-ment of modern history, rather than the whole of that movement. It is, nevertheless, the most important politi-cal result of civilization as Mill sees it; and the ultimate victory of democracy, he insists, depends

not . . . upon the opinion of any individual or set of in-dividuals that it ought to triumph, but upon the natural laws of the progress of wealth, upon the diffusion of read-ing, and the increase of the facilities of human inter-

---

[40] *LR* ii [*WR* xxxi], 125.
[41] *LWR* iii/xxv. 1–28; *DD* i. 160–205.
[42] *LWR* iii/xxv. 3; *DD* i. 163.

course . . . he must be a poor politician who does not know, that whatever is the growing power in society will force its way into the government, by fair means or foul. The distribution of constitutional power cannot long continue very different from that of real power, without a convulsion.[43]

Mill sees two rational ways of meeting this situation: one who thinks the masses ready for power will assist, or at least not hinder, the democratic movement; while one who thinks them as yet unready will do his utmost, first, to prepare them for it, and second, to stimulate the energies and improve the intellects and characters of 'the opulent and lettered classes' in order 'to create a power which might partially rival the mere power of the masses, and might exercise the most salutary influence over them for their own good'.[44] This argument is intimately linked with Mill's subsequent discussion of the 'moral effects' of civilization, especially its tendency to a 'relaxation of individual energy', and with his critical examination, in this connexion, of English education, especially at the Universities. Into this we need not go. But it is important to notice the emergence in Mill's thought of the notion of a power to *rival* that of the masses; for this is a new element. Hitherto Mill had largely pinned his faith to the people's ability to choose wise rulers. Now he is beginning to fear tendencies in the masses which must be offset by some other power in society. It is no surprise to find him now discriminating between 'the political party calling themselves Conservatives' and 'a truer spirit of Conservatism' which 'lives in many who are determined enemies of those [established] institutions in their present state'.[45] It is interesting to compare what Mill says of his *Review* in his first letter to de Tocqueville on 11 June 1835:

---

[43] *LWR* iii/xxv. 8–9; *DD* i. 172–3.
[44] Cf. *LWR* iii/xxv. 9; *DD* i. 173-4.
[45] Cf. *LWR* iii/xxv. 10; *DD* i. 176.

La Revue a la prétention de représenter ce qu'il y a de plus avancé dans les doctrines démocratiques . . .[46]

with what he says in a letter to Bulwer on 23 November 1836:

The review ought to represent not Radicalism, but Neo-Radicalism, a Radicalism which is not democracy, not a bigoted adherence to any forms of government, or to one kind of institutions, and which is only to be called Radicalism inasmuch as it does not palter nor compromise with evils, but cuts at their roots. . . .[47]

When, however, we return to Mill's active political life at the end of 1837, we do not find much indication that this underlying movement of his political thought was affecting his attitude. The possibility of a dynamic Radical party, even a Radical ministry, headed by Lord Durham, roused him to an almost feverish enthusiasm; and an article intended to persuade well-intentioned non-Radicals that Radicalism, properly understood, could and must be reconciled with Conservatism, properly understood, had to give way to an attempt to answer the question—

. . . what ought now to be done by the Parliamentary Radicals. And by Radicals we here mean, those who believe in the absolute necessity of what Lord John Russell says he will never consent to—the Ballot, with or without an extension of the suffrage.[48]

Mill's correspondence with Fonblanque in the early part of 1838[49] makes his position clear: he was more than ever conscious of the differences between him and the orthodox Radicals:

---

[46] OPC vi (1), 292.
[47] Elliot, i. 103.
[48] Cf. LWR vi/xxviii. 503–4, 506.
[49] M–T Coll. xlix/8, 9, 10.

Do you in your conscience think that my opinions are at all like theirs? Have you forgotten, what I am sure you once knew, that my opinion of their philosophy has for years been *more* unfavourable by far than your own? . . . In the face of this, it is rather hard to be accused of ascribing all wisdom and infallibility to a set from whom I differ more than from the Tories;[50]

but the political exigencies of the moment made it impossible for him to break the connexion:

. . . while I myself seek the radical party where it *is*, not where it is *not*, and endeavour to rest upon the general body of radical opinion in the country, I will not throw overboard the most honest men in public life for standing nobly in the breach on a great occasion. I will rather risk myself with them even at the hazard of being accused by you of being exactly what it is my special object, my principle and also my interest to show that I am not.[51]

The high hopes of 1838 were disappointed: in the event, Mill was to do more for Durham's cause than Durham did for Mill's. Illness removed Durham from the political stage, and with him there went both Mill's dream of an effective Radical party and the consequent justification of the trouble and expense of the *Review*. But Mill did not give up till he had published, first, the article on 'Reorganization of the Reform Party' which summed up his political aims at this period,[52] and second, the essay on Coleridge which marked his final severance from orthodox Radicalism.[53]

The thesis of the first of these articles is this:

---

50 M–T Coll. xlix/8, ff. 15*v*–16*r*: Mill to Fonblanque, 30 Jan. 1838.

51 M–T Coll. xlix/8, f. 16*r*–*v*.

52 *LWR* x/xxxii. 475–508.

53 *LWR* xi/xxxiii. 257–302; *DD* i. 393–466.

When we call the party which we desire to see formed a Radical party, we mean not to circumscribe it by any partial or sectional limitation. We call it Radical because the modern Radicals are in possession of a part of the ground on which it is necessary that the combination should be built, because the measures with which they, and we may add, with which any leader they may select, must be identified, the Ballot and Household Suffrage, or something equivalent to it, are a portion of those which must be comprehended in the practical policy of such a party. But we well know that the Reform party of the empire ought not to be, cannot be, Radical in any narrow or sectarian sense. There may be many *coteries* in a country, but there can be only two parties. What we must have to oppose the great Conservative party is the whole Liberal party, not some mere section of it . . . a phalanx stretching from the Whig-Radicals at one extremity to the Ultra-Radicals and the Working Classes on the other.[54]

Mill sees the basis of this essential two-party division in the clash of interests between the 'privileged' and the 'disqualified' classes. He insists again that effective radicalism must base itself on the middle class:

No practical and judicious statesman could . . . take his stand anywhere but on the middle class . . . it does not follow, that he is obliged to take their policy; it follows only, that he must be able to make them take his. . . . He cannot therefore, attempt Universal Suffrage. To extend the suffrage to the whole middle class, to equalise its distribution among that class, to enable that class to exercise it freely, all this he can and ought to aim at.[55]

But with the working class thus indefinitely excluded from voting rights, it is, Mill once more emphasizes, essential that Radicals serve the interests of that class:

---

[54] *LWR* x/xxxii. 475–6.
[55] Ibid., p. 493.

What then has a liberal statesman to offer to the working classes? The greatest thing of all; and a thing which must precede Universal Suffrage—if Universal Suffrage is ever to come without a civil war. *He must redress the practical grievances of the working classes.* . . . The motto of a Radical politician should be, Government *by means of* the middle for the working classes.[56]

There is, in fine, little variation in Mill's 'practical views' throughout the 1830's except what is attributable to the changing year-to-year circumstances of the political struggle. To the end of the decade (and for that matter beyond) he adhered for the most part to the accepted policies of the Radical party—the ballot, gradual extension of the franchise, shorter parliaments, payment of M.P.s, abolition of the hereditary second chamber. But it is probably fair to say that it was only because circumstances precluded any rapid advance towards universal suffrage that Mill was able to remain in alliance with the Radicals with even the very moderate comfort he experienced at the end of the decade. When we examine the writings which reveal the deeper currents of his thought, we see how powerful were the forces which at this time were dragging him away from that alliance.

The famous companion essays on Bentham and Coleridge, published respectively in August 1838 and March 1840, give a measure of the extent to which Mill had by now diverged from the radicalism of his inheritance. Limiting our scrutiny as strictly as possible to his view of democracy and representation, we find him in the first of these essays[57] arguing that Bentham's theory of government affords the right answer—the only correct answer—to one of the three fundamental questions in politics. Representation is indeed, as Bentham maintained, the means of securing the people against governmental abuse of power. But representation, properly organized,

---

[56] Ibid., p. 494.
[57] *LWR* vii/xxix. 467–506; *DD* i. 330–92.

necessarily confers power on the numerical majority of a
society; and the matter can be left there only if we answer the first of the three questions—'to what authority
is it for the good of the people that they should be subject'?—by saying, 'that of a majority among themselves'.[58]
But this answer now seems very dubious to Mill; and his
doubts are the greater because he apprehends that more
than mere political authority is at stake—it is a question
of 'the despotism of Public Opinion' in every sphere of
social life. The majority in any society, Mill argues,
'must consist of persons all standing in the same social
position, and having, in the main, the same pursuits,
namely, unskilled manual labourers', and to leave this
mass without any counterbalancing power must be 'to
make one narrow, mean type of human nature universal
and perpetual'.[59] Mill does not question the claim of
the majority to 'paramount power':

> But it is necessary that the institutions of society should
> make provision for keeping up, in some form or other, as
> a corrective to partial views, and a shelter for freedom of
> thought and individuality of character, a perpetual and
> standing Opposition to the will of the majority.[60]

In default of such opposition to the ruling power, societies in the past have either 'been hardened into Chi-
nese stationariness, or fallen into dissolution'. This develops more explicitly the suggestion in 'Civilization' that
a rival power to that of the mass must be created; but it
still leaves the reader largely in the dark as to how this
'Opposition' is to be organized. Along this path we are
taken a little farther by the essay on Coleridge.

So far as politics is concerned, the central theme of
Mill's essay on Coleridge is expressed in the long passage afterwards quoted in his *System of Logic* as an il-

58 Cf. *LWR* vii/xxix. 497; *DD* i. 376–7.

59 Cf. *LWR* vii/xxix. 497–8; *DD* i. 378–9.

60 *LWR* vii/xxix. 499; *DD* i. 380.

lustration of the kind of generalizations about society which can be raised by the inverse deductive, or historical, method 'to the rank of scientific truths'.[61] Briefly recapitulated, the argument is that there are three conditions essential to a stable civil society: first, 'a system of *education* . . . of which . . . one main and incessant ingredient was *restraining discipline*'; second, 'the existence, in some form or other, of the feeling of allegiance, or loyalty'; and third, 'a strong and active principle of nationality'.[62] The acceptance of these principles, however, does not, in Mill's view, entail purely reactionary conclusions. He concedes that a philosophy of society is at present possible only in the form of a philosophy of history;[63] but on the other hand he argues, 'when society requires to be rebuilt, there is no use in attempting to rebuild it on the old plan'.[64] Mill, then, does not waver in his advocacy of reform. But he now urges that reformers can learn much from such a Conservatism as Coleridge's; and the lessons he points to are intimately connected with the movement we have already observed in his own political thought.

First, he strongly supports Coleridge's notion of a national 'clerisy', 'an endowed class, for the cultivation of learning, and for diffusing its results among the community'.[65] This notion readily fused in Mill's mind with ideas he had acquired earlier from the Saint Simonians and more recently from Comte, whose *Cours de philosophie positive* had first come to Mill's notice in 1837.[66]

---

[61] *Logic*, vi. x. 5; 8th edn., 1872, ii. 519 ff. The fact that this passage was reprinted in this context in every edition of the *Logic* published in Mill's lifetime ought to be reckoned with in any assessment of the extent to which Mill reacted in later life against the influence of Coleridgean ideas.

[62] Cf. *LWR* xi/xxxiii. 271–5; *DD* i. 416–21.

[63] Cf. *LWR* xi/xxxiii. 277; *DD* i. 425.

[64] *LWR* xi/xxxiii. 276; *DD* i. 423.

[65] *LWR* xi/xxxiii. 289; *DD* i. 445.

[66] Cf. W. Knight, 'Unpublished Letters of J. S. Mill to Prof. Nichol', *Fortnightly Review*, lxi, Jan.–June 1897, p. 674: Mill to

Second, Coleridge's theory of the Constitution inspires Mill to a more drastic reconsideration of the Benthamite theory of representation than anything in his previous writings:

> Let us take . . . the Benthamic theory. The principle of this may be said to be, that since the general interest is the object of government, a complete control over the government ought to be given to those whose interest is identical with the general interest. . . . What can a philosopher make of such complex notions as 'interest' and 'general interest', without breaking them down into the elements of which they are composed? . . . as that end (the general good) is a very complex state of things, comprising as its component elements many requisites which are neither of one and the same nature, nor attainable by one and the same means, political philosophy must begin by a classification of these elements. . . . This preliminary classification being supposed, things would in a perfect government be so ordered, that corresponding to each of the great interests of society, there would be some branch or some integral part of the governing body, so constituted that it should not be merely deemed by philosophers, but should actually and constantly deem itself, to have its strongest interests involved in the maintenance of that one of the ends of society which it is intended to be the guardian of.[67]

When we recall what Mill had written less than five years before, in reviewing Bailey, of the concept of representation of interests, it is evident how far and how fast

---

Nichol, 21 Dec. 1837; also L. Lévy-Bruhl (ed.), *Lettres inédites de John Stuart Mill à Auguste Comte*, Paris, 1899, p. 2: Mill to Comte, 8 Nov. 1841. The first of these letters also shows how lively Mill's interest in the Saint Simonians still was: 'by-the-bye, I should like soon to have these St. Simonian books again, one is always wanting them'.

[67] *LWR* xi/xxxiii. 292–3; *DD* i. 449–51.

his thought has moved. He is even prepared to admit that in England and other countries where there are large landed properties, the 'interest of permanence' is, as Coleridge argues, connected with the land, so that there is a case for the House of Lords as representative of that interest.[68]

There is ample evidence elsewhere to confirm the impression that in 1840 the conservative trend in Mill's thought was reaching a climax. In conversation with Caroline Fox on 10 April, he said of the republican experiment in America:

> . . . it has failed and ever must fail for want of the two contending powers which are always requisite to keep things in proper order—Government and Public Opinion. America subjects herself to the latter only. . . . These two contending motive powers are essential to the well-being of a State; if either gains supremacy, it becomes, like all self-willed, unsubdued, spoilt beings, very troublesome. Its existence in excess changes its nature from good to evil.[69]

Reviewing an anonymous volume of *Essays on Government* in the *Westminster Review* for September, Mill returned to the problem of representation and delegation in a tone detectably gloomier than that of 1835:

> We think that democracy *can* govern: it can make its legislators its mere delegates to carry into effect its preconceived opinions. We do not say that it *will* do so. Whether it will, appears to us the great question which

---

[68] Cf. *LWR* xi/xxxiii. 290–1; *DD* i. 447–8.
[69] Caroline Fox (ed. H. N. Pym), *Memories of Old Friends*, 2nd edn., London, 1882, i. 165. The references to America in this conversation strongly suggest that Mill was reading de Tocqueville's second part, of which he had 'finished one careful perusal' a month later (cf. *OPC* vi (1), 327: Mill to de Tocqueville, 11 May 1840).

futurity has to resolve, and on the solution of which it depends whether democracy will be that social regeneration which its partisans expect, or merely a new form of bad government, perhaps somewhat better, perhaps somewhat worse, than those which preceded it.[70]

Finally, in October, appeared Mill's second review of de Tocqueville. From this it is clear that Mill has become much more sympathetic with de Tocqueville's fears of the 'tyranny of the majority', especially its tyranny over intellectual and moral independence. He now shares de Tocqueville's fear

> not of too great liberty, but of too ready submission; not of anarchy, but of servility; not of too rapid change, but of Chinese stationariness.[71]

Mill, however, sees the ultimate source of these dangers, not, with de Tocqueville, in 'equality of conditions', but in a far more general and profound movement of social development—the progress of civilization itself, the growth of commercial and industrial prosperity:

> It is not because the individuals composing the mass are all equal, but because the mass itself has grown to so immense a size, that individuals are powerless in the face of it; and because the mass, having, by mechanical improvements, become capable of acting simultaneously, can compel, not merely any individual, but any number of individuals, to bend before it.[72]

Thus, while Mill agrees with de Tocqueville in seeing democratic institutions themselves, and the practical political education they afford, as the best cure for the evils of democracy, he feels that the more deep-seated evils of

[70] WR xxxiv. 519.
[71] ER lxxii. 35; DD ii. 56.
[72] ER lxxii. 41; DD ii. 67.

a 'mass society' call for moral and political remedies of a
different kind. Morally, what is wanted is a conviction
among 'the more generous and cultivated minds' that
the commercial spirit must be resisted and checked. Politically,

> What is requisite . . . for the same end, is not that pub-
> lic opinion should not be, what it is and must be, the
> ruling power; but that, in order to the formation of the
> best public opinion, there should exist somewhere a great
> social support for opinions and sentiments different from
> those of the mass. The shape which that support may best
> assume is a question of time, place, and circumstance; but
> (in a commercial country, and in an age when, happily
> for mankind, the military spirit is gone by), there can be
> no doubt about the elements which must compose it: they
> are, an agricultural class, a leisured class, and a learned
> class.[73]

The three elements named at the end of this passage
(which has some claim to be regarded as the high-water-
mark of Mill's conservatism) represent in reverse order
the stages by which he had moved away from orthodox
Benthamism. From the St. Simonians and from Coleridge
(and later from Comte) he took the notion of a 'learned
class' with an indispensable social function. His first reflections on de Tocqueville's book led him in the mid-
1830's to the notion of a leisured class as an essential
security against majority tyranny. Lastly, he fell, for a
time at least, under the sway of the belief that 'the agri-
cultural spirit' was a necessary counterpoise to 'the commercial spirit'. None of these ideas ever wholly lost its
effect on Mill's thought: if the influence of the last is less
apparent in his political thought, narrowly construed, it
is appropriate to remember his growing preoccupation, in
later life, with peasant proprietorship and cognate topics.

---

[73] *ER* lxxii. 45; *DD* ii. 73.

II

The first half of the ensuing decade is a period when there is a singular dearth of evidence about Mill's political ideas. There is nothing relevant in his published writings for the early 1840's, and even his private correspondence is not very helpful. It was, of course, a period of withdrawal for Mill: his social life became more and more restricted, and the manifold influences that had been at work on his mind, one by one, dropped out—his friendship with Carlyle was broken, Sterling died, the correspondence with de Tocqueville failed to live up to its early promise of genuine intimacy. The only important new contact was with Comte; and here differences of a profound kind were not slow to show themselves. In politics, Mill's mood was inevitably one of disillusionment after the excitement of the preceding few years. He told Macvey Napier, it is true, that his adhesion to the *Edinburgh Review* was 'in a certain sense political as well as literary';[74] and the conduct of the Whigs in 1841 won his warm approval.[75] But a truer notion of Mill's political attitude during these years is probably given by a letter he wrote to Barclay Fox in the autumn of 1842:

As for politics I have almost given up thinking on the subject. Passing events suggest no thoughts but what they have been suggesting for many years past; and there is nothing for a person who is excluded from active partici-

---

[74] *Selections from the Correspondence of the late Macvey Napier, Esq.*, London, 1879, p. 329: Mill to Napier, 21 Sept. 1840.

[75] Cf. Caroline Fox (ed. H. N. Pym), *Memories of Old Friends*, 2nd edn., London, 1882, ii. 327–8: Mill to R. B. Fox, 24 July 1841; and E. B. de Fonblanque, *The Life and Labours of Albany Fonblanque*, London, 1874, p. 32: Mill to Fonblanque, 1841 (exact date unknown, but must be between June and August, when Melbourne resigned).

pation in political life to do, except to watch the signs
which occur of real improvement in mankind's ideas on
some of the smaller points, and the too slender indications
of some approach to improvement in their feelings on the
larger ones. . . . There never was a time when ideas went
for more in human affairs than they do now . . . although, in comparison with the mountain of evil to be
removed, I never felt disposed to estimate human capabili-
ties at a lower rate than now.[76]

This is characteristic in its emphasis on the need for 'improvement in mankind's ideas' and 'feelings'. A month
or so later, Mill said this in a letter to Comte:

Vous avez très bien fait sentir que la régénération so-
ciale dépend maintenant de l'essor spirituel, ce qui devient
au reste de plus en plus évident aux esprits éclairés, par
l'impuissance aujourd'hui constatée de toutes les tentatives
théoriques et pratiques qu'on fait depuis bientôt cent ans
pour renouveler l'état de l'homme par les seules institutions. Je crois même cette heureuse révolution spéculative
plus avancée dans ce pays-ci que partout ailleurs, désen-
chantés comme nous sommes des institutions soi-disant
libres, à raison d'une plus intime familiarité pratique.[77]

In this frame of mind Mill could see Comte's theory of a
reconstituted 'spiritual power', rigorously separated from
temporal authority, as a clearer formulation of his own
notion of the need for 'organised antagonism' in a
healthy and progressive society.[78] He found the same
insight in Guizot:

---

[76] Caroline Fox, op. cit. ii. 335–6: Mill to R. B. Fox, 9 Sept.
1842.

[77] L. Lévy-Bruhl, *Lettres inédites de John Stuart Mill à Auguste Comte*, Paris, 1899, pp. 121–2: Mill to Comte, 23 Oct.
1842.

[78] Cf. Lévy-Bruhl, op. cit., pp. 28–29: Mill to Comte, 25
Feb. 1842.

We believe with M. Guizot that modern Europe presents the only example in history, of the maintenance, through many ages, of this co-ordinate action among rival powers naturally tending in different directions. And, with him, we ascribe chiefly to this cause the spirit of improvement, which has never ceased to exist, and still makes progress, in the European nations.[79]

To be 'disenchanted with so-called free institutions', however, and consequently to stand aloof from the consideration of political problems, were positions too sharply at odds with the habits of a lifetime to be maintained. Though the salt of politics had lost its savour, Mill never wholly suspended his interest in public affairs. His ventures into journalism at this period (very rare in the years from 1840 to 1843) were confined to limited topics and largely to monetary and fiscal problems. But in the *Edinburgh Review* for April 1846 he at last resumed the discussion of wider political questions. Reviewing two books by the French writer Charles Duveyrier,[80] Mill seems to have had his own thought on political organization set in motion again by some of the ideas he found there. Every people, Duveyrier argued, comprises two societies—an *administration* and a *public*. The former (which corresponds, it may be noted, fairly closely with the 'Universal Class' of Hegel's *Philosophy of Right*) has 'the general interest' for its 'supreme law'; its composition is not hereditary but based on 'the principle . . . of classing its members according to their merit, and rewarding them according to their works'. The *public*, on the other hand, comprising landed proprietors, capitalists, and workers, has inheritance as its 'supreme law' and is characterized by the predominance of personal interest and competition.[81] 'These two societies',

---

[79] *ER* lxxxii, Oct. 1845, p. 393; *DD* ii. 237.

[80] *ER* lxxxiii. 453–74; extracts reprinted, *DD* ii. 78–83.

[81] Cf. Duveyrier, *La Pairie dans ses rapports avec la situation politique* . . . , &c., Paris, 1842, p. 12: quoted by Mill, *ER* lxxxiii. 462; *DD* ii. 78.

says Duveyrier, 'serve naturally as a counterpoise; they continually act and react upon each other.' All this chimed in very well with Mill's own views on the need both for an equilibrium of forces in the state and for a professional Civil Service 'to introduce' (in Duveyrier's words) 'more and more into the mass of the public, elements of order and forethought'. Mill was sceptical about the probable success of Duveyrier's attempt to induce the French Chamber of Peers to regard itself as representing the administration; but he endorsed the general theory, and linked it with his own anxieties about 'the irresistible tendency of modern society towards democracy';

> It is not the uncontrolled ascendancy of popular power, but of any power, which is formidable. There is no power in society, or capable of being constituted in it, of which the influences do not become mischievous as soon as it reigns uncontrolled. . . . To render its ascendancy safe, it must be fitted with correctives and counteractives, possessing the qualities opposite to its characteristic defects. Now, the defects to which the government of numbers . . . is most liable, are precisely those of a public, as compared with an administration. Want of appreciation of distant objects and remote consequences; where an object is desired, want both of an adequate sense of practical difficulties, and of the sagacity necessary for eluding them; disregard of traditions, and of maxims sanctioned by experience; an undervaluing of the importance of fixed rules, when immediate purposes require a departure from them —these are among the acknowledged dangers of popular government; and there is the still greater, though less recognised, danger, of being ruled by a spirit of suspicious and intolerant mediocrity.[82]

Mill goes on to argue that, where historical circumstances allow any choice, the 'principle of the French Upper House'—which he compares to the Roman Senate—a

---

[82] *ER* lxxxiii. 464; *DD* ii. 80–81.

body comprising 'those who are or have been public functionaries', is the best means of counterbalancing the 'defects of Representative Assemblies', which 'are, in substance, those of unskilled politicians'.[83]

To this, however, Mill adds something further. He
asks whether legislation itself, properly understood, is a
matter fit to be entrusted to 'a popular body of 658 or 459
members, not specially educated for the purpose, having
served no apprenticeship, and undergone no examination'. He suggests that the proper functions of such a
body are

> *discussing* all national interests; . . . giving expression to
> the wishes and feelings of the country; and granting or
> withholding its consent to the laws which others
> make . . . ,

the 'others' to be a

> skilled Senate, or Council of Legislation, which, whatever
> might be its special constitution, must be grounded upon
> some form of the principle which we have now consid-
> ered.[84]

Thus Mill at this stage had not separated (as he did in
the *Representative Government*) the arguments for a
Second Chamber and those for a Legislative Council
distinct from the representative assembly. But what is
most interesting in this 1846 article is that in it Mill tries
for the first time to give some institutional shape to his
ideas of Antagonism and Opposition in society. A large
part of the thought he devoted to political questions during the next fifteen years was spent on this problem.

Two features characterize Mill's political development
in the later 1840's. On the one hand, there was a marked
revival of his concern with current politics. The winter

---

83 Cf. *ER* lxxxiii. 463–5; *DD* ii. 78–82.
84 *ER* lxxxiii. 465–6; *DD* ii. 82–83.

of 1846–7 was one of his most productive periods of journalism: between October and April he wrote over sixty leading articles for the *Morning Chronicle*; and while most of these dealt with Irish affairs, their production reveals a very different attitude to public affairs from that which he had adopted between 1841 and 1845. The other feature of these years is a reinvigoration of his radicalism and a growing concern with working-class conditions and problems: 'I have even ceased to think', he wrote to Austin in 1847,

> that a leisured class, in the ordinary sense of the term, is an essential constituent of the best form of society. What does seem to me essential is that society at large should not be overworked, nor over-anxious about the means of subsistence.[85]

This is, of course, the period when the *Principles of Political Economy* was being prepared in close collaboration with Harriet Taylor—a period when her influence was working on Mill to the virtual exclusion of all others.

The French Revolution of 1848 was welcomed by Mill, in this frame of mind, with enthusiasm: as early as 18 March he was defending the Provisional Government in *The Spectator*. And the renewed discussion of Parliamentary Reform in the summer reopened old lines of thought in Mill's mind. He saw in the Commons division of 6 July the dissolution of the Reform alliance between Whigs and Radicals which went back to 1830, and he welcomed the 'reform minority' which aimed

> at rendering the representation of the people real by distributing the representation in proportion to population, by increasing the number of electors, by affording the honest voter the protection of the ballot, and by shortening the tenure of power confided to members of parliament.[86]

---

85 Elliot, i. 131: Mill to Austin, 13 Apr. 1847.
86 *Daily News*, 8 July 1848, p. 3.

In a subsequent article Mill dealt with the alleged deficiency of the lower orders in the qualities required by 'this great transitional period in opinions and institutions':

> This objection assumes as the natural and intended effect of popular institutions, that the crude opinions and unguided instincts of the working classes would be the directing power in the state. We have no such expectation from any extension of the franchise. Reformers have always maintained, and the example of France is now before us to show, that views of things taken from the peculiar position of the working classes are not likely to predominate or have at all more than their just influence, even in a legislature chosen by universal suffrage. . . .

Yet the admission of the workers to the franchise would mean

> A gain beyond all price. . . . This gain does not consist in turning the propertied classes out of the government . . . but in compelling the propertied classes to carry it on in a manner which they shall be capable of justifying to the unpropertied.
> This, however, is only one, and the most obvious of the benefits. . . . Nothing can be imagined which would tend so much to regenerate the intellectual vigour of the classes who are now letting the powers of government perish in their hands from mere mental feebleness. . . . The conflict now going on is between the . . . interests of the propertied classes and those of the unpropertied. This opposition of interests—partly real, partly only apparent—is at present the grand difficulty of government. Now of these two opposing forces . . . one only is represented in the British parliament. . . .
> Is it not . . . one of the principal and acknowledged uses of parliament, that all which agitates and divides society should make itself felt by a corresponding agitation and division there? Ought not parliament to be the place

of discussion for adverse interests and principles, the arena where opposing forces should meet and fight out their battle, that they may not find themselves reduced to fight it in a less peaceful field?[87]

These two articles (followed on 25 July by one on electoral districts) are of great interest. They show, first, how unswerving was Mill's support for established radical policies—including the ballot and shorter parliaments. Second, they show that he has moved still closer to the idea of representation of interests—this being clearly associated with the change, noted above, in his conception of the proper functions of representative assemblies. Third, there is, momentarily at least, an optimism about Mill's outlook reminiscent of the 1830's and far removed from the 'disenchantment' of the early 40's.

In *The Westminster Review* for April 1849 Mill published his most elaborate defence of the Revolution of 1848, and incidentally discussed once again some general problems in politics. Defending Carnot's assertion that the making of laws and a constitution should be reserved to 'the intellectual *élite* of France', Mill argued as he had done in 1846 that legislation ought not to be entrusted to 'a numerous representative assembly':

> The office of a representative body is not to make the laws, but to see that they are made by the right persons, and to be the organ of the nation for giving or withholding its ratification of them.[88]

It is noteworthy how exactly this echoes Mill's earlier argument about the relation between the people and their representatives: it is not for the people to govern, but only to choose a well-qualified assembly to govern for them; it is not for that assembly to make laws, but only to see that they are made by a panel of experts.

---

[87] *Daily News*, 19 July 1848, p. 2.
[88] *WR* li. 20; *DD* ii. 365.

The Constitution of the Second Republic, Mill says, is 'a digest of the elementary doctrines of representative democracy',[89] and he comments on some of its features. His remarks on the unicameral legislature are especially interesting in view of his discussion in 1846 of the potentialities of a properly constituted second chamber. 'The arguments for a Second Chamber,' he now says,

> when looked at from one point of view, are of great force; being no other than the irresistible arguments for the necessity or expediency of a principle of antagonism in society—of a counterpoise somewhere to the preponderant power in the State. It seems hardly possible that there should be permanently good government, or enlightened progress, without such a counterpoise.[90]

But, he now argues, a legislative second chamber is likely to be a mere obstacle to improvement. Better to find a place for the 'antagonism' in society, rather than in the state, in universities rather than in 'Senates or Houses of Lords'.

Meddling by the legislature in the executive or judicial branches of government is vigorously condemned. Mill likewise condemns the injudicious extension of the elective principle:

> We dissent altogether from the common opinion of democratic republicans, which tends to multiply the conferring of offices by popular election. The sovereign Assembly . . . must of necessity be so elected. But, with this exception, it appears to us certain . . . that judges, administrators, functionaries of all sorts, will be selected with a much more careful eye to their qualifications, if some conspicuous public officer, a President or a minister has the choice of them imposed on him as part of his public business. . . . It seems equally certain that the President,

---

[89] WR li. 42; DD ii. 401.
[90] WR li. 42; DD ii. 402.

or prime minister, will be better selected by the people's representatives, than by the people themselves directly. . . .[91]

The executive, so chosen, and removable also by the assembly, should, Mill subsequently argues, have the power of dissolution. Such an executive, he says,

> would probably be a more effectual check than any second Chamber upon the conduct of an Assembly engaged in a course of hasty or unjust legislation.[92]

Thus the optimism and enthusiasm of 1848 did not remove Mill's caution as to extravagant democratic devices. Nor did the optimistic frame of mind long survive unimpaired. By the beginning of 1850 Mill was despondent enough to write this:

> We have come, I think, to a period, when progress even of a political kind is coming to a halt, by reason of the low intellectual and moral state of all classes, and of the rich as much as of the poorer classes only.[93]

For the best part of a decade he was to publish no substantial discussion of topics that are relevant here; and before we examine such evidence as there is for the development of his ideas during that period of silence, it seems reasonable to pause and review the stage now reached. By the end of the 1840's Mill had 'worked up' to many of the doctrines of his *Representative Government*. Certain lines of thought had been firmly laid down—notably the indispensable need for skilled professional administration, and the need for some kind of counterpoise to the power of the majority which must soon predominate in society. Yet Mill remained faithful

---

[91] *WR* li. 45–46; *DD* ii. 407.
[92] *WR* li. 47; *DD* ii. 410.
[93] Elliot, i. 153: Mill to Edward Herford, Jan. 1850.

to most of the orthodox Radical platform. One of the outstanding problems before us is that of how, when, and why he abandoned the ballot, payment of M.P.s, and shorter parliaments. But the major gap in Mill's theory of representative government as it stood in 1849 was the lack of any satisfactory institutional embodiment of the principle of balance or antagonism, of a sure defence against 'majority tyranny'. From this lack arose his growing preoccupation with the mechanics of voting.

III

From 1849 to 1851—from the period of John Taylor's illness and death to that of Mill's marriage to his widow —we have virtually no evidence for Mill's political opinions; and thereafter for seven years or so most of the evidence occurs sporadically in Mill's letters. But there is also the pamphlet, published eventually in 1859 as *Thoughts on Parliamentary Reform*, but written, as Mill tells us, 'some years previously, on the occasion of one of the abortive Reform Bills'.[94] This seems to mean the Bill of 1852, that of 1854 being ruled out because we know that the pamphlet, in its original form, had been completed by the beginning of January 1854.[95] Those parts of it, therefore, which are not known to be later additions, can probably be taken as embodying Mill's views in the latter part of 1852.

In this light, *Thoughts on Parliamentary Reform* shows Mill advocating as a necessary principle of any perfect representative system the granting of the suffrage to every adult. He admits, however, that the unfitness of many to vote as things were, imposed a gradual approach to the goal of universal suffrage.[96] Mill now rejected the view that electoral districts should be so organized as to give each vote an equal value. The reason

---

[94] *Autobiography*, World's Classics edn., p. 218.
[95] Hayek, pp. 187–8: Mill to his wife, 9 Jan. 1854.
[96] Cf. DD iii. 16–18.

clearly was his preoccupation with the question of giving additional weight to the votes of the educated classes; what is not clear is the nature of his solution to the problem at this period. Not for several years did he adopt the notion of plural voting based on educational qualifications. He did, however, now explicitly advocate an educational test for the suffrage, insisting that

> We must never lose sight of the truth, that the suffrage for a member of Parliament is power over others, and that to power over others no *right* can possibly exist. Whoever wishes to exercise it, is bound to acquire the necessary qualifications.[97]

More striking than any of this, however, is the fact that Mill now, undoubtedly influenced and prompted by his wife,[98] abandoned the ballot, which he had still supported, at least implicitly, in his *Daily News* articles of 1848. What had been for him the touchstone of progressive political opinions in the 1830's now became something which would 'produce far more evil than good'. The risk of coercion by landlords and others had, in Mill's view, grown less than the danger of 'the selfishness, or selfish partialities of the voter himself'. The 'progress of circumstances', political and social, has 'done the work of the ballot' by strengthening the lower classes in relation to the higher; and therefore the ballot can no longer be defended as a necessary evil—the only ground on which it could ever be defended.[99]

Early in 1853 Mill's attention was drawn to a device for securing the representation of minorities. Lord Monteagle, the former Whig Chancellor of the Exchequer, sent him what Mill in his reply variously designates a

---

[97] Ibid., p. 24–25.

[98] Cf. *Autobiography*, World's Classics edn., p. 218: '. . . hostility to the Ballot (a change of opinion in both of us, in which she rather preceded me) . . .'.

[99] Cf. DD iii. 32–44.

'paper' or 'memorandum' on the subject. This was almost
certainly a proof copy of *Minorities and Majorities: their
relative rights,* by Monteagle's son-in-law, James Garth
Marshall. Mill replied on 20 March 1853 in a letter
which, besides specifying three 'great and perfectly safe
improvements, which could hardly be successfully resisted if a Government proposed them'—abolition of unduly small constituencies, introduction of a minimal educational qualification, and admission of women to the
franchise on the same terms as men—commented favourably on Marshall's principal idea. This was the 'cumulative vote', allowing a voter to distribute at his discretion
a number of votes equal to the number of candidates to
be elected. Mill, with the proviso that the number should
be not less than three to avoid giving minorities undue
influence, approved of this device:

> To allow the cumulative vote would be one of the best
> ways which occur to me of enabling quality of support to
> count as well as quantity.[100]

He had some reservations, however. When Marshall
asked to be allowed to use Mill's letter to his father-in-law
when publishing his pamphlet, Mill acceded to his request, but stipulated that Marshall must not imply

> that I am a positive supporter of your plan—for, though
> it is very likely I may become one, I have not yet seen it
> sufficiently discussed, to be aware of all the objections to
> which it may possibly be liable.[101]

---

[100] Cf. Elliot, i. 173–5.

[101] King's College, Cambridge, MS. K.162: Mill to James
Garth Marshall, 7 Jan. 1854. The correspondent is unnamed; but
the context makes clear that it was Marshall, and the letter enables us to identify the document sent to Mill by Monteagle as a
proof of Marshall's pamphlet. Mill's qualified permission came too
late, his reply having been delayed by his absence abroad. Marshall's pamphlet had been published before the end of 1853.

The insertion in the Reform Bill of 1854 of an alternative device for minority representation led to some discussion of the problem and some reference to Marshall's pamphlet in the reviews that year.[102] It seems likely that this caused Mill and his wife to come down in favour of Marshall's plan and to incorporate it in a revised draft of *Thoughts on Parliamentary Reform*. There is, however, no evidence to show exactly when this was done.

Not until the end of 1857 do we find evidence which enables us to proceed farther. Replying on 11 December in that year to a request to sign a petition for an 'Educational Franchise', Mill definitely advocates Marshall's plan as a means of preventing the swamping of minorities and reiterates his support for an educational *qualification*. (He also expresses his support for the Parliamentary representation of London University.)[103] But he decidedly rejects the petitioners' main object. The notion of creating a special constituency or group of constituencies composed of the educated classes (the 'educational franchise' thus conferred to be enjoyed in addition to any vote the individual might have on other grounds) had been before the public since at least 1853, when a pamphlet on the subject was published. Mill may or may not have read this; but he certainly knew of its proposals from the favourable account of them given in the *Edinburgh Review* for October 1853. In 1857 his opinion was this:

> I quite agree in the opinion that educated persons should count in a greater ratio than that of their mere numbers in the constituency of the country. But I have not seen any method proposed by which persons of educated minds can be sifted from the rest of the community. All that could well be done is to give votes to a limited number of what are called liberal professions, on the presumption

---

[102] Cf. *Quarterly Review*, xciv. 558 ff. (Marshall is summarily dealt with on p. 592) and *Edinburgh Review*, c. 226–35.

[103] Cf. Elliot, i. 200.

(often a very false one) that every member of those professions must be an educated person. But nearly all the
recognised professions have, as such, interests and partialities opposed to the public good, and the members of
Parliament whom they would elect, if organised apart
would, I apprehend, be much more likely to represent
their sentiments and objects as professional, than as educated men.[104]

About the same period Mill was losing faith in the
desirability of paying Members of Parliament. Writing
on 8 July 1858 to Chapman, the Prime Minister of Victoria, Mill says his earlier view on this has been 'to say
the least, very much shaken'. Such payment, he now
fears, would raise up 'a class of men without any fixed
occupation but that of being in Parliament'; and he
illustrates from America the undesirability of this.[105]
Mill is not, strictly speaking, in contradiction with his
earlier views. He had desired the payment of members
in order to make legislation a profession. But he now
believed that, in principle, legislation should be a matter
not for representative assemblies but for small bodies of
experts. To pay members of the assemblies would now
be to create a class of professional 'politicians' in the
worst sense. That the experts should be professionally
trained and competitively recruited for this and for other
governmental work Mill, of course, now believed more
strongly than ever. It is to be recalled that this is the
period at which Mill played his part in furthering the
adoption of the Northcote–Trevelyan report and defended the existing administration of India against what
he feared would be its surrender to political jobbery.
Whatever doubts Mill may have had about democracy,
his faith in professional administration never wavered:
he said of the Northcote–Trevelyan report that 'the

---

104 Elliot, i. 199–200.
105 Ibid., p. 210.

scheme is the greatest thing yet proposed in the way of *real* reform'.[106]

Thoughts on Parliamentary Reform was published in February 1859. With one exception, all its main proposals had been agreed on by Mill and his wife for several years: grouping small boroughs into districts, a gradual approach to universal suffrage, an educational qualification, minority representation through the cumulative vote, rejection of the ballot. But the exception is a point of first importance for the understanding of Mill's ultimate conception of representative government: it is also almost alone among the later changes in his political thought in having been entirely uninfluenced by his wife. Mill now admits the desirability of an educational franchise similar in some respects to what he had rejected little more than a year earlier. There are two important differences. First, Mill's plan, instead of setting up separate constituencies of educated voters, would merely confer upon such voters additional votes in the existing constituencies. This, he implies, would remove or reduce the risks he had mentioned when refusing to sign the educational franchise petition.[107] Second, his scheme establishes a graduated scale of presumptive educational attainments, awarding, at the bottom, one additional vote to a skilled labourer and two to a foreman, and, at the top, as many as five to professional men, writers and artists, public functionaries, university graduates, and members of learned societies.[108] It is also important to observe that Mill postulates the attainment of universal suffrage before the introduction of plural voting on this basis.[109]

---

[106] Hayek, p. 200: Mill to his wife, 9 Mar. 1854.

[107] Cf. especially *DD* iii. 23–24n.

[108] Cf. ibid., pp. 21–22.

[109] Cf. op. cit., pp. 22–23: 'The perfection, then, of an electoral system would be, that every person should have one vote, but that every well-educated person in the community should have more than one. . . . And neither of these constituents of a perfect representative system is admissible without the other.'

Within a month of Mill's publication of his long-
matured pamphlet, that part of it relating to the representation of minorities was rendered obsolete by his discovery of Proportional Representation as advocated by
Thomas Hare in his *Election of Representatives*:

> You appear to me to have exactly, and for the first time,
> solved the difficulty of popular representation—and by
> doing so, to have raised up the cloud of gloom and un-
> certainty which hung over the futurity of representative
> government and therefore of civilization.[110]

In April he made his conversion public in the article
'Recent Writers on Reform'.[111] Here, among other
things, Mill reverts to a Radical position in respect of
which his attitude had been at least equivocal in earlier
years—the rejection of 'the sophistical doctrine of a representation of interests'.[112] He also argues that his own
scheme for plural voting is 'perfectly compatible' with
Hare's plan, though he thinks it may be rendered 'ultimately unnecessary' by the adequate representation of
minorities.[113] Above all, however, Mill in this article
evinces the overwhelming faith in the potentialities of
Hare's system which hereafter dominated his conception
of representation. What is to be noticed here is the close
connexion between this faith and the constant emphasis
we have seen in Mill's thought on the *quality* of representatives. On the one hand, the system 'would prodi-
giously improve the *personnel* of the national representation. . . . An assembly thus chosen would contain the
élite of the nation'; on the other, every elector would be
able to feel himself to have, personally, 'the opportunity,
if he chose, of tendering his vote for the ablest and best

---

[110] Elliot, i. 215: Mill to Thomas Hare, 3 Mar. 1859.

[111] *Fraser's Magazine*, lix, Apr. 1859, pp. 489–508; *DD* iii.
47–96.

[112] *Fraser's Magazine*, p. 499; *DD* iii. 73.

[113] *Fraser's Magazine*, p. 504; *DD* iii. 85.

man in the Empire, who is willing to serve'.[114] It is perhaps worth underlining two further points which display the continuity of Mill's thought on these subjects. The first is his sense of urgency in the face of rising democracy:

> We can never do enough in pressing forward Mr. Hare's plan. . . . It is an uphill race, and a race against time, for [? if] the American form of Democracy overtakes us first, the majority will no more relax their despotism than a single despot would. . . .[115]

The second is his reiteration that properly conceived reform is the best kind of conservatism:

> It will be, as it has been through all my lifetime, that in every real pinch, Radicals have had to do duty as Conservatives often in opposition to those they were attempting to save . . . ;[116]

and again:

> As this plan [*sc.* of Hare's] would be essentially, and in the best sense of the word, Conservative, as well as, also in the best sense, Liberal and Democratic, it ought to unite both parties in supporting it. . . .[117]

It remains to consider whether Mill added anything of major import in the *Considerations on Representative Government*. It is evident that in this, his most extensive treatment of the subject, he dealt more systematically and at greater length with such basic questions as the nature of the preconditions for representative government. And much of the book's permanent value and interest derives

---

[114] *Fraser's Magazine*, pp. 502, 506; *DD* iii. 80–81, 89.
[115] M–T Coll. lvii/2: Mill to Henry Fawcett, 5 Feb. 1860.
[116] Ibid.
[117] Elliot, i. 233: Mill to Edwin Chadwick, 20 Dec. 1859.

from these early chapters. Similarly in the closing chapters of the book Mill deals with topics hardly touched on elsewhere in his writings—local government, nationality, federalism, the government of dependencies; but these are peripheral to our main theme here. Our question is whether the central chapters, which sum up Mill's conception of representative government, contain anything of significance which we have not seen emerging in his earlier writings. In chapter XI Mill at last cautiously withdraws his support from the Radical demand for shorter Parliaments: the existing period of seven years is, he admits, 'of unnecessary length', but it 'is hardly worth altering for any benefit likely to be produced'; and in general, 'Where . . . democracy is the ascendant power . . .' a term of 'less than five years would hardly be a sufficient period to prevent timid subserviency' of representatives to constituents.[118] This is new, but hardly of fundamental importance—we have noticed that the demand for shorter parliaments had never bulked big in Mill's 'practical views'. For the rest, the *Considerations* embody elaboration and clarification rather than new departures. The elucidations are often valuable—notably, that which distinguishes clearly between the functions of the 'Legislative Commission', as Mill now terms it, and those of a Second Chamber. But they add nothing to the substance of his thought.

The conception of representative government to which Mill was brought by this long-drawn-out development has been widely criticized. It has been condemned for its excessive rationalism, its exaggerated faith in the efficacy of institutional devices, its underestimate—indeed its neglect—of the force of such factors as the party system. It is not our present business to meet these criticisms, though answers to some of them are implicit in what Mill himself says. There is point in Mill's contention that

---

[118] Cf. *Considerations*, pp. 298–300.

From despairing of a cure, there is too often but one step to denying the disease; and from this follows dislike to having a remedy proposed, as if the proposer were creating a mischief instead of offering relief from one.[119]

There is, however, one criticism which bears so closely on the theme of this analysis that it must be briefly considered by way of conclusion. According to Mr. R. P. Anschutz, there is a contradiction between Mill's argument for proportional representation and his argument for plural voting.[120] If so, the conception of representative government put forward in the *Considerations* is logically untenable, for that conception involves both devices.[121] The allegation of inconsistency, however, appears to rest upon a mistake about Mill's intention. Two distinctions are essential to Mill's theory. First, the distinction between true and false *democracy*. The latter, by distorting the representative system in favour of the majority, is a travesty of democracy; and this can be corrected only by adequate proportional representation of minorities. But there still remains the second distinction—between democracy, however true, and properly representative government. Democracy in the last resort fails by Mill's standards because it rests on an assumption which ran counter to all that he had believed and preached for thirty years—the assumption that men are equal in the moral and intellectual qualities required by the exercise of political power. Quotations could be multiplied to illustrate the point, but the following may suffice:

---

[119] Op. cit., p. 260.

[120] *The Philosophy of J. S. Mill* (Oxford, 1953), p. 45n.

[121] It is true that Mill came to see the impracticability in existing political and social circumstances of introducing an acceptable scheme of plural voting; and already in 1861 his faith in Hare's plan was sufficient to enable him to contemplate universal suffrage combined with proportional representation without undue alarm. But I have found no evidence to suggest that he abandoned plural voting as a theoretically desirable improvement.

. . . it is to me evident that in this direction [*sc.* of plural voting] lies the true ideal of representative government; and that to work towards it, by the best practical contrivances which can be found, is the path of real political improvement. . . .

. . . I do not propose the plurality as a thing in itself undesirable, which, like the exclusion of part of the community from the suffrage, may be temporarily tolerated while necessary to prevent greater evils. I do not look upon equal voting as among the things which are good in themselves, provided they can be guarded against inconveniences. I look upon it as only relatively good; less objectionable than inequality of privilege grounded on irrelevant or adventitious circumstances, but in principle wrong, because recognising a wrong standard, and exercising a bad influence on the voter's mind. It is not useful, but hurtful, that the constitution of the country should declare ignorance to be entitled to as much political power as knowledge. . . .[122]

As a moral philosopher Mill has suffered, rightly or wrongly, from the imputation of being an inconsistent Utilitarian. He ought not to suffer, as a political theorist, from being represented as an inconsistent democrat. A consistent viewpoint unites Mill's political thought from start to finish; but it is not, in the strict sense he would himself have adopted, the viewpoint of a democrat.

---

[122] *Considerations*, pp. 286, 288.

MILL AND LIBERALISM

BY

Maurice Cowling

The present writer's account of the content of
Mill's doctrine of Liberalism suggests that that doctrine
was less libertarian and less simply individualistic than
other writers have been willing to allow. On his view
Mill's political, ethical, sociological and religious writings were an attempt to fill the place left vacant by the
decrepitude of Christianity, and to provide a doctrine or
religion which all men would find suitable as they passed
out of the theological and metaphysical stages of world
history, as Comte had conceived it, into the positive,
scientific age which was about to arrive. Like Marx,
Mill believed that his doctrine was particularly suitable
to the historical conditions by which mankind was now
confronted: like Marx he was assured of its indefeasi-
bility. Mill's Liberalism no less than Marx's Marxism

From *Mill and Liberalism*, by Maurice Cowling, pp. 77–105,
copyright 1963, Cambridge University Press. Reprinted by permission of the author and the publisher.

The present selections were chosen by Mr. Cowling for this
volume. He also wrote some introductory and connective paragraphs, and altered the text very slightly.

claimed superiority over all competing doctrines. In the
hands of both, a combination of spiritual self-confidence,
synthetic history, unargued rhetoric and one-dimensional
analysis of human existence produced a body of thinking whose object was to insinuate into the minds of men
both an understanding of the nature of existence and a
way of living practically in it which was characteristic of
the orthodoxies against which Mill appeared to be pro-
testing.

Since this view of Mill's system is contested by other
interpreters, it is desirable to justify it. Justification depends to a large extent on the author's analysis of Book
VI of *A System of Logic*.[1] Book VI of *A System of Logic*
however, is not the work by which most readers know of
Mill: if we are to provide a convincing justification for
them, we must examine *On Liberty* also.

Examination of *On Liberty* is the more necessary in
that there can at first sight be no mistaking the libertarian character of the great body of Mill's expressions in
this work. Chapter V of *On Liberty* is offered by Mill as
an assault on the 'despotism of custom', conformity and
mediocrity, a sustained plea for eccentricity, diversity and
individual liberty. *On Liberty*, as a whole, looks like
unambiguous criticism of the tendency, in all European
societies, to destroy '[the] remarkable diversity of character and culture' prevailing a century before Mill wrote,
the expression of doubt about the tendency said to characterize the education given in Mill's day, 'to bring people
under common influences and give them access to the
general store of facts and sentiments', and a protest
against the 'ascendancy of public opinion in the State'.[2]
These criticisms lead to the conclusion that 'the combination of all these causes forms so great a mass of
influences hostile to Individuality' that it is only by
making 'the intelligent part of the public . . . see that it
is good there should be differences, even though not for

---

[1] To be found in Chapter III of *Mill and Liberalism*.
[2] *On Liberty*, pp. 64–5.

the better' that the disagreeable situation will be avoided in which 'all deviations . . . from one uniform type . . . [are] considered impious, immoral, even monstrous and contrary to nature'.[3] This must seem plain, and writers may be excused who feel no obligation to probe further.

However, the fact that Mill claims for his doctrine the respectability of Freedom need not make us accept his rhetoric at its face value. Mill was addicted to the rhetoric of Freedom as much as to the rhetoric of Truth: but about both it is necessary to ask questions. In particular, we must ask what it is that freedom is supposed to replace, what it is that individuality is supposed to do, and what sort of individuality it is to which men are obliged to move. For, once these questions are answered, Mill's principles seem no more than preferences for one type of polity and character over another. There is nothing self-evident about his preferences: neither Truth nor variety of human accomplishment are preserves of any particular type; there is no need to credit Mill's principles with greater rationality or necessary capacity for maximizing diversity. To establish this is important. For, if it can be established that *individuality* in his writing includes less than all the ends to which men might want to move, then the principle of individuality is designed to detract from human freedom, not to maximize it.

In order to understand the nature of Mill's purpose, it is essential to avoid detailed entanglement in the principles by which relations between government, public opinion and individual action are to be regulated. Instead, we have to ask why Mill wants their respective spheres delimited. We must examine the *objective* to which the principle is directed, rather than the application of the principle itself. Professor Rees has interesting things to say about its practical relevance. The present writer accepts his view that, when Mill defines the 'principle of self-protection' to mean that 'the only part

---

[3] *Op. cit.,* p. 66.

of the conduct of anyone, for which he is amenable to society, is that which concerns others', he implies 'a division of conduct into actions which either do or do not affect *the interests* of other persons rather than . . . what has generally been supposed to have been the division, namely, into conduct having or not having *effects* on others'.[4] This is an important distinction. It removes the impression that the principle is so general as to give no advice whatever about its application. Mill, it is true, gives a number of applications in the second part of the pamphlet: but it is difficult to establish *any* connection between this general formulation and the detailed applications.

It is, however, far from clear that the drift of Mill's argument is, on Professor Rees' view, more libertarian than it seemed before. The principle, on his interpretation, leaves the impression, indeed, of being more definitively inquisitorial than on the old. The interest of a man is not, in Mill's usage, his interest in a vulgar selfish sense: a man's interest is his interest as a progressive being—a progressive being with an obligation to be concerned for the well-being of society as a whole, and to maximize the greatest amount of happiness altogether. Often, as we have seen, there is no conflict between individual self-interest and the interest of society as a whole, but where there is, the individual's duty is to consider, not his own happiness, but the greatest amount of happiness altogether.

Now the greatest amount of happiness altogether is not maximized if men insist on following their selfish interests at the expense of general happiness: nor will it be maximized if they follow their lower, sensual natures at the expense of the higher. It will not be maximized, either, if they refuse to be educated, decline to be persuaded to the rational conclusions enjoined by their

---

[4] J. C. Rees, 'A Re-reading of Mill *On Liberty*', *Political Studies*, vol. VIII, no. 2, 1960, p. 123.

higher natures or refuse to give that deference to superiority of intellect and the higher sociology which Mill assumes rational, educated men will always wish to give. From this it follows that, if the duty of society (or government) is to restrict individuality (when necessary) in order to maximize general utility, then individuality is likely to flourish only so long as it is connected with the higher cultivation of the sentiments. The sort of social or governmental pressure which might, therefore, be admissible on this principle is more searching than superficial attention to the principle suggests. For, if interference with individual liberty *can* be justified on the ground that interference is in the interest of others, and if the interest of others is taken to lie in producing the greatest amount of higher happiness possible, then the injunction is no less vague than before in defining the *amount* of legitimate social (or governmental) pressure, but much more specific in determining the *purpose* to which interference should be put.

Mill distinguishes, it is true, between actions which do injury to the interests of others, and those which do not; and observes that 'the inconveniences which are strictly inseparable from the unfavourable judgement of others, are the only ones to which a person should ever be subjected for that portion of his conduct and character which concerns his own good, but which does not affect the interest of others in their relations with him'.[5] Social action is not appropriate in these cases. In cases where the interests of other people *are* affected, moral disapproval is desirable, not only of the actions themselves but of the dispositions which produce them.[6] But 'the self-regarding faults . . . are not properly immoralities . . . They may be proofs of any amount of folly . . . but . . . the term duty to oneself, when it means anything more than prudence, means self-

[5] *On Liberty*, p. 69.
[6] *Op. cit.*, p. 70.

respect or self-development', and, along with other duties
to ourselves, '[is] not socially obligatory, unless circumstances render them at the same time duties to others'.[7]
This limits the extent to which Mill will tolerate interference with individuality and might seem to make his
principle more libertarian than we are suggesting. But
it is necessary to ask: why is liberty to be absolute at this
point? why, when no assignable damage is done to the
interest of others, should a man be left free to do what he
likes with himself? And Mill's answer is, not so much
because diversity of individual character is desirable *in
itself*, but 'because for none of [these duties to oneself]
is it *for the good of mankind* that [a man] be held
accountable to [his fellow creatures]',[8] and because
'the inconvenience [which society suffers from self-
regarding, self-affecting faults] is one which society can
afford to bear *for the sake of the greater good of human
freedom*'.[9]

'For the sake of the greater good of human freedom', it
may be objected, dismisses the view we are taking of
Mill's doctrine, and it must, on the face of it, be agreed,
that it does. Again, however, it is desirable to ask what
freedom in Mill is for, and what is the *good of mankind*
to which the convenience of bringing social pressure to
bear is to be postponed. When the question is asked in
this way, the answer will not be disappointing. For the
answer is, as it always is in Mill—general social utility,
the end and justification of *all* social action.

General utility for Mill means, as we know, maximization, not of *any* happiness, but of the higher happiness,
the freedom of men to engage in 'rational' pursuit of
disinterestedness and truth. Maximization of the higher
happiness comes when men are left free (from mediocre
social pressure) to reflect on, and choose, the right action

---

[7] *On Liberty*, p. 70.
[8] *Ibid.*
[9] *Ibid.*, p. 73.

rather than the wrong one. The object of right social policy is to find the best means to achieve this end. 'The merely contingent . . . injury which a person causes to society, by conduct which neither violates any specific duty to the public, nor occasions perceptible hurt to any assignable individual except himself' *does* damage society, so far as it diminishes the stock of mental cultivation.[10] The fact that damage *is* done, however, does not mean that society should interfere. Interference would produce consequences no less disagreeable than the consequences that flow from refusing to interfere: once the differing consequences are compared, interference must be rejected. It must be rejected because, in pursuit of 'the good of mankind' and 'for the sake of the greater good' which 'human freedom' brings, non-interference will be more conducive to utility. Where assignable damage *is* done to the interests of others, then the assignable damage outweighs the damage done by restriction of individual liberty, and punishment, or disapprobation, *has* to be imposed. But where assignable damage is not done (or, perhaps, Mill might add, cannot be measured), then men are more likely to maximize utility (despite the inconvenience) by allowing full individual liberty, than by preventing the damage a free man may do by perversely misusing his freedom.

For, even when men are free of governmental or social disapprobation, society still has means of inducing them to act rationally, disinterestedly and with a view to maximizing utility. Because the obvious, formal (and perhaps, in a way, Mill thinks, crude) agencies of public pressure are not used, it is not, therefore, to be supposed that public pressure cannot be brought to bear. Nor does Mill think that pressure ought not to be brought to bear. Pressure ought not to be contemporary society's mediocre pressure to conform to ill-conceived, unsystematic prejudice. Nevertheless,

---

[10] *Op. cit.*, p. 73.

the existing generation is master both of the training and the entire circumstances of the generation to come; it cannot indeed make them perfectly wise and good . . . but it is perfectly well able to make the rising generation, as a whole, as good as, and a little better than, itself. If society lets any considerable number of its members grow up mere children, incapable of being acted on by rational consideration of distant motives, society has itself to blame for the consequences. Armed not only with all the powers of education, but with the ascendancy which the authority of a received opinion always exercises over the minds who are least fitted to judge for themselves . . . let not society pretend that it needs, besides all this, the power to issue commands and enforce obedience in the personal concerns of individuals, in which, on all principles of justice and policy, the decision ought to rest with those who are to abide the consequences.[11]

The best way of achieving a rational consensus, in other words, is to leave men as free as possible to be led into it by rational education. To maximize freedom can, in some circumstances, do damage to utility, but not as much as would be done by restricting it. When the damage done by leaving a man free is clear and assignable, then he must, regrettably, be punished: but where no assignable damage is done, then the *only* rational way to maximize utility is to leave men's minds absolutely open to the working of rational education—because it is only through rational education that unforced assent to the right means of determining the right course of action will take root.

Mill does not, in his *Applications*,[12] emphasize these conclusions, though he believed that education should be compulsory. But Mill was attempting in *On Liberty* to protect the élite from domination by mediocrity. How he would have applied his principles in a system where the

---

11 *On Liberty*, pp. 73–4.
12 *Ibid.*, ch. 5.

élite had triumphed, and to what extent it could have operated individualistically where a 'rational' consensus had prevailed, is another question. *On Liberty*, in the form in which it was written, so far from being an attempt to free men from the impositions of *all* doctrine, is an attempt to free them from customary, habitual, conventional doctrine. Convention, custom and the mediocrity of opinion are the enemies in Mill's mythology: the freedom he gives is given in order to subject men's prejudices to reasoning authority. *On Liberty* does not offer safeguards for *individuality*; it is designed to propagate the individuality of the elevated by protecting *them* against the mediocrity of opinion as a whole. Convention, custom, habit and public opinion are never to be trusted: all history has been a battle against them. History shows them to be oppressive: oppressions of this kind must be resisted. Once the oppressive consensus has been removed, a better one must replace it: but it would be foolish to expect an imposed consensus to achieve the objects which a rational consensus might. Mill, in fact, had grasp of an important truth—that it is no use *expecting* success from imposing a consensus by force, but that does not make him abandon the attempt to have a consensus. On the contrary: the consensus imposed by mediocrity is bad, and liberty in relation to *it* ought to be as great as possible. The means of achieving a rational consensus will not be discovered by pursuing the intuited views on which conventional opinions depend. But that does not alter the fact that the purpose in allowing men liberty, the justification of individuality, is not diversity in itself, but diversity informed by the rationally agreed education and sociology which the higher minds alone can provide. Education is desirable and self-development an obligation because both maximize the same sort of happiness. Mill, in short, feared democracy and loved individuality, not so much because individuality would induce diversity, as because, by breaking up existing rigidities, it would make the world safe for 'rational' education, 'rational' thinking, 'rational' sociology and the assured leadership of the 'rational' clerisy.

* * *

The position we are maintaining is that Mill's fundamental principles have neither proof nor philosophical authority, but are commitments to action, the outcome of assertions to claim knowledge of the nature of the world and the direction men's duty ought to take within it: and that they cannot sustain claims to be something other, or something more, than this. Mill seems sometimes to suggest that they perform one function—a philosophical, or even a positive, scientific one—but at times that they perform the other, practical one. He does not always think that they have scientific authority: at moments when he is most explicit, he does not say so at all. Nevertheless, where assumptions are made without scrutiny, he seems to think it; and it is difficult to avoid feeling that much of what we will characterize as his *arrogance* is connected with want of clarity at this point.

The statements we have been discussing are religious: Mill himself says so. The principle of utility enjoins maximization of the finest things of which men are capable: and this is what Mill means by the Religion of Humanity.

Not only does all strengthening of social ties, and all healthy growth of society, give to each individual a stronger personal interest in practically consulting the welfare of others: it also leads him to identify his *feelings* more and more with their good. . . . He comes, as though instinctively, to be conscious of himself as a being who *of course* pays regard to others. The good of others becomes to him a thing naturally and necessarily to be attended to, like any of the physical conditions of our existence. . . . This mode of conceiving ourselves and human life, as civilisation goes on, is felt to be more and more natural. Every step in political improvement renders it more so, by removing the sources of opposition of interest, and levelling those inequalities of legal privilege between individuals or classes, owing to which there are large portions of mankind whose happiness it is still practicable to disregard. In an improving state of the human mind, the influences are constantly on the increase, which tend to generate in each individual a feeling of unity with all the rest; which, if perfect, would make him never think of, or desire, any beneficial condition for himself, in the benefits of which they are not included. If we now suppose this feeling of unity to be taught as a religion, and the whole force of education, of institutions, and of opinion, directed, as it once was in the case of religion, to make every person grow up from infancy surrounded on all sides both by the profession and the practice of it, I think that no-one who can realise this conception, will feel any misgiving about the sufficiency of the ultimate sanction for the Happiness morality.[13]

Utilitarianism is capable of attracting all the sanctions given to any other religion. The higher minds perform the functions once performed by the clergy: one of the ideal objects to which attention should be turned, in substitution for the ideal object of Christianity, is altruistic elevation of the feelings. To describe by the word 'morality' the injunction to identify oneself, not just with one's own interests, but with the whole human race is, says Mill, to claim 'too little for it; [it is] a real religion, of which as of other religions, outward good works (the utmost meaning usually suggested by the word morality) are only a part, and are indeed rather the fruits of religion than the religion itself'.[14] The theological temper and theological interests of Mill cannot be doubted. What sort of temper was it, and what was the content of the position?

Mill did not have, in any normal sense, a religious upbringing. In his father's house, except in Mill's earliest childhood, there was no religion. So far as Mill came in

---

[13] *Utilitarianism*, p. 195.
[14] *Three Essays on Religion*, p. 109.

time to take religion seriously, there was disagreement, but his hostility to prevailing orthodoxies involved no breach with the religion of his family. It involved, on the contrary, self-confident protest against what he thought of as the mediocrity of prevailing opinion. Unlike Sidgwick, Hobhouse, Leslie Stephen, and other post-Christian agnostics of the generations following, Mill had never, properly speaking, had a religion. Through his wife's family and connections he had indirect knowledge of various sorts of English dissent: through Romantic literature he understood something of the sentimental religion of the heart. But of the religion of the churches he was ignorant, and profoundly contemptuous. That is not to say that his contempt was always expressed. There is about Mill's treatment of Christianity a caution more suitable to tactical proselytizing than to earnest propagation of the truth. His attempt to distinguish the teachings of Christ (for whom he expressed admiration) from later theological accretions (for which he did not) was probably a genuine expression of his own conviction. The recurrent assertion that Utilitarianism does not conflict with the Christian message may well have been part of a deep-rooted desire to reconcile all truths with all others. There seems no reason to doubt the sincerity of the assertion that 'other ethics than any which can be evolved from exclusively Christian sources', so far from totally superseding Christian teaching, 'must exist side by side with Christian ethics to produce the moral regeneration of mankind'.[15] These positions are genuine intellectual conclusions which follow consistently from the need for comprehensiveness and 'antagonistic modes of thought'; it may be no more than muddle which neglects the significance of the Christian claim to know the truth about God's nature, and supposes that 'the good' from Christianity can be retained once this central claim has been rejected. Yet, it is difficult to avoid feeling that the strength of contemporary Christian feeling, and the dam-

[15] *On Liberty*, p. 45.

age Mill feared from attacking it openly, increased the
ambiguity of his public statements. The specifically
religious writings do, indeed, go a long way to expose his
attitude towards Christian claims. When they were published after his death they were less hostile to Christianity than Mill's friends had expected, but they were
more hostile than anything he published in his lifetime.
What emerges from them is commitment to general cultivation, and recognition that *some* Christians have *some*
part to play in providing it. There is no unambiguous
statement of his willingness (in certain circumstances) to
see Christianity rejected altogether, and nothing to match
the assertion, made privately to John Sterling in 1831,
that 'in France, where Christianity has lost its hold on
men's minds . . . a Christian would be positively less fit
than a St. Simonian (for example) to form part of a
national church'.[16] Mill was conscious of the power of
Christian feeling in England: reluctance to play a part
in destroying, without replacing, an established doctrine, was one consideration which made him unwilling
openly to reject Christianity. It is, however, possible, at
least, that genuine reluctance was strengthened by tactical awareness that moralists who wanted to propagate *his*
general injunctions would do well to take pains to 'adopt
(as far as without hypocrisy they can) those means of
addressing the feelings and the conscience to which a
connection with Christianity has given potency'.[17]

However, if we are to consider what Mill thought (in
private) as well as what he published, one may say that,
for Christian theology, and for the developments imposed
by generations of theologians on the moral message of
the 'founder of Christianity', Mill had a fundamentalist's
aversion. Mill is not, in these circumstances, it might
seem, promising material for theological comment. Nevertheless, for Mill, no less than for any other Victorian

---

[16] J. S. Mill to John Sterling, Oct. 20–22, 1831. Elliot, *Letters
of J. S. Mill*, vol. 1, p. 5.

[17] *Three Essays on Religion*, p. 194.

moralist, religion was a major preoccupation. He was hostile to Christendom, not indifferent: his agnosticism (if that is the right word) has about it a quality of inquisitorial certainty; he displays at considerable length an active theological concern with three of the most important questions with which theology has to deal—the character of Nature, the knowability of God, the existence of evil: if we wish to understand the character of his utilitarianism, it is necessary to understand what he has to say about them.

In Mill's view, Nature—the world untouched by Man—is not in itself good, and does not testify to the existence of a Good God. It may be held to testify to the existence of an author of Nature, the Creator of the world, 'a Being of great but limited powers . . . of great, and perhaps unlimited intelligence':[18] but contemplation of Nature as it is without human intervention lends no weight whatever to the belief that the Creator of the world is a being of great moral power. 'There is no evidence in Nature', he writes 'for divine justice, whatever standards of justice our ethical opinions may lead us to recognise. There is no shadow of justice in the general arrangements of Nature: and what imperfect realisation it obtains in any human society . . . is the work of man himself . . . making to himself a second nature far better and more unselfish than he was created with'.[19]

Nor does the dogmatic religion of the churches help to establish that God's character has moral quality. The doctrine of atonement and belief in Hell (which Mill thinks inessential additions to the original body of Christ's teaching) make it difficult to accept the Christian God as a tolerable moral being. Not content with creating a world in which there is no moral order, God subjects men to injustices and indignities, punishments and torments which they have not merited. Christ, regarded by Mill as the founder of Christianity rather than the Son

---

[18] Three Essays on Religion, p. 194.
[19] Ibid., pp. 113–14.

of God, was, indeed, a being of great moral grandeur: but how is it possible to reconcile His 'beauty and benignity and moral greatness' with 'recognition . . . [in Christianity] of the object of highest worship in a being who could make a Hell, and who could create countless generations of human beings with the certain foreknowledge that he was creating them for this fate'? 'Is there' he asks 'any moral enormity which might not be justified by imitation of such a Deity? And is it possible to adore such a one without a frightful distortion of the standard of right and wrong'?[20]

Reconciliation of these two standards—the standard of the highest human aspiration (as seen, among other places, in Christ's teaching) and the nature of the Creator of the World—has central relevance to utilitarianism *and* religion. Mill's epistemology is empirical and anti-transcendental. He directs sharp philosophical comments at the practical effects of Intuitionism: this hostility extends to its theology. Mill's religion is a religion of Sense-Experience. It insists, against transcendentalist claims to direct knowledge of God's nature or direct intuition of his goodness, that men can know God's nature only as they know other natures—i.e. phenomenally. Men can, says Mill, know the effects of other men's wills, not other men themselves, and can do no more than *infer* their characters from them. In the same way, we can know God only by inference from the effects of his works, not by knowledge of his character in isolation from its consequences. Our knowledge of God, therefore, is relative, not absolute, the outcome of a particularly human activity, not the infusion of a Divine afflatus or ignition of a Divine spark. It follows from this that, although we know little about God, what little we do know must be described in the language we apply to men. Words must not be used to mean one thing when applied to God, and another when applied to his creatures. Divine action must be judged by the standards we apply

20 *Ibid.*

to human actions; we must avoid the temptation to twist words like *good* and *bad* in order to represent the evil inherent in the order of Nature as the beneficence of God's Providence.

> Unless I believe God to possess the same moral attributes which I find, in however inferior a degree, in a good man, what ground of assurance have I of God's veracity? All trust in a Revelation presupposes a conviction that God's attributes are the same, in all but degree, with the best human attributes.

> If [Mill goes on] instead of the 'glad tidings' that there exists a Being in whom all the excellencies which the highest human mind can conceive, exist in a degree inconceivable to us, I am informed that the world is ruled by a Being whose attributes are infinite, but what they are we cannot learn, nor what are the principles of his government, except that 'the highest human morality which we are capable of conceiving' does not sanction them: convince me of it, and I will bear my fate as I may. But when I am told that I must believe this, and at the same time call this being by the names which express and affirm the highest human morality, I say in plain terms that I will not. Whatever power such a being may have over me, there is one thing which he shall not do: he shall not compel me to worship him. I will call no being good, who is not what I mean when I apply that epithet to my fellow creatures: and if such a being can sentence me to hell for not so calling him, to hell I will go.[21]

It may be legitimate to argue that men cannot grasp the character of God's Providence or the nature of His Goodness, to maintain, that is to say, a total agnosticism about it: but Mill is emphatic about the need, in practical moral judgement, where God's work is under consideration, to reject what is unknowable as being, for

---

[21] J. S. Mill, *An Examination of Sir William Hamilton's Philosophy* (1865), London 1878, pp. 128–9.

that reason, irrelevant. That which is knowable—the phenomenal world—is alone relevant: moral standards there
must be the outcome of human judgement because they
are created by human wills through human words.
Knowledge of goodness, and judgement of what is good,
are part of the human effort to improve, elevate, amelio-
rate the Nature which God has provided as the area of
human activity: and we must *always* use 'good' to mean
what we mean by it in normal usage.

> The proposition, that we cannot conceive the moral attri-
> butes of God in such a manner as to be able to affirm of
> any doctrine or assertion that it is inconsistent with them,
> has no foundation in the laws of the human mind: while,
> if admitted, it would not prove that we should ascribe to
> God attributes bearing the same name as human qualities,
> but not to be understood in the same sense; it would prove
> that we ought not to ascribe any moral attributes to God
> at all, inasmuch as no moral attributes known or conceiv-
> able by us are true of him, and we are condemned to ab-
> solute ignorance of him as a moral being.[22]

Whatever goodness God himself may have, however
greatly human goodness has been increased in earlier
stages of civilization by men's belief that God supports
particular moral systems, it is an anthropocentric and
specifically human standard which ought now, in the
Religion of Humanity, to determine men's judgement of
the right courses to take in the struggle against evil.

Mill's religion, then, is not a supernatural one. Its
authority does not depend on supernatural sanctions; Mill
is anxious to establish that morality can be damaged when
stress is laid on the supernatural character of its authority. He does not deny that supernatural religions have
in the past—especially in the theological phase of human
history—buttressed the laws and conventions of particular societies. Religion has, to a certain extent he admits,

---

[22] *Op. cit.*, pp. 134–5.

been useful in providing that measure of social solidarity which stable societies need. But supernatural religion is not *essential* to stable morality. Morality (Mill means *any* morality) can maintain itself so long as parents, public opinion and the educational system are committed to maintaining it. Though religion is usually credited with 'all the influence in human affairs which belongs to any generally accepted system of rules for the guidance and government of human life',[23] it is not the religious content which is effective, but the fact that *something* is taught, and taught definitively. 'Vast efficacy belongs naturally to *any* doctrine received with tolerable unanimity as true and impressed on the mind from the earliest childhood as duty'; 'a little reflection will . . . lead us to the conclusion that it is this which is the great moral power in human affairs, and that religion only seems so powerful because this mighty power has been under its command'.[24]

Not only, moreover, is religion unnecessary, it is often in these respects positively damaging. A healthy society is not, in Mill's picture, a society where men accept a morality because it has been accepted in the past, or because it has been promulgated by unreasoning authority. The only homogeneous society worth considering, in Mill's writing, is a society where *all* men are actively engaged in recurrent reasoning about the character of goodness and its relevance to the problems by which they are confronted. They may defer to the authority of cultivated minds, but rational men will do so only because the cultivated mind does better than most men what all men would do for themselves if they could. Deference to this sort of authority is not arbitrary: it is a natural exercise of the practical reason, and will disappear once the minds to whom deference is given cease to give evidence of superior cultivation. Deference of this sort is rooted in human judgement and reason, but

[23] *Three Essays on Religion*, p. 78.
[24] *Ibid.*

does not supersede them. Deference to supernatural authority induces an arbitrary, unreflective conservatism, and a damaging tendency to silence rational argument. Human reasoning will be maintained only by constant effort: the effort will not be sustained if deference predominates. The moral consensus must be neither arbitrary nor imposed; it must be the outcome of individual striving. Striving should be guided by an education in Humanity: this process of inculcating moral attitudes and positive knowledge will speed the spread of the three most important pillars of untranscendental religion—utility, disinterestedness and mental cultivation. These are the comprehensive ethical injunctions, but they are at no point free from human scrutiny: they are, so far from being the conclusions of supernatural religion, the basis of the most wholly terrestrial of all—the Religion of Humanity.

The Religion of Humanity has for its chief end the principle of utility in the widest sense. It is a religion, in Mill's view, because it performs the social functions of a religion, and commands authority because it contains, in a peculiarly powerful form, 'the essence of religion, the strong and ardent direction of the emotions and desires towards an ideal object'. 'The ideal object' is a benevolent desire for the elevation of humanity. To establish that the Religion of Humanity is *a* religion does not, however, establish that anyone is *obliged* to conform to its precepts. Obligation will seem weak unless it is not only *a religion*, but also the only religion worth attending to. If it is not the best religion, then it may be an open question whether its precepts should be obeyed: and apologists who claimed only that it was a *possible* religion would not be thought to have said very much in its favour.

It is sometimes supposed, by Mill's critics and by his friends, that Mill was not a proselytizer—that, since his objective was as wide a variety of human accomplishment and disposition as possible, he could not have believed in a best religion. Mill's liberalism, it has been supposed, is an invitation to *every* sort of human experiment. Examination of Mill's words, however, makes this seem unlikely. He wished, at one level, to encourage scrutiny and questioning of every established habit, religion and institution: he was opposed to every sort of received (arbitrarily received) orthodoxy. Nevertheless, his liberalism does not involve replacing authoritative commitment with a vacuum. He is claiming to free men from wrong, inadequate or arbitrary postures: he is not freeing them from religious postures altogether. On the contrary, he is committed, not merely to believing that the Religion of Humanity is *a* religion: he is committed also to believing that it is 'a better religion than any of those which are ordinarily called by that title'[25]; and, since this is a large claim of great consequences, we must ask why he supposes that he is entitled to make it.

He feels entitled to make it, in the first place, because the Religion of Humanity is the outcome, not of authoritative dictate, but of the efforts of all those highest minds which, in the course of history, have turned their attention to the problems of human conduct. Mill's view of history shows in some places the impress of an intelligent relativism, but in others he is not only not relativistic, but is positively dogmatic in imputing a monopoly of merit in any particular situation to the cause, or person, whose opinions or actions he admires. *On Liberty,* though not the only point at which he establishes a synthetic history for himself, provides the best examples. There he assumes that the history of the world provides evidence of a strand of recurrent resistance to mediocrity, a gallery of enlightened heroes, whose cumulative wisdom and authority constitute a validation of his doctrine. That the gallery is arbitrarily selected, that the majority *can* in some situations be right: that Socrates *was* a corrupter of youth, and that it is by no means clear that *he* is to be respected and his critics condemned, are not, at this point in his argument, positions Mill thinks it desirable

---

25 *Three Essays on Religion,* p. 110.

to consider. There is, it is true, reiteration of the belief
that no man has a monopoly of truth, and that majorities,
or dominant opinions, are not infallible. But, if dominant
opinions are *not* infallible, nor are defeated opinions
either; and it is not easy to see why the opinions of
Socrates should necessarily be thought better, when detached from the context in which they were enunciated
and the consequences they produced, than the opinions
of those by whom he was driven to death.

Whatever we may think of it, Mill believes he can
discern an antinomian, libertarian tradition of this kind,
issuing in his own time in an obligation to support franchise reform, hostility to Governor Eyre, remedying of
Irish grievances, admiration of Bismarck and the destruction of the aristocratic power which dominated the polity Mill knew best. He believes that this tradition of
thinking has provided mankind with an 'ideal object of
reverence', and that its general beneficence and rational
altruism supply substitutes to replace the sanctions which
fear of punishment supplied to the moral dictates of supernatural religions. The fellowship of the best minds,
and the moral approbation of humanity, provide, indeed,
a secular version of the Communion of Saints: for 'the
thought that our dead parents or friends would have approved our conduct is a scarcely less powerful motive
than the knowledge that our living ones do approve it;
and the idea that Socrates, or Howard, or Washington,
or Antoninus, or Christ would have sympathised with us
. . . has operated on the very best minds as a strong
incentive to act up to their highest feelings and convictions'.[26] It is this combination of certainty that these are
the best men, that they are advocating both the *best* and
the *same* courses, and that these 'highest minds, even
now, live in thought with the great dead, far more than
with the living, and next to the dead, with those ideal
human beings yet to come', which gives Mill such super-
stitious confidence in them. Not only is the tradition a

---

[26] *Op. cit.*, p. 109.

communion of the best minds, it is also a comprehensive junction of the best doctrines. Mankind, in its constant struggle to improve the world, has, through this work of resistance to mediocrity, enunciated elevated doctrines: the history of mankind is a record of their progressive accumulation. Once gained, truths of this sort are not lost. Once uttered by a powerful moral teacher, they become the permanent possession of mankind: and the process of trial and acceptance, to which all doctrines are subjected, guarantees that, in the highest minds, all that is best in all the best doctrines will be comprehended.

The Religion of Humanity, then, consists of the 'best' doctrines that have been propagated by the 'best' minds, and may, almost by definition, be taken to be, not only a good religion, but the best one. Even if this is so, however, it is still doubtful whether mere assertion that it *is*, would give it binding authority—particularly when the supernatural sanction is rejected. In order to do this, it is necessary, on utilitarian grounds if on no other, to make claims about the consequences of adopting it. This Mill does not fail to do: indeed, so far from failing, he claims for the Religion of Humanity the sort of comprehensive consequence which supporters of almost all religions have almost always made for commitment to them.

We have talked already about *disinterestedness* in Mill's utilitarianism: but it is necessary to repeat once more that the principle of utility and the Religion of Humanity alike are supposed to induce a higher disinterestedness than any that has ever been advocated by the highest ethical doctrines in the past. *Disinterested* concern for the welfare of mankind is the first, and central, injunction in Mill's practical doctrine, and provides essential direction of the higher faculties towards an 'ideal object'. Disinterestedness has been made part of the higher human ethic: disinterested concern for all humanity provides spiritual and moral satisfaction on the one hand, and fulfilment of human nature on the other. Kant would have agreed: 'in the golden rule of Jesus of Nazareth we read the complete spirit of the ethics of utility'[27]; where the highest minds concur, there can be no doubt of the categorical character of the injunction. As humanity is improved, and desire for immortality diminishes, the Religion of Humanity will be even more appropriate than in the past. 'Mankind can', says Mill, 'perfectly well do without the belief in a Heaven': 'what is odious in death is not death itself, but the act of dying and its lugubrious accompaniments'.[28] A time may come when 'human nature' will reach the point at which it begins to find 'comfort, and not sadness, in the thought that it is not chained through eternity to a conscious existence which it cannot be assured that it will always wish to preserve'. And when that time comes, so long as 'the Religion of Humanity [is] as sedulously cultivated as the supernatural religions are, . . . all who had received the customary amount of moral cultivation would up to the hour of death live ideally in the life of those who were to follow them'.[29]

The Religion of Humanity has, furthermore, the beneficial consequence of providing greater opportunity than there would have been otherwise, for general participation in human activity and the working of society. Mill does not write, as Marx or Hegel did, about alienation: he is not concerned with the problem in the same form. Nevertheless, he is interested in *participation*, in the attempt to find means whereby those who have recently emerged from feudal or aristocratic tutelage, should feel that they belong in a rationally ordered society. Mill fears the consequence of failing to extend this sense of participation. Nothing can prevent manual labourers exercising an influence over social policy: nothing would be more dangerous than a class of fundamentally uneducated persons making their irrational mark on social habit and governmental action. Mill wishes to cultivate the faculties of the uneducated—because cultivation

---

27 *Utilitarianism*, p. 179.

28 *Three Essays on Religion*, p. 120.

29 *Op. cit.*, p. 119.

maximizes happiness, and makes labour more 'salutary'
by making the labourer more intelligent: and because
education would give, as well as to all other classes of
philistines, to this dangerous one also, a sense of participation, not merely in the animal side of life, but in
that higher cultivation of the sensibilities which is essential to rational living. It has been difficult, in a disordered
society, to provide the emancipated classes with stable
opinions; much industrial labour, in Mill's view no less
than in Marx's, is mere drudgery. But if the injunctions of the Religion of Humanity are propagated extensively, greater solidarity will be achieved.

This sense of participation is not just a passive acceptance of authority, the docile assenting to its propositions.
It involves active critical self-examination; energetic pursuit in every particular of the closest approximation to
Truth. Mill's society is a society of seekers after Truth:
Truth has a sacred position in his scripture. He reserves
for it the unctuousness which an unctuous religion will
reserve for God: he means by it as many, and elusive,
things as others might mean by *Salvation* or *the end of
human history*. Truth is what all men are seeking, or
supposed to seek: it appears in many forms. An essential
prerequisite is to see the arbitrariness of habitual commitment for what it is. The struggle to be free of prejudice and habit (so far as habit had not been renovated
by reflection) lead, also, to a communal approach to that
form of highest happiness in which knowledge of Truth
consists. All men, whatever their class, temperament or
social standing, are capable of making the approach.
This sort of life 'is even now the lot of many': and 'the
present wretched educational and social arrangements
are the only real hindrance to its being obtainable by
almost all'.[30] The religion has, in other words, an oecu-
menical quality characteristic of all the world's great
faiths.

It is, finally, a comprehensive account of the destiny
to which all men should be committed, leaves nothing

---

[30] *Utilitarianism*, p. 175.

uncertain (at the level with which it is concerned) about the manner of ascertaining men's duties, and is the best of all religions, because it is founded, not on unquestionable supernatural *authority*, but in the needs, desires and higher natures of men. It is utility *and* goodness *and* moral grandeur, the search after truth and the elevation of the sentiments: it is a view of the past and an account of men's duties in it: and an attempt to overcome the limitations of existence by providing rationally binding chains which, slowly but certainly, free men from the arbitrary finiteness of their condition. It is, one may say in critical conclusion, either an arbitrary injunction or a contentless one; but, in whichever light it is viewed, it shows Mill to be, not a meek, fumbling liberal, not a man of 'surprising, gentle humanity'[31] or 'hesitant, sceptical spirituality'[32]: not even 'an exceptionally good . . . truly modest man . . . too gentle to express contempt for other men'.[33] It reveals neither 'an infinite patience', 'catholicity of temper',[34] nor 'single-minded devotion to the cause of toleration and reason . . . unique even among the dedicated lives of the nineteenth century'.[35] It exposes, on the contrary, a socially cohesive, morally insinuating, proselytizing *doctrine*. Mill was a proselytizer of genius: the ruthless denigrator of existing positions, the systematic propagator of a new moral posture, a man of sneers and smears and pervading certainty. It is in this light that the present generation should view this major prophet of the half-articulated 'truths' which hang flabbily in the atmosphere of modern liberalism.

---

[31] Donald G. Macrae, *Ideology and Society*, London 1961, p. 172.

[32] D. M. Mackinnon, *A Study in Ethical Theory*, London 1957, p. 230.

[33] John Plamenatz, *The English Utilitarians*, Oxford 1958, p. 123.

[34] H. J. Laski, Introduction (World's Classics) to Mill's *Autobiography*, London 1924, p. xiv.

[35] Sir Isaiah Berlin, *John Stuart Mill and the Ends of Life*, London 1959, p. 4.

SOME RECENT
INTERPRETATIONS OF
JOHN STUART MILL

BY

R. J. Halliday

It is usual to interpret Mill's understanding of liberty in terms deriving from his distinction in *On Liberty*
between self-regarding and other-regarding conduct.
Granted this distinction and Mill's genuine concern to
define and defend it, it remains a relevant question why
he attached so much importance to it. This raises a less
familiar theme in Mill, namely the inter-connection of
self-regarding and other-regarding conduct. An uncom-
mitted reading of the main texts suggests an equivalent
value is attached to this. Mill clearly and constantly asserts a close connection between each person's own attempt to improve himself, to cultivate his 'affections and
will', and the social and political structure in which he
acts. Self-regarding virtue and responsible social conduct
are interdependent; the quality of each depends upon

Reprinted by kind permission of the author and the Editor from
Philosophy, Vol. XLIII, No. 163 (John Stuart Mill number),
January 1968.

the quality of the other. A fuller recognition of this and its central place in Mill's revision of Bentham may be of help in examining some of the particular problems raised by recent scholarship on Mill.

In this article I am mainly concerned with the interpretations of Cowling and Rees.[1] Cowling has written of the Mill attracted by positivism, the 'liberal' who stressed deference to and implied opinion-forming by an élite. He makes Mill's basic value a consensus, a unanimity of opinion which facilitates a non-empirical science of politics; the doctrine is superficially libertarian, the practice distinctly authoritarian. Rees, on the other hand, is concerned with Mill's defence of individuality. The case for liberty is founded on his respect for personal freedom; Mill qualifies it only in his recognition of the need to guarantee the interests and rights of other persons. My suggestions can be introduced by first considering the interpretation of Rees.

If I interpret him correctly, Rees tends not to weight Mill's concern for the quality of individual character and the need for its improvement at all heavily. He does not demonstrate the connections Mill makes between personal character and the nature of the social and political structure. In part this may be due to his stress on the distinction in *On Liberty* between that part of a person's life which concerns only himself and that which concerns other persons. He interprets this as in effect asserting that actions and conduct move out of the self-

---

[1] Maurice Cowling, *Mill and Liberalism* (Cambridge University Press, 1963). John Rees, *Mill and his Early Critics* (University of Leicester Press, 1956). Also the following articles in *Political Studies*: 'A Phase in the Development of Mill's Ideas on Liberty', Vol. VI, No. 1 (1958, 33–44); 'A Re-reading of Mill on Liberty', Vol. VIII, No. 2 (1960, 113–129); 'Was Mill for Liberty?' Vol. XIV, No. 1 (1966, 72–77). There is also a reference to the short piece on Mill by Alan Ryan, *The Listener*, Vol. LXXIV, No. 1908 (October 21, 1965, 620–622).

It ought, perhaps, to be made clear that the article 'Was Mill for Liberty?' is a critical review of Cowling's book.

regarding category only when the interests and rights of
other persons are either threatened or actually affected.
A person's conduct is clearly self-regarding if this is not
the case. (When discussing the other-regarding category
Mill has chiefly in mind conduct that harms others. But
other-regarding conduct also includes actions that help
or benefit others. Rees concentrates exclusively upon conduct harmful to others.) If it is the case, there remains a
margin of discretion as to whether interference is or is
not likely to promote the general welfare. Mill's assertion
that conduct becomes other-regarding when it violates
distinct and assignable obligation owed to other persons
(conduct remaining self-regarding if it occasions no perceptible hurt to any person other than the agent), is seen
by Rees as a principle which limits social control of personal conduct to precisely those cases where the interests
and rights of others are actually affected or threatened.
As a principle it defines Mill's 'overwhelming concern'
for individuality and spontaneity.[2] If this is the meaning,
or sense, of the principle upon which the case for liberty
is built, it does at least raise problems for a consistent
interpretation of Mill's doctrines in other works.

> I hold that it is allowable in all, and in the more thought-
> ful and cultivated often a duty, to assert and promulgate,
> with all the force they are capable of, their opinion of
> what is good or bad, admirable or contemptible, but not
> to compel others to conform to that opinion; whether the
> force used is that of extra-legal coercion, or exerts itself
> by means of the law.[3]

---

[2] This survey is compiled from the two articles, 'A Re-reading
of Mill on Liberty' and 'Was Mill for Liberty?'. Rees is revising
his interpretation of the principle to include more consideration of
'rights' and how they connect with Mill's idea of justice. Some of
my criticism may in this sense be premature.

[3] *Principles of Political Economy*, Book V, Ch. XI, Section 2
(University of Toronto Press, 1965), p. 938. All quotations and
references in the article are from the editions of the works cited.

Clearly this is a duty to others, an obligation owed to other persons; a person might in some sense 'lecture' himself but one cannot *assert* and *promulgate* to oneself. It is at least assignable in a general sense (to the more thoughtful and cultivated). Nor can it be a duty some people owe to other people out of self-respect or from considerations of self-development. Mill puts it beyond doubt that these, at the very most, are duties to oneself alone.[4] To be compatible with the Rees interpretation of the principle, a failure to perform this duty (of assertion and promulgation, etc.) would come within the other-regarding category only if it actually affected or threatened the interests and rights of another person or persons. The issue to be settled, presumably, would be whether there was a right to expect, or an interest in, the performance of this duty. In short, general questions of duty are separable from particular questions of whether actual harm was done or threatened. This is both consistent and reasonable. The problem remains, however, of reconciling it with the account of duty given in at least some parts of *Utilitarianism*.

> Duty is a thing which may be *exacted* from a person, as one exacts a debt. Unless we think that it may be exacted from him, we do not call it his duty. Reasons of prudence, or the interests of other people, may militate against actually exacting it; but the person himself, it is clearly understood, would not be entitled to complain.[5]

Mill's point is a specific one. There might be things we would like or wish people to do, but unless we think they can be exacted without injustice we do not call them duties. Hence, on a strict interpretation of the principle, a failure to assert and promulgate, etc., comes within the other-regarding category and is sanctionable. This might be thought trivial argument; perhaps one ought not to

---

[4] *On Liberty* (Everyman Edition), p. 135.

[5] *Utilitarianism* (Everyman Edition), p. 45.

expect a thoroughly consistent doctrine. It does, however, raise one important question. If Mill was prepared to accept a duty of this sort (the passage remained unchanged in all editions of *The Principles*) and yet was not prepared to use compulsion to exact it, what other inducements or persuasions are compatible with his principle? This is a valid question. Part of Mill's intention was to define the kinds of power which could rightfully be exercised over individuals; also to determine which of the necessary restraints upon action did not have pernicious or degrading effects. The first point of substantive disagreement with the Rees interpretation is that he fails to consider this in sufficient depth. The whole question can be raised in the context of the arguments in the introduction to *On Liberty*.

Mill argues that society can and does execute its own mandates. Society practises a tyranny (more formidable than many kinds of political oppression) when it either issues wrong mandates instead of right ones, or 'mandates at all in things with which it ought not to meddle'. The practical question, he says, is one of limit—'how to make the fitting adjustment between individual independence and social control'.

> All that makes existence valuable to anyone, depends on the enforcement of restraints upon the actions of other people. Some rules of conduct, therefore, must be imposed, by law in the first place, and by opinion on many things which are not fit subjects for the operation of law. What these rules should be is the principal question in human affairs; . . .[6]

There have to be rules imposed by law and rules imposed by opinion. Mill's main objection in the introduction is to any attempt to make adherence to custom a foundation for these rules. Customary opinion or prefer-

---

[6] *On Liberty*, p. 69.

ence is in effect mere liking or disliking. Custom operates to prevent 'any misgiving respecting the rules of conduct which mankind impose on one another', and avoids an appeal to reason. In practice, it is the 'likings and dislikings of society or of some powerful portion of it' which lay down the rules for general observance.[7] The point again is a specific one. Rules of conduct must appeal to reasons and not to mere likes or dislikes. Opinion can impose a rule 'on many things which are not fit subjects for the operation of law' if it appeals to reasons. This is the general framework for Mill's attempt in *On Liberty* to consider the nature and extent of the control which can rightfully be exercised over the individual. It raises two particular questions. What reasons, if any, could be given for rules of conduct imposed 'by opinion' on a person whose conduct had not either affected or threatened the interests and rights of another person or persons? Also what reason could be given for interfering with conduct by the sanction of law? The Rees interpretation of the principle is, in effect, geared to answering only the last of those questions. It is difficult to see how it could address itself to the first since Rees interprets the principle as one which was, at least in part, specifically drawn up to exclude the pressure of opinion. He tends to refer the categories of self- and other-regarding conduct to the problem of protecting individual choice and spontaneity from social jurisdiction in general and mediocre mass-opinion in particular. The effect of this interpretation is to reduce Mill's principle to an assertion of a clear distinction of individuality on the one hand, and social jurisdiction on the other; to keep the categories of

---

[7] The introduction indicates the influence of Bentham's view of what a true principle consists in. See Chapter 2 of *The Principles of Morals and Legislation*. It also confirms what Mill said elsewhere; that the effective restraints on freedom of opinion and discussion stem 'from the general habit, both in opinion and conduct, of making adherence to custom the rule of life'. *Principles*, p. 935.

self- and other-regarding strictly apart and to underwrite Mill's preference for a good use of personal freedom. This is clear in chapter two of *Mill and his Early Critics* and in the way Rees assesses Mill's reaction to Tocqueville.

He argues that it was Tocqueville who gave an urgency to Mill's misgivings about government by the numerical majority and stimulated a more vigorous and definite anticipation 'of one of the main themes of *On Liberty*, namely the importance of the free development of individual character in the face of the many obstacles modern society was putting in its way'.[8] This does not do full justice to Mill's assessment of Tocqueville in *The Autobiography*. An equally important theme, the 'collateral subject' on which Mill derived benefit from Tocqueville, was the question of centralisation. Tocqueville's understanding of the importance of the 'practical political activity' of the people in performing as much of 'the collective business of society, as can safely be so performed', clearly impressed Mill. His assessment of Tocqueville on centralisation was one of the foundations of the laissez-faire principle. It amounts to a clear recognition that a training of one's own conduct through participation makes possible participation in a responsible political system.

> He viewed this practical political activity of the individual citizen, not only as one of the most effectual means of training the social feelings and practical intelligence of the people, so important in themselves and so indispensable to good government, but also as the specific counteractive to some of the characteristic infirmities of democracy, and a necessary protection against its degenerating into the only despotism of which, in the modern world, there is real danger—the absolute rule of the head of the executive

---

[8] 'A Phase in the Development of Mill's Ideas on Liberty', p. 39.

over a congregation of isolated individuals, all equals but all slaves.[9]

The Rees interpretation not only obscures the need for the principle of self- and other-regarding conduct to be compatible with imposed rules of opinion, it also reduces Mill's understanding of the reasons that can be given for rules of conduct. One reason for the existence of any rule regulating human behaviour is that it makes possible for each person a development of social feeling and a growth in practical intelligence. Mill was genuinely distressed by the idea of private persons having little sense of duty to society. In *Representative Government* he argued that the absence of a 'school of public spirit' can only produce the minimal obligation of obedience to the law and submission to the government.[10] An interpretation of Mill which implies a radical distinction between individuality and social jurisdiction cannot capture Mill's general understanding of politics and the crucial laissez-faire distinction between authoritative and unauthoritative government agency.

Mill makes it clear in Book V, chapter eleven of *The Principles* that laissez-faire is not to be understood as a principle which limits government action to the protection of person and property from force and fraud. This would be an impossible definition since it would exclude 'some of the most indispensable and unanimously recognised of the duties of government'.[11] Mill distinguishes between two types of government agency which differ in their nature and effects and in the 'motives' which could justify them. Authoritative government extends to controlling the free agency of individuals (government by sanction and prohibition). Unauthoritative government consists in the giving of advice and the promulgation of information, and also in supplementing individual

---

[9] *Autobiography* (World's Classics Edition), p. 163.

[10] *Representative Government* (Everyman Edition), p. 217.

[11] *The Principles of Political Economy*, p. 936.

agency with 'side by side' agencies of its own.[12] Mill
puts beyond doubt his belief that 'there is a part of the
life of every person who has come to years of discretion,
within which the individuality of that person ought to
reign uncontrolled either by any other individual or by
the public collectively'. What is relevant to the Rees interpretation of Mill is that both authoritative and unauthoritative government agency depend not upon choice
per se but upon a type of choice; not just upon free individual agency but upon agency of a certain kind. Unauthoritative government, in its function of creating 'side
by side' agencies, does leave individuals free, but only
'free to use their own means of pursuing any object of
general interest' [emphasis mine]. Authoritative government, on the other hand, can only avoid 'the degradation
of slavery' if 'the conscience of the individual goes freely
with the legal restraint'.

> Scarcely any degree of utility, short of absolute necessity,
> will justify a prohibitory regulation, unless it can also be
> made to recommend itself to the general conscience; un-
> less persons of ordinary good intentions either believe al-
> ready, or can be induced to believe, that the thing prohib-
> ited is a thing which they ought not to wish to do.[13]

This confirms the validity of asking what inducements
or persuasions are compatible with the principle, also the
point on enforcement of restraints in the introduction to
On Liberty. The exercise of power over others (in the
form of prohibitory regulation) may well demand persuasion of some sort and the categories of self- and other-
regarding conduct depend upon both rules of law and
rules of opinion. Free choice can mean choices which
persons of 'ordinary good intentions' have already made,
or choices which they ought to make. In this sense the
much-quoted example of Mill invoking the 'tyranny of

---

[12] *Op. cit.*, p. 937.
[13] *Ibid.*, p. 938.

opinion' to decrease the size of families in the labouring class is compatible with his principle and explicable in terms of his general theory of government agency.[14]

If the opinion were once generally established among the labouring class that their welfare required a due regulation of the numbers of families, the respectable and well-conducted of the body would conform to the prescription, and only those would exempt themselves from it, who were in the habit of making light of social obligations generally; and there would be then an evident justification for converting the moral obligation against bringing children into the world who are a burden to the community, into a legal one.[15]

The argument is again that of laissez-faire. Authoritative government (government by sanction and legal prohibition) is justified in creating a legal obligation when responsible choices have actually been made, or, in the case of those 'in the habit of making light of social obligations', when a choice has not been made which ought to have been made. The implications of this for any interpretation of Mill's liberalism are considerable. There is not the one value of free, unhindered choice as Rees implies. There is the additional value attaching to a responsible individuality which either does exist or can be brought into existence, short of compelling individuals to act and think in a certain way. It seems clear that the Rees interpretation of the principle needs to be set off against the very direct interconnection between the self- and the other-regarding categories.

This is not a perverse or merely contentious exercise. For if Cowling over-simplifies Mill by refusing to grant

[14] See for instance Sheldon S. Wolin, *Politics and Vision* (London, 1961), Ch. 9, p. 349. He interprets Mill as proposing 'that the tyranny of opinion be invoked in order to promote some of his own pet causes'.

[15] *Principles*, Bk. II, Ch. XIII, Section 2, p. 372.

the valuation of liberty and diversity for their own sakes, Rees undervalues the extent to which Mill's case for individual free choice presumes a responsible use of that choice. Mill's understanding of liberty was governed by his belief that social coherence depended, ultimately, upon each person's sense of social responsibility. This clear attachment to a type of individual choice stems from the belief that it will have a beneficial influence upon the social and the political structure. Mill's point in the major writings is that respect for the rights and interests of other people depends upon each person's attempt to improve his own conduct and character. A distinction between self- and other-regarding conduct is possible, in part, because of this. Mill assumes that people do recognise, and ought to recognise, the inter-action of self-regarding character and social conduct. The principle must then require an active concern with other people's conduct. This is the rule of conduct which can and ought to be imposed by 'opinion'. Mill can speak for himself:

> It would be a great misunderstanding of this doctrine to suppose that it is one of selfish indifference, which pretends that human beings have no business with each other's conduct in life, and that they should not concern themselves about the well-doing or well-being of one another, unless their own interest is involved. Instead of any diminution, there is need of a great increase of disinterested exertion to promote the good of others.[16]

Granted the laissez-faire understanding of government agency and Mill's acceptance of rules of conduct imposed by opinion (for which a reason can be given), it would seem the distinction of self- and other-regarding conduct exists in conjunction with the belief in an essential interconnection of the two categories. This may be

---

[16] *On Liberty*, p. 132.

an expansion of the view of morality expressed in a letter to Sterling. 'The spirit of all morality' is 'right self-culture'; 'all I mean is that it is culture of the man's self, of his feelings and will, fitting him to look abroad and see how he is to act'.[17] Whether it is plausible or not to grant this belief the status of a 'principle', the evidence for Mill's attachment to the interdependence of self-culture and social education is fairly impressive. It is, perhaps, clearest in the essay on Bentham.

The essay attempts to establish at least one criterion for an adequate system of ethics. An ethical system must 'aid individuals in the formation of their own character'. If it does this it will make possible a responsible regulation of conduct which is social in character.

> Morality consists of two parts. One of these is self-education; the training, by the human being himself, of his affections and will. That department is a blank in Bentham's system. The other and co-equal part, the regulation of his outward actions, must be altogether halting and imperfect without the first: for how can we judge in what manner many an action will affect even the worldly interests of ourselves or others, unless we take in, as part of the question, its influence on the regulation of our, or their, affections and desires?[18]

Bentham's theory was 'deficient'. In doing nothing for the conduct of the individual it was doing nothing for the conduct of society. It may facilitate the prescription of rules 'by which it (society) may protect its material interests', but, it does not 'suffice of itself even for the material interests'. The existence of these interests and

---

[17] Letter to Sterling, London, 24th May 1832. Letter 50, p. 101, *The Earlier Letters of John Stuart Mill*, ed. F. E. Mineka, Collected Works, Vol. XII (University of Toronto Press).

[18] *Mill on Bentham* (Leavis) London, 1959, p. 71. The survey of Mill's argument is taken from pp. 70–74. See also pp. 66–68.

of society depends on 'national character'. 'A philosophy
of laws and institutions, not founded on a philosophy
of national character, is an absurdity.' Mill's point is
clear. Bentham limited himself to 'prescribing some of
the more obvious dictates of worldly prudence, and outward probity and beneficence', hence his ethical system
could do nothing for the conduct of the individual and,
ultimately, nothing for a responsible regulation of social
behaviour. Given this account of the argument, it is difficult to see how Ryan can use the essay to support his
view that where the agent only is involved the matter is
not a moral one. Mill charged Bentham with overlooking
'the moral part of man's nature, in the strict sense of the
term—the desire of perfection, or the feeling of an ap-
proving or of an accusing conscience'. Mill does not say
that morality is 'essentially concerned with the business
side of life, with preserving minimal forbearances'.[19]
This is precisely the view which Mill is criticising. Bentham had devised an ethical system which was only useful for 'the merely *business* part of the social arrangements. Whatever can be understood or whatever done
without reference to moral influences, his philosophy is
equal to'; the essay supports what was said in the introduction to *On Liberty*. Some rules of conduct must be
imposed by opinion in those areas where the law cannot
go. If one's training of one's own character does facilitate
a responsible regulation of social actions, then self-
regarding character cannot remain outside all rules of
conduct. Nor are the rules the minimum necessary for
effective social organisation; they are not reducible to the
merely 'business part'. This central point in the revision
of Bentham had been expounded in the less well known
Remarks on Bentham's Philosophy written early in

---

[19] *Listener*, p. 620. This may be unfair to Ryan. I have only
seen the (reduced?) *Listener* version of his account. Nor does his
interpretation rest solely on this point, but he cannot use the
essay on Bentham to show that Mill made morality concerned
with preserving minimal forbearances.

1833.[20] In this Mill charged Bentham with ignoring the connection of acts and habits with character; once a moralist overlooked this connection 'his estimation even of the consequences of the very act itself, is rendered imperfect'. This Mill argued was not necessarily fatal to a philosophy of legislation, but it probably would be fatal to an adequate consideration 'of the greater social questions'; 'for those (unlike the details of legislation) to be duly estimated, must be viewed as the great instruments of forming the national character'. Hence even Bentham's speculations on government were inadequate, since 'it never seems to have occurred to him to regard political institutions in a higher light, as the principal means of the social education of a people'. Mill's criticism might then be properly reduced to one accusation; that Bentham had not understood the interdependence of self-culture and social education, the close connections which exist between personal character and social and political institutions. The problem remains of demonstrating this belief in the essay *On Liberty*.

It is true that Mill asserts no self-regarding fault can be called immoral. Presumably no self-regarding virtue is properly moral.[21] If this is so, then he would seem to have relinquished the notion of self-education as the first part of morality. In this sense the self- and other-regarding categories would be clearly distinct. There could be no sensible talk of private morality or immorality; an area of life and conduct would simply not be amenable to moral praise or blame. For my argument, however, it seems sufficient to show that 'rules of opinion'

---

[20] Reprinted as Appendix B in Edward Lytton Bulwer's *England and the English* (Paris, 1834, 376–388). Mill wrote this piece at Bulwer's request and, contrary to expectation, it was reprinted '*ipsissimis verbis*'. For Mill's comments on this criticism see letters 72 (p. 152), 82 (p. 172) and 111 (p. 236) in *The Earlier Letters of John Stuart Mill*.

[21] *On Liberty*, p. 135, 'unlike the self-regarding faults previously mentioned, which are not properly immoralities, and to whatever pitch they may be carried, do not constitute wickedness'.

can be imposed and that self-regarding conduct is not
beyond persuasion and judgment (which will be effective
and direct). This judgment, too, must not be undertaken
merely as a concession to the material interests of society
since the rules are not just concerned with the 'business
part' of the social arrangements. Chapter four does substantiate these points. Self-regarding faults, such as 'rash-
ness, obstinacy, self-conceit' and the pursuit of 'animal
pleasures at the expense of those of feeling and intellect',
do concern only the person himself, but they can be
'judged'. A person can be called a fool. He can be told
that he is a being of an inferior order. One person can
'honestly point out to another that he thinks him in fault'
and has a right to act on his opinion by avoiding the
other person's company. Mill puts one thing beyond
doubt:

> In these various modes a person may suffer very severe
> penalties at the hands of others for faults which directly
> concern only himself . . .[22]

These are natural penalties, 'spontaneous consequences
of the faults themselves'. They do not warrant punishment (through the agencies of law, government and society) though a person 'must expect to be lowered in the
opinion of others and to have a less share of their favourable sentiments'; Mill then states:

> but of this he has no right to complain, unless he has
> merited their favour by special excellence in his social
> relations, and has thus established a title to their good
> offices, which is not affected by his demerits towards him-
> self.[23]

This is crucial. A person who is specially excellent in his
social relations has a right to complain about the penal-

---

[22] *Op. cit.*, p. 134.
[23] *Ibid.*, pp. 134–135.

ties attaching to 'rules of opinion'. Mill's point seems to be that if a person can responsibly regulate his other-regarding conduct without being excellent in his character then he is entitled to conduct his own affairs free from persuasive opinion. Only if defects of character translate into defects of social conduct can a person rightfully suffer 'severe penalties at the hands of others'. This seems compatible with asserting a 'principle' of inter-connection as well as of distinction between self- and other-regarding conduct. Genuine problems remain for interpreting other passages, but at least one clear point has emerged.[24]

On Liberty is not a text granting equal value to all self-regarding preferences and conduct. Both categories of human action are subject to rules and open to persuasion, either by opinion or sanction. Faced with one or both forms of 'persuasion', a person has a 'right to complain' only if he has demonstrated that his social conduct is responsible. The assumption seems to be that self-regarding deficiency will manifest itself in social conduct. In *On Liberty* Mill leaves the possibility open of this not being so. Hence the principle does not presume it desirable that a person should employ his free agency to cultivate standards and habits inappropriate for responsible social conduct. One's right to freedom from pressures and persuasions depends essentially on the use one makes of liberty. Rees is correct. Mill does not say 'men will be coerced or pressed into a life of higher culti-

---

[24] There are many problem passages. In particular, perhaps, those on the theories of social right advanced by the United Kingdom Alliance (the temperance pressure group) and the 'illegitimate interference with the rightful liberty of the individual' achieved by Sabbatarian legislation. *On Liberty*, pp. 144–147. It should be stressed, however, that the interpretation being offered is not intended to exclude the clear distinction between self-regarding and other-regarding 'areas' and conduct; it suggests only a modification in how this might be approached.

vation of the mind'.[25] Men are free to enjoy whatever form of art and literature they care to choose. This does not, however, imply a freedom from persuasion and inducement. Mill recognises that society has other means than sanctions to bring 'its weaker members up to its ordinary standard of rational conduct'. Society does not need 'the power to issue commands and enforce obedience in the personal concerns of individuals'.[26]

The relevant question for Mill was that of which kinds of persuasion were compatible with liberty; could persuasion, in fact, be distinguished from compulsion? This is important for an adequate interpretation of Mill's doctrine. If persuasion cannot be distinguished from compulsion there is little point in the categorisation of human behaviour into self- and other-regarding conduct. There must be effective inducements for a person to act responsibly which are different in kind from legal and political sanctions. The principle depends upon the education of both the self- and the other-regarding virtues. The business of education, as Mill said, is to cultivate both.[27] One major objection to both the Cowling and the Rees interpretations of Mill is their underestimation of the importance of this. Both interpret education or persuasion in a sense much narrower than did Mill himself.

Cowling's attempt to demonstrate the positivist in Mill leads him to interpret education as a means to truth. Mill recognises the need for unanimity and hence educa-

---

[25] *Was Mill for Liberty?*, p. 76.

[26] *On Liberty*, p. 139. Cowling does give full weight to this in chapter five of his book. Much of Mill's point, however, is obscured by arguing, as Cowling does, that to understand 'the nature of Mill's purpose, it is essential to avoid detailed entanglement in the principles by which relations between government, public opinion and individual action are to be regulated' (p. 98). Cf. p. 331 in this volume.

[27] *On Liberty*, p. 133.

tion is a species of rational enquiry to prepare the way for rule by an élite.[28] Participation is a means of promoting the feeling of belonging 'in a rationally ordered society'; it is a beneficial consequence of the Religion of Humanity and leads individuals to seek after Truth. Rees seems to think that, in the main, the problem of education for Mill is one of organising a diversified system of schooling.[29] This reduction of Mill's meaning is clear in both interpretations. Neither systematically attempts to relate the Mill of the main texts on politics and ethics to the Mill who argued for property redistribution and peasant proprietorship, individual participation in free institutions and co-operative practices in industry. Yet these are the means of persuasion, the means of educating both self-regarding virtue and other-regarding conduct. Neither in fact gives much credit to Mill's 'cash value' as a socialist which was perfectly compatible with the laissez-faire principle. The empirical testing of social theories (such as socialism and Communism) is, in Mill's sense, educational. The attempt to work out a theory in practice is a way of teaching 'lessons', a way of drawing out the faculties of man by practical activity.[30] Poverty and human misconduct are 'at least failures in the social

---

[28] Mill's 'purpose', says Cowling, is to 'make the world safe for "rational" education, "rational" thinking and the assured leadership of the "rational" clerisy'. This accounts for his fear of democracy and his love of individuality (p. 105). Cf. pp. 337–338 in this volume.

[29] Rees does appreciate Mill's dislike of learning by cram and his support of any activity as 'educational' which draws out the different faculties of the mind. Rees, 'H. O. Pappe on Mill,' *Political Studies*, Vol. X, No. 2 (1962, 199). As far as I know, he has never specified the implications of this for the self- and other-regarding category. The review of Cowling discusses Mill on education in the context of the 'overwhelming importance' attached 'to individuality and diversity in general conduct and opinions' (p. 73).

[30] *Principles*, Bk. V, Ch. IX, Sect. 7, 903–904.

arrangements'. 'Bad education or want of education' is admitted to be 'the fault of those arrangements—it may almost be said the crime'.

> I am speaking loosely and in the rough, for a minuter analysis of the sources of faults of character and errors of conduct would establish far more conclusively the filiation which connects them with a defective organisation of society, though it would also show the reciprocal dependence of that faulty state of society on a backward state of the human mind.[31]

The practice of laissez-faire—the belief that man gains his moral and political education through individual participation—leads Mill to reject Communist associations. An indispensable condition of human progress is 'that human nature should have freedom to expand spontaneously in various directions, both in thought and practice; that people should both think for themselves and try experiments for themselves'.[32] Mill had seen this in Tocqueville, and throughout his life he believed individual conduct and character was largely formed by activity and experiment. In this he was fairly unusual. Many of his contemporaries stressed the genetic determination of character.[33] For Mill, passivity reduced the possibility

---

[31] *Chapters on Socialism* (American Book Exchange, New York, 1880), p. 266.

[32] *Op. cit.*, p. 396.

[33] This needs to be stressed to indicate how far away Mill was from the popular evolutionary understanding of choice and character. Evolutionary theories of ethics characteristically asserted man's determination by inherited experience of utility. It is both significant and interesting that Darwin thought Mill's 'most serious blemish' was his belief that the moral faculties were acquired and not innate. *Descent of Man* (2nd Edition, London, 1877) Ch. IV, p. 98. Mill's notion of an adequate epistemology is relevant here; what was needed was a 'more complete analysis' of the psychological process by which 'original tendency' is modified by ulterior or

that a person would transcend the private pleasure and the particular interest. What was ethically desirable became more possible when the individual was free from excessive dependence on hired labour and where, if practicable, the benefits of property were widely spread. For an individual to broaden his concerns, for him to understand the needs of the system as a whole, he must act within a social structure which 'schools' him. Co-operative associations in industry were educational; 'if public spirit, generous sentiments, or true justice and equality are desired, association, not isolation, of interests is the school in which these excellences are nurtured'.[34] Social experiment is not something optional, it is something necessary because educational. It is one way of teaching the lesson for a modern nation, 'that the well-being of a people must exist by means of the justice and self-government, the δικαιοσύνη and σωφροσύνη, of the individual citizens'.[35] For the same reason democratic political institutions are educational, since they nourish public spirit and develop intelligence. The ownership of property is also an educational influence. It teaches self-control and is particularly valuable in producing a direct prudential check to population growth. As Mill said,

> It is difficult to imagine what theory of education that can be, which can attach no importance to such an instrument. Books and schooling are absolutely necessary to education; but not all sufficient. The mental faculties will be most developed where they are most exercised; . . .[36]

---

interpreted experience. See 'Bain's Psychology', *Dissertations and Discussions*, Vol. III (2nd Ed. London, 1875), in particular, pp. 146–148.

[34] *Principles*, Bk. IV, Ch. VII, Sect. 4, p. 768.

[35] *Ibid.* Sect. 2, p. 763.

[36] *Ibid.* Bk. II, Ch. VII, Sect. 2, p. 280. My quotation follows the MS and the '48 and '49 editions of the *Principles*. The edition does not, however, affect the general point.

The *Autobiography* establishes the point which is in Mill's mind. Social transformation depends upon an equivalent change of character. The capacity 'to labour and combine', 'for public and social purposes' can never be extinct; 'the hindrance is not in the essential constitution of human nature'.

> The deep-rooted selfishness which forms the general character of the existing state of society, is *so* deeply rooted, only because the whole course of existing institutions tends to foster it; and modern institutions in some respects more than ancient, since the occasion on which the individual is called on to do anything for the public, without receiving its pay, are far less frequent in modern life, than in the smaller commonwealths of antiquity.[37]

The reform of social and political arrangements is central to Mill's understanding of liberty, since without it the persuasion and inducement to act responsibly will not exist. This reform, in turn, depends upon an improvement of individual character. As he explained in his *Remarks on Bentham's Philosophy*, all increases in human happiness which were due merely to a change of circumstances and were 'unaccompanied by changes in the state of the desires' were hopeless. 'Not to mention', says Mill, 'that while the desires are circumscribed in self' there would not be an adequate motive for attempting to modify external circumstances 'to good ends'.[38] This is crucial both to Mill's understanding of education and to his understanding of liberty. To underwrite it or ignore it, as Rees and Cowling do, must result in a failure to appreciate fully that Mill's arguments on free choice and diversity of conduct interacted with his understanding of social and political structures. In particular that his belief, whether permanent or occa-

---

[37] *Autobiography*, pp. 197–198.
[38] *Remarks on Bentham's Philosophy*, p. 386.

sional, in the value of consensus was partly governed by his understanding of modern society as socially mobile, increasingly literate and directly faced with the problems of population growth and property redistribution.[39] This suggests a major deficiency in the way Cowling has interpreted Mill's doctrine of liberty. If he does believe—and he seems to—that the concern with proselytising a type of character and rational judgment was due to Mill's desire for a life of certainty and science in politics, he has misunderstood what is instrumental about liberty. Liberty is instrumental in developing character and hence in training individual conduct to act responsibly. Liberty is essential to the coherence of the social structure and to democratic government since these ultimately depend upon responsible individual acts. Liberty will assist in preventing a passive acceptance of custom, hence it will reduce the number of rules based merely on preference and 'likings'. It will also reduce relations of dependence founded upon the mental and material subjection of one group by another. Liberty (to put it somewhat crudely) is one of the elements which 'unfreezes' the social structure and makes possible persuasion as well as sanction. The responsible use of power depends upon responsible choice. Cowling is right to stress deference to an élite and to interpret the function of individuality as one of breaking up existing rigidities. Part of Mill's point, however, and this is nowhere clearer than in Book Four of *The Principles,* is that it cannot and ought not to be a deference to personal authority of the sort characteristic of hierarchical systems. Critical deference founded upon respect and intelligence demands a social and political structure which is characteristically 'modern' in its outlook and organisation. Mill argued this with

---

[39] *The Subjection of Women* is the most revealing essay I know of for Mill's general arguments on social mobility. See, in particular, Ch. 1, Sect. 13–15, pp. 44–47 (Stanton Coit edition, London, 1906).

specific reference to England in a letter to D'Eichthal.[40] Unless there was an alteration in 'those parts of our social institutions and policy which at present oppose improvement, degrade and brutalise the intellects and morality of the people', there would not be 'a *pouvoir spirituel* capable of commanding the faith of the majority, who must and do believe on authority'. In a postscript Mill made the same point with more precision. It was an error to suppose that mankind could be perfected by teaching them St Simonism; the 'adoption of St Simonism, if that doctrine be true, will be the natural result and effect of a high state of moral and intellectual culture previously received'. Deference is possible only in an educated society and the élite itself is a means of raising the intelligence of the non-élite. What Mill called the 'natural tendency' 'towards collective mediocrity' would in part be checked by the improved education of the non-élite 'whose minds would be insensibly raised by the influence of the minds with which they were in contact, or even in conflict'.[41] The élite is just one of the means of persuasion. Persuasion, as distinct from sanction, is possible only given a certain social and political structure; free institutions are necessary and not merely useful,[42] without them there could not be the education of character and the training of conduct that Mill

---

[40] London, 9th February 1830. Letter 29, pp. 48–49. *The Earlier Letters of John Stuart Mill.*

[41] *Representative Government*, pp. 266–267. It should be made clear the élite will not be a separate ruling 'group' or 'party'; it is simply a means of persuasion (education) institutionalised in government.

[42] Cowling argues the reverse of this on p. 159. For Mill's considerable scepticism concerning the practicality and desirability of élite rule, see the review article 'Centralisation', *Edinburgh Review* (April, 1862), pp. 323–358, in particular pp. 349–350. Also the review of 'Guizot's Essays and Lectures on History', in *Dissertations and Discussions*, Vol. II, pp. 218–282. See in particular p. 238.

wanted; there would be little point in distinguishing self-regarding from other-regarding conduct.

There is a genuine problem remaining in Mill's attraction to positivism;[43] in effect Cowling rests his case upon demonstrating the characteristic positivist themes in his writings. They are the familiar ones; the belief in transition from 'critical' to 'organic' periods; the commitment to an observational science of politics made possible by connecting historical generalisation with 'laws' of human nature; a stress on consensus and deference. Were these themes fully documented they would not, however, validate the general interpretation Cowling offers. Mill's sociology is organised around the assumption that the human race is progressive. The laws of progress can only be discovered by combining observation with the study of the evolution of mind and the growth of character. Character and intelligence, as data for politics and sociology, are inseparable from particular social and political structures. The claim of political and social science to be considered 'sciences', or 'science', presumes their use in modifying these structures. Mill was not concerned with claiming the power positively to predict the formation of a type of character since, for his purposes, it was sufficient to understand tendencies—a knowledge of tendencies made possible the shaping of circumstances.[44] Cowling's suggestion that his view of problem-solving involved the assumption that particular questions could be freed from the limitations inherent in particular situations also runs counter to much that Mill wrote. Science to Mill was a guide to judgment and not a substitute for it; all adequate judgment involved a study of the particular case and the circumstances peculiar to

---

[43] A good deal of the relevant evidence for Mill's views on positivism in general and Comtism in particular has been assembled in chapter seven of W. H. Simon's *European Positivism in the Nineteenth Century*, Cornell, 1963.

[44] *A System of Logic*, Vol. II (7th Edition, London 1868), pp. 454–455.

it.[45] The fact he had constantly before him was the dependence of individual intelligence and character on the social and political institutions of a modern democracy. It might be suggested that much of his liberalism consisted in his recognition of this. Rees and Cowling in underwriting the connections made between character and conduct and, ultimately, between systems of ethics and systems of politics, may not be saying a great deal about this liberalism. One cannot ignore Mill the 'socialist'[46] and interpret his understanding of liberty either in terms of a single distinction or as a mere means of preparing for rule by an élite.

---

[45] Mill's clearest statement of this is, perhaps, with regard to Political Economy. See his speech on 'Maguire's Motion on the State of Ireland' (March 1868). This is reprinted in *Chapters and Speeches on the Irish Land Question* (London, 1870), pp. 108–125. See in particular pp. 117–118.

[46] Mill believed that social and political experimentation was educational; it made possible the improvement of individual conduct and character. A 'socialist' was anyone committed to questioning the system of private property and competition with this end in view. See in particular his review of Newman's 'Lectures on Political Economy', *The Westminster and Foreign Quarterly Review*, October 1851, Vol. LVI, pp. 83–101.

AN INTRODUCTION TO MILL'S THEORY OF AUTHORITY*

BY

Richard B. Friedman

I

The object of this essay is to define a new approach to the controversial theory of authority John Stuart Mill first stated in *The Spirit of the Age* (1831).[1] No doubt the notion of authority is itself one of the most controversial and confusing concepts in political thought. It is therefore well worth emphasizing at the very outset of

* This essay is part of a work in progress, and, as it deals with certain highly speculative matters, I regard it as subject to revision. I wish to express my gratitude to Mr. Hubert Forbes, Professor Michael Oakeshott, and Mr. J. B. Schneewind for conversations which helped me to understand my subject better, and to The International Dimensions Program of the University of Pittsburgh for a grant that permitted me to study in London.

[1] In this study, all references to *The Spirit of the Age* will be to the edition reprinted in John Stuart Mill, *Essays on Politics and Culture*, ed. Gertrude Himmelfarb (Anchor Books: Garden City, New York, 1963), and will be hereinafter cited as *Spirit*.

this study that Mill was concerned with authority in a highly specific sense. He did not identify it with the legitimate possession of coercive power, as twentieth-century social science has for the most part. Rather, he was concerned with deference on the part of some persons to the moral and political beliefs of others. Mill, that is to say, was concerned with believing on authority; and this involved more exactly: (1) believing the opinions of someone else even though the believer does not, or even cannot, comprehend the particular grounds on which those opinions are supposed by the latter person to rest, (2) because of some characteristic of the person thus deferred to, such as his social standing or religious claims, by virtue of which his opinions are taken by the believer to be credible. Thus, when a person accepts a belief on authority, he is understood by Mill to be abdicating his own judgment as to the validity of that belief out of deference to the judgment of someone else.[2] Mill was thus concerned with authority in the realm of beliefs; and beginning with the publication of *The Spirit of the Age*, he made a systematic attempt to introduce a justification of authority so conceived into his political philosophy.[3]

Mill did not deny that a defense of authority in the realm of beliefs constituted a "reaction" against "the

---

[2] This definition of authority should be regarded as provisional, as merely a way of beginning; it will be enlarged upon at several points further on.

[3] Among Mill's many subsequent discussions of authority, the following are especially important to the development of his views. "The Rationale of Political Representation," *London Review*, I (July 1835), 341–71; "Tocqueville on Democracy in America," *London Review*, II (October 1835), 85–129; "Coleridge," *London and Westminster Review*, XXXIII (March, 1840), 257–302; "Tocqueville on Democracy in America," *Edinburgh Review*, LXXII (October 1840), 1–47; *On Liberty* (1859), particularly ch. 3; *Representative Government* (1861), particularly ch. I–VII; *Auguste Comte and Positivism* (1865); "The Utility of Religion" in *Three Essays on Religion* (1874).

philosophy of the eighteenth century" in which he had been originally educated. He was acutely conscious that it was precisely this sort of authority that had been repudiated by Bentham and James Mill. His "first instructors," Mill acknowledged, "had always identified deference to authority with mental slavery and the repression of individual thought."[4] Moreover, Mill knew that Benthamite utilitarianism was publicly regarded as a philosophy which scorned authority in the realm of beliefs, and which appeared to be destructive not only of this or that belief, but of belief as such. Mill's doctrine of authority thus raises in a most obtrusive fashion the question of its continuity with Benthamite utilitarianism—as well as the more subtle question of the internal continuity of Mill's own thought from the "authoritarianism" of *The Spirit of the Age* to the "libertarianism" of the essay *On Liberty*.

The Spirit of the Age contained the first public statement of Mill's doctrine of authority. But that is not all: it was also his initial general revision of the utilitarian moral and political philosophy. It contained the first published expression of what Mill called his "new opinions."[5] These are the opinions Mill formed for himself following the famous "mental crisis" that had left him dissatisfied with the teachings of his "first instructors" and had exposed him to the "new mode of political thinking" being cultivated at the time in France and Germany.[6] *The Spirit of the Age* can thus be recognized as standing at, or near, the beginning of the subject that has probably engrossed students of Mill's thought more than any other: his sustained effort to revise utilitarianism. Inquiry into Mill's theory of authority is thus unavoidably involved with this larger effort; and a principal task of such an inquiry must be to seek to determine why Mill

---

[4] *The Early Draft of John Stuart Mill's Autobiography,* ed. Jack Stillinger (Urbana, 1961), p. 188.

[5] *Autobiography* (New York, 1924), p. 122.

[6] *Early Draft,* p. 189 and *Autobiography,* p. 114.

initially embarked on this revisionary effort in the field
of political philosophy by constructing a theory of authority.

The Spirit of the Age was neglected by students of
Mill's thought for over a century, but it is now recognized as a work of crucial significance to his political
philosophy. It has also become a subject of widespread
controversy among students of his thought. Oddly enough,
however, this controversy does not turn precisely on the
interpretation of The Spirit of the Age itself, but instead
on its relationship to Mill's subsequent writings. The
meaning of The Spirit of the Age has been regarded
as evident or taken for granted, and the dispute has
come to center on its influence over, or, at any rate, its
continuity with, Mill's later work. More specifically,
what is taken for granted is that the political theory of
The Spirit of the Age constitutes a fundamental break
with Benthamite utilitarianism, that it is in fact nothing
less than "a Saint-Simonian tract,"[7] and that the critically
decisive evidence for both these claims lies primarily in
Mill's defense of authority. A recent comment typifies
this stock view: "initially he rejected Benthamism and
identified himself with an alternative outlook that in
large part was derived from the writings of the St. Simonians . . . particularly . . . the elitism he found there."[8]
While this interpretation of The Spirit of the Age and
Mill's other early "authoritarian" writings is widely
accepted, nevertheless it is also recognized to raise an
acute and perplexing problem as to the development of

---

[7] Edward Alexander, Matthew Arnold and John Stuart Mill
(London, 1965), p. 37.

[8] Joseph Hamburger, Intellectuals in Politics: John Stuart Mill
and the Philosophic Radicals (New Haven, 1965), pp. 78, 81. See
also Frederick A. von Hayek, "John Stuart Mill at the Age of
Twenty-Five," in The Spirit of the Age (Chicago, 1942), pp.
XXVIII–XXIX; I. W. Mueller, John Stuart Mill and French
Thought (Urbana, 1956), ch. 2; Shirley Robin Letwin, The Pursuit of Certainty (Cambridge, 1965), p. 244.

Mill's thought. For Mill's later work, especially the essay *On Liberty*, is widely regarded as the classic expression of liberalism. And the critical question therefore arises as to whether Mill subsequently abandoned the authoritarian doctrine of *The Spirit of the Age* or whether he somehow managed to continue to hold it, so that the essay *On Liberty* is not what it has long appeared to be. Thus, out of this critical question, two different interpretations of the relation between *The Spirit of the Age* and the later, "liberal" writings have been generated.

The first interpretation[9] is that *The Spirit of the Age* and *On Liberty* are fundamentally incompatible because of the genuine authoritarianism of the former and the genuine libertarianism of the latter. Furthermore, it is thought that *The Spirit of the Age* represents "the height of his [Mill's] reaction against his earlier [Benthamite] views,"[10] and that when Mill speaks of having "completely turned back from what there had been of excess in my reaction against Benthamism,"[11] it was specifically the authoritarian doctrine of *The Spirit of the Age* that he was recanting. This view, then, denies that *The Spirit of the Age* belongs to Mill's "mature" thought, the part preserved for posterity, although that essay is nevertheless recognized to possess a certain unique significance in Mill's intellectual biography, as the most extreme published expression of his reaction against Benthamism following his "mental crisis."

Protagonists of the second interpretation[12] contend, on the other hand, that *The Spirit of the Age* and *On*

---

[9] See Mueller, ch. 2 and 3; Karl Britton, *John Stuart Mill* (London, 1953), pp. 34–35; Hayek, p. XXXII; also John C. Rees, "The Reaction to Cowling on Mill," *The Mill News Letter*, vol. I, no. 2 (Spring 1966) 2–11, for discussion of this interpretation.

[10] Hayek, p. VIII.

[11] *Autobiography*, p. 161.

[12] Maurice Cowling, *Mill and Liberalism* (Cambridge, 1963); Letwin, Introduction and Part III.

Liberty are highly compatible; that *The Spirit of the Age* does indeed constitute an essential break with Benthamism on account of its authoritarian doctrine; but that Mill never abandoned that doctrine and never "made his way back to the easy-going tolerance of . . . Bentham."[13] The essay *On Liberty* is thus seen to differ from *The Spirit of the Age* in a tactical way at most, the argument being that Mill came to advocate individual liberty not for its own sake, but as a highly effective and indeed indispensible means for detaching men from their old loyalties and thus for bringing about the final destruction of the old order, so that the enterprise of setting up a new authority could go ahead without impediment. Liberty, that is to say, is an indispensible tool for forwarding the course of history towards the realization of a form of society not itself notably distinguished by liberty. This second interpretation, in effect, revives the vehement attack leveled against Mill by James Fitzjames Stephen in *Liberty, Equality, Fraternity* (1873). Stephen argued that *On Liberty* is the expression of a new humanitarian "faith" or "dogma" as intolerant of the Christian faith as Mill had alleged the Christian had been of its rivals.[14] Stephen's criticism is thus extended backward in time so as to include *The Spirit of the Age* (which Stephen does not seem to have known). From this standpoint, *The Spirit of the Age* is seen to be distinguished from the rest of Mill's work by being merely the most outspoken expression of his sustained commitment to the realization of a new authoritarian "faith." In this way, then, Mill is viewed as a typical nineteenth-century thinker seeking one more secular substitute to fill the place left vacant by the decline of Christianity. Thus, whereas the upshot of the first interpretation is to reduce *The Spirit of the Age*

---

[13] Letwin, p. 300.

[14] James Fitzjames Stephen, *Liberty, Equality, Fraternity* (London, 2nd ed., 1874), pp. 2, 4, 85–86.

to a form of youthful excess, the result of the second is to blacken Mill's reputation as a "liberal."

In spite of their differences, these two interpretations share at least two features in common. First, they both hold that *The Spirit of the Age*, because of its doctrine of authority, constitutes a fundamental break with Benthamite utilitarianism (and it is on this score that *The Spirit of the Age* is also seen as basically Saint-Simonian). Secondly, they both regard the preceding point as so glaringly obvious that the only thing left for the student to puzzle over is the relationship between *The Spirit of the Age* and Mill's subsequent work. Now it seems to me that the first claim is mistaken, and that there is, accordingly, much to puzzle over in *The Spirit of the Age* itself. Both interpretations seem to me to suffer from a failure to consider the *kind* of justification of authority that Mill offered, as if all justifications of authority (with respect to beliefs) are and must be of the same order. The possibility is not entertained that there might be various ways of justifying authority and that utilitarianism has its way too. Rather, the expressed or tacit assumption upon which every commentary on Mill's doctrine of authority has been based is that a mere defense of authority in the realm of beliefs is incompatible as such with utilitarianism, so that Mill's defense must be incompatible too. But this assumption is mistaken; and the specific object of this paper is to bring out the precise way in which utilitarianism may be made to yield a particular kind of justification of authority which can be recognized to differ in essentials from the sort Mill found in the Saint-Simonians and in other authors of "the reaction of the nineteenth century against the eighteenth."

The purpose of this essay is to propose a new analytical and historical approach to the study of Mill's early theory of authority and thus, by implication, to the subsequent development of his political philosophy. My procedure will be to consider the sense in which utilitarianism is capable of furnishing an argument for authority. To do this, it will be useful to examine an explicit construction of a utilitarian justification of authority. Fortunately, such a case is available, although it has been completely ignored by students of Mill's thought. This is John Austin's defense of authority in the third lecture of *The Province of Jurisprudence Determined* (published in 1832, but delivered as lectures beginning in 1829). In this little-known part of his celebrated work, Austin quite explicitly constructed a utilitarian theory of authority. He did not, however, present that theory in the context of a philosophy of history; nor did he deal with the "emergence of the masses," as Mill had done. *The Spirit of the Age* certainly differs from *The Province* with respect to the overt historical and "sociological" consciousness it exhibits. But this very difference can be regarded as a virtue for purposes of the study of Mill, just because the utilitarian character of Austin's doctrine shows up so clearly in being isolated from these other matters. The following examination of Austin on authority is thus intended to delineate some of the chief characteristics of what may be called the utilitarian mode of treating authority.

There is also an historical purpose behind this examination of Austin's views. Undoubtedly the chief obstacle hindering recognition of the utilitarian character of Mill's own doctrine of authority is the belief that Mill acquired that doctrine from the Saint-Simonians and Comte, that in fact *The Spirit of the Age* is a "Saint-Simonian tract." Thus, a usual way in which students of Mill's thought have proceeded to elucidate *The Spirit of the Age* is by citing parallels with Saint-Simonian doctrine, a doctrine that seems patently incongruous with Benthamite utilitarianism. This practice has often seemed sufficient to back up the assumption that in defending authority, Mill broke with utilitarianism. In an appendix to this paper, it will therefore be shown that it is at least as likely that Mill was indebted to Austin's lectures for his theory of authority as he was to the Saint-Simonians and Comte. However, these historical considerations are not central to this study, and I wish to make it clear that my aim is not simply the detection of the pedigree of Mill's ideas, but also and primarily the elucidation of the ideas themselves. My claim is, then, that by examining Austin's views on authority, in order to determine exactly how Austin impressed a utilitarian character on his understanding of authority, it also becomes possible to comprehend Mill's own theory more precisely. Moreover, this approach will make possible a sharper contrast of Mill's theory of authority with that of the Saint-Simonians, and bring out the fundamental differences between them.

No attempt will, however, be made in this paper to provide a detailed, critical analysis of Mill's treatment of authority in *The Spirit of the Age* and in subsequent writings. That would require a study far longer than this. Indeed, one aim of this restricted study is to make it apparent that such a critical analysis is a far more intricate and difficult enterprise than has been recognized by those current students of Mill's thought who have been in fact the first to take notice of *The Spirit of the Age*. The following discussion of Austin's views is intended, then, to be a prolegomena to the study of Mill's views. At certain points along the way, however, some important comparisons between Austin and Mill will be drawn, and some significant contrasts with the Saint-Simonians pointed out.

II

It is widely believed that Austin's *Province* is, or at any rate was intended to be, nothing more than a morally neutral piece of "analytical jurisprudence." It is true that Austin did attempt to keep separate the two questions: What is law? and What should the law be? But this is not to say that he did not treat the latter question in *The Province*. In fact several sections are devoted to the elucidation and application of utilitarian ethical and political theory, and also to the criticism of the only ethical theory Austin was prepared to recognize as a significant rival to utilitarianism, namely Intuitionism.[15] In this connection, it is worth observing that Mill praised *The Province* as the "best" attempt so far made to present "the utilitarian scheme" as to "first principles."[16] Austin's treatment of authority in Lecture III is an explicit example of his normative concerns. But in spite of the attention received by Austin's work, his treatment of authority, like almost all the other explicitly normative passages of *The Province*, has been neglected. Indeed, it is a remarkable and puzzling fact that there is no discussion of Austin's treatment of authority in any one of the many studies of his thought. This is a fact that partly accounts for the belief that Mill, alone among the utilitarians, developed a theory of authority. In any case, Austin devoted the whole of Lecture III to the vindication of authority in the realm of beliefs, and he could not have been more explicit in basing his vindication on utilitarian premises.

Thus, in Lecture III, he argues in behalf of a "system of rules," both "moral and legal," whose content "might be known by all or most. But all the numerous reasons, upon which the system would rest, could scarcely be compassed" by any but "the comparatively few."[17] Austin is perfectly candid in calling this a system of "authority" because, first of all, "most of those who observe them [the rules]" would "be unable to perceive their ends, and be ignorant of the reasons on which they were founded, or of the proofs from which they were inferred";[18] and, secondly, this "multitude" would none-

---

[15] See John Austin, *The Province of Jurisprudence Determined*, ed. H. L. A. Hart (London, 1954), pp. 33–118 and 127–33, 295–99. Hereinafter cited as *Province*.

[16] John Stuart Mill to John Pringle Nichol, October 14, 1834 in *The Earlier Letters of John Stuart Mill*, ed. Francis E. Mineka, *Collected Works*, v. XII (Toronto, 1963), p. 236.

[17] *Province*, p. 62.

[18] *Ibid.*, p. 61.

theless accept these rules as possessing such reasons and proofs on the "authority" or "testimony" of a certain few they "trust."[19] Austin is, then, working with the same conception of authority as Mill.

Now the point to be stressed is that Austin explicitly derived this system of authority from utilitarianism, and to bring out the way he did so, it is necessary to follow his line of advance. Austin arrives at this system by entertaining and then rejecting a particular "objection to the theory of general utility." This objection runs as follows. According to the theory of utility, "legal and moral rules" are supposed to be "fashioned on the principle of utility . . . [that is] obtained by observation and induction from the tendencies of human actions" to promote "the general happiness."[20] But this requirement means that "the multitude," who plainly cannot master the inductive science of the tendencies of actions, cannot therefore know what rules they ought to obey. The inductive evidence for fashioning rules is evidence "to which the great bulk of mankind has scarcely the slightest access";

> since they are busied with earning the means of living, the many are unable to explore the field of ethics, and to learn their numerous duties by learning the tendencies of actions.[21]

The "perplexing" objection to utilitarianism is, then, that the many are "debarred" from the very kind of knowledge upon which moral conduct is supposed to be based. But that is not all: for this same objection cannot be leveled against Intuitionism. Intuitionism is conceived by Austin, in this connection, as asserting that all human beings possess an "immediate consciousness" of moral

---

[19] *Ibid.*, p. 79.
[20] *Ibid.*, p. 60.
[21] *Ibid.*, p. 60.

values in that they are "endowed with a *moral sense,*
or with a *common sense,* or with a *practical reason . . .*"
or "conscience."[22] Now, on this ethical theory, the
"multitude" may still be seen as people debarred from
access to inductive knowledge. But since moral judgment
is not founded on inductive knowledge, their scientific
ignorance does not also constitute moral ignorance.
". . . duties . . . would be subjects of immediate consciousness, and completely exempted from the jurisdiction
of observation and induction."[23] Intuitionism is thus used
by Austin to highlight the above objection to utilitarianism: for unlike the Intuitionist, the Utilitarian apparently finds himself in the "absurd and monstrous"
position of proposing a criterion of moral decision which
ordinary men and women cannot use to guide themselves.[24]

In setting forth this "objection" to utilitarianism, Austin can be recognized to have adopted for his own use
"the Benthamite simplification of the issues" of ethical
theory.[25] According to this simplification, "the hypothesis or theories which attempt to resolve this question
[of an "index" of right conduct], may be reduced, I
think, to two"[26]—namely "moral sense" and "utility."
Now the point to be stressed is that this reduction, by
shaping Austin's definition of the "objection" to utilitarianism, also shapes his answer; and this answer is his
doctrine of authority. Austin meets the objection, then,
by contending that utilitarianism can still be upheld in
practice, in spite of the limited knowledge of the multitude, insofar as the multitude are prepared to "trust on
authority" the rules proposed by "the comparatively few,

---

22 *Province,* p. 46; cf. p. 37.
23 *Ibid.,* p. 46; cf. p. 36.
24 *Ibid.,* p. 60.
25 J. B. Schneewind, "Moral Problems and Moral Philosophy
in the Victorian Period," *Victorian Studies* (September 1965), p.
30–32 n.
26 *Province,* p. 35.

who study the science assiduously."[27] To quote one key passage at length:

> If ethical science must be gotten by consulting the principle of utility, if it rest upon observation and induction applied to the tendencies of actions, if it be a matter of acquired knowledge and not of immediate consciousness, much of it (I admit) will ever be hidden from the multitude, or will be ever taken by the multitude on authority, testimony or trust. For an inquiry into the tendencies of actions embraces so spacious a field, that none but the comparatively few, who study the science assiduously, can apply the principle extensively. . . .[28]

Here Austin is insisting on a stark contrast between utilitarianism and intuitionism in order to bring out how necessary authority is to utilitarianism. For Austin, it is the central utilitarian demand that moral and legal rules be fashioned on inductive knowledge, together with the fact of widespread ignorance, that renders authority necessary to utilitarianism, if utilitarianism is actually to prevail as the mode of rule-making in society. And, on the same score, authority of this sort appears to Austin to be unnecessary on the intuitionist ethical theory.

Parenthetically, it may be recognized here that Austin's treatment of authority has some limited bearing on the current philosophical controversy over the role of rules in utilitarianism.[29] This controversy in turn illuminates Austin's doctrine. Austin wishes to avoid forcing ordinary men "on the dangerous process of calculating specific consequences" every time they have to make a moral decision.[30] For they have neither the know-

---

[27] *Ibid.*, pp. 73, 81–82.

[28] *Ibid.*, p. 73, also pp. 60–62.

[29] See particularly J. B. Rawls, "Two Concepts of Rules," *Philosophical Review*, LXIV (1955), 3–32, but especially p. 19–22 n. on Austin.

[30] *Province*, p. 60.

ledge nor the time to do so. He proposes to avoid this
"danger" by arguing that "Our rules would be fashioned
on utility; our conduct, on our rules."[31] Now the crucial
point for Austin is that he thinks this use of rules avoids
the danger of calculating specific consequences not only
because men thereby have rules to obey, but also because these rules are to be taken on authority by most
men. This suggests that even if Austin (and, for that
matter, Mill) is interpreted as a so-called "act-utilitar-
ian," for whom exceptions can properly be made to rules
when utility is better promoted by not following the
rules, nevertheless as far as the "multitude" are concerned no such exception can be allowed. For the multitude do not have access to the knowledge by reference
to which they might justifiably take it upon themselves
to make an exception to a rule. Another way of expressing this same point is by recognizing the special sense
in which Austin's "few" compose a moral elite. They are a
moral elite not precisely in the sense that they must meet
more exacting moral standards than ordinary men and
accordingly have higher privileges and rights. Rather
they alone are permitted, if any one is permitted, to make
exceptions to the rules all men ought to follow.[32]

Austin then proceeds to complete his argument for
authority by again entertaining and meeting an "objection" to utilitarianism. This is that the "few" who have
"affected to inquire into ethics" and into "legislation,
politics, and political economy" are in fact divided among
themselves as to the tendencies of actions. There is thus
no unified "body of doctrine" to be taken on trust by the
multitude; and since the very ignorance of the multitude
which makes authority necessary in the first place also

---

[31] *Province*, p. 47.

[32] Cf. John Stuart Mill, *Utilitarianism* in *Utilitarianism, Liberty*, etc. (London and New York, 1910), p. 22: ". . . the beliefs
which have thus come down are the rules of morality for the multitude, and for the philosopher until he has succeeded in finding
better."

makes it impossible for them to decide between the competing doctrines of the few, no system of authority is in practice possible. Fundamental intellectual controversy between the few thus issues in the same result as the ignorance of the many: it makes utilitarianism incapable of realization.

> Now how can the bulk of mankind, who have little opportunity for research, compare the respective merits of these varying and hostile opinions, and hit upon those of the throng which accord with utility and truth? Here, testimony is not to be trusted. There is not *that concurrence or agreement of numerous and impartial inquiries,* to which the most cautious and erect understanding readily and wisely defers. With regard to the science of ethics, and to all the various sciences which are nearly related to ethics, invincible doubt, or blind and prostrate belief, would seem to be the doom of the multitude . . . whilst every authority, whereon they may hang their faith, wants that mark of trustworthiness [i.e. unity] which justifies reliance on authority.[33]

The answer to this objection, Austin claims, depends on first understanding why the "few" disagree among themselves. They do so not because moral disagreements are necessarily irresolvable by the application of scientific methodology to the study of human action, but rather because inductive social science has not progressed far enough, as compared to the progress of physical science. The progress of the former has been inhibited because of the failure on the part of the few who cultivate it to do so in an unprejudiced fashion. The few who are capable of generating a unified "body of doctrine" have permitted their own "interests" to influence their study, thus frustrating the advance of social science. Here again it is worth quoting Austin at considerable length.

---

[33] *Province,* pp. 63–64. Austin's italics.

It was the opinion of Mr. Locke, and I fully concur in the opinion, that there is no peculiar uncertainty in the *subject* or *matter* of these sciences: that the great and extraordinary difficulties, by which their advancement is impeded, are extrinsic; are opposed by sinister interests, or by prejudice. . . . [But if] the writers would attend to the suggestions of Hobbes and of Locke, and would imitate the method so successfully pursued by geometers . . . [then] this patience in investigation, this distinctness and accuracy of method, this freedom and "indifferency" in the pursuit of the useful and the true, would thoroughly dispel the obscurity by which the science is clouded. The wish, the hope, the prediction of Mr. Locke would, in time, be accomplished: and "ethics would rank with the sciences which are *capable of demonstration*." The adepts in ethical, as well as in mathematical science, would commonly agree in their results: And, as the jar of *their* conclusions gradually subsided, a body of doctrine and authority to which the multitude . . . might trust would emerge from the existing chaos. . . . In *the unanimous or general consent of numerous and impartial inquirers,* they would find that mark of trustworthiness which justifies reliance on authority. . . .[34]

Austin's theory of authority thus presupposes the truth of the claim that there are no moral disagreements among men (or, at any rate, among the "few") which cannot be resolved in principle by scientific inquiry into the consequences of human action. This claim rests on the cardinal tenet of utilitarian ethics, that to justify a course of action is to provide evidence showing that it produces a greater balance of good over bad results than the alternatives. Austin's argument for authority is, then, that if the scientific resolution of moral disagreements is to be accepted by all members of society, then the "many" must accept that resolution on the authority of the "few" who grasp its scientific basis. Two theses can thus be recog-

---

[34] *Province,* pp. 74, 77–78, 79.

nized to compose Austin's vindication: first, the utilitarian view of the nature of moral justification; second, the "sociological" thesis that society is in fact inhabited chiefly by people who cannot comprehend the substance of a utilitarian justification.

This, then, in outline, is Austin's theory of authority; and, at this point, it is worth calling attention to six features of his theory, all but the first of which are bound up with its basis in utilitarian ethical theory. These six features are by no means exhaustive of its implications, but they will all be found to have a significant bearing on Mill's attempt to forge a justification of authority.

(1) To begin with, it should be observed that Austin was working with a highly specific conception of authority. This is a consideration worth stressing in the study of Austin's (and Mill's) theory for a special reason. It is a notorious fact that nineteenth- and twentieth-century political and social theory exhibits a ceaseless, acrimonious, and confusing controversy over the "meaning" of authority. Nor has contemporary empirical political science managed to remain immune from this controversy, what with its repeated attempts to delineate the field of political study by framing definitions of power, authority, legitimacy, etc. The result has been a series of loose and general notions of authority, such as legitimate power[35] or anything that regularly procures obedience from people.[36] The merits and demerits of these definitions aside, the point is that it would be a grave mistake to confound the conception of authority that is to be found in the *Province* (or in *The Spirit of the Age*) with any of these widely-held conceptions, which are distinguished by their tendency to run au-

[35] Max Weber, *The Theory of Social and Economic Organization*, trans. Talcott Parsons (New York, 1947), p. 56; T. D. Weldon, *The Vocabulary of Politics* (London, 1953), pp. 51–56.
[36] Robert Michels, "Authority," *Encyclopedia of the Social Sciences*, v. I, p. 319; David Easton, *A Systems Analysis of Political Life* (New York, 1965), p. 208.

thority and power together. It is of critical importance to
recognize that, on Austin's notion of authority, it is possible to distinguish sharply between authority and power;
and this means in turn that, for Austin, deference to
authority is quite compatible with liberty of action.
"Power" is here being used in the narrow sense in which
it specifically involves coercion rather than in the broad
sense in which it refers to any means of getting a man
to do one's bidding, all the way from the use of physical
force to persuasion by rational argument. Power in the
narrow sense had long been the subject of careful scrutiny by thinkers in the utilitarian tradition. James Mill,
for example, wrote

> A man's power means the readiness of other men to obey
> him. Now one man obeys another, from the prospect,
> either of good if he obeys, or of evil if he does not obey.
> Wealth is the great means of procuring obedience,
> through the medium of good. . . . The power of inflicting
> evil, in case of disobedience, and of procuring services
> by fear, is what in the more peculiar sense, is meant by the
> term Power.[37]

Further, the utilitarians all conceived of liberty by reference to the absence of power in this "peculiar sense."
Thus Austin says that "when liberty is not exactly synonymous with right it means, and can mean nothing else,
but exemption from restraint or obligation"[38] (obligation
means to Austin, being liable to incur an evil from the
person commanding in case of disobedience[39]). Now
the reason for recalling these definitions is that Austin
did not conceive of the act of accepting authority as
restraint and therefore as nullifying liberty. Rather he
speaks of "deference" and "trust" as distinguishing the

[37] *Analysis of the Phenomena of the Human Mind* (2 vols.,
London, 1869), II, p. 208. Originally published in 1829.
[38] *Province*, p. 187; cf. p. 269.
[39] *Ibid.*, p. 18.

act of accepting authority. What he means is that one person defers to the authority of another person when the former accepts the latter's "opinions" (including opinions about what rules it is desirable to obey), without making that acceptance conditional upon a "direct examination"[40] of the grounds on which those opinions are supposed to rest. And such deference to the opinions of another is paid because of something about the source (i.e., his "mark") from which those opinions come, by virtue of which they are taken to be credible. (On Austin's own doctrine, that "mark" is "the unanimous or general consent of numerous and impartial inquirers".) For Austin, then, the distinguishing feature of the authority relationship is not compulsion, but the voluntary abdication of one's "private judgment" and the acceptance of someone else's judgment as a reason for believing.

It should be observed that it is this same notion of authority that Austin uses when he argues against reliance on authority, as well as when he argues for it. Thus, there are passages of the *Province* which seem to suggest that Austin intends his system of authority to replace one already in existence. By establishing his system of authority, Austin declares, "the multitude . . . might be freed from the dominion of authority: from the necessity of blindly persisting in hereditary opinions and practices."[41] Here the "mark" of authority is what Austin calls "custom" or "tradition"; and he writes that "the bulk of the community" obey government at present not because of any assessment of its policies in the light of "the principle of general utility," but because that government is recognized to act in the customary way.[42] Here again, the same two distinguishing features of the authority relationship are present, namely, (i) non-

---

[40] *Ibid.*, p. 79. For a similar *notion* of authority, see Jeremy Bentham, *The Handbook of Political Fallacies*, ed. Harold A. Larrabee (New York, 1962), pp. 23–26.

[41] *Province*, p. 73.

[42] *Ibid.*, p. 299.

examination of the content of that which one is being asked to obey, (ii) the acceptance of a particular "mark" as justifying this sort of "trust." And such a relationship is not coercive.

The above discussion of Austin's notion of authority is merely a preliminary sketch, and is not intended to take the place of either an extended analysis or an assessment of its validity for political philosophy. Such a comprehensive discussion is, in any case, best undertaken in connection with a detailed examination of the views of Mill and of "the reaction of the nineteenth century." The above sketch should, however, help to forestall certain confusions about authority that have hindered comprehension of Mill's theory. In connection with Mill, one further point may be made.

Since, on the above analysis, deference to authority is understood to be a different mode of obedience from submission to coercive power, it follows that an argument in behalf of authority is not to be construed as an argument for limiting liberty. A justification of authority is not logically incompatible with a justification of liberty. When Mill sets about in *On Liberty* "to assert one very simple principle" which is intended to state how far civilized adults should be left free to do what they choose, he takes this enterprise to be equivalent to fixing a limit on the justifiable exercise of coercion over them. But since deference to authority is not coercion, it follows that such deference cannot be construed as a violation of Mill's principle of liberty. No case of trusting to authority properly so-called can be said to violate Mill's limitation on coercion (whatever that limitation is) because to defer to authority is not to be compelled. (Mill is quite explicit that a man's "own good, either physical or moral, is not a sufficient warrant" for *coercing* him, but it may be for "remonstrating," "reasoning," "persuading," or "entreating" him.[43]) This distinction between

---

[43] *On Liberty*, p. 73. Compare the important passage in *On Liberty* in which Mill says that "the sovereign Many have let

authority and coercion is not, however, meant to imply that Mill intends to place no restriction whatever on the scope of authority, but only that such a restriction cannot be couched in the form of a limitation on coercion. The question how far men should defer to authority, is a different question from the question how much coercion is desirable. For in the first question we are asking how far it is desirable that men should form their own moral and political judgments, not how far they should be exempt from coercion. Thus, if the political philosophy of the essay *On Liberty* is at odds with the political philosophy of *The Spirit of the Age*, this cannot simply be due to the fact that the former includes a justification of liberty and the latter a justification of authority.

(2) There is no suggestion or hint anywhere in *The Province of Jurisprudence* that the utilitarian ethical theory might somehow come into conflict with the argument for authority presented there. On the contrary, it is the only other ethical theory recognized by utilitarianism, namely, intuitionism, that Austin sees as standing in opposition to the kind of defense of authority he offers. Indeed, for Austin, this opposition is overwhelmingly obvious. By (allegedly) treating ultimate moral values as "self-evident," Intuitionism *begins* with the *prima facie* claim that authority is unnecessary. For authority can be justified only when it can be shown that it is desirable for a person to abdicate his own "private judgment" and accept on trust the utterances of someone else. But a necessary (though not sufficient) condition that has to be satisfied for it to be right for a person to abdicate his judgment is that he is incapable of grasping the matter at hand through the exercise of his own judgment. It appears to Austin that this condition is rejected as such

---

themselves be guided (which in their best times they have always done) by the counsels and influence of a more highly gifted and instructed One or Few" (p. 124). Mill is explicit that he is here speaking of non-coercive "influence." Cf. *Spirit,* p. 36, on the "voluntary acquiescence" involved in authority; also pp. 9–10.

by intuitionism. Since the cardinal thesis of intuitionism is, as Austin understands it, that immediate access to moral truths is available "to all mankind,"[44] it follows that (at least to begin with) there is no call for anyone to abdicate his own judgment in moral matters. But, likewise for Austin, there is no *prima facie* opposition to authority from the utilitarian ethical theory. For since utilitarianism denies cognitive status to "private judgment" (or "conscience," "practical reason," etc.) in moral matters, it follows that the utilitarian at least does not *begin* his consideration of authority with the handicap, that to submit to authority is to cut oneself off from the source of moral truth. Thus implicit in Austin's treatment of authority is a parallel between the very idea of authority as involving the surrender of private judgment and the central utilitarian denial of cognitive status to private judgment. Hence the confidence with which Austin as a utilitarian proceeds to the task of vindicating authority.

To this consideration may be added another of a similar sort. As a utilitarian Austin also rejects the (intuitionist) thesis that the moral value of an *act* depends on the moral quality of the motive from which it springs. It follows that he does not begin his treatment of authority with the conviction that submission to authority is a derogation from the moral dignity of one's conduct (or even the destruction of its moral worth, if it is held that "the principle of autonomy is the sole principle of ethics"). Thus Austin declares that a man can be said to have satisfied the demands of morality by obeying a rule, even though the moral agent be "ignorant of the reasons" why the rule is right, i.e., produces desirable consequences.[45]

What we are here dealing with may be called the principle of the availability of a concept. In Austin's eyes, the concept of authority is available to utilitarian-

---

[44] *Province,* p. 36.
[45] *Ibid.,* p. 61. Also pp. 109–11, 115–16.

ism in a way that it is not available to intuitionism. This is not to say, however, that intuitionism cannot possibly support authority. The form assumed by an "intuitionist" justification of authority must be that authority is so indispensable to the very existence of a moral life, given the imperfect character of men as they are, that in spite of the *prima facie* undesirability of authority, it still may be justified as a necessary evil. Unfortunately, Austin never contrasts his theory of authority with this venerable doctrine, though it was still very much alive in nineteenth-century England.

(3) I come now to the logical form of Austin's justification of authority. This is critically significant for the understanding of its implications in political theory. According to Utilitarianism, the proper method for justifying any rule, practice, or institution is to provide inductive evidence to show that the observation of that rule, etc., would produce a greater balance of good over evil results than the alternative(s). The point to be stressed, however, is that Austin does not provide, or think it necessary to provide, any such inductive evidence in behalf of his "system" of authority. He does not subject the authority-relationship itself to the usual utilitarian method of justification. Rather, his argument is that if the utilitarian method of justification is in fact to be employed in a society for the evaluation and formulation of its rules, then the very use of that method requires the acceptance of authority in that society, insofar as it is inhabited by an "uninstructed" multitude. For since the multitude do not comprehend the "reasons" for those rules, it follows that the only way voluntary obedience can be procured from them is through their "trusting" those who promulgate the rules. For Austin, then, the utilitarian method of justification entails authority, quite apart from any inductive evidence in its behalf, other than that society is in fact inhabited by such a multitude as he describes. (Nor can this conclusion be avoided by subjecting a society organized around Austin's system of authority to the test of inductive evidence, since,

whatever the results of that test, the "multitude" would still have to take those results on "trust" from the "few" capable of performing the "test." Hence, even the desirability of dispensing with authority would have to be taken on authority.) In this study, I will call Austin's justification a "meta-political" form of justification since it follows from the adoption of the utilitarian method, rather than from being itself subjected to the utilitarian test.

One special implication of this "meta-political" form of justification should be noted here. It is, in a precise sense, wholly abstract. For it does not follow from this *kind* of justification of authority, that any particular rules should be accepted on authority. The rules that should be accepted on trust are only those which have, as it were, passed the ordinary utilitarian test as to inductive evidence of their consequences. So it should be observed that Austin is not himself prepared to delineate a system of rules or beliefs to be taken on authority: he does not think social science has advanced far enough to provide such a system. In the meantime, therefore, it becomes possible to claim that the actual establishment of a system of authority would be unjustified. What we have here, then, is an incipient temporal, if not historical, complement to the doctrine of authority, in which two "periods" akin to Mill's present transitional period and future "natural state of society" are already implicit. This raises the question (among others): what, if anything, does the Saint-Simonian theory of history contribute in principle to this rationalist picture of a possible history of mankind?

(4) In presenting his argument for authority, Austin passes over in silence one critical aspect of the utilitarian ethical theory. The utilitarians saw that in order for moral questions to be decided by an appeal to inductive evidence alone, there must be a single ultimate end. For if more than one ultimate end were admitted, a decision between the various ends when they came into conflict could not be taken on the basis of inductive evidence

alone. Further, this end must itself belong among the class of things capable of being known empirically, since otherwise inductive science could not determine what course of action most effectively promotes that end. Hence, the utilitarians conceived of a single ultimate end, happiness, in terms of the satisfaction of the desires men actually have (rather than those they ought to have). Accordingly, scientific investigation into what course of action is most effective in promoting happiness so understood must presumably be preceded by an investigation into *what* pleases and pains men. But the question then arises as to whether Austin's doctrine of authority is compatible with this side of utilitarianism. The difficulty is that the prior investigation into what pleases men would seem to require that the investigators somehow consult the many as to what pleases them; and the authority of the few would, then, apparently be restricted to serving the aims of the many by placing at their disposal the means by which those aims can be realized, but leaving it up to the many to decide whether they will accept those means on trust.

Yet, plainly, Austin makes no provision in his doctrine for such consultation of the few with the many. In fact, he by-passes this problem altogether by employing a practice used by other utilitarians too. What Austin does is to substitute for an inductive investigation into what men actually desire, a deductive argument from a conception of human nature. This is well illustrated by his significant discussion of "the inestimable science of political economy" for some seven pages out of the twenty-three that make up his lecture on authority.[46] There, he makes several deductions "from the condition of man upon earth" in order to demonstrate that, *whatever* men actually desire in a world characterized by "the niggardliness of nature," the institution of private property and prudent policies founded upon "the true principle of population detected by the sagacity of Mr. Malthus" are indis-

[46] *Province*, pp. 66–72.

pensible to the optimum gratification of desires.[47] More-over, Austin is also prepared to contend that the few should both attempt to dispel certain "prejudices" of the many (that, for example, private property is the chief cause of their "penury" and "drudgery") and to teach the many so far as possible "the true reasons which call for private property."[48] In this connection, Austin distinguishes between the "nicer points" of economics which "the multitude . . . will never understand distinctly . . . [and will] be always taken from authority" and the "commanding truths" (such as "the effect of the principle of population on the price of labour") which can be "clearly apprehended by the many."[49] (Note that at the same time that the truths of political economy are to be diffused among the people—some to be taken on trust, others to be clearly apprehended—Austin is also arguing that "the many are unable to explore the field of ethics" because "they are busied with earning the means of living."[50])

The critical point is, then, that by the use of such deductive reasoning as a surrogate for inductive investigation, the few need not consult the many at all. Not only the rules, but also "the general happiness" the rules are designed to promote, can then be determined by the few apart from any participation by the many. (Austin was in fact no democrat.[51]) In this way, the authority of the few is not impaired. It scarcely needs to be added that

---

[47] *Province*, pp. 67–68.

[48] *Ibid.*, p. 70.

[49] *Ibid.*, pp. 71–72. But is there anything about the nature of economic science that insures that its "commanding truths" are going to go on being the ones that the multitude can understand themselves? Is this not just a happy, but fortuitous, coincidence so far? Mill seems to have thought so: see "Tocqueville on Democracy in America (Vol. I)," in *Essays on Politics and Culture, op. cit.*, p. 196–98 n.

[50] *Province*, p. 60; cf. pp. 63–64.

[51] See the autobiographical preface to his *A Plea For The Constitution*, second ed. (London, 1859), p. vi; also p. 15.

this kind of argument has a bearing on Mill's concept of "rational democracy" in which the rulers will have wide discretion because "the many will not only defer to their authority, but cheerfully acknowledge them as their superiors in wisdom, and the fittest to rule."[52]

(5) It is now appropriate to consider Austin's view of the possibility of the historical realization of his system of authority. His discussion of this matter suffers from excessive brevity, and the terms in which it is cast are liable to be misconstrued. And when compared with Mill's extensive concern with this question, the paucity of argument by Austin becomes itself significant. One thing he does clearly insist upon is that, at present, the few are divided among themselves as to "the science of ethics," that this disunity springs from their failure to pursue ethical and political science with "due 'indifferency,'" and that this "existing chaos" is so great and conspicuous that "the ignorant" have scarcely any opinions to "hang their faith upon," except some "truths" of economics.[53] As to the establishment of authority, Austin's argument seems to run as follows. He contends that authority may justifiably be established only if the few come to agree among themselves. He insists that in this agreement the multitude "would find that mark of trustworthiness which justifies reliance on authority." Such an authority would "satisfy the most scrupulous reason."[54] Austin's reasoning here seems to be that since the few cannot reach agreement among themselves *except* by shedding their "prejudices" and achieving "indifference" or "impartiality," it follows that the doctrine upon which they agree must itself be free from "prejudice" and "sinister interest." That is, Austin seems to

[52] "Tocqueville on Democracy," *op. cit.*, p. 196–98 n. See also "The Rationale of Political Representation," *London Review*, I (July 1835), 341–71, for Mill's fullest discussion of "rational democracy."

[53] *Province*, pp. 74, 79–81; cf. pp. 295–300.

[54] *Ibid.*, p. 79.

hold that the very establishment of his utilitarian authority presupposes the eradication of prejudice among the few who are to possess that authority. So it is that he confidently asserts that agreement among the few justifies reliance on their authority.

At first glance, it may appear that Austin has with this argument abandoned the standard utilitarian view of human nature in political contexts, and is claiming that his scientific elite is different from all other aristocracies in that it is capable of somehow divesting itself of its egotism and transforming itself into a collection of "altruists" through its commitment to the promotion of "the general happiness." On this interpretation, the historical realization of the system of authority is made to depend on a transformation of human nature. (Critics of Mill's similar theory of authority seem to attribute just such a view to Mill, thereby supposedly adding further evidence that he rejected utilitarian political theory.[55]) Nevertheless, there is no evidence whatever in *The Province* for this psychological interpretation of what Austin means by the "indifferency" of the few. It seems plausible only as long as it is thought to represent the only thing he could have meant. However, a careful inspection of Austin's words strongly suggests another and quite different interpretation, which once again points on to Mill and to certain characteristic themes in his thought.

This second interpretation depends on recognizing that Austin was employing the connected terms "indifferency," "impartiality," "freedom from prejudice," etc., in a special way characteristic of the Enlightenment. His citation of Locke, from whom he took the word "indifferency," also points to this Enlightenment source. From this standpoint, Austin understood prejudice as a refusal to evaluate one's commitments in the light of some "external standard." Thus he explicitly defines "prejudice" as a sustained adherence to something simply because one is already committed to it and is already paying "ha-

---

[55] Hamburger, p. 81; Letwin, pp. 7, 250–52, 302–11.

bitual obedience" to it. Then the fact that one is "fond" of it seems a sufficient reason for continuing one's commitment to it.[56] Prejudice, on this view, is seen as a refusal to call one's loyalties to a moral accounting. And its opposite, "indifference," is thus seen as a certain kind of "freedom." In this connection, Austin quite explicitly speaks of indifference as a readiness to

> scrutinize established institutions, and current or received opinions, fearlessly, but coolly; with the freedom which is imperiously demanded by general utility, but without the antipathy which is begotten by the dread of persecution, and which is scarcely less adverse than "the love of things ancient" to the rapid advancement of science.[57]

If the passage in Locke on indifference that Austin uses is traced back to the *Essay Concerning Human Understanding*, Locke will also be found using the concept of indifference to mean "freedom" from "the well-endowed opinions in fashion." This freedom, Locke says, is a necessary condition for placing "morality amongst the sciences capable of demonstration."[58] If, on the other hand, we turn to Mill, he will also be found speaking in *The Spirit of the Age* of "the lesson of indifference, so earnestly, and with such admirable effect, inculcated by Locke upon *students,* for whom alone that great man wrote. . . ."[59] Mill identifies this "indifference" with a willingness to "assert . . . liberty of thought, [and] discard all authority."[60] In the light of this passage on "indifference" by Mill (which certainly suggests a borrowing from Austin), and those from Austin and Locke, it becomes clear that the distinction between "prejudice"

[56] *Province*, p. 299.
[57] *Ibid.*, p. 79.
[58] Locke, *Essay Concerning Human Understanding*, IV, iii, 18, and 20.
[59] *Spirit*, p. 15.
[60] *Ibid.*

and "indifferency" is not to be identified with the distinction between self-interest and altruism, but rather with the distinction between a refusal to question established opinions and a willingness to question them. The distinguishing feature of "indifferency" is what Kant called courage, in a famous passage on the nature of Enlightenment that illuminates the doctrines of Austin and Mill:

> Enlightenment is man's release from his self-incurred tutelage. Tutelage is man's inability to make use of his understanding without direction from another. Self-incurred is this tutelage when its cause lies not in lack of reason but in lack of resolution and courage to use it without direction from another. *Sapere aude!* "Have courage to use your own reason!"—that is the motto of enlightenment.[61]

I am suggesting, then, that when Austin argues that the few can become impartial, he is not to be understood to mean that in them self-interest will be eradicated and they will become altruists (which is to impose a Comtian gloss that, in the case of Mill, might seem quite plausible on the assumption that he got his theory of authority from Comte and the Saint-Simonians). Indifferency involves, rather, devotion to free criticism, and is not then to be understood to imply a rejection of the utilitarian conception of human nature. It may even be conceived of as a subtle expression of self-love, what Mill called the desire for "individuality" in the passage of the essay *On Liberty* in which he discusses the few men who are disposed to question established opinions, thereby asserting "their own nature," as contrasted with the majority who, declining to judge established ways, efface "their own nature."[62]

This interpretation puts in a different perspective Austin's thesis that agreement among the few justifies re-

---

[61] Immanuel Kant, "What Is Enlightenment?" in *On History*, ed. Lewis White Beck (Indianapolis, 1963), p. 3.

[62] *On Liberty*, p. 119.

liance on their authority inasmuch as such agreement cannot take place unless the few achieve "indifferency." What Austin would appear to mean is that if there is free scrutiny of all opinions before they are received as authoritative, then this practice will justify reliance on their authority. Unfortunately he does not enlarge on this claim, but the very use of the phrase "the freedom which is imperiously demanded by utility" suggests that he is here relying on the standard utilitarian argument about the connection between freedom and utility. This is the argument employed by James Mill in "Liberty of the Press" (1819)—which the utilitarians accepted as a paradigm—as well as by John Stuart Mill in his early writings,[63] including *The Spirit of the Age*, and in the famous second chapter of *On Liberty*. The argument is that there is a sufficient reason for believing an opinion to be sound only if it has withstood criticism; or, in the words of *The Spirit of the Age*, "that every objection which can suggest itself has been duly examined by competent judges, and found immaterial."[64] There is, however, no reason to believe an opinion could resist criticism unless men are free to criticize it and are disposed to engage in criticism. Hence "freedom" is a necessary condition for presuming an opinion to be true. (It should be noted that the freedom required here is not only absence of external restraint on public expression but, as Austin and Mill both perceive, the courage to criticize.) But since the utilitarian ethical theory requires knowledge of the tendencies of actions, this sort of freedom is required by the utilitarian method too. Thus it follows that the utilitarian justification of freedom is, like the utilitarian justification of authority, of the "metapolitical" type. That is, no inductive evidence need be produced that free expression has desirable consequences

---

[63] See *Prefaces to Liberty: Selected Writings of John Stuart Mill*, ed. Bernard Wishy (Boston, 1959), especially p. 42.

[64] *Spirit*, p. 14; see also n. 49 above for a further reference to this argument in Mill.

since such freedom is a necessary condition for assessing any claim to knowledge of the consequences of actions. Now *if* this standard utilitarian argument is a correct interpretation of what Austin intended, then what he would seem to be suggesting is that the multitude have sufficient reason for believing any opinions agreed upon by the few because such opinions must have resisted all counter-arguments. Only then could an "indifferent" few all have agreed upon them. Hence Austin's teaching, on this interpretation, is that the historical realization of his system of authority is both possible and justified only if there is a coincidence of superior knowledge and courage to engage in free inquiry on the part of the few. Utilitarianism appears to Austin to require both free criticism as a condition of the growth of knowledge and authority to insure that it is acted upon.

It is hardly necessary to add that there is a certain tension or even paradoxical character in this picture of the few as being at once free thinkers themselves and possessors of authority over others. It suggests a temptation that Mill was to come to recognize, Comte could not resist. The difficulty here is not that the few will have to become altruists, but rather that they will have to continue to be "indifferent" and to criticize established ways even after those ways have become theirs and have been established by them. Yet the distinguishing feature of the Enlightenment concept of indifference is a readiness to judge established ways, and it is quite possible that "indifferency" can be sustained in the "individual" only in so far as he remains in opposition and stands over against established ways. The difficulty, in other words, is that the "few" depicted in the writings of Mill and Austin are not merely possessors of the science which provides the knowledge needed to fit means to ends: they also may be recognized to possess the character of "individuals" in the sense in which the German Idealists gave an unrivaled account of that character, i.e., men who achieve a sense of self-identity through distinguishing themselves from society and setting themselves over against it as critics. One may wonder, then, whether this character can be sustained after the man who bears it acquires authority. It may be suspected that Mill came to recognize this in his own way, and that a great deal of his concern with political "opposition" in his later writings reflects this recognition.

This discussion of "indifference" leads to one further consideration concerning the historical realization of Austin's system of authority. For it should be emphasized that Austin chose to say relatively little about the whole matter, and what little he did say is expressed in conditional language. Austin never asserts that such "indifferency" will or must be achieved by the few. He only says that, *if* it is, then and only then will it be desirable for those with superior knowledge also to possess authority. This suggests something further about the "historical" aspect of Austin's theory, briefly discussed under (2) above. First of all, Austin's language implies that as long as the few are not "indifferent," namely at the present time, the establishment of authority is unjustified. But secondly and more significantly, his system has an ambiguous historical status, since the realization of that system depends upon the satisfaction of an uncertain condition: the achievement of indifference by the few and their subsequent agreement. And while Austin is prepared to speak of a moral science of the tendencies of human actions, he is silent about an historical science of the succession of entire social systems. The critical consideration is that while Austin contends that a system of authority whose rules are consciously based on inductive knowledge is both possible and desirable, he does not contend that such a system could itself be brought into existence by action taken in accordance with the knowledge supplied by an inductive science of history. It was just the latter claim that Comte and the Saint-Simonians made, and they drew the obvious conclusion. Since the new authoritative social order can be brought about by action taken in accordance with the "natural law of de-

velopment . . . which prescribes for each epoch . . . the
political course it is possible to pursue,"[65] and since this
law is comprehended by the few "savants" alone, it followed for Comte that the rational activity of founding
the new order must itself involve the use of authority
and "vivid pictures" to procure from the many adherence
to this founding enterprise.

> The mass of mankind will never be inspired with a passion
> for any system, by proving to them that it is one which the
> progress of civilization has prepared. . . . A truth of this
> nature is accessible to a very limited circle. . . .[66]

And so:

> To reestablish harmony no other expedient is admissible
> but that of entirely proscribing any discussion of the plan
> laid down.[67]

Comte thus surrounded the activity of establishing the
new society with the authority that Austin insisted on
confining to that society itself. Now this contrast between Comte and Austin helps to define one of the well-
known issues on which Mill was to clash with Comte.
Mill's criticism of Comte in this respect is not simply that
it is morally odious to impose the new order on men, but
rather that to do so in accordance with supposed knowledge of historical laws is to destroy that free inquiry
which is the indispensible condition of assuming the
new authoritative doctrine to be true. So he wrote in the
year he brought out *The Spirit of the Age:*

---

[65] Auguste Comte, "Plan of the Scientific Operations Necessary
For Reorganising Society" (May 1822) trans. Henry Dix Hutton,
reprinted in *System of Positive Polity* (Paris, 1854), 4 vols., v.
4, p. 565. This is the work of the Saint-Simonian school that first
fully captured Mill's interest. See the Appendix below.

[66] *Ibid.*, p. 567.
[67] *Ibid.*, p. 564.

In the present age of transition, everything must be subordinate to *freedom of inquiry:* if your opinions, or mine, are right, they will in time be unanimously adopted by the instructed classes, and *then* it will be time to found the national creed upon the assumption of their truth.[68]

Mill's commitment to free inquiry stems from the same source as does Austin's: "the freedom which is imperiously demanded by general utility." Accordingly, Mill identified the historical process by which the new order could be realized with the process of free inquiry rather than with authoritative political action. But it was not until many years later that he fully acknowledged the crucial implication of this identification; and that is that the historical realization of the new order becomes highly uncertain, as it was for Austin.

A time such as M. Comte reckoned upon may come; unless something stops the progress of human improvement, it is sure to come: but after an unknown duration of hard thought and violent controversy. . . . the hope of such accordance of opinion among sociological inquirers as would obtain, in mere deference to their authority, the universal assent which M. Comte's scheme of society requires, must be adjourned to an indefinite distance.[69]

However, Mill's prudence, his recognition that the attempt to close the gap between the ideal and the actual through political action would pervert the ideal, is only one aspect of his criticism of Comte's doctrine which can

---

[68] John Stuart Mill to John Sterling, October 20–22, 1831 in *Earlier Letters,* v. 12, 75–77. Mill wrote this passage in the year he published *Spirit,* and it is quite possible that he had in mind the work from Comte from which the quotes above are taken.

[69] John Stuart Mill, *Auguste Comte and Positivism* (Ann Arbor, 1961), pp. 120–21. Cf. *On Liberty,* pp. 114–15: "At present . . . while mankind are imperfect there should be different opinions . . ."

be traced back to his commitment to utilitarianism. Austin helps us to see this.

(6) Whereas the preceding point concerned Austin's conception of the few who are supposed to hold authority, this last point will deal with his conception of the multitude who are supposed to be under authority. Discussion of the latter consideration will lead directly to another fundamental difference between the utilitarian theory of authority and the Saint-Simonian.

Austin provides no account whatever of what might be called the psychology of deference to authority. All that he says is that insofar as the few can reach agreement among themselves, then this unity will be readily recognized by the multitude as a "mark" of authority and so they will defer to those few. And here there is a grave difficulty. Austin seems to have assumed that the justification of authority he is offering on utilitarian grounds will itself be understood by the multitude and supply their motive for deferring. This assumption has two dimensions. First, Austin seems to think that the very ignorance on the part of the multitude that makes authority necessary in the first place, will yet be recognized *by* the multitude as ignorance and that they will therefore defer to "the adepts in ethics" *as a remedy for their own ignorance*. Secondly, he assumes that the multitude will also recognize who the few are who are entitled to deference (according to Austin's theory) by recognizing the very quality by virtue of which those few (on Austin's theory) deserve that deference, namely their superior knowledge. That is, the many will recognize the wise as wise apart from any "mark" such as wealth or social position or office, as if wisdom were socially visible in the way the foregoing conventional "marks" are. (It is perhaps arguable that Austin presupposed that the utilitarian intellectuals—"the adepts in ethics"—were already socially visible in his own society, as when he speaks of Malthus and the economists. But then Austin *was* assuming that the few were recognized by some quality other than their superior knowledge, namely, their occupation of the emergent office of secular intellectual.) What has happened here is that Austin's concern to vindicate the authority of superior knowledge has led him to lose sight of the concept of authority with which he is working. As a result, he never considers the possibility that the exercise of authority by the few over the many might require as a complement a form of non-rational persuasion and non-rational "marks" of authority which are accessible to the multitude. Yet his very use and justification of the concept of deferential authority certainly suggests such a possibility.

This criticism of Austin raises certain subtle questions about the concept of authority which require careful and extended treatment by themselves. Suffice it to say here that Austin simply side-steps or ignores the above problem in that he does not allow for the possibility that the multitude may be impelled to accept authority for reasons other than that authority can receive a utilitarian justification in terms of superior knowledge. To be more specific, he does not allow for the possibility (which is central to "the reaction of the nineteenth century" and to Saint-Simonianism) that the multitude might assent to the authority of some few not because they believe those few to be wiser than themselves, but instead because submission would relieve them of the burden of having to make their own choices; that, in short, what vexes the multitude about "the existing chaos" of conflicting opinions depicted by Austin, is the acute psychological strain it generates in them, rather than the lack of scientific progress in the study of society. Austin does speak of the multitude "turning and veering, for want of directing principles, with every wind of doctrine."[70] But he takes no account of the psychological disorientation that might be generated by this "turning and veering." It is, however, just this disorientation which is the decisive point of departure of the Saint-Simonian doc-

[70] *Province*, p. 73.

trine of authority. For the concept of authority conveys precisely the idea of a surrender of individual judgment and hence the obliteration of that "individualism," hostility to which is the animating heart of Saint-Simonianism. In conclusion, it is therefore worth briefly contrasting the Saint-Simonian approach to authority with Austin's.

John Stuart Mill referred to the Saint-Simonians (and Comte) as among the chief representatives of "the reaction of the nineteenth century against the eighteenth."[71] Their central teaching consisted of an interpretation of "modern" history or "progress" that was, in Mill's eyes, a reaction against the Enlightenment and utilitarian teaching on progress. In this connection, their central thesis was that authority was indispensible to modern society *not in spite of but because of its so-called progress.*[72] Progress had indeed taken place, in the sense of the downfall of the hierarchy, tradition, and religion of the old order. As a result of the destruction of the authoritative moral consensus of the old order, each man was unavoidably thrown back on his own moral and mental resources, such as they were, and burdened with the responsibility of having to make his own choices. Men had been, as it were, "forced to be free." In fact, progress had done its work so well that it destroyed most of what most people had once relied on for external guidance and internal consolation, leaving them in a state of moral suspense from which only some new form of authority could rescue them. The multitude have been dispossessed of their beliefs, but remained as credulous as ever. From this perspective, it appeared to be an illusion to think that most men really desired the independence that had been thrust upon them by rapid social change.

---

[71] *Autobiography*, p. 113.

[72] *The Doctrine of Saint-Simon: An Exposition, First Year, 1828–1829*, trans. Georg G. Iggers (Boston, 1958), pp. 5–6, 140–46, 229; Comte, "Plan of the Scientific Operations . . ." pp. 527–39; cf. Mill, *Early Draft*, pp. 188–89 on authority and progress.

How sweet it is to obey when we can enjoy the happiness . . . of being conveniently discharged, by sage and worthy leaders, from the pressing responsibility of a general direction of our conduct.[73]

What progress had seemingly produced, then, on this view, was not a society of self-determined "individuals," but instead the "masses" understood (in the generic sense of that key term in modern political vocabulary) as a people living under the exacting conditions of "modern" life, but devoid of the guidance provided by a common set of authoritative beliefs and thus susceptible to the appeals of whatever new forms of authority and subordination seem able to fill the vacuum left by the downfall of the old order. As Nietzsche put it, "having learnt not to believe in one authority, [modern men] sought to find another."[74]

The student of modern political and social thought cannot be unaware that this *kind* of interpretation of the "transition" to modernity is characteristic of much nineteenth- and twentieth-century thought, and that it involves a network of interlocking problems—philosophical, "methodological," moral, and political—that its nineteenth-century originators certainly did not pause to distinguish and that are perhaps even today not adequately understood. Nevertheless, the point may be stressed here that this "historical" interpretation provides a wholly different sort of starting-point for the speculations on authority of the Saint-Simonians and the other writers of "the reaction of the nineteenth century." Their point of departure is not a philosophical theory about the place of reason and knowledge in ethics, which is Austin's

[73] Comte, *Cours de Philosophie Positive,* 4th ed., vol. IV (Paris, 1877), p. 439, as quoted by Herbert Marcuse, *Reason and Revolution: Hegel and the Rise of Social Theory,* 2nd edition (New York, 1954), p. 350.

[74] Nietzsche, *Nachlass,* p. 554, as quoted by Arthur C. Danto, *Nietzsche as Philosopher* (New York, 1965), p. 31.

point of departure, but instead a conception of social equilibrium expressed in terms of an interpretation of the causes and consequences of social change. From this standpoint, the authority-relationship, in which a man abdicates his individual judgment, appeared to be the definitive characteristic of the social bond itself; and the justification of authority the Saint-Simonians offered was that authority would nullify the "egotism," "isolation," "doubt," and "consuming sickness" characteristic of the present age of "individualism."[75] Accordingly, those who should be under authority do not then appear, as in Austin's theory, merely as an analytical category of an ethical theory (i.e., those who have limited understanding of inductive science), but as a concrete collection of humans thrown up by the process of becoming modern. Now, it is this generic notion of the masses that is missing from Austin's theory and, accordingly, so is a parallel concern with the psychological function of authority in maintaining a certain kind of social order. His view of the multitude is entirely governed by his utilitarian philosophy, and the idea seems not to have occurred to him that authority may be accepted and indeed desired by men because they "do not desire liberty."[76] In conclusion, then, it may be recognized that this distinction between Austin's approach to authority and the Saint-Simonian helps again to define a central problem of Mill's treatment of authority. For the question remains, although it cannot be answered here, how far, if at all, Mill understood the Saint-Simonian approach to authority in developing a theory of authority akin to Austin's. This is a question that has not even been raised by those who assert unequivocally that *The Spirit of the Age* is Saint-Simonian. That question, however, becomes critical to the understanding of Mill's thought once it is recognized that he was working within the utilitarian framework in developing his theory of authority.

[75] *The Doctrine of Saint-Simon*, pp. 5–6, 232, 245, 246, 259.
[76] *On Liberty*, p. 122.

Discussion of the preceding six points is intended to help define an approach to Mill's treatment of authority in *The Spirit of the Age* and in his subsequent writings. These points are by no means exhaustive of what may be learned from Austin. But they will have made clear that the widespread belief that Mill's theory of authority simply constitutes a fundamental departure from utilitarianism and that it is fundamentally a Saint-Simonian theory can no longer be accepted. And anyone who wishes to claim that Mill himself must have thought that in developing his theory of authority, he was departing fundamentally from utilitarianism, must reckon with the example before Mill of Austin's explicitly utilitarian theory of authority.

APPENDIX

This appendix is concerned with certain historical questions raised by the recognition that Austin developed a theory of authority similar to Mill's in several respects.

First of all, is there any evidence that Mill was receptive to Austin's treatment of authority when he came to develop his own? Mill was acquainted with Austin's lectures prior to the publication of *The Province of Jurisprudence Determined* in 1832. Mill's letters show that he was attending Austin's lectures from the very beginning (Fall 1829), and that he continued to attend them at least through March 1833.[1] Far more important is the consideration that Mill certainly heard Austin deliver the third lecture on authority, and took notes on it which he preserved. Thus, when the extended edition of Austin's lectures was published posthumously in 1861, the editor called attention to the fact that he used Mill's "notes of the original lectures" because they were "found

---

[1] See Mill's correspondence in *Earlier Letters*, XII, pp. 51, 107, 134, 141, 147. Also H. Hale Bellot, *University College, London, 1826–1926* (London, 1929), pp. 97–99.

so accurate and full in the parts where the printed lectures [i.e., *The Province* of 1832] are complete, that
they may be confidently relied on for supplying the
lacunae . . ."[2] Lecture III was one of the lectures that
possessed gaps filled by Mill's notes.[3] And while the
notes of Mill used to supply lacunae in Lecture III are
slight, and add nothing material to what Austin published originally, they constitute certain evidence that
Mill knew Austin's presentation of that particular lecture in its original form. To this fact may be added the
consideration that in Mill's 1832 review of *The Province*,
it was Austin's lecture on authority that he mainly
dwelled on (unlike subsequent commentators). Mill
quoted extensively from four pages of the third lecture
in which Austin was arguing that (to quote from Mill's
quotation), "The adepts in ethics . . . would commonly
agree in their results; and . . . a body of doctrine and
authority, to which the *multitude* might trust, would
emerge from the existing chaos."[4] There is, then, no
reason to doubt Mill's statement, many years later, that
Austin's original lectures "left an indelible impression on
the minds of those who heard them delivered."[5] Mill,
then, not only heard but very likely had reflected on Austin's lecture on authority; and he could not then have
thought that he alone, among avowed utilitarians, was
offering a justification of authority at the time.

Moreover, Mill held Austin in high intellectual es-
teem. He judged *The Province* as "the very highest au-

---

[2] "Advertisement," in John Austin, *Lectures on Jurisprudence*,
ed. Robert Campbell (London, 1861), 2 vols., I, p. v. It should
also be noted that Austin's own plans for an enlarged edition of
the lectures (which never materialized) included consultation
with Mill. See letter of Mill to Harriet Taylor, January 27, 1849,
in F. A. Hayek, *John Stuart Mill and Harriet Taylor* (London,
1951), p. 132.

[3] See Austin, *Lectures,* Lecture III.

[4] "Austin's Lectures on Jurisprudence," *Tait's,* II (December
1832), pp. 347–48.

[5] See *Edinburgh Review* (October 1863), p. 448.

thority on what may be called the metaphysics of law."[6]
As to its ethics, Mill wrote in 1834 that "Of all views I
have yet seen taken of the utilitarian scheme, I like Austin's best, in his book on *The Province* . . ."[7] But there
is one statement in Mill's *Autobiography* that is especially revealing. This is a neglected passage in the chapter on "the crisis in my mental life":

> Among the persons of intellect whom I had known of old,
> the one with whom I had now most points of agreement
> was the elder Austin. I have mentioned that he had al-
> ways set himself in opposition to our early sectarianism;
> and latterly he had, like myself, come under new in-
> fluences . . . the influences of German literature. He
> attached much less importance than formerly to outward
> changes; unless accompanied by a better cultivation of
> the inward nature. He held, with the French Economists,
> that the real security for good government is "un peuple
> éclairé", which is not always the fruit of popular institu-
> tions, and which if it could not be had without them,
> would do their work better than they. Like me he never
> ceased to be a utilitarian. He professed great disrespect for
> what he called "the universal principles of human nature
> of the political economists", and insisted instead on the evi-
> dence which history and daily experience afford of the
> "extra-ordinary pliability of human nature" . . .[8]

Bearing in mind that Mill and Austin were developing
similar doctrines of authority in which sectarianism was
rejected and agreement among all "the instructed" was
advocated, this passage can now be better understood,
even though Austin never published his views on many
of the subjects alluded to above. (But consider the fol-

---

[6] "Recent Writers on Reform," in *Essays on Politics and Culture*, p. 335.

[7] Letter to John Pringle Nichol, October 14, 1834, *Earlier
Letters, op. cit.*, XII, p. 236.

[8] *Autobiography*, pp. 124–25.

lowing report of a conversation: Austin argued "strenuously that the Reformation has, on the whole, been an
evil to mankind . . . [because] it has produced sectarianism . . . [and] rendered theological questions popular.
Austin argues in nearly the same tone against the French
Revolution."[9])

Mill's intellectual affinity with Austin, probably beginning at least as early as Fall 1829, points up something of further significance in understanding Mill's
development. Mill's well-known dissatisfaction with the
"sectarian" character of "the people called utilitarians"
and consequent disaffection from "orthodox" utilitarian
circles[10] is presented in all studies of him as an isolated,
individual revolt which is to be traced back to his personal "mental crisis." But it is now apparent that Austin
shared this same dissatisfaction on ostensibly utilitarian
grounds, and it is possible that several others associated
with utilitarianism did so also. Thus, Mill reviewed Samuel Bailey's "excellent 'Rationale of Representation'"
(1835) as a utilitarian treatment of representative government. But Mill took it that Bailey was arguing in that
work for a "rational democracy" in which the "instructed" would be given wide discretion in making policy because the "multitude" would be deferential.[11] More
important, however, was G. C. Lewis's *Essay on the Influence of Authority in Matters of Opinions* (1849),
which Mill first encountered in an early draft in 1837.
Lewis's work, which still has its readers today, is explicitly based on Austin's third lecture (which he too

[9] G. C. Lewis to Sir Edmund Head, December 18, 1839, and
January 4, 1840, in *Letters of Sir George Cornewall Lewis,* ed.
Reverend Sir Gilbert Frankland Lewis (London, 1870), pp.
105-8.

[10] Letter to Thomas Carlyle, January 12, 1834, and to J. P.
Nichol, October 14, 1834, *Earlier Letters, op. cit.,* XII, 207 and
236.

[11] Letter to Joseph Blanco White, April 15, 1835, *Earlier Letters,* p. 258. For Mill's review of Bailey's book, see "Rationale of
Political Representation," *op. cit.*

had attended); and in all essentials, Lewis follows Austin in his treatment of authority. Mill wrote to Lewis that "the principles it inculcates are, as I have long thought so extremely needed at the present day."[12] But these "principles" were largely Austin's.[13] Lastly, it should be mentioned that Austin extended his ideas on authority further in *A Plea for the Constitution* (1859), which Mill described as "the most intellectual" attack of the day on "further reform."[14] One passage is especially worth quoting because of its similarity to *The Spirit of the Age.*

> The only remedy for the anarchical dispositions by which the more civilized nations have long been disturbed or menaced, is the diffusion of sound political and economic principles amongst the body of the people; or, at the least, amongst such a number of the more intelligent of them as would suffice to form an authority for the safe guidance of the rest.[15]

And in this tract, Austin is prepared to use "the sentiment of legitimism" to procure an attachment to the constitution.[16]

It would seem, then, that Mill was not the only utilitarian concerned to defend deferential authority, and that it is at least possible that his intellectual disaffection with sectarian utilitarianism (circa 1829) was part of an

---

[12] Letter to G. C. Lewis, November 24, 1837, *Earlier Letters,* XII, 360–61.

[13] George Cornewall Lewis, *An Essay on the Influence of Authority in Matters of Opinion* (London, 1849), pp. 3–6, 50, 399. For Austin's "influence" on Lewis, see also Walter Bagehot, "Sir George Cornewall Lewis" in *Works,* ed. Forrest Morgan (Hartford, 1889), 5 vols., III, 252–55; and *Letters of . . . Lewis,* pp. 56, 159.

[14] "Recent Writers on Reform," in *Essays on Politics and Culture,* p. 340.

[15] *A Plea for the Constitution,* p. 21.

[16] *Ibid.,* p. 37.

internal conflict between two groups of "utilitarians"
which (on account of Austin's involvement) may very
well have antedated Mill's "mental crisis" (circa 1826–
28, the years in which Austin was apparently preparing
his lectures on jurisprudence). However, the last statement is highly speculative, and the chief consideration
remains that it is very probable that Mill himself was
quite receptive to Austin's lecture on authority when
he first heard it delivered.

The question remains whether there is any evidence
showing that Mill's interest in Austin's treatment of authority antedates his interest in Saint-Simonianism, especially Comte's *Système de Politique Positive* (1822).
The evidence known to me appears inconclusive. But
the interesting consideration here is that it was apparently in Fall 1829 that Mill first read Comte's work with
care (Comte's work being the first Saint-Simonian treatise that impressed Mill).[17] This was the same period
in which Austin began lecturing (and Macaulay leveled
his notorious attack on James Mill's *Essay on Government*). Without attempting to trace Mill's growing interest in Saint-Simonianism thereafter, two final points
may be made. First, Mill claimed (in the *Early Draft*
of his autobiography, but deleted from the published version) that "the only very strong impression which I received from anything connected with Saint-Simonianism
was derived from an early writing of Auguste Comte,"
viz., the *Politique Positive*. This impression had to do,
Mill says, with "one important point in the parallelism
[between the physical sciences and the moral sciences]
much insisted on by M. Comte, [which] had not occurred to me."[18] This "one point" was that freedom of
conscience has no place in the physical sciences because
of the accumulation of a body of scientific truths all
scientists concur in. "Hitherto it had not occurred to me

17 Letter to Gustave d'Eichthal, October 8, 1829, *Earlier Letters*, XII, p. 35.
18 *Early Draft*, pp. 187–88.

that the case would be the same in the moral, social and political branches of speculation if they were equally advanced with the physical."[19] This "point" was argued by Mill in *The Spirit of the Age,* and it is absent from *The Province.* Nevertheless, as Mill says, it rests on the parallelism between physical science and moral science, together with the utilitarian denial of cognitive status to conscience. And both of the latter were views Mill (and Austin) already held. This brings me to the last point. Mill repeatedly declares that "These ideas, I knew, were not peculiar to the St. Simonians"[20] and that "I had much changed from what I was before I read any of their publications; but it was their works which gave order and system to the ideas which I had already imbibed from intercourse with others."[21] It is quite possible that some of these ideas imbibed from others were Austin's, and it may well have been the example of Austin working out a *utilitarian* theory of authority that allowed Mill to respond to Comte's doctrine.

---

[19] *Ibid.,* p. 188.

[20] *Autobiography,* p. 115.

[21] Letter to Gustave d'Eichthal, February 9, 1830, *Earlier Letters,* p. 45.

THE AUTONOMY OF
SOCIOLOGY

BY

Karl Popper

A concise formulation of Marx's opposition to psychologism[1], i.e. to the plausible doctrine that all laws of social life must be ultimately reducible to the psychological laws of 'human nature', is his famous epigram: 'It is not the consciousness of man that determines his existence—rather, it is his social existence that determines his consciousness.'[2] The function of the present chapter

From Chapter 14, "The Autonomy of Sociology," in *The Open Society and its Enemies*, Vol. II: *The High Tide of Prophecy: Hegel, Marx, and the Aftermath*, Princeton University Press, 4th Edition revised, 1963; Copyright © 1963 by Karl Raimund Popper, and Routledge and Kegan Paul, Ltd., 5th Edition, 1966. Reprinted by permission of the author and the publishers.

[1] Cp. note 19 to the last chapter.

[2] Cp. Marx's Preface to *A Contribution to the Critique of Political Economy*, quoted also in note 20 to chapter 13 and in text to notes 13 to chapter 15 and 3 to chapter 16; cp. *H.o.M.*, 372 = *Capital*, p. xvi. See also Marx and Engels, *German Ideology* (*H.o.M.*, 213 = *GA*, Series I, vol. v, 16): 'It is not consciousness that determines life, but life that determines consciousness.'

as well as of the two following ones is mainly to elucidate this epigram. And I may state at once that in developing what I believe to be Marx's anti-psychologism, I am developing a view to which I subscribe myself.

As an elementary illustration, and a first step in our examination, we may refer to the problem of the so-called rules of exogamy, i.e. the problem of explaining the wide distribution, among the most diverse cultures, of marriage laws apparently designed to prevent inbreeding. Mill and his psychologistic school of sociology (it was joined later by many psychoanalysts) would try to explain these rules by an appeal to 'human nature', for instance to some sort of instinctive aversion against incest (developed perhaps through natural selection, or else through 'repression'); and something like this would also be the naïve or popular explanation. Adopting the point of view expressed in Marx's epigram, however, one could ask whether it is not the other way round, that is to say, whether the apparent instinct is not rather a product of education, the effect rather than the cause of the social rules and traditions demanding exogamy and forbidding incest[3]. It is clear that these two approaches correspond exactly to the very ancient problem whether social laws are 'natural' or 'conventional' (dealt with at length in chapter 5). In a question such as the one chosen here as an illustration, it would be difficult to determine which of the two theories is the correct one, the explanation of the traditional social rules by instinct or the explanation of an apparent instinct by traditional social rules. The possibility of deciding such questions by experiment has, however, been shown in a similar case, that of the apparently instinctive aversion to snakes. This aversion has a greater semblance of being instinctive or 'natural' in that it is exhibited not only by men but also by all anthropoid apes and by most mon-

---

[3] Cp. M. Ginsberg, *Sociology* (Home University Library, 130 ff.), who discusses this problem in a similar context, without, however, referring to Marx.

keys as well. But experiments seem to indicate that this
fear is conventional. It appears to be a product of education, not only in the human race but also for instance
in chimpanzees, since[4] both young children and young
chimpanzees who have not been taught to fear snakes do
not exhibit the alleged instinct. This example should be
taken as a warning. We are faced here with an aversion
which is apparently universal, even beyond the human
race. But although from the fact that a habit is not universal we might perhaps argue against its being based
on an instinct (but even this argument is dangerous
since there are social customs enforcing the suppression
of instincts), we see that the converse is certainly not
true. The universal occurrence of a certain behaviour
is not a decisive argument in favour of its instinctive
character, or of its being rooted in 'human nature'.

Such considerations may show how naïve it is to
assume that all social laws must be derivable, in principle, from the psychology of 'human nature'. But this
analysis is still rather crude. In order to proceed one
step further, we may try to analyse more directly the
main thesis of psychologism, the doctrine that, society
being the product of interacting minds, social laws must
ultimately be reducible to psychological laws, since the
events of social life, including its conventions, must be
the outcome of motives springing from the minds of individual men.

Against this doctrine of psychologism, the defenders
of an autonomous sociology can advance *institutionalist*
views[5]. They can point out, first of all, that no action
can ever be explained by motive alone; if motives (or
any other psychological or behaviourist concepts) are to
be used in the explanation, then they must be supplemented by a reference to the general situation, and es-

---

[4] Cp., for instance, *Zoology Leaflet* 10, published by the Field
Museum of Natural History, Chicago, 1929.

[5] For institutionalism, cp. especially chapter 3 (text to notes 9
and 10) and chapter 9.

pecially to the environment. In the case of human actions, this environment is very largely of a social nature; thus our actions cannot be explained without reference to our social environment, to social institutions and to their manner of functioning. It is therefore impossible, the institutionalist may contend, to reduce sociology to a psychological or behaviouristic analysis of our actions; rather, every such analysis presupposes sociology, which therefore cannot wholly depend on psychological analysis. Sociology, or at least a very important part of it, must be autonomous.

Against this view, the followers of psychologism may retort that they are quite ready to admit the great importance of environmental factors, whether natural or social: but the structure (they may prefer the fashionable word 'pattern') of the social environment, as opposed to the natural environment, is man-made; and therefore it must be explicable in terms of human nature, in accordance with the doctrine of psychologism. For instance, the characteristic institution which economists call 'the market', and whose functioning is the main object of their studies, can be derived in the last analysis from the psychology of 'economic man', or, to use Mill's phraseology, from the psychological 'phenomena . . . of the pursuit of wealth'[6]. Moreover, the followers of psychologism insist that it is because of the peculiar psychological structure of human nature that institutions play such an important rôle in our society, and that, once established, they show a tendency to become a traditional and a comparatively fixed part of our environment. Finally—and this is their decisive point— the *origin as well as the development* of traditions must be explicable in terms of human nature. When tracing back traditions and institutions to their origin, we must find that their introduction is explicable in psychological terms, since they have been introduced by man for some

---

[6] Cp. Mill, *A System of Logic*, VI; IX, § 3. (Cp. also notes 16–18 to chapter 13.)

purpose or other, and under the influence of certain motives. And even if these motives have been forgotten in
the course of time, then that forgetfulness, as well as
our readiness to put up with institutions whose purpose
is obscure, is in its turn based on human nature. Thus
'all phenomena of society are phenomena of human
nature'[7], as Mill said; and 'the Laws of the phenomena
of society are, and can be, nothing but the laws of the
actions and passions of human beings', that is to say,
'the laws of individual human nature. Men are not, when
brought together, converted into another kind of substance. . . .'[8].

This last remark of Mill's exhibits one of the most
praiseworthy aspects of psychologism, namely, its sane
opposition to collectivism and holism, its refusal to be
impressed by Rousseau's or Hegel's romanticism—by a
general will or a national spirit, or perhaps, by a group
mind. Psychologism is, I believe, correct only in so far
as it insists upon what may be called 'methodological
individualism' as opposed to 'methodological collectivism'; it rightly insists that the 'behaviour' and the 'actions'
of collectives, such as states or social groups, must be
reduced to the behaviour and to the actions of human
individuals. But the belief that the choice of such an individualistic method implies the choice of a psychological
method is mistaken (as will be shown below in this chapter), even though it may appear very convincing at first
sight. And that psychologism as such moves on rather
dangerous ground, apart from its commendable individualistic method, can be seen from some further passages of Mill's argument. For they show that *psychologism is forced to adopt historicist methods*. The attempt
to reduce the facts of our social environment to psy-

---

[7] Cp. Mill, *op. cit.*, VI; VI, § 2.

[8] Cp. Mill, *op. cit.*, VI; VII, § 1. For the opposition between
'methodological individualism' and 'methodological collectivism',
see F. A. von Hayek's *Scientism and the Study of Society*, Part
II, section VII (*Economica*, 1943, pp. 41 ff.).

chological facts forces us into speculations about origins and developments. When analysing Plato's sociology, we had an opportunity of gauging the dubious merits of such an approach to social science (compare chapter 5). In criticizing Mill, we shall now try to deal it a decisive blow.

It is undoubtedly Mill's psychologism which forces him to adopt a historicist method; and he is even vaguely aware of the barrenness or poverty of historicism, since he tries to account for this barrenness by pointing out the difficulties arising from the tremendous complexity of the interaction of so many individual minds. 'While it is . . . imperative', he says, '. . . never to introduce any generalization . . . into the social sciences until sufficient grounds can be pointed out in human nature, I do not think any one will contend that it would have been possible, setting out from the principle of human nature and from the general circumstances of the position of our species, to determine *a priori* the order in which human development must take place, and to predict, consequently, the general facts of history up to the present time.'[9] The reason he gives is that 'after the first few terms of the series, the influence exercised over each generation by the generations which preceded it becomes . . . more and more preponderant over all other influences'. (In other words, the social environment becomes a dominant influence.) 'So long a series of actions and reactions . . . could not possibly be computed by human faculties. . . .'

This argument, and especially Mill's remark on 'the first few terms of the series', are a striking revelation of the weakness of the psychologistic version of historicism. If all regularities in social life, the laws of our social environment, of all institutions, etc., are ultimately to be explained by, and reduced to, the 'actions and passions of human beings', then such an approach forces upon us

---

[9] For this and the following quotation see Mill, *op. cit.*, VI; X, § 4.

not only the idea of historico-causal development, but also the idea of the *first steps* of such a development. For the stress on the psychological origin of social rules or institutions can only mean that they can be traced back to a state when their introduction was dependent solely upon psychological factors, or more precisely, when it was independent of any established social institutions. Psychologism is thus forced, whether it likes it or not, to operate with the idea of a *beginning of society*, and with the idea of a human nature and a human psychology as they existed prior to society. In other words, Mill's remark concerning the 'first few terms of the series' of social development is not an accidental slip, as one might perhaps believe, but the appropriate expression of the desperate position forced upon him. It is a desperate position because this theory of a pre-social human nature which explains the foundation of society—a psychologistic version of the 'social contract'—is not only an historical myth, but also, as it were, a methodological myth. It can hardly be seriously discussed, for we have every reason to believe that man or rather his ancestor was social prior to being human (considering, for example, that language presupposes society). But this implies that social institutions, and with them, typical social regularities or sociological laws[10], must have existed prior to what some people are pleased to call 'human nature', and to human psychology. If a reduction is to be attempted at all, it would therefore be more hopeful to attempt a reduction or interpretation of psychology in terms of sociology than the other way round.

This brings us back to Marx's epigram at the beginning of this chapter. Men—i.e. human minds, the needs, the hopes, fears, and expectations, the motives and aspirations of human individuals—are, if anything, the product of life in society rather than its creators. It must be

---

[10] I am using the term 'sociological laws' to denote the natural laws of social life, as opposed to its normative laws; cp. text to notes 8–9 to chapter 5.

admitted that the structure of our social environment is man-made in a certain sense; that its institutions and traditions are neither the work of God nor of nature, but the results of human actions and decisions, and alterable by human actions and decisions. But this does not mean that they are all consciously designed, and explicable in terms of needs, hopes, or motives. On the contrary, even those which arise as the result of conscious and intentional human actions are, as a rule, *the indirect, the unintended and often the unwanted by-products of such actions*. 'Only a minority of social institutions are consciously designed, while the vast majority have just "grown", as the undesigned results of human actions', as I have said before[11]; and we can

---

[11] Cp. note 10 to chapter 3. The passage is a quotation from p. 122 of part II of my article, *The Poverty of Historicism* (*Economica*, N.S. xi, 1944).

I owe the suggestion that it was Marx who first conceived social theory as the study of the *unwanted social repercussions of nearly all our actions* to K. Polanyi, who emphasized this aspect of Marxism in private discussions (1924).

* (1) It should be noted, however, that in spite of the aspect of Marxism which has been just mentioned and which constitutes an important point of agreement between Marx's views on method and mine, there is a considerable disagreement between Marx's and my views about the way in which these unwanted or unintended repercussions have to be analysed. For Marx is a *methodological collectivist*. He believes that it is the 'system of economic relations' as such which gives rise to the unwanted consequences—a system of institutions which, in turn, may be explicable in terms of 'means of production', but which is not analysable in terms of individuals, their relations, and their actions. As opposed to this, I hold that institutions (and traditions) must be analysed in individualistic terms—that is to say, in terms of the relations of individuals acting in certain situations, and of the unintended consequences of their actions.

(2) The reference in the text to 'canvas-cleaning', and to chapter 9 is to notes 9 to 12, and the text, of this chapter.

(3) Concerning the remarks in the text (in the paragraph to which this note is appended, and in some of those which follow)

add that even most of the few institutions which were
consciously and successfully designed (say, a newly
founded University, or a Trade Union) do not turn out
according to plan—again because of the unintended social repercussions resulting from their intentional creation. For their creation affects not only many other social
institutions but also 'human nature'—hopes, fears, and
ambitions, first of those more immediately involved, and
later often of all members of the society. One of the consequences of this is that the moral values of a society—the
demands and proposals recognized by all, or by very
nearly all, of its members—are closely bound up with its
institutions and traditions, and that they cannot survive
the destruction of the institutions and traditions of a
society (as indicated in chapter 9 when we discussed
the 'canvas-cleaning' of the radical revolutionary).

All this holds most emphatically for the more ancient
periods of social development, i.e. for the closed society,
in which the conscious design of institutions is a most ex-

---

about the unintended social repercussions of our actions, I wish
to draw attention to the fact that the situation in the physical
sciences (and in the field of mechanical engineering and technology) is somewhat similar. The task of technology is here also
largely to inform us about unintended consequences of what we
are doing (e.g. that a bridge may become too heavy if we
strengthen certain of its components). But the analogy goes even
further. Our mechanical inventions do rarely turn out according
to our original plans. The inventors of the motor car probably did
not foresee the social repercussions of their doings, but they certainly did not foresee the purely mechanical repercussions—the
many ways in which their cars broke down. And while their cars
were altered in order to avoid these breakdowns, they changed
beyond recognition. (And with them, some people's motives and
aspirations changed also.)

(4) With my criticism of the Conspiracy Theory (further down
in the text), cp. my addresses *Prediction and Prophecy and their
Significance for Social Theory* (in *Proceedings of the Xth International Congress of Philosophy*, 1948, vol. i, 82 ff.; see especially
87 f.), and *Towards a Rational Theory of Tradition* (*The Rationalist Annual*, 1949, 36 ff., see especially 40 f.).*

ceptional event, if it happens at all. To-day, things may begin to be different, owing to our slowly increasing knowledge of society, i.e. owing to the study of the un-intended repercussions of our plans and actions; and one day, men may even become the conscious creators of an open society, and thereby of a greater part of their own fate. (Marx entertained this hope, as will be shown in the next chapter.) But all this is partly a matter of degree, and although we may learn to foresee many of the unintended consequences of our actions (the main aim of all social technology), there will always be many which we did not foresee.

The fact that psychologism is forced to operate with the idea of a psychological origin of society constitutes in my opinion a decisive argument against it. But it is not the only one. Perhaps the most important criticism of psychologism is that it fails to understand the main task of the explanatory social sciences.

This task is not, as the historicist believes, the prophecy of the future course of history. It is, rather, the discovery and explanation of the less obvious dependences within the social sphere. It is the discovery of the difficulties which stand in the way of social action—the study, as it were, of the unwieldiness, the resilience or the brittle-ness of the social stuff, of its resistance to our attempts to mould it and to work with it.

In order to make my point clear, I shall briefly de-scribe a theory which is widely held but which assumes what I consider the very opposite of the true aim of the social sciences; I call it the *'conspiracy theory of society'*. It is the view that an explanation of a social phenomenon consists in the discovery of the men or groups who are interested in the occurrence of this phenomenon (some-times it is a hidden interest which has first to be re-vealed), and who have planned and conspired to bring it about.

This view of the aims of the social sciences arises, of course, from the mistaken theory that, whatever happens in society—especially happenings such as war, unemploy-

ment, poverty, shortages, which people as a rule dislike—
is the result of direct design by some powerful individuals
and groups. This theory is widely held; it is older even
than historicism (which, as shown by its primitive theistic
form, is a derivative of the conspiracy theory). In its
modern forms it is, like modern historicism, and a certain
modern attitude towards 'natural laws', a typical result
of the secularization of a religious superstition. The belief
in the Homeric gods whose conspiracies explain the history of the Trojan War is gone. The gods are abandoned.
But their place is filled by powerful men or groups—
sinister pressure groups whose wickedness is responsible
for all the evils we suffer from—such as the Learned
Elders of Zion, or the monopolists, or the capitalists, or
the imperialists.

I do not wish to imply that conspiracies never happen.
On the contrary, they are typical social phenomena. They
become important, for example, whenever people who believe in the conspiracy theory get into power. And people
who sincerely believe that they know how to make
heaven on earth are most likely to adopt the conspiracy
theory, and to get involved in a counter-conspiracy
against non-existing conspirators. For the only explanation of their failure to produce their heaven is the evil
intention of the Devil, who has a vested interest in hell.

Conspiracies occur, it must be admitted. But the striking fact which, in spite of their occurrence, disproves the
conspiracy theory is that few of these conspiracies are
ultimately successful. *Conspirators rarely consummate
their conspiracy.*

Why is this so? Why do achievements differ so widely
from aspirations? Because this is usually the case in social
life, conspiracy or no conspiracy. Social life is not only a
trial of strength between opposing groups—it is action
within a more or less resilient or brittle framework of institutions and traditions and it creates—apart from any
conscious counter-action—many unforeseen reactions in
this framework, some of them perhaps even unforeseeable.

To try to analyse these reactions and to foresee them

as far as possible is, I believe, the main task of the social sciences. It is the task of analysing the unintended social repercussions of intentional human actions—those repercussions whose significance is neglected both by the conspiracy theory and by psychologism, as already indicated. An action which proceeds precisely according to intention does not create a problem for social science (except that there may be a need to explain why in this particular case no unintended repercussions occurred). One of the most primitive economic actions may serve as an example in order to make the idea of unintended consequences of our actions quite clear. If a man wishes urgently to buy a house, we can safely assume that he does not wish to raise the market price of houses. But the very fact that he appears on the market as a buyer will tend to raise market prices. And analogous remarks hold for the seller. Or to take an example from a very different field, if a man decides to insure his life, he is unlikely to have the intention of encouraging some people to invest their money in insurance shares. But he will do so nevertheless. We see here clearly that not all consequences of our actions are intended consequences; and accordingly, that the conspiracy theory of society cannot be true because it amounts to the assertion that all results, even those which at first sight do not seem to be intended by anybody, are the intended results of the actions of people who are interested in these results.

The examples given do not refute psychologism as easily as they refute the conspiracy theory, for one can argue that it is the sellers' *knowledge* of a buyer's presence in the market, and their *hope* of getting a higher price—in other words, psychological factors—which explain the repercussions described. This, of course, is quite true; but we must not forget that this knowledge and this hope are not ultimate data of human nature, and that they are, in their turn, explicable in terms of the *social situation*—the market situation.

This social situation is hardly reducible to motives and to the general laws of 'human nature'. Indeed, the interference of certain 'traits of human nature', such as our susceptibility to propaganda, may sometimes lead to deviations from the economic behaviour just mentioned. Furthermore, if the social situation is different from the one envisaged, then it is possible that the consumer, by the action of buying, may indirectly contribute to a cheapening of the article; for instance, by making its mass-production more profitable. And although this effect happens to further his interest as a consumer, it may have been caused just as involuntarily as the opposite effect, and altogether under precisely similar psychological conditions. It seems clear that the social situations which may lead to such widely different unwanted or unintended repercussions must be studied by a social science which is not bound to the prejudice that 'it is imperative never to introduce any generalization into the social sciences until sufficient grounds can be pointed out in human nature', as Mill said[12]. They must be studied by an autonomous social science.

Continuing this argument against psychologism we may say that our actions are to a very large extent explicable in terms of the situation in which they occur. Of course, they are never fully explicable in terms of the situation alone; an explanation of the way in which a man, when crossing a street, dodges the cars which move on it may go beyond the situation, and may refer his motives, to an 'instinct' of self-preservation, or to his wish to avoid pain, etc. But this 'psychological' part of the explanation is very often trivial, as compared with the detailed determination of his action by what we may call the *logic of the situation*; and besides, it is impossible to include all psychological factors in the description of the situation. The analysis of situations, the situational logic, plays a very important part in social life as well as in the social sciences. It is, in fact, the method of economic analysis. As to an example outside economics, I

---

[12] See the passage from Mill's *Logic*, quoted in the text to note 8 to the present chapter.

refer to the 'logic of power'[13], which we may use in order to explain the moves of power politics as well as the working of certain political institutions. The method of applying a situational logic to the social sciences is not based on any psychological assumption concerning the rationality (or otherwise) of 'human nature'. On the contrary: when we speak of 'rational behaviour' or of 'irrational behaviour' then we mean behaviour which is, or which is not, in accordance with the logic of that situation. In fact, the psychological analysis of an action in terms of its (rational or irrational) motives presupposes —as has been pointed out by Max Weber[14]—that we

---

[13] Cp. note 63 to chapter 10. Important contributors to the logic of power are Plato (in Books VIII and IX of the *Republic*, and in the *Laws*), Aristotle, Machiavelli, Pareto, and many others.

[14] Cp. Max Weber's *Ges. Aufsaetze zur Wissenschaftslehre* (1922), especially pp. 408 ff.

A remark may be added here concerning the often repeated assertion that the social sciences operate with a method different from that of the natural sciences, in so far as we know the 'social atoms', i.e. ourselves, by direct acquaintance, while our knowledge of physical atoms is only hypothetical. From this, it is often concluded (e.g. by Carl Menger) that the method of social science, since it makes use of our knowledge of ourselves, is psychological, or perhaps 'subjective', as opposed to the 'objective' methods of the natural sciences. To this, we may answer: There is surely no reason why we should not use any 'direct' knowledge we may have of ourselves. But such knowledge is useful in the social sciences only if we generalize, i.e. if we assume that what we know of ourselves holds good for others too. But this generalization is of a hypothetical character, and it must be tested and corrected by experience of an 'objective' kind. (Before having met anybody who does not like chocolate, some people may easily believe that everybody likes it.) Undoubtedly, in the case of 'social atoms' we are in certain ways more favourably situated than in the case of physical atoms, owing not only to our knowledge of ourselves, but also to the use of language. Yet from the point of view of scientific method, a social hypothesis suggested by self-intuition is in no different position from a physical hypothesis about atoms. The latter may also be suggested to the physicist by a kind of intuition

have previously developed some standard of what is to be considered as rational in the situation in question.

My arguments against psychologism should not be misunderstood[15]. They are not, of course, intended to show that psychological studies and discoveries are of little importance for the social scientist. They mean, rather, that psychology—the psychology of the individual—is one of the social sciences, even though it is not the basis of all social science. Nobody would deny the importance for political science of psychological facts such as the craving for power, and the various neurotic phenomena connected with it. But 'craving for power' is undoubtedly a social notion as well as a psychological one: we must not forget that, if we study, for example, the first appearance in childhood of this craving, then we study it in the setting of a certain social institution, for example, that of our modern family. (The Eskimo family may give rise to rather different phenomena.) Another psychological fact which is significant for sociology, and which raises grave political and institutional problems, is that to live in the haven of a tribe, or of a 'community' approaching a tribe, is for many men an emotional necessity (especially for young people who, perhaps in accordance with a parallelism between ontogenetic and phylogenetic development, seem to have to pass through a tribal or

---

about what atoms are like. And in both cases, this intuition is a private affair of the man who proposes the hypothesis. What is 'public', and important for science, is merely the question whether the hypotheses could be tested by experience, and whether they stood up to tests.

From this point of view, social theories are no more 'subjective' than physical ones. (And it would be clearer, for example, to speak of 'the theory of subjective values' or of 'the theory of acts of choice' than of 'the subjective theory of value': see also note 9 to chapter 20.)

[15] The present paragraph has been inserted in order to avoid the misunderstanding mentioned in the text. I am indebted to Prof. E. Gombrich for drawing my attention to the possibility of such a misunderstanding.

'American-Indian' stage). That my attack on psychologism is not intended as an attack on all psychological considerations may be seen from the use I have made (in chapter 10) of such a concept as the 'strain of civilization' which is partly the result of this unsatisfied emotional need. This concept refers to certain feelings of uneasiness, and is therefore a psychological concept. But at the same time, it is a sociological concept also; for it characterizes these feelings not only as unpleasant and unsettling, etc., but relates them to a certain social situation, and to the contrast between an open and a closed society. (Many psychological concepts such as ambition or love have an analogous status.) Also, we must not overlook the great merits which psychologism has acquired by advocating a methodological individualism and by opposing a methodological collectivism; for it lends support to the important doctrine that all social phenomena, and especially the functioning of all social institutions, should always be understood as resulting from the decisions, actions, attitudes, etc., of human individuals, and that we should never be satisfied by an explanation in terms of so-called 'collectives' (states, nations, races, etc.). The mistake of psychologism is its presumption that this methodological individualism in the field of social science implies the programme of reducing all social phenomena and all social regularities to psychological phenomena and psychological laws. The danger of this presumption is its inclination towards historicism, as we have seen. That it is unwarranted is shown by the need for a theory of the unintended social repercussions of our actions, and by the need for what I have described as the logic of social situations.

In defending and developing Marx's view that the problems of society are irreducible to those of 'human nature', I have permitted myself to go beyond the arguments actually propounded by Marx. Marx did not speak of 'psychologism', nor did he criticize it systematically; nor was it Mill whom he had in mind in the epigram quoted at the beginning of this chapter. The force of this epigram is directed, rather, against 'idealism', in its Hegelian form. Yet so far as the problem of the psychological nature of society is concerned, Mill's psychologism can be said to coincide with the idealist theory combated by Marx[16]. As it happened, however, it was just the influence of another element in Hegelianism, namely Hegel's Platonizing collectivism, his theory that the state and the nation are more 'real' than the individual who owes everything to them, that led Marx to the view expounded in this chapter. (An instance of the fact that one can sometimes extract a valuable suggestion even from an absurd philosophical theory.) Thus, historically, Marx developed certain of Hegel's views concerning the superiority of society over the individual, and used them as arguments against other views of Hegel. But since I consider Mill a worthier opponent than Hegel, I have not kept to the history of Marx's ideas, but have tried to develop them in the form of an argument against Mill.

---

[16] Hegel contended that his 'Idea' was something existing 'absolutely', i.e. independently of anybody's thought. One might contend, therefore, that he was not a psychologist. Yet Marx, quite reasonably, did not take seriously this 'absolute idealism' of Hegel; he rather interpreted it as a disguised *psychologism*, and combated it as such. Cp. *Capital*, 873 (italics mine): 'For Hegel, the *thought process* (which he even presents in disguise under the name "Idea" as an independent agent or subject) is the creator of the real.' Marx confines his attack to the doctrine that the thought process (or consciousness, or mind) creates the 'real'; and he shows that it does not even create the social reality (to say nothing about the material universe).

For the Hegelian theory of the dependence of the individual upon society, see (apart from section iii of chapter 12) the discussion, in chapter 23, of the social, or more precisely, the interpersonal element in scientific method, as well as the corresponding discussion, in chapter 24, of the inter-personal element in rationality.

MILL'S WORKS

The University of Toronto Press has begun the publication of the first collected edition of Mill's works in English. The volumes issued so far display impeccable scholarship, the plans call for the inclusion of numerous articles and letters previously uncollected, and the introductions to the separate volumes promise to be of considerable value. So far the *Principles of Political Economy*, ed. J. M. Robson, 1965, and the *Earlier Letters*, ed. F. E. Mineka, 1963, have been published.

Ney MacMinn, J. R. Hainds, and James McNab have edited a *Bibliography of the Writings of John Stuart Mill*, Northwestern University Studies in the Humanities, No. 12, 1945, which is in fact the text of a list Mill himself made of his writings. It is almost complete. For up-to-date bibliographical information, and for the most complete list of secondary works on Mill, the student should consult the *Mill Newsletter*, ed. John M. Robson, University of Toronto Press and Victoria College, 1965–, which contains brief reviews and notices of work in progress on Mill as well as bibliographies. A good bibliography of nineteenth-century writings on Mill is available as an appendix to W. L. Courtney's *Life of John Stuart Mill*, but the bibliography being compiled by D. Hascall and John M. Robson for the *Mill Newsletter* will be fuller.

The following list mentions only Mill's main works:

Auguste Comte and Positivism. Reprinted from the *Westminster Review*, London, 1865. 3rd ed., 1882.

Autobiography. (Edited by Helen Taylor), London, 1873. A more complete version is the one published by Columbia University Press, New York, 1924, edited by John Jacob Coss. See also *The Early Draft of John Stuart Mill's Autobiography*, ed. J. Stillinger, Urbana, 1961.

Considerations on Representative Government. London, 1861, 3rd ed., 1865.

Dissertations and Discussions. 2 vols., London, 1859. 3 vols., 1867. 4 vols., 1875.

Essays on Some Unsettled Questions of Political Economy. London, 1844. 2nd ed., 1874.

An Examination of Sir William Hamilton's Philosophy. London, 1865. 5th ed., 1878.

On Liberty. London, 1859. 3rd ed., 1864.

Principles of Political Economy. 2 vols., London, 1848. 7th ed., 1871.

The Subjection of Women. London, 1869. 4th ed., 1878.

A System of Logic. 2 vols., 1843, 8th ed., 1872.

Thoughts on Parliamentary Reform. London, 1859.

Three Essays on Religion: Nature, The Utility of Religion, and Theism. (With an introductory notice by Helen Taylor), London, 1874.

Utilitarianism. Reprinted from *Fraser's Magazine* (1861), London, 1863. 4th ed., 1871.

Chapters on Socialism. Reprinted from the *Fortnightly Review*, 1879, as *Socialism*, ed. W. D. P. Bliss, New York, 1891.

In 1869 Mill, along with Alexander Bain, Andrew Findlater, and George Grote, published an edition of James Mill's *Analysis of the Phenomena of the Human Mind*, 2 vols., London. Each of the editors added notes as he pleased, agreeing or (more usually) disagreeing with James Mill's text. Most of the notes are of little interest now, but J. S. Mill's, and some of Bain's, are well worth consulting.

Note: The essay entitled "On Social Freedom," ed. D. Fosdick, New York, 1941, has been attributed to Mill, but this attribution is mistaken. See J. C. Rees, *Mill and His Early Critics*, Leicester, 1956.

There are numerous reprints of many of Mill's works. Standard volumes include A. D. Lindsay's collection, in the Everyman's Library series, and M. Cohen's, in the Modern Library series. Some of the shorter and less well-known pieces are reprinted now in various of the following volumes:

G. Himmelfarb, ed., *Essays on Politics and Culture*, Doubleday and Co., New York, 1962;

J. B. Schneewind, ed., *Mill's Essays on Literature and Society*, and *Mill's Ethical Writings*, both Collier Books, New York, 1965;

J. M. Robson, ed., *John Stuart Mill: A Selection of His Works*, St. Martin's Press, New York, 1966.

The Liberal Arts Press has reprinted the *Three Essays on Religion* in two separate volumes, one containing "Nature" and "The Utility of Religion," the other containing "Theism." They have also reprinted the Coss edition of the *Autobiography*. *The System of Logic* is available, and there is a good abridgment of it by E. Nagel, *J. S. Mill's Philosophy of Scientific Method*. B. Wishy, in *Prefaces to Liberty*, Boston, 1959, has assembled a number of Mill's minor writings relevant to *On Liberty*.

MILL'S LIFE AND LETTERS

The standard biography of Mill is now *The Life of John Stuart Mill*, by M. St. J. Packe, London, 1954, but it can usefully be supplemented by two older works: Alexander Bain's *John Stuart Mill*, London, 1882, which enjoys the advantage of having been written by one who knew Mill fairly well; and W. L. Courtney's brief *Life of John Stuart Mill*, London, 1889. *The Letters of John Stuart Mill*, ed. H. S. R. Elliott, 2 vols., London, 1910, will remain indispensable until the edition being published by the University of Toronto Press is completed: F. E. Mineka's two volumes of *Earlier Letters*, Toronto, 1963, now supersede Elliott for the period up to 1848. The student should consult F. A. Hayek's *John Stuart Mill and Harriet Taylor*, London, 1951, not only for the interesting letters it contains but also for Hayek's introduction. For the most reasonable assessments of Mill's relations to Mrs. Taylor, see H. O. Pappe, *J. S. Mill and the Harriet Taylor Myth*, Melbourne, 1960, and John M. Robson, "Artist and Scientist: Harriet Taylor and John Stuart Mill," *Queen's Quarterly*, 73, 1966. Further investigation of Mill's life may be begun on the basis of the extensive bibliography contained in Packe's *Life*. It has been announced in the *Mill Newsletter* that Gertrude Himmelfarb is working on a new biography of Mill.

HISTORICAL BACKGROUND

The Age of Improvement, by Asa Briggs, London, 1959, is one of the best introductions to English history from the period of the French Revolution to the Reform Bill of 1867. For more detailed studies, N. Gash's *Reaction and Reconstruction in English Politics, 1832–1852*, Oxford, 1965, is a brilliant analysis of political developments following the first Reform Bill, and W. L. Burn, *The Age of Equipoise*, London, 1964, a fascinating investigation of British life in the 1850s and 1860s. S. G. Checkland, *The Rise of Industrial Society in England*, London, 1964, and, more briefly, W. H. B. Court, *Concise Economic History of Britain*, Cambridge, 1954, survey economic developments.

Elie Halvey's *Growth of Philosophic Radicalism*, London, 1928, is the indispensable study of the Benthamites and their doctrines on morals, politics, population, and economics. The first two volumes of Sir Leslie Stephen's *English Utilitarians*, London, 1900, deal with Bentham and James Mill: the third volume is a study of J. S. Mill, and all three remain valuable. Mill is discussed in innumerable histories of philosophy, political theory, economics, and literature. The student wishing to consider him in the light of the literary culture of his age may wish to consult Jerome H. Buckley, *The Victorian Temper*, Cambridge, Massachusetts, 1951, or the richer, if more diffuse, volume by Walter E. Houghton, *The Victorian Frame of Mind*, New Haven, 1957. Basil Willey's *Nineteenth Century Studies*, London, 1949, and *More Nineteenth Century Studies*, 1956, contain a number of interesting essays on various major and minor intellectuals of the Victorian and pre-Victorian periods. *Victorian England: Portrait of an Age*, by G. M. Young, Oxford, 1936, is a masterpiece in a category all its own.

The journal *Victorian Studies*, edited by Michael Wolff and George Levine, regularly carries relevant articles and publishes a bibliographical survey of work on the Victorian period once each year.

RECENT BOOKS AND
ARTICLES ON MILL

The following list is by no means an exhaustive bibliography of recent work on Mill. It emphasizes writings relevant to Mill's philosophy and to his social and political thought, omitting studies of his economics. It does not list standard histories of philosophy, literature, etc., in which Mill is discussed, nor does it note the numerous volumes of history, biography, and philosophy in which reference is made to him. Articles included in the present volume are not listed.

ABRAMS, M. H. *The Mirror and the Lamp: Romantic Theory and the Critical Tradition*, New York, 1953.

ACTON, H. B. "Comte's Positivism and the Science of Society," *Philosophy*, 26, 1951.

AIKEN, HENRY DAVID. "Definitions, Factual Premises, and Ethical Conclusions," *Philosophical Review*, 61, 1952. Reprinted in *Reason and Conduct*, New York, 1962.

———. "Utilitarianism and Liberty: John Stuart Mill's Defense of Freedom," in *Reason and Conduct*, New York, 1962.

ALEXANDER, EDWARD. *Matthew Arnold and John Stuart Mill*. New York, 1965.

———. "Mill's Theory of Culture: The Wedding of Literature and Democracy," *University of Toronto Quarterly*, 35, 1965.

ANSCHUTZ, RICHARD PAUL. "J. S. Mill, Carlyle, and Mrs. Taylor," *Political Science*, 7, 1955.

———. *The Philosophy of J. S. Mill*, Oxford, 1953.

APPLEMAN, PHILIP, WM. A. MADDEN, AND MICHAEL WOLFF, EDS., *1859: Entering an Age of Crisis*, Bloomington, Ind., 1959.

ATKINSON, R. F. "J. S. Mill's 'Proof' of the Principle of Utility," *Philosophy*, 32, 1957.

BEARCE, GEORGE D. *British Attitudes Toward India 1784–1858*, Oxford, 1961.

BEDAU, HUGO. "Justice and Classical Utilitarianism," in C. J. Friedrich and J. W. Chapman, eds., *Justice*, New York, 1963.

BERLIN, ISAIAH. *John Stuart Mill and the Ends of Life*, London, 1960.

BETH, EVERT W. AND JEAN PIAGET. *Mathematical Epistemology and Psychology*, Dordrecht, 1967.

BORCHARD, RUTH. *John Stuart Mill: the Man*, London, 1957.

BRITTON, KARL. *John Stuart Mill*, Baltimore and Harmondsworth, 1953.

———. "The Nature of Arithmetic. A Reconsideration of Mill's Views," *Proceedings of the Aristotelian Society*, 48, 1947–48.

———. "Utilitarianism: The Appeal to a First Principle," *Proceedings of the Aristotelian Society*, 60, 1959–60.

BURNS, J. H. "Was Mill a Democrat?" *History Today*, 8, 1958.

———. "Utilitarianism and Democracy," *Philosophical Quarterly*, 9, 1959.

CARR, ROBERT. "The Religious Thought of John Stuart Mill: A Study in Reluctant Scepticism," *Journal of the History of Ideas*, 23, 1962.

CLARK, GEORGE A. "Mill's 'Notorious Analogy,'" *Journal of Philosophy*, 56, 1959.

CLARK, PAMELA M. "Some Difficulties in Utilitarianism," *Philosophy*, 29, 1954.

CRANSTON, MAURICE. *John Stuart Mill*, London, 1958.

CUMMING, ROBERT D. "Mill's History of His Ideas," *Journal of the History of Ideas*, 25, 1964.

DEVLIN, PATRICK. *The Enforcement of Morals*, London, 1965 especially I, VI, and VII.

DURHAM, JOHN. "The Influence of John Stuart Mill's Mental Crisis on his Thought," *American Imago*, 20, 1963.

EBENSTEIN, WILLIAM. "John Stuart Mill: Political and Economic Liberty," in C. J. Friedrich, ed., *Liberty*, New York, 1962.

FEUER, LEWIS S. "John Stuart Mill and Marxian Socialism," *Journal of the History of Ideas*, 10, 1949.

FLOWER, ELIZABETH. "Mill and Some Present Concerns about Ethical Judgments," in C. J. Friedrich, ed., *Liberty*, New York, 1962.

FREGE, G. *Foundations of Arithmetic*, trans. J. L. Austin, Oxford, 1953.

HAINDS, JOHN R. "John Stuart Mill and the St. Simonians," *Journal of the History of Ideas*, 7, 1946.

———. "J. S. Mill's *Examiner* Articles on Art," *Journal of the History of Ideas*, 11, 1950.

HAMBURGER, JOSEPH. *Intellectuals in Politics: John Stuart Mill and the Philosophic Radicals*, New Haven, Conn., 1965.

HANCOCK, ROGER. "Ethics and History in Kant and Mill," *Ethics*, 68, 1957.

HARRIS, ABRAM L. *Economics and Social Reform*, New York, 1958.

HART, H. L. A. *Law, Liberty, and Morality*, Stanford, Calif., 1963.

——— AND A. M. HONORÉ. *Causation in the Law*, Oxford, 1959.

HAYEK, F. A., ED. *The Spirit of the Age* by J. S. Mill, Chicago, 1942.

HOLLOWAY, HARRY A. "Mill and Green on the Modern Welfare State," *Western Political Quarterly*, 13, 1960.

JACKSON, REGINALD. "Mill's Joint Method," *Mind*, 46, 1937 and 47, 1938.

———. *Examination of the Deductive Logic of J. S. Mill,* London, 1941.

JACOBS, HERBERT. *Rechtsphilosophie und politische Philosophie bei John Stuart Mill,* Bonn, 1965.

KAUFMAN, F. *Methodology of the Social Sciences,* New York, 1958.

KENDALL, W. "The Open Society and its Fallacies," *American Political Science Review,* 54, 1960 (and see discussion the following year).

KORT, FRED. "The Issue of a Science of Politics in Utilitarian Thought," *American Political Science Review,* 46, 1952.

KRETZMANN, NORMAN. "Desire as Proof of Desirability," *Philosophical Quarterly,* 8, 1958.

KROOK, DOROTHEA. *Three Traditions of Moral Thought,* Cambridge, England, 1959.

KUBITZ, OSKAR A. *The Development of J. S. Mill's System of Logic,* Urbana, Ill., 1932.

LEAVIS, F. R. "Mill, Beatrice Webb, and the 'English School,'" *Scrutiny,* 16, 1949.

———. *Mill on Bentham and Coleridge,* London, 1950.

LENNARD, REGINALD V. "Mill-and others-on Liberty," *Hibbert Journal,* 57, 1959.

LETWIN, SHIRLEY ROBIN. *The Pursuit of Certainty,* Cambridge, England, 1965.

LEVI, A. W. "The 'Mental Crisis' of John Stuart Mill," *Psychoanalytic Review,* 32, 1945.

———. "The Writing of Mill's Autobiography," *Ethics,* 61, 1951.

LINDQUIST, EMORY K. *John St. Mill's Essay on Liberty: A Centennial Review,* Wichita, Kansas, 1959.

MC CLOSKEY, H. J. "Mill's Liberalism," *Philosophical Quarterly,* 13, 1963.

MC CREADY, H. W. "The Defence of Individualism," *Queen's Quarterly,* 52, 1945.

MACK, MARY P. "The Fabians and Utilitarianism," *Journal of the History of Ideas,* 16, 1955.

MC NEILLY, F. S. "Pre-moral Appraisals," *Philosophical Quarterly,* 8, 1958.

MC RAE, ROBERT. "Phenomenalism and J. S. Mill's Theory of Causation," *Philosophy and Phenomenological Research*, 9, 1948.

MAGID, H. M. "Mill and the Problem of Freedom of Thought," *Social Research*, 21, 1954.

MILLER, K. E. "J. S. Mill's Theory of International Relations," *Journal of the History of Ideas*, 22, 1961.

MUELLER, IRIS WESSEL. *John Stuart Mill and French Thought*, Urbana, 1956.

NAKHNIKIAN, GEORGE. "Value and Obligation in Mill," *Ethics*, 62, 1951.

ONG, WALTER J. "J. S. Mill's Pariah Poet," *Philological Quarterly*, 29, 1950.

PANKHURST, R. J. P. *The St.-Simonians, Mill and Carlyle*, London, 1957.

PAPPE, H. O. "The Mills and Harriet Taylor," *Political Science*, 8, 1956.

———. "Mill and Tocqueville," *Journal of the History of Ideas*, 25, 1964.

PLAMENATZ, JOHN. *Mill's Utilitarianism*. Oxford, 1949.

POPKIN, RICHARD H. "A Note on the 'Proof' of Utility in J. S. Mill," *Ethics*, 61, 1950.

POWERS, RICHARD H. "John Stuart Mill: Morality and Inequality," *South Atlantic Quarterly*, 58, 1959.

PREYER, ROBERT. "The Utilitarian Poetics: John Stuart Mill," *University of Kansas City Review*, 19, 1953.

PRICE, H. H. "Mill's View of the External World," *Proceedings of the Aristotelian Society*, 27, 1926–27.

RAPHAEL, D. D. "Fallacies in and about Mill's Utilitarianism," *Philosophy*, 30, 1955.

REES, J. C. "A Phase in the Development of Mill's Ideas on Liberty," *Political Studies*, 6, 1958.

———. "A Re-reading of Mill on Liberty," *Political Studies*, 8, 1960.

———. "H. O. Pappe's 'John Stuart Mill and the Harriet Taylor Myth,'" *Political Studies*, 10, 1962.

ROBBINS, L. "Packe on Mill," *Economica*, 24, 1957.

RYLE, GILBERT. "The Theory of Meaning," in C. A. Mace, ed., *British Philosophy in the Mid-Century*, London, 1957.

SAKAI, NAOYOSHI. *J. S. Mill's Conception of Freedom*, Zürich, 1957.

SAMPSON, R. V. "J. S. Mill: an Interpretation," *Cambridge Journal*, 3, 1950.

SCANLON, J. P. "J. S. Mill and the Definition of Freedom," *Ethics*, 68, 1958.

SCHAPIRO, J. S. "J. S. Mill, Pioneer of Democratic Liberalism in England," *Journal of the History of Ideas*, 4, 1943.

SPENCE, G. W. "The Psychology Behind J. S. Mill's Proof," *Philosophy*, 43, 1968.

SPIEGELBERG, HERBERT. "Accident of Birth: a Non-Utilitarian Motif in J. S. Mill's Philosophy," *Journal of the History of Ideas*, 22, 1961.

STEWART, H. L. "J. S. Mill's 'Logic': A Post-centenary Appraisal," *University of Toronto Quarterly*, 17, 1947.

STILLINGER, J. "The Text of John Stuart Mill's Autobiography," *Bulletin of the John Rylands Library*, 43, 1960.

STRONG, EDWARD W. "William Whewell and John Stuart Mill: Their Controversy about Scientific Knowledge," *Journal of the History of Ideas*, 16, 1955.

TEN, C. L. "Mill on Self-Regarding Actions," *Philosophy*, 43, 1968.

THOMPSON, MANLEY H. "J. S. Mill's Theory of Truth: A Study in Metaphysics," *Philosophical Review*, 56, 1947.

VINER, JACOB. "Bentham and J. S. Mill: The Utilitarian Background," in *The Long View and the Short*, Glencoe, Ill., 1958.

WALSH, H. T. "Whewell and Mill on Induction," *Philosophy of Science*, 29, 1962.

WELLMAN, CARL. "A Reinterpretation of Mill's Proof," *Ethics*, 69, 1959.

WEST, E. G. "Liberty and Education: John Stuart Mill's Dilemma," *Philosophy*, 40, 1965.

WHITMORE, C. E. "Mill and Mathematics: An Historical Note," *Journal of the History of Ideas*, 6, 1946.

WINCH, PETER. *The Idea of a Social Science*, London, 1958, esp. Ch. III.

WOLFSON, H. A. "The Philonic God of Revelation and his Latter-day Deniers," *Harvard Theological Review*, 53, 1960, reprinted in *Religious Philosophy*, Cambridge, Mass., 1961.

ZINKERNAGEL, P. "Revaluations of J. S. Mill's Ethical Proof," *Theoria*, 19, 1952.